University of
Hertfordshire

College Lane, Hatfield, Herts, AL10 9AB

This item must be returned if
reserved.

Fines are charged for the late
return of reserved items.

Helpdesk@herts.ac.uk +44(0)1707 284678

WARFARE IN HISTORY

Henry of Lancaster's Expedition to Aquitaine, 1345–46

WARFARE IN HISTORY

ISSN 1358–779X

Series editors
Matthew Bennett, Royal Military Academy, Sandhurst, UK
Anne Curry, University of Southampton, UK
Stephen Morillo, Wabash College, Crawfordsville, USA

This series aims to provide a wide-ranging and scholarly approach to military history, offering both individual studies of topics or wars and volumes giving a selection of contemporary and later accounts of particular battles; its scope ranges from the early medieval to the early modern period.

New proposals for the series are welcomed; they should be sent to the publisher at the address below.

Boydell and Brewer Limited, PO Box 9, Woodbridge, Suffolk IP12 3DF

Previously published volumes in this series are listed at the back of this volume

Henry of Lancaster's Expedition to Aquitaine, 1345–46

Military Service and Professionalism in the Hundred Years' War

Nicholas A. Gribit

THE BOYDELL PRESS

First published 2016
The Boydell Press, Woodbridge

ISBN 978-1-78327-117-7

The Boydell Press is an imprint of Boydell & Brewer Ltd
PO Box 9, Woodbridge, Suffolk IP12 3DF, UK
and of Boydell & Brewer Inc.
668 Mt Hope Avenue, Rochester, NY 14620–2731, USA
website: www.boydellandbrewer.com

A CIP catalogue record for this book is available
from the British Library

The publisher has no responsibility for the continued existence or accuracy of
URLs for external or third-party internet websites referred to in this book, and
does not guarantee that any content on such websites is, or will remain, accurate
or appropriate

This publication is printed on acid-free paper

Patri Meo

Contents

Illustrations

Maps

Map 1 authored by Simon J. Harris and Guilhem Pépin. Maps 2–7 produced by
Simon J. Harris with the direction of Nicholas A. Gribit.

Tables

The publication of this book has been made possible by a grant from The Scouloudi Foundation in association with the Institute of Historical Research.

Preface and Acknowledgements

What follows is the culmination of several years of research which has led me through the doors of numerous archives and libraries in England and 'across the way' in France. The search through voluminous original documents and records, and the consultation of published primary sources, has been a lengthy process; such a task cannot be completed without enduring some level of tedium, but feelings of this sort are easily eclipsed by the excitement of discovering new pieces of evidence which, however significant, can throw further light on the subject of medieval English armies and the lives of the individuals who constituted them.

From the outset of this research it was my intention to write a clear and 'rounded' account of an English military expedition (1345–46) that would appeal to students, academic researchers and the general reader alike. In this fashion I have endeavoured to further our understanding of medieval warfare, but if this present work only succeeds in sparking the interest of a curious mind, or aids the research of somebody else, then I shall be replete.

There are a handful of individuals and institutions to whom I am greatly indebted for their generous help and support in bringing this current work to fruition. Firstly, I wish to acknowledge the grant made by the Scouloudi Foundation in association with the Institute of Historical Research, which helped make this publication possible. An award from the Extraordinary Research Fund, made by the University of Leeds School of History, enabled me to undertake archival research in France, and I was warmly welcomed by the community of scholars at Université de Bordeaux III (now Université Bordeaux Montaigne) who permitted my use of the research institute, Ausonius – UMR 5607, during my brief sojourn in the regional capital. The Ranulf Higden Society has also provided a stimulating environment in which I have had numerous queries regarding the translation of complex medieval documents answered.

David Simpkin, David Green and Philip Caudrey have been particularly generous in sharing their research findings. They have offered specialist advice on the careers of those men who fought in the reigns of Edward I and Edward II, who belonged to the affinity of Edward, the Black Prince, and who originated from Norfolk, respectively. James Ross provided valuable help during my numerous visits to The National Archives at Kew; our discussions on the subject of the royal financial administration were always fruitful. I have also benefited greatly from the expert advice of Guilhem Pépin, who has been a constant source of knowledge on all things Gascon.

Clifford J. Rogers has kindly allowed me access to his transcript of the unpublished Saint-Omer chronicle – this has saved me countless hours that would have otherwise been spent on translating the document.

A warm debt of gratitude is owed to the following colleagues who made time to read draft chapters of the book: Andrew Ayton for his valuable comments on the chapters focusing on Henry of Lancaster's military retinue (his extensive work on medieval English armies has been a perennial source of inspiration for my own work); Adrian Bell for his constant support, and for his insightful comments on the final chapter; and Mark Ormrod, who has been a source of encouragement, and has given valuable advice on the subject of war finance.

There are three scholars in particular who deserve special acknowledgement. Simon J. Harris has read and commented on several draft chapters and was the chief architect of the cartography. My doctoral supervisor, Alan V. Murray, also deserves special praise. After a desultory start, our academic partnership flourished – his logical approach to the sources has influenced my own understanding of medieval armies and, not least, the final structure of this work has benefited greatly from lengthy discussions in his office. Alan was also kind enough to read a draft of the entire manuscript. The person to whom I perhaps owe the most gratitude is Paul H. W. Booth. He generously read the entire work and meticulously checked my translation of the document that appears in Appendix A. Paul has been a voice of guidance since my undergraduate days – it was his special subject classes on the Black Prince which first sparked my interest in the Hundred Years' War; from him I have learnt a great deal.

My final thanks are for my family and friends. Thomas Entwistle was kind enough to loan his camera (which has borne witness to many of our shared adventures) on countless occasions to photograph the majority of the documents upon which this research is based. I need not mention here others who have supported my academic endeavours, they know who they are. I should add though that the sometimes seemingly interminable periods of writing are made easier when my brother, and the Frys and the Ramms of this world are around. My Auntie Rowena and Uncle Joe have provided considerable financial support over the course of my research, so to them I say a big thank you. For my parents I need to say little, other than that I owe it all to them; it is my father who inculcated me with a love of the medieval world, and it is to him that this book is dedicated. The last acknowledgement goes to my partner in crime, Layne Harrod, who makes everything I do possible. She has endured the undulating emotions of writing this book – and, I dare say, will be partly glad to see Henry of Lancaster and his men leave both of our lives (at least for a short while). Thank you, Layney.

Nicholas A. Gribit
Hyde Park, Leeds
October 2015

Abbreviations

AL	Archives municipales de Libourne (Libourne)
AN	Archives nationales (Paris)
BIHR	*Bulletin of the Institute of Historical Research*
BM	Bibliothèque municipale
BnF	Bibliothèque nationale de France (Paris)
BPR	*Register of Edward the Black Prince*, ed. and trans. M. C. B. Dawes (London: HMSO, 1930–1933)
Cal. Anc. Corr.	*Calendar of Ancient Correspondence Concerning Wales*, ed. J. Goronwy Edwards (Cardiff: University Press Board, 1935)
CCR	*Calendar of Close Rolls*
CFR	*Calendar of Fine Rolls*
CIPM	*Calendar of Inquisitions Post Mortem*
CP	George Edward Cokayne, *The Complete Peerage of England, Scotland, Ireland, Great Britain and the United Kingdom: Extant, Extinct or Dormant*, 14 vols (London: St Catherine, 1910–1998)
CPP	*Calendar of Entries in the Papal Registers Relating to Great Britain and Ireland: Petitions to the Pope*, ed. W. H. Bliss (London: Eyre and Spottiswoode, 1896)
CPR	*Calendar of Patent Rolls*
Crécy and Calais	*Crécy and Calais, From the Original Records in the Public Record Office*, ed. George Wrottesley (London: [n. pub.], 1898)
EHR	*English Historical Review*
Foedera	*Foedera, Conventiones, Litterae etc.*, ed. T. Rymer, rev. edn A. Clarke, F. Holbrooke and J. Caley, 4 vols (London: George Eyre and Andrew Strahan, 1816–1869)
Norwell	Norwell, William de, *The Wardrobe Book of William de Norwell 12 July 1338 to 26 May 1340*, ed. M. Lyon and others (Brussels: Académie Royale de Belgique, Commission Royale d'Histoire, 1983)

Oeuvres   Jean Froissart, 'Chroniques', in *Oeuvres de Froissart*,
                             ed. Kervyn de Lettenhove, rev. edn, 25 vols
                             (Osnabrück: Biblio Verlag, 1967)
ODNB   *Oxford Dictionary of National Biography*, Oxford
                             University Press 2004, online edn
Scrope and Grosvenor   Nicolas N. Harris, ed., *The Scrope and Grosvenor
                             Controversy*, 2 vols (London: Samuel Bentley,
                             1832)
Somerville   Robert Somerville, *History of the Duchy of
                             Lancaster*, 2 vols (London: Chancellor and
                             Council of the Duchy of Lancaster, 1953–2000), I
                             (1953)
TRHS   *Transactions of the Royal Historical Society*

All documents cited in this work are housed at The National Archives, Kew,
unless stated otherwise.

Note on Money and Names

The main system of currency in medieval England was pounds sterling. It was a silver coinage expressed in the three units of pounds (£), shillings (s) and pence (d), with twelve pence in a shilling, and twenty shillings in a pound (i.e. £1 = 20s = 240d). Another currency unit in England was the mark, only ever 'money of account' (not actual coinage), which was worth two-thirds of a pound (13s 4d). Other currencies referred to in this study are the florin of Florence and the French *écu* and *livre tournois*. The two former were gold coins of high denomination which fluctuated significantly in value in the fourteenth century (specific valuations are provided in the footnotes), and the latter was a silver coin (worth 4s sterling) which became the principal currency in France during the fourteenth century. Gold coins were often high-denomination and used for commerce and international exchange, whereas silver based moneys were lower denomination and used in everyday life.

Personal names are given in their original form. Hence, the duke of Normandy's name is rendered as Jean (Valois), whereas the forename of the Gascon lord known as Captal de Buch is given as Johan (de Grailly), but the name of the Norfolk banneret who served in the retinue of Henry of Lancaster appears in the English form of John (de Norwich). Similarly, the name of the Welsh esquire who hailed from Kidwelly is given as Gruffudd (Dwn) rather than the anglicised 'Griffith'.

The term Gascon is either used specifically to refer to individuals who originated from the region of Gascony, an area within the duchy of Aquitaine which roughly stretched from the Atlantic coast to Agen and from Bordeaux down to the Pyrenees (see Map 1), or broadly to refer to military contingents recruited from the duchy of Aquitaine. Hence, 'Gascon forces' or 'Gascon lords' refer to men from different regions of the duchy and who might not strictly be Gascon. The general term Aquitanian denotes a person who originates from the duchy of Aquitaine, which might naturally also include a Gascon.

Introduction

In the summer of 1345 Henry of Lancaster, earl of Derby, led an English royal army to the duchy of Aquitaine in south-west France. The expedition was a remarkable achievement for the English and marked the first successful land campaign of the Anglo-French conflict which has come to be known as the Hundred Years' War (1337–1453). More importantly, the enterprise signified the beginning of a string of military victories for the English in different theatres of war from 1345 to 1347. In 1345 the earl led an outnumbered force to two major victories during the early stages of the expedition, first at the town of Bergerac and then at the battle of Auberoche; these events were the prelude to Edward III's great voyage to Normandy the following year which culminated in his decisive defeat of the French at the battle of Crécy and the subsequent capture of Calais (1347). The success of the expedition in Aquitaine set the tone for the highly effective multi-front warfare launched by Edward III in the mid 1340s, resulting in victories over the Scots at Neville's Cross (1346) and over the French at La Roche-Derrien (1347), and the subsequent capture of the French king, Jean II, at the battle of Poitiers in 1356 which ultimately compelled the French to accept the ignominious Treaty of Brétigny-Calais in 1360.

It is, indeed, probably the shortness of the period between Lancaster's success in the duchy and Edward III's victory at Crécy which has caused historians to overlook the true significance of what has, in many ways, become a 'forgotten war'. It not only delivered the first blow to the flower of French chivalry, but also provided a vital psychological boost to English armies that were fighting, or were preparing to fight, in other theatres of war. It helped legitimise Edward III's dynastic claim to the French throne, provided an impetus to military recruitment at home and, ultimately, divided the French forces which itself helped pave the way for Edward's decisive victory against the French king, Philippe VI. 'The way of Normandy' (*viage de Normandie*), as it was known at that time, therefore, has largely diminished the importance of the events which had unfolded in Aquitaine the previous year.

This book is a detailed study of the army and the expedition that Lancaster led in 1345–46, with a particular focus on the individuals who served in the earl's own military retinue. By putting a single campaign under the microscope, so to speak, it aims to throw light on several different aspects of military organisation during a period of major reform in English armies. The expedition to Aquitaine was undertaken at an important period of military development, whereby changes in the composition, structure and recruitment of armies, as well as the tactics and strategies used by the military commanders who led them overseas, had transformed England into a front-rank military power by the end of the first phase of the Hundred Years' War.[1] These various elements of army organisation pertaining to the expeditionary force in 1345 will be analysed in detail. Lancaster's army is one of the best documented of the first half of the fourteenth century, and the entire study is underpinned by the wealth of original sources, largely produced by the English medieval royal administrative system. It is for these reasons that Lancaster's expedition to Aquitaine is of particular significance.

Only one attempt has previously been made to treat a single campaign 'in the round' which, by happenstance, also relates to an English expedition in Aquitaine. Herbert J. Hewitt's pioneering study of the Black Prince's expedition to the duchy in 1355, published over half a century ago, provided a comprehensive account of the expedition but it was not firmly based on prosopographical evidence of the military personnel of the prince's army. Hewitt also acknowledges two other shortcomings in his work. The first is the lack of attention given to the 'Gascons' (men who were native to the duchy) and to the Welshmen who took part in the expedition; the second is the omission of any discussion of the financial administration of the army because 'it is inextricably bound up with the general finance of the war … and it is also the subject of specialist study'.[2] This study of Lancaster's army investigates both areas that Hewitt felt unable to address and therefore attempts to bridge an important gap in the historiography of English medieval warfare. It is the first complete study of a single campaign undertaken during the French war which analyses the recruitment, composition, military preparations and financial administration of the army, as well as the course of events of the expedition in Aquitaine. In addition it provides an in-depth study of the individuals who took up arms in Lancaster's retinue.

There has been great scholarly interest in England's involvement in the Hundred Years' War for more than a century. This has led to studies of campaigns, tactics and strategies of war, and other aspects of the conflict

---

[1] For a detailed discussion on these major reforms in military organisation, see Andrew Ayton, *Knights and Warhorses: Military Service and the English Aristocracy under Edward III* (Woodbridge: Boydell, 1994), pp. 19-25; Clifford J. Rogers '"As if a New Sun had Arisen": England's Fourteenth-Century RMA', in *The Dynamics of Military Revolution, 1300–2050*, ed. MacGregor Knox and Williamson Murray (Cambridge: Cambridge University Press, 2001), pp. 15–34; Michael Prestwich, 'Was There a Military Revolution in Medieval England?', in *Recognitions: Essays Presented to Edmund Fryde*, ed. Colin Richmond and Isobel Harvey (Aberystwyth: National Library of Wales, 1996), pp. 19–38.

[2] Herbert J. Hewitt, *The Black Prince's Expedition of 1355–1357* (Manchester: Manchester University Press, 1958), pp. vii–viii.

have received attention at some point or other, from the recruitment and organisation of armies, and the role of the gentry and nobility, who have come to be regarded as the 'warrior class', to the impact that warfare had on society.[3] For Henry of Lancaster's expedition in 1345–46, however, apart from a couple of studies that focus on the course of events in the duchy, it is only Kenneth Fowler (the earl's biographer) and Jonathan Sumption who have attempted to treat the campaign in any detail.[4] Sumption's masterful narrative of the Hundred Years' War provides an excellent account of the expedition in Aquitaine from both English and French perspectives, but the very purpose of his work does not permit a detailed analysis of Lancaster's army. Fowler's study, by contrast, is based on the life and career of the earl, and his coverage of the expedition to the duchy has a slightly stronger focus on military organisation. Although the biography does include a study of Lancaster's entourage and household which elucidates the relationships between the earl and the men most closely associated with him, it provides only a brief assessment of the size and composition of the English force in 1345, as well as of the assembling and financing of the army.

A substantial part of this study is concerned with the individual soldiers who served in Lancaster's retinue in Aquitaine which, in some ways, builds on Fowler's earlier investigation into the men who had an attachment to the earl.[5] Who were these people who took up arms with Lancaster, what were their motivations for service and how experienced were they in warfare? What was their affiliation with Lancaster and, in addition, to what extent did they

---

[3] On the tactics and strategies of war deployed by Edward III, see Clifford J. Rogers, *War Cruel and Sharp: English Strategy under Edward III, 1327–1360* (Woodbridge: Boydell, 2000). For some of the early and most important studies on Edwardian armies, see John E. Morris, *The Welsh Wars of Edward I* (Oxford: Clarendon Press, 1901); Albert E. Prince, 'The Strength of English Armies in the Reign of Edward III', *EHR*, 46 (1931), 353–71; N. B. Lewis, 'The Organisation of Indentured Retinues in Fourteenth-Century England', *TRHS*, 4th ser., 27 (1945), 29–39. For later studies on English armies see various publications by Andrew Ayton, Adrian Bell and Anne Curry in the Bibliography. On the subject of the role of the gentry and nobility, see Nigel Saul, *Knights and Esquires: The Gloucestershire Gentry in the Fourteenth Century* (Oxford: Clarendon Press, 1981); Simon Walker, *The Lancastrian Affinity 1361–1399* (Oxford: Clarendon Press, 1990).

[4] Kenneth Fowler, *The King's Lieutenant: Henry of Grosmont, First Duke of Lancaster, 1310–1361* (London: Elek, 1969); Jonathan Sumption, *The Hundred Years War I: Trial by Battle* (London: Faber and Faber, 1999), pp. 455–88, 541–50. Alfred H. Burne gives an account of the English expedition in Aquitaine, although it is not consistent in accuracy or detail. Clifford Rogers provides a comprehensive and detailed account of the short campaign undertaken by Lancaster at the beginning of the expedition which culminated in the capture of Bergerac. Alfred H. Burne, *The Crécy War: A Military History of the Hundred Years War from 1337 to the Peace of Brétigny, 1360* (London: Eyre & Spottis-woode, 1955); Clifford J. Rogers, 'The Bergerac Campaign (1345) and the Generalship of Henry of Lancaster', *Journal of Medieval Military History*, 2 (2004), 89–110.

[5] Fowler, *The King's Lieutenant*, pp. 172–86.

have an association with each other? These are a few of the basic but fundamental questions that we must seek to answer. The in-depth analysis of a retinue for a single campaign can provide a sharper focus than is possible in Fowler's biographical study, and it enables us to explore the entire careers of hundreds of men and create portrayals of colourful (and sometimes insipid, it has to be said) careers in arms. The campaign is also placed in the context of the more recent historiography that has furthered our understanding of the 'military community' in England, and of the networks and affiliations that underpinned those individuals who took up arms in war.[6] Andrew Ayton, for example, has demonstrated that English armies and 'the military retinue' – the group of men attendant on a captain in time of war – were an institutional and social phenomenon that embodied a multitude of social networks, as well as the personal and hierarchical relationships that existed in everyday life.

In addition it is necessary to consider not just the 'vertical' ties between the earl and the men who served him but also the 'horizontal' connections that existed between the men themselves based, among other things, on family and friendship, lordship and land, and a shared history of military service. This approach to the sources can provide a valuable insight into the characteristics and dynamics of the war retinue in 1345 and illuminate its various attributes, such as cohesion, formation and structure. The military careers of men in Lancaster's retinue and the evidence of their patterns of service with different captains and in different theatres of war can also be used to inform the wider debate on the emergence of military professionalism in fourteenth-century England. It is these individuals who will provide a connecting thread throughout the succeeding chapters of this book.

The principal source upon which this research is based is a retinue roll housed at The National Archives (TNA), Kew, which contains the names of the men who served in Henry of Lancaster's retinue in 1345–46. This document would have been drawn up after the campaign ended and presented to the Exchequer together with other administrative documents when the earl accounted for his service. It consists of three parchment membranes which have been sewn head to foot and it provides a nominal list of soldiers grouped by order of rank and status; thus, bannerets are listed first, followed by knights, esquires and then archers. At some point over the course of the six centuries following the earl's expedition, the final two membranes

---

[6] The concept of the 'military community', which is based on all those who participated in warfare, was created by Philip Morgan and later developed by Andrew Ayton. Philip Morgan, *War and Society in Medieval Cheshire, 1277–1403* (Manchester: Manchester University Press, 1987), pp. 149–84; Andrew Ayton, 'Armies and Military Communities in Fourteenth-Century England', in *Soldiers, Nobles and Gentlemen: Essays in Honour of Maurice Keen*, ed. Peter Coss and Christopher Tyerman (Woodbridge: Boydell, 2009), pp. 215–39.

became detached and were subsequently misfiled by their custodians. Only the first membrane, containing the list of names of bannerets and knights, has therefore, up to now, been available for consultation by historians.[7] But through good fortune and scholarly astuteness, the missing membranes were recently rediscovered at The National Archives by Andrew Ayton who, with characteristic generosity, brought them to the attention of the author of the present work.[8] As a result we now have a complete list of names of soldiers who served in Lancaster's retinue, and it has turned out to be the largest retinue of the first half of the fourteenth century for which the identities of all of the soldiers are known.

Because of the size of the retinue, and the completeness of the documentation, it is possible, therefore, to undertake a collective study of Lancaster's retinue based on mini-biographies of the individual soldiers.[9] A career profile of each man, containing qualitative data such as his history of military service, place of origin or residence, administrative position held, and so on, can be assembled by drawing on a wide range of nominal evidence. The retinue roll discussed above has been employed together with a wealth of other source materials, largely produced by the royal administration, which are spread across various classes of documents at The National Archives. Thousands of administrative records, such as letters of protection and general attorney, charters of pardon, writs of exoneration and the testimonies given at the Court of Chivalry in the 1380s, have been used in the research. The prosopographical study of Lancaster's men has also benefited from the use of the online database and calendar edition created by *The Soldier in Later Medieval England* and *The Gascon Rolls* projects respectively, which have provided invaluable evidence of the military service undertaken by men in the later fourteenth century.[10] The Gascon Rolls calendar was particularly helpful in revealing the

---

[7]   E 101/25/9, m. 3. The first membrane of the retinue roll has been analysed in Kenneth Fowler, 'Henry of Grosmont, First Duke of Lancaster, 1310–1361', 2 vols (unpublished doctoral thesis, University of Leeds, 1961) and Nicholas A. Gribit, 'Henry de Lancaster's Army in Aquitaine, 1345: Recruitment, Service and Reward during the Hundred Years' War' (unpublished doctoral thesis, University of Leeds, 2013).

[8]   E 101/35/2/10.

[9]   Andrew Ayton, 'The English Army at Crécy', in *The Battle of Crécy, 1346*, ed. Andrew Ayton and Sir Philip Preston (Woodbridge: Boydell, 2005), pp. 159–253 (p. 160). The benefit of creating biographies of individuals in order to understand the nature of medieval society in England was first noted by K. B. McFarlane in the 1950s, but the method of prosopography was fully developed by Ayton in order to understand the nature of English armies and military communities. K. B. McFarlane, 'Bastard Feudalism', *BIHR*, 20 (1945), 161–81, (p. 173). For examples of monographs based on the prosopography of military service, see Adrian R. Bell, *War and the Soldier in the Fourteenth Century* (Woodbridge: Boydell, 2004); David Simpkin, *The English Aristocracy at War: From the Welsh Wars of Edward I to the Battle of Bannockburn* (Woodbridge: Boydell, 2008).

[10] www.medievalsoldier.org; www.gasconrolls.org. All documents cited hereafter by class number C 61 have been consulted via the Gascon Rolls website.

administrative and martial activities of men in the duchy of Aquitaine and in illuminating different aspects of Anglo-Gascon relations at the beginning of the Hundred Years' War.[11]

This monograph is divided into three parts. The first focuses on the army itself. In Chapter 1 the historical background is set out in brief, together with the political context in which Lancaster's expedition was launched in 1345. Chapter 2 provides an assessment of the different types of troops which set out for Aquitaine, and is followed in Chapter 3 by a comprehensive account of how the army was raised. Chapter 4 analyses the efficiency with which the army was paid and financially administered over the course of the eighteen months that it spent in the field. It also investigates how the 'money chain' worked, based on a systematic study of the extant pay records, and a reconstruction of the schedule of payments made to the English retinue captains.

Part two outlines the course of events of the expedition. The narrative in Chapters 5 and 6 is based on a wide range of chronicles, but I should point out here one unpublished chronicle in particular, written by someone connected with the garrison of Saint-Omer, which has not been previously used by historians, and which offers an accurate and detailed account of the French siege of Aiguillon in 1346.[12]

The third part of the book focuses on the military retinue of Henry of Lancaster and is based on the prosopographical evidence for those men who took up arms with the earl. Two chapters (7 and 8) investigate the structure, formation, cohesion and stability of what was the largest war retinue to have been put in the field by that time. These chapters attempt to answer the basic questions of how Lancaster was able to assemble a retinue of such an unprecedented size, and how it turned out to be such a formidable fighting force. In Chapter 9 the military careers and the evidence of patterns of service of the earl's men are analysed in order to afford a contribution to the wider topic of military professionalism in England in the fourteenth century. The study ends with some reflections on the significance of the expedition, and on the importance of Lancaster himself as a military leader in Aquitaine in the mid 1340s. It is intended to lead to a reassessment of the campaign as well as of Lancaster's crucial part in England's military successes during the first phase of the Hundred Years' War.

[11] The calendar was originally directed by Dr Paul Booth and Dr Malcolm Vale, and was later continued by Professor Anne Curry and Dr Philip Morgan.
[12] The chronicle was recently rediscovered by Clifford Rogers and has only been utilised in his account of the Bergerac campaign. *Saint-Omer Chronicle*, ed. and trans. Clifford J. Rogers (typescript for edition in preparation), passage quoted from BM Saint-Omer, MS 707, fols 206–33.

I

Henry of Lancaster and the English Army: Soldiers, Payment and Recruitment

1

Henry of Lancaster and the English Expedition to Aquitaine, 1345–46

Historical Background

The military expedition led by Henry of Lancaster to Aquitaine in 1345 was part of a long-running conflict between England and France which is known by historical tradition as The Hundred Years' War (1337–1453). This intermittent and protracted war dominated politics and society in western Europe in the later Middle Ages, and enveloped a swathe of kingdoms which played an integral role in the course of events that ensued. The Iberian kingdoms of Aragon, Castile, Navarre and Portugal, the counties and duchies of Artois, Brabant, Hainault, Holland, Jülich, Luxemburg, Namur and Zeeland that constituted the Low Countries, as well as the Holy Roman Empire, Scotland and the states that form modern-day Italy, were, along with other kingdoms, drawn into the apparently interminable conflict.[1] A plethora of alliances were made between these ruling powers and between them and the two protagonists of the war, the longest lasting of which was the union between France and Scotland which threatened England, on and off, from the 'Auld Alliance' in 1295 until a Scottish king, James VI, also became king of England in 1603.[2] In fact the term, Hundred Years' War, or *Guerre de cent ans*, its French precedent, is a misnomer of nineteenth-century historians that obscures the context of a wider Anglo-French conflict which had begun in the reign of Henry II (1154–89), the first Plantagenet king of England.[3] At the heart of hostilities were English-held

---

[1] For a brief outline of events which occurred in these lands and the influence that they had on the Anglo-French war, see Kelly DeVries, 'The Hundred Years War: Not One But Many', in *The Hundred Years War (Part II): Different Vistas*, ed. L. J. Andrew Villalon and Donald J. Kagay (Leiden: Brill, 2008), pp. 3–34 (pp. 8–32).

[2] Anne Curry, *The Hundred Years War*, 2nd edn (Basingstoke: Palgrave Macmillan, 2003), pp. 118–19. For an introduction to the Auld Alliance which was established in Paris (1295), and then in Dunfermline (1296), see Elisabeth Bonner, 'Scotland's "Auld Alliance" with France, 1295–1560', *History*, 84 (1999), 5–30.

[3] This term for Anglo-French hostilities from 1337 to 1453 was first coined by historians in the 1860s and has become widely accepted ever since: Curry, *Hundred Years War*, pp. 5–27. The term of this artificial periodisation, however, is itself misleading as

territories in France, and the duchy of Aquitaine in particular, which came into English possession through Henry's marriage to Eleanor, the heiress to the duchy, and had remained in the hands of his royal successors since the mid-twelfth century. Other territories that formed part of the Angevin empire – the assemblage of lands under Plantagenet control – at its greatest extent included Normandy, Maine, Anjou, Touraine and Poitou, but by 1204 only Aquitaine remained in English possession.[4] In the successive reigns of Richard I and John hostilities between the kingdoms of England and France persisted, but in the reign of Henry III (1216–72) the relationship between the two monarchs was redefined at the Peace of Paris of 1259. English kings held Aquitaine thereafter as a fief of the French crown.[5] In practice this meant that English kings were now obliged to pay liege homage to their feudal overlord, the French king, in return for their tenure of Aquitaine and, following Edward I's marriage to Eleanor of Castile in 1279, also for the county of Ponthieu. This produced a novel dynastic dilemma for the English kings as one monarch now held superior feudal status over another, and the perennial desire of both rival kingdoms to exercise their own authority and power in Aquitaine inevitably led to future strife in the duchy.

It was the confiscation of Aquitaine by the French kings that caused the outbreak of war in the duchy in 1294 and 1324, and it was again largely the cause of the reopening of hostilities in 1337. The English kings, Edward I and Edward II, had both organised military campaigns against their cross-channel neighbours prior to Edward III's declaration of war, and hostilities against England's old adversary were reignited by all of the successors to the English throne up to the early sixteenth century.[6] The expulsion of the last English troops from Aquitaine in 1453 marked the end of the king-dukes' governance in the duchy, but the city of Calais, which had been captured

the 'The Hundred Years' War' in fact covers a period of 116 years. In some ways the reign of William the Conqueror marked the beginning of Anglo-French hostilities as it was his invasion of England and subsequent succession to the throne that first brought about the intractable problem that was inherited by future kings, namely that a king of England held continental land possessions.

[4] In 1279 the Plantagenet inheritance included the county of Ponthieu following Edward I's marriage to Eleanor of Castile. Malcolm G. A. Vale, *The Origins of the Hundred Years War: The Angevin Legacy, 1250–1340* (Oxford: Clarendon Press, 1996), pp. 9–21; Anne Curry, *The Hundred Years' War, 1337–1453* (London: Routledge, 2003), pp. 11–12. The term Angevin derived from Henry II's holding of Anjou.

[5] At the Treaty of Paris Henry III reinforced his vassal status and ceded his claim to all other Angevin lands to the French king, Louis IX: Vale, *Origins of the Hundred Years' War*, pp. 48–63; Curry, *Hundred Years' War, 1337–1453*, pp. 11–12.

[6] Edward IV and Henry VIII, for example, attempted to symbolically reopen the Hundred Years' War by launching attacks on France based on the same dynastic premise which underpinned Edward III's French war in the fourteenth century. W. Mark Ormrod, *Edward III* (New Haven, CT: Yale University Press, 2011), p. 588.

by Edward III in 1347, did not return to French possession until 1553.[7] It was within this long era of Anglo-French hostilities that the Hundred Years' War was fought, a period characterised by a succession of naval and land-based wars punctuated by long periods of truce and temporary peace. One of the distinctive features of the war, which set it apart from other periods of fighting, was Edward III's dynastic claim to the French throne through his mother, Isabella, following the death of the last Capetian king, Charles IV, in 1328. As nephew of Charles, Edward was the closest heir to the dead king but he was deemed ineligible to inherit on account of the female line from which his claim derived and, consequently, Philippe of Valois was made king of France. Whether the pursuit of the French crown was a realistic ambition of Edward in 1337 is uncertain, but his aim to recover the French territories that had been held by previous kings of England from generation to generation cannot be doubted.

It was during the first phase of the war (1337–60) that Henry of Lancaster, earl of Derby, the king's cousin, led his army to spectacular victories over French forces in Aquitaine (1345), which were a precursor to the series of English military successes at Crécy (1346), Neville's Cross (1346), La Roche-Derrien (1347) and Calais (1347). The momentum of English success reached an apogee in the mid 1350s when the French king, Jean II, was captured by Edward, prince of Wales (more commonly known as the Black Prince) at the battle of Poitiers, which allowed Edward to dictate advantageous terms for England at the Treaty of Brétigny-Calais following the king's last overseas expedition in 1359.[8] The intensity and longevity of the war gave rise to patriotism in both countries on either side of the Channel and laid the foundations for the future development of a national consciousness. In this phase of the war the English were able to recover from the humiliation of the defeat by the Scots at Bannockburn (1314), and successfully adopt new battle tactics that focused on a defensive mode of fighting with a combinative use of longbowmen and dismounted men-at-arms. The potential benefits of utilising such a strategy – which formed a major part of what has been labelled the 'medieval military revolution' – had been demonstrated against the Scots at the battle of Halidon Hill (1333), but it was not until the following decades that England became a dominant military power in Europe.

After the resounding success of the military enterprises of the mid 1340s

---

[7] The battle of Castillon (1453), in which an English army led by John Talbot was defeated near Bordeaux, is considered to be the last battle of the Hundred Years' War. On the English occupation of Calais, see Georges Daumet, *Calais sous la domination anglaise* (Arras: Répressé-Crépel et fils, 1902).

[8] For the crippling terms accepted by the French at the Treaty of Brétigny, see Jean Le Patourel, 'The Treaty of Brétigny, 1360', in *Feudal Empires: Norman and Plantagenet*, ed. Michael Jones (London: Hambledon, 1984), pp. 19–39.

an enthusiasm for war amongst the 'military community' proliferated in England. The creation of the prestigious Order of the Garter enshrined the recent victories in perpetuity and embodied the chivalric code that under-pinned the principles of one of England's most vigorous warrior-kings. It was perhaps Edward's ability to foster intimate and mutually beneficial relation-ships with the English nobility that represented one of the most successful traits of his kingship, and his creation of six new earls on the eve of the outbreak of the French war in 1337 was a testament to his designs. Among this crop of newly promoted men, who were intended to become the king's foremost military captains, was Henry of Lancaster, earl of Derby (1310–61). The earl was a contemporary of the king who, as a soldier, diplomat and administrator, went on to become one of the most influential figures in the first phase of the French war.

In the first eight years of the war Edward III deployed a variety of strategies against his French adversary, albeit with mixed success. A shift in focus to the theatre of war in Aquitaine followed Edward's failed attempts to win a decisive land battle against Philippe VI on the north east frontier of France from 1338 to 1340, and in Brittany in 1342. A diplomatic offensive launched by Edward in 1337 had secured alliances with the nobility and princes of the Low Countries and, later on, with the Holy Roman Emperor, Ludwig IV of Bavaria, as a result of which the imperial vicariate was bestowed upon him in 1338.[9] The main advantage of Edward's imperial appointment was that it enabled him to summon to arms the emperor's vassals in the Low Countries, including Jan III, duke of Brabant, Wilhelm V, margrave of Jülich and Wilhelm II, count of Hainault. However, in spite of this grand northern European coalition the subsequent campaigns in the northern French counties of Cambrai, Vermandois and Thiérarche (1339), as well as the unsuccessful siege of Tournai (1341), failed to provide either side with an opportunity for a decisive military encounter.[10] Furthermore, Edward's expensive foreign policy of building alliances abroad based on grants of subsidies and royal favours provoked a major political crisis in England which almost lost him control of his own parliament.[11]

English fortunes of war could not have been more different at sea. The stunning naval victory at Sluys in 1340 ensured English dominance of the Channel and undoubtedly boosted the confidence of the Plantagenet regime while helping to legitimise Edward's dynastic claim to the French throne

[9] Henry Stephen Lucas, *The Low Countries and the Hundred Years' War, 1326–1347* (Ann Arbor, MI: University of Michigan, 1929), pp. 339–48.
[10] Rogers, *War Cruel and Sharp*, pp. 157–73; 199–216. Sumption, *Trial by Battle*, pp. 239–90.
[11] Gerald L. Harriss, *King, Parliament and Public Finance in Medieval England, to 1369* (Oxford: Clarendon Press, 1975), pp. 231–93.

which he had made earlier that year.[12] It was not until the Breton succession dispute erupted in the following year, however, that Edward was able to make strategic gains of any significance on land. The death of Jean III, duke of Brittany in the spring of 1341, and the war of succession in his duchy that ensued, provided a proper 'cause of war' (*casus belli*) for the rival kings; the military intervention by Edward on behalf of Jean de Montfort, the English candidate, and French support for the opposing contender, Charles de Blois, ended in a truce at Malestroit in January 1343.[13] Consequently, the English were able to establish a foothold in the north-western duchy which ensured a safe crossing for both the commercial and military sea traffic bound for Aquitaine and the west of France. More significantly, the control of parts of the Breton peninsula offered a staging point from which Plantagenet forces could penetrate into the French interior. A new front in the Anglo-French war had thereby been opened which would facilitate a sustainable and successful military strategy three years later.[14]

By 1343 the interests of English diplomacy had also penetrated into the Iberian peninsula where Edward hoped to secure a powerful ally in the form of Alfonso XI of Castile through a marriage alliance between his son, Pedro, and Edward's daughter, Joan. An alliance with Alfonso would bring with it the prospect of the support, or at least the neutrality, of the Castilian fleet, a supreme maritime power which the French king had been able to utilise since 1336 when he made an alliance with Castile.[15] To achieve this end and to establish good relations with the other Iberian kingdoms of Aragon and Portugal Henry of Lancaster and Richard, earl of Arundel, were appointed as the king's lieutenants in Aquitaine and Languedoc in 1344. Meanwhile, the state of affairs in the duchy of Aquitaine had rapidly deteriorated since the outbreak of war in 1337 and both the financial and military situation in the duchy had reached a critical point.[16] Since the kings of England had ruled as dukes of Aquitaine, affairs in the duchy had been largely administered by the two principal offices of the lieutenancy and the seneschalcy of Aquitaine. The lieutenancy was an occasional office irregularly used by the kings of England, usually in times of war or strife, and the appointee, as was the case in 1344, was often a close relative of the king. The seneschal was responsible for judicial matters, the general governance and the administration of the duchy, and was supported by the constable of Bordeaux,

---

[12] For an assessment of the tactics and strategy used by the English at Sluys, see Graham Cushway, *Edward III and the War at Sea* (Woodbridge: Boydell, 2011), pp. 90–100.

[13] Christopher T. Allmand, *The Hundred Years War: England and France at War, c. 1300–c. 1450*, rev. edn (Cambridge: Cambridge University Press, 2001), p. 14.

[14] Sumption, *Trial by Battle*, pp. 370–410.

[15] Peter E. Russell, *The English Intervention in Spain and Portugal in the Time of Edward III and Richard II* (Oxford: Clarendon Press, 1955), pp. 1–11.

[16] Fowler, *King's Lieutenant*, pp. 39–52.

who was the chief financial officer in Aquitaine. In the duchy's two principal cities of Bayonne and Bordeaux, administrative powers devolved to the office of mayor. All these positions in the ducal administration, except for the mayor of Bayonne, were traditionally held by Englishmen.

After the French invasion of the duchy in 1324 and the subsequent War of Saint-Sardos (1324–25), the areas under English control and the number of Gascon lords loyal to the king-duke had diminished.[17] The situation was exacerbated further by the renewal of hostilities thirteen years later; a period of constant fighting in the duchy culminated in strategic losses for the English as the French penetrated into Bordelais from Saintonge and Agenais, which almost resulted in the capture of Bordeaux, the ducal capital, in 1339. The success of French military operations had been followed up by the distribution of pardons to tempt the lords of towns into Philippe VI's allegiance.[18] The fickle nature that characterised the duchy's nobility was often exploited by the French king, who, as sovereign lord of Aquitaine, could hear and pass judgment on any appeals from the duke's courts made by its inhabitants. In turn, the native nobility benefited greatly from the feudal structure of the duchy's lordship and its complex political structure. In particular their immediate ruler – Edward III – was normally resident overseas, which provided them with a greater degree of autonomy than if he had ruled personally in the duchy, and Philippe VI's ultimate lordship over Aquitaine meant that the nobility could circumvent and undermine the duchy's judicial system by petitioning the French king directly in Paris.

By the end of the 1330s the Bordeaux administration was unable to meet its financial commitments to the Gascon lords who had been retained in Edward III's service and provided him with military support. The impecuniousness of the English was compounded by the decreasing revenue which had resulted from its progressive shrinkage, as well as the costs of pensions and other payments which were tailored to ensure that the Gascons did not switch to French obedience. The defence of the duchy had largely been left to the indigenous nobility whose loyalty to their duke in the defence against increasing French encroachment had left its coffers empty. In reality, the inability of the ducal administration to pay for military service performed by Gascons in the late 1330s left both the English king-duke and his subjects in the duchy near to bankruptcy, and the dire financial situation is borne out by the desperate petitions of impoverished lords who sought recompense from the king years later.[19] As a result, military operations in

---

[17] Vale, *Origins of the Hundred Years War*, pp. 227–65. The term 'Gascon lords' refers to the nobility who were indigenous to Aquitaine rather than to the specific region of Gascony, which formed a linguistic region within the duchy.

[18] Sumption, *Trial by Battle*, p. 159.

[19] In his petition to Edward III in 1344 Hélias de Pommiers, for example, claimed that 'he had nothing to maintain his position or allow him to continue in the king's

the south west were financed by the English Exchequer and not by the ducal revenue as had originally been intended. By 1340 the territories under English control were limited to the narrow coastal strip between the mouth of the Gironde and the Pyrenees, as the French had taken control of the Garonne valley and advanced down the Dordogne valley as far as Libourne. Most places in the duchy were in allegiance with the Valois king, apart from the coastal towns of Bayonne and Bordeaux, and Saint-Sever and their immediate surroundings.[20]

At the beginning of 1345 the rival kingdoms had reached a political impasse, and the breakdown of Anglo-French peace negotiations at the papal court in March presaged hostilities that were soon to follow. The events which had transpired during the opening years of the Hundred Years' War had a dual effect: they reaffirmed the importance of Edward's principal war aim of luring Philippe VI on to the battlefield, and they ultimately shaped his plans that would fulfil that aim. The preparations for a new offensive in 1345 were based on the unprecedented idea of launching a coordinated and simultaneous attack on the French on several different fronts. On this occasion military operations would not be restricted to the duchy, or to a particular region in France, and the abandonment of Edward's earlier policy of recruiting large mercenary armies meant that the men who prosecuted these campaigns would be predominantly English. The aim of this newly adopted multi-front warfare was to divide the French forces, and to bring to fruition Edward's desire for a decisive engagement with Philippe.[21]

The preparations for Edward III's grand strategy were well under way by the spring of 1345. Four armies were to be assembled. The first comprised around 500 men and was to be led to Brittany by William de Bohun, earl of Northampton.[22] The second, of the much greater size of 2000 men, is the focus of this study, and was placed under the command of Henry of Lancaster who would operate in Aquitaine. The third, and largest of the expeditionary forces, was to be led by Edward himself. This force, the largest hitherto raised in England, was of up to 20,000 men and was intended to land in northern France, although the exact destination is unknown.[23] The armies led by the earls of Lancaster (as Henry became upon his father's

service' on account of the wars in the duchy. C 61/56, m. 11. For numerous letters to the constable of Bordeaux ordering him to settle the accounts of service and pay wages owed to men who had performed service in Aquitaine up to seven years earlier, see C 61/56.

[20] Fowler, *King's Lieutenant*, pp. 41–53. For English-held land in Aquitaine prior to the outbreak of war in 1337 and surrounding territories, see Map 1.

[21] Rogers claims Edward III's aim since the beginning of the Hundred Years' War had been to draw Philippe VI into a pitched battle and win a decisive victory against the French. Rogers, *War, Cruel and Sharpe*, pp. 238–72.

[22] *Foedera*, III, p. 36; Sumption, *Trial by Battle*, p. 454.

[23] Ormrod, *Edward III*, p. 264; Ayton, *The English Army at Crécy*, pp. 159–252.

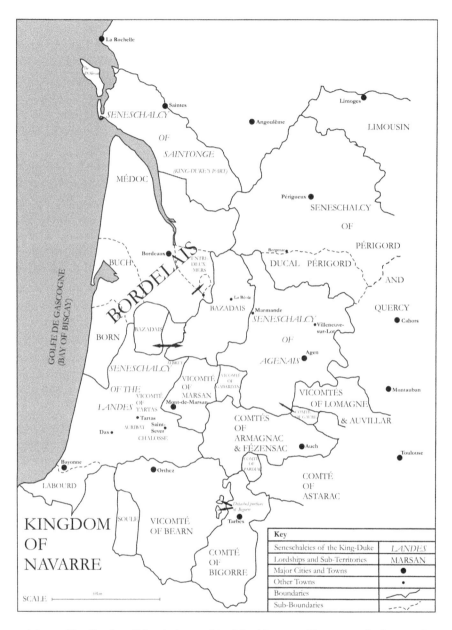

Map 1. The Duchy of Aquitaine and its Neighbouring Territories (before 1337)

death, in the course of the campaign) and Northampton were to be supplemented by troops raised by English allies in Brittany and Aquitaine. The
fourth expeditionary force was comparatively small and was placed under
the command of Sir Thomas Ferrers, whose aim was to capture the French
garrison of Castle Cornet on the island of Guernsey.[24] The control of this
strategically important Channel island was intended to ensure safe sea-cross-
ings for the English armies and, therefore, was an important preliminary to
the overall operations. It was in the context of this grand scheme of events
that the recruitment and mobilisation of Lancaster's army began.

Henry of Lancaster

Henry of Lancaster, or Henry of Grosmont as he was commonly known in
order to distinguish him from his father and namesake, was born around
1310, probably at his father's castle of Grosmont in the South Wales marcher
lordship of the Three Castles. As second cousin of Edward III and a third
generation of the house of Lancaster, Henry belonged to an illustrious
ancestry that had been prominent in England's affairs for more than half a
century. He was the grandson of Edmund Crouchback (1245–96), who was
made first earl of Lancaster and first earl of Leicester in 1267 by his older
brother, Edward I, and nephew of the formidable Thomas of Lancaster
(c.1278–1322) who led the baronial opposition against Edward II and was
summarily executed outside the walls of Pontefract castle following his final
rebellion in 1322.[25] Henry's father, the third earl of Lancaster (c.1280–1345),
was also a staunch opponent of Edward II whom he captured and imprisoned
at Kenilworth in 1326 after joining the invading army of Queen Isabella and
her lover, Roger Mortimer, earl of March. The latter then forced the king
to relinquish his throne and subsequently established his own rule during
the minority regime of Edward III. The older Henry was appointed the
guardian of Edward III following his coronation a year later, and in response
to the growing threat of Mortimer's rule he played an integral part in the
military coup against Mortimer in 1330 which safely delivered the throne
to the young king.[26] Indeed, Edward's reliance upon Lancastrian support to
accomplish his ambitions continued throughout his long reign and rested

[24] Ferrers was Governor of the Channel Islands (1337–41; 1343–48) and led a military
force of 30 men-at-arms and 86 archers in 1345: E 101/25/6, m. 1.
[25] For the careers of Edmund and Thomas, see Andrew M. Spencer, *Nobility and Kingship in Medieval England: The Earls and Edward I, 1272–1307* (Cambridge: Cambridge
University Press, 2014), pp. 175–258; John R. Maddicott, *Thomas of Lancaster, 1307–1322:
A Study in the Reign of Edward II* (Oxford: Oxford University Press, 1970).
[26] On the political events that led to the downfall of Edward II, see J. R. Seymour
Phillips, *Edward II* (New Haven, CT: Yale University Press, 2010).

squarely on the shoulders of the younger Henry of Lancaster, who became one of the most distinguished English statesmen in the fourteenth century.

In the last year of his life Henry had accumulated the titles of 'duke of Lancaster, earl of Derby, Lincoln and Leicester, steward of England, lord of Bergerac and Beaufort' and, after Edward, the Black Prince, was the wealthiest magnate in England.[27] Before 1345, however, he only held the titles of 'lord of Kidwelly' and 'earl of Derby'.[28] It was not until 1347, two years after his father's death, that Henry would take up his family inheritance and continue the process of recovering the ancestral lands which had been forfeited by Thomas of Lancaster.[29] The earldom of Derby was granted to Henry in 1337, but a large part of the Lancastrian lands in South Wales had been granted to him by his father four years earlier, including the castles of Skenfrith, Grosmont and Kidwelly, as well as lands in Carnwyllion and Ogmore and Ebboth manor. The older Henry also granted him the Yorkshire manors of Barlow and Kilburn, as well as the profits from Pickering forest eyre.[30] His Welsh landholdings were augmented in 1334 when he secured the custody of the lands of Isabella de Hastings during the minority of Laurence de Hastings (future earl of Pembroke) – most notably Abergavenny castle – to which were later added Carreg Cennen castle and Iscennen.[31] In the following decade Henry was also granted the keeping of Carmarthen (castle, town and county) and the lordship of Cantref Mawr for ten years.[32]

As earl of Derby he held the extensive honour of Tutbury in Staffordshire and Derbyshire. To support his new title Henry was endowed by the Crown with an annuity of 1000 marks that was partly converted soon after to a grant of some Norfolk and Yorkshire manors, and he also received a pension of £20 a year from the revenues of the shrievalty (office of sheriff)

---

[27] John Nichols, *A History of the Wills of the Kings and Queens of England* (London: J. Nichols, 1790), pp. 83–7.

[28] Henry styled himself 'lord of Kidwelly' in writs and warrants in 1334 and in later years. *Somerville*, p. 38, n. 2. The evidence of Henry's landholdings and franchises discussed in this and the following paragraph has been taken from *Somerville*, pp. 37–41.

[29] Henry's father had begun the piecemeal process of recovering his family estates within months of Thomas' death by petitioning Edward II and, in later years, Roger Mortimer and Edward III in an attempt to restore the Lancastrian inheritance. *Somerville*, pp. 31–7.

[30] The forest eyre was granted to Henry in October 1334 and the Yorkshire manors in January 1338.

[31] Laurence de Hastings was granted livery of his lands by Edward III in 1339, except for the lands in the custody of Henry of Lancaster, who presumably retained part of Hastings' inheritance until the latter came of age in 1341. Andrew Ayton, 'Hastings, Laurence, twelfth earl of Pembroke (1320–1348)', *ODNB*, Oct 2008 [accessed 28 February 2015].

[32] Carmarthen and Cantref Mawr were committed to Henry's keeping on 17 February 1342. *CFR, 1337–47*, pp. 263–4, 335.

of Derbyshire.[33] In the same year that Henry became earl, his father granted him and his wife Isabella the Hampshire and Wiltshire manors of Hannington, Inglesham, Longstock, Hartley Mauditt and West Patrick that had come into the Lancastrian inheritance through his mother Maud Chaworth.[34] Over the next eight years he acquired a handful of manors in the counties of Lancaster (Ulnes Walton), Stafford (Shenston) and Leicester (Hallaton), as well as the shrievalty of Staffordshire. In addition, Henry leased the honour of Pontefract from Queen Philippa for the term of his life in 1342 and thus regained the principal Lancastrian *caput* in the north of England.[35] It was in 1347 and subsequent years that Henry made substantial additions to the family inheritance, most of which derived from royal grants as a reward for his military feats in the duchy of Aquitaine. The greatest honour was bestowed on him in 1351 when he was elevated to the rank of duke and granted palatine powers in Lancashire.

Of Henry's early life very little is known, but according to his own memoir and devotional treatise written in 1354, *Le Livre de Seyntz Medicines* (*The Book of Holy Medicines*), he was good looking in his youth – tall, blond and svelte.[36] Such looks were matched by charm, and despite being a man of piety Henry confesses to being troubled by his lapses of chastity. The skills of literacy do not seem to have come naturally to him, as it was not until later in life that he claimed to have learned to write and he often struggled with Anglo-Norman, the dialect of the social elite in England at that time. In *Le Livre* we glean the impression of a man who indulged in court splendours and the pleasures of a noble life: rich food, fine clothes, hunting, dancing, jousting, flirtation and knightly prowess.[37] The treatise is an allegorical account of Henry's sins and penance which characterises his devout religious beliefs, and reveals his particular devotion to the Virgin Mary. Henry's mother died before he reached his teenage years, and although we cannot be certain of Henry's movements during the

---

[33] On 3 October 1337 the earl's annuity which had been granted on the customs of the ports of London, Boston and Kingston-upon-Hull, was partly converted to a grant on the manor of Wighton and the hundred of North Greenhoe (Norfolk), and the manor of Laughton-en-le-Morthen (Yorkshire). *CPR, 1334–38*, p. 538.

[34] A rent from the manor of King's Somborne (Hampshire) also formed part of this package of grants, all of which were re-granted to Henry's father for his lifetime.

[35] Henry's father had obtained confirmation of his rights in the honour of Pontefract in 1330. *CPR, 1330–34*, p. 19.

[36] For a comprehensive translation of the treatise, see Henry of Grosmont, First Duke of Lancaster, *Le Livre de Seyntz Medicines: The Book of Holy Medicines*, trans. with notes and introduction by Catherine Batt (Tempe, AZ: ACMRS, 2015).

[37] M. Teresa Tavormina, 'Henry of Lancaster, *The Book of Holy Medicines*', in *Cultures of Piety: Medieval English Devotional Literature in Translation*, ed. Anne Clark Bartlett and Thomas H. Bestul (Ithaca, NY: Cornell University Press, 1999), pp. 19–40 (pp. 19–21).

tumult of the 1320s it is unlikely that he had any direct involvement in the Lancastrian rebellions against the king.[38]

At twenty years of age Henry married Isabella, the daughter of Henry, Lord Beaumont, a prominent northern baron who was a notable adherent of his uncle and a close friend of his father.[39] Isabella bore him two daughters (i.e. co-heiresses), Maud and Blanche, the latter of whom would marry John of Gaunt and sire the future king of England, Henry of Bolingbroke. The union between the houses of Beaumont and Lancaster was augmented further by the marriage of Henry's sister, Eleanor, to Lord Beaumont's son and heir, John, who was thus brother-in-law to Henry twice over.[40] In 1330 Henry was knighted, and on account of his father's blindness he took an active part in the earl's council and represented him in parliament. It was around this time that Henry emerged as a political figure in his own right and an intimate association between himself and the king began to develop.[41] The two men were of a similar age (Edward was two years older) and shared the same interests in the tournament and romance literature, among other things; both were imbued with chivalric values and emulated the practices of the Arthurian legend – a view borne out in 1344 by Henry's leading role in the inauguration ceremonies of Edward III's new knightly order based on the Round Table society which provided inspiration for, and was superseded by, the Order of the Garter four years later.[42] Indeed, it has even been suggested, somewhat unconvincingly, that Lancaster himself was the patron of the Arthurian alliterative poem *Sir Gawain and the Green Knight*.[43] In 1331 he accompanied the king on a secret mission to France. Later that year he attended a royal joust at Cheapside, then went abroad to Brabant. He attended parliament regularly over the next twelve months.[44] In the following March he was granted an annuity of 500 marks at the Exchequer 'for the special affection which the king bore him … and also for his better maintenance in the king's service'.[45] The intimacy between the two men grew and perhaps the most notable act of affection was

---

[38]   Fowler, *King's Lieutenant*, p. 26.

[39]   Henry married Isabella before 24 June 1330. DL 41/10/34, m. 44; Fowler, *King's Lieutenant*, p. 26.

[40]   Eleanor and John were married between 1 September and 6 November 1330. Fowler, *King's Lieutenant*, p. 26.

[41]   W. Mark Ormrod, 'Henry of Lancaster, first duke of Lancaster (*c*.1310–1361)', *ODNB*, Jan 2008 [accessed 28 February 2015].

[42]   D'Arcy J. D. Boulton, *The Knights of the Crown: The Monarchical Orders of Knighthood in Later Medieval Europe, 1325–1520* (Woodbridge: Boydell, 1987), pp. 104–5, 109–10.

[43]   W. G. Cooke and D'Arcy J. D. Boulton, '*Sir Gawain and the Green Knight*: A Poem for Henry of Grosmont?', *Medium Ævum*, 68 (1999), 42–54.

[44]   Fowler, *King's Lieutenant*, pp. 27–8.

[45]   *CPR, 1330–34*, p. 265 (27 March 1332).

when Henry submitted to imprisonment in Brussels in 1340 as one of the sureties for debts due by Edward III to the Leuven and Mechelen creditors who had bank-rolled the king's alliance with the rulers in the Low Countries.[46]

The trust that the king placed in Henry of Lancaster is reflected by the appointments to high military command and also by the diplomatic missions undertaken by the earl during his eventful career up to 1345. On two occasions he served as the king's lieutenant in Scotland (1336, 1341), and he shared the office in Aquitaine with the earl of Arundel in 1344. By the time of the 1345 expedition Lancaster was in the prime of life and had taken part in no fewer than ten military expeditions on the Continent and in Scotland, including the naval battle of Sluys.[47] The Scottish wars in the 1330s and the opening campaigns of the Hundred Years' War proved as much a training ground for Lancaster as they had done for Edward III. The earl's daring raid to rescue the earl of Athol's widow who was besieged at Lochindorb castle in 1336, for example, highlighted the benefits of conducting a highly mobile force not only as part of a battle-seeking strategy, but also as an effective means of avoiding the Scottish enemy. Similarly, the earl experienced the advantages of attacking with speed when he took part in a lightning raid on the island of Cadzand, in Zeeland, the following year. Such valuable experiences of warfare no doubt influenced the earl's own tactics and military strategies which he later deployed in Aquitaine.

By 1345 Lancaster's reputation as a military commander was very high, and in addition his personal skills as an orator and a negotiator enabled him to excel in the field of diplomacy. From 1340 to 1344 Henry took part in five separate diplomatic missions which included treating with representatives of the pope at Valenciennes (1340), negotiating the truce of Esplechin (1340) and brokering a marriage alliance with Alfonso XI (1343). It was during this last embassy that Henry and William Montague, earl of Salisbury, crusaded with the king of Castile against the Moors at Algeciras and in North Africa. It was, perhaps, these crusading exploits that inspired the character of Geoffrey Chaucer's knight in the prologue of *The Canterbury Tales*, who 'In far Granada at the siege was he, Of Algeciras and ridden in Bani'.[48] By the mid 1340s Henry had emerged as one of the king's most influential and talented captains, and Edward's strategy of launching a multi-pronged attack against the Valois forces provided him with the opportunity to lead

[46] Fowler, *King's Lieutenant*, pp. 34–6.

[47] For a detailed discussion of Lancaster's military and diplomatic missions up to 1345, see Fowler, *King's Lieutenant*, pp. 29–52.

[48] Russell, *English Intervention in Spain*, p. 8. Geoffrey Chaucer, *The Riverside Chaucer*, ed. Larry D. Benson, 3rd edn (Boston: Houghton Mifflin, 1987), p. 24, lines 56–7: 'In Grenade at the seege eek hadde he be, Of Algezir, and riden in Belmarye'.

an army overseas and win fame and fortune, but above all, to demonstrate his talent as a military commander. It was in the summer of 1345 that he led an expeditionary force to Aquitaine which won stunning victories against the French and dramatically swung the course of the Hundred Years' War in England's favour.

2

English and Welsh Soldiers:
Troop Types in Lancaster's Army

On Sunday 13 March 1345 the king entered into an indenture, or formal contract of service, with Henry of Lancaster, whereby Henry agreed to go to Aquitaine as the king's lieutenant and command an army of 2000 men who were to assemble at Southampton on 14 May, ready to embark for the duchy.[1] The bulk of the cost of the expedition was to be financed by the accumulated clerical and lay subsidies, forms of extraordinary direct taxation granted to the king by parliament two years earlier. The indenture stipulated that the army was to comprise 500 men-at-arms, 500 Welsh infantry and 1000 archers (half mounted, half on foot). It also set out, amongst other things, the extensive military and judicial powers that Lancaster was to have as the king's lieutenant, and stated that he was to serve in the duchy for an initial period of six months. The terms embodied in the indenture of service are discussed in greater detail in the next chapter, but, first, an important prerequisite to an in-depth study of Lancaster's army is an examination of the typical soldiers who were required to serve under the earl's command. Although the various troop types which constituted English armies in the fourteenth century have been discussed extensively in previous studies, there remains some ambiguity surrounding the terminology used both by contemporary clerks and present-day scholars to describe men of different rank and status.[2] A brief definition of each type of soldier that served with Lancaster is therefore needed. It is necessary to determine how they were equipped, to analyse the various terms used by clerks to describe such men and where they fitted in the overall structure of the army, and how they related to medieval society in general.

The conventional view that medieval armies were made up of 'cavalry' and 'infantry' contingents does not fit with the English armies of the fourteenth century. As Michael Prestwich points out, it would be problematic to define

---

[1]   E 159/123, m. 254; see Appendix A for a transcription and translation of the document.
[2]   Adrian Bell, for example, uses terms such as 'dukes' and 'earls' to denote different ranks, but these are essentially social titles and should not be regarded as military ranks. Bell, *War and the Soldier*, p. 49.

a soldier by whether he fought on horseback or on foot,[3] not least because the developments in army organisation in Edward III's reign had transformed the military role, and sometimes the status, of the medieval soldier. These changes in warfare were paralleled by the nuanced changes in the military nomenclature used by royal clerks. For example, no fewer than twenty different words are recorded in the royal administrative documents relating to combatants who served in Lancaster's expedition in 1345.[4] Obviously, each term does not refer to a different 'type' of soldier, but it can give a clear idea of how one soldier differed from another, whether it be the status that he held, the type of equipment that he owned, or by his role on the battlefield.

It is common practice in current historiography to distinguish soldiers in military terms simply by the two ranks of archer and man-at-arms, but this approach can be misleading considering that the word 'rank' connotes a hierarchical structure and sense of command, in terms of either the social or the military order.[5] The main difference between an archer and a man-at-arms – besides the stark contrast in their social status – is how they were equipped and fought on campaign; furthermore, there were clear differences of rank within each of these two categories of soldier. Therefore, the more neutral term of 'troop type' rather than 'rank' has been used in the following discussion to distinguish between archers and men-at-arms. In the cases of Henry of Lancaster and William of Greystoke, for example, it is apparent that both men belonged to the category of man-at-arms, but it is their titles of 'Counte' and 'Baron', recorded by the Exchequer clerks, which reflect their standing in the military community.[6] It is problematic, therefore, to define a soldier solely by the commonality of his troop type, and would seem more accurate, rather, to define a soldier by his troop type, his military rank and, where possible, his social status. Soldiers in Lancaster's army can be categorised by three main troop types; that is, men-at-arms, archers (mounted and foot) and Welsh infantry.[7]

---

[3] Michael Prestwich, *Armies and Warfare in the Middle Ages: The English Experience* (New Haven, CT: Yale University Press, 1996), p. 12.

[4] Terms used by royal clerks in 1345: earl, baron, banneret, knight, man-at-arms, esquire (*scutifer, armiger, valettus*), sergeant, armoured man on horse, armoured man on foot, mounted archer, foot archer, Welsh spearman, Welsh foot archer, *centenar, vintenar, ductor*, constable and marshal.

[5] Adrian R. Bell et al., *The Soldier in Later Medieval England* (Oxford: Oxford University Press, 2013), p. 8.

[6] E 101/25/9, m. 3. They are recorded as 'Counte de Lancastre' and 'le Baron de Craystok' in the retinue roll attached to Lancaster's particulars of account.

[7] Albert Prince uses a similar classification of troops, although he includes the Welsh infantry among 'other footmen and the auxiliaries' rather than forming a separate and discrete troop type: Albert E. Prince, 'The Army and Navy', in *The English Government at Work, 1327–1336*, ed. James F. Willard et al., 3 vols (Cambridge, MA: Mediaeval

Men-at-arms

A man-at-arms (*homo ad arma*) was broadly defined as a heavily armoured, mounted, soldier who fought on horseback or on foot as circumstances demanded. This troop type, or category of soldier, encompassed the three military ranks of banneret, knight and esquire. For a typical man-at-arms the lance, shield and sword remained the main form of weaponry, while bascinets (light helmets) and other accoutrements for the field were incorporated into battle-armour. The rapid move towards the full-scale adoption of plate-armour during the Hundred Years' War resulted in cuisses (thigh-defences), vambraces (arm-defences), gauntlets and leg-harnesses with poleyns (knee-defences) becoming commonplace for men-at-arms. There were various other forms of weaponry such as the mace, for example, which were often wielded by the elite on the battlefield.[8] We should normally, of course, expect knights to have owned equipment of a better quality than men of lower rank or status.[9] Although the general introduction in the 1340s of extra payment to captains called *regard* may have been designed to help troops with the growing costs of plate armour, inevitably a proportion of soldiers, particularly at the beginning of the war, would not have been able to afford such costs – so we might expect a typical man-at-arms to have worn a combination of traditional armour with more advanced accoutrements.[10] A warhorse invariably remained the most valuable piece of his equipment.

Banneret, or knight banneret, to use the fuller term, was the highest rank of man-at-arms. This elite status was not hereditary, but contingent on both wealth and social precedence, as bannerets were expected to recruit

---

Academy of America, 1940–50), I (1940), pp. 332–93 (p. 336). The 'hobelar', a lightly armed horseman who emerged in Ireland in the late thirteenth century, constitutes a fourth troop type that commonly featured in English armies from the 1320s to 1340s. Hobelars, however, did not fight in Lancaster's army in 1345 and therefore are not included in the following discussion. On the origins and use of hobelars in English armies, see Morgan, *War and Society*, pp. 38–9.

[8] Prestwich, *Armies and Warfare*, p. 23.

[9] Most knights would probably have worn a helm (an all-enclosing steel helmet) over a bascinet, as well as a breast plate and jack (quilted surcoat). For an illuminating example of a high quality suit of armour and weaponry, although dating from a later period, see the harness for war owned by a royal household knight, Sir Robert Salle, in the 1370s: Shelagh Mitchell, 'The Armour of Sir Robert Salle: An Indication of Social Status?', in *Fourteenth Century England, VIII*, ed. J. S. Hamilton (Woodbridge: Boydell, 2014), pp. 83–94 (pp. 85–7).

[10] For a definition and discussion of the purpose of *regard*, see Chapter 4. If armour was captured on the battlefield we might expect a general rise in the quality of accoutrements worn by men-at-arms following an emphatic military victory, or series of victories, as was the case for men who served in English armies from 1345 to 1347.

and lead a sizeable following of men to war.[11] In 1348, for example, Edward III rewarded the newly promoted Sir Thomas Cok with a life annuity (or pension) of 200 marks 'for his better maintenance of the estate of banneret'.[12] It was *banneretti* who traditionally fulfilled a prominent role of command on the battlefield, and all five retinue captains who led their own constituent forces on the 1345 expedition held this rank. There were exceptions, though. The appointment of Sir John Chandos to lead a retinue of forty men-at-arms in 1361, amongst whom was a banneret, despite Chandos not yet having attained that rank himself, shows that, on occasion, martial prowess, reputation and, above all else, ability to command effectively, were of greater importance than one's position in the hierarchical structure of the army.[13] The second military rank was filled with the ordinary knights, or 'knights bachelor', who were distinguishable on the battlefield by the simple pennant (a flag in the shape of a swallow's tail) that they bore on the end of their lance, as opposed to the rectangular banners displayed by bannerets.[14] In contemporary and modern opinion, the knight – *miles* (Latin), or *chivaler* (Anglo-Norman) – is the paradigm of a medieval warrior.[15] As well as being a well-equipped combatant, he fulfilled a traditional role in the recruitment and leadership of men, and was typically drawn from the 'gentry' of medieval society. They, however, did not constitute the most numerous rank of men-at-arms.

It was the rank immediately below knight, that of esquire, which furnished most of the men-at-arms in a fourteenth-century English army. Most of these men belonged to gentry families and therefore were part of the same social stratum as knights, which was a title that they aspired to attain. There are, however, numerous examples of esquires who eschewed knighthood over the course of their military careers and some had a degree of moderate

---

[11] It had been the conventional view of historians in the 1930s that elevation to the rank of banneret 'was based primarily upon military pre-eminence': Prince, *Army and Navy*, p. 337.

[12] *CPR, 1348–50*, p. 23. The annuity was also granted to support Cok in the office of seneschal of Aquitaine for one year and because he was retained to stay with the king for life.

[13] Chandos was appointed as Edward III's lieutenant in France and Normandy in 1361 to redress any violations of the Treaty of Brétigny. Prestwich, *Armies and Warfare*, p. 15; E 101/28/7 (indenture of service made between Chandos and Edward III).

[14] When Chandos was eventually elevated to banneret at the battle of Najera in 1367, for example, Froissart describes how the Black Prince cut the long tail from the knight's pennant, enabling Chandos to unfurl his silk banner for the first time. *Oeuvres*, VII, pp. 195–9.

[15] The concept of the knight as the embodiment of a warrior is inextricably linked to the contemporary terminology used to describe him. *Chivaler*, for example, has connotations with chivalry and *miles* derives from the classical Latin term meaning 'soldier'. Bell et al., *The Soldier in Later Medieval England*, p. 54.

wealth that would have surpassed some relatively poor knights.[16] In the mid 1340s this level of the military hierarchy was much less defined than the two preceding ranks, and an array of synonymous terms was used to refer to men of this rank. The royal administrative documents produced in connection with Lancaster's expedition in 1345, for example, include no fewer than seven different words to denote men-at-arms of sub-knightly rank, including the Latin terms *armiger* (armour-bearer) and *scutifer* (shield-bearer) and its Anglo-Norman equivalent, *esquier*.[17] It was the latter term, however, which became most commonly used as the century progressed and by the 1360s 'esquire' was recognised as a social gradation.[18] The term of esquire, therefore, is used in general hereafter to denote men of such rank.

Another functional term for soldiers of this rank can be found in the particulars of account of Sir James Lord Audley of Heighley, who was one of five retinue leaders in Lancaster's army. This document, which provides a detailed breakdown of the captains' expenses, records a payment of wages for a *miles* and *homines ad arma*.[19] In this instance 'men-at-arms' is used specifically to denote soldiers of sub-knightly rank rather than as a reference to a particular troop type. The distinction between the knight and the other men-at-arms is evident by the clerk's use of terminology and the different rates of pay offered by the Crown. Sir John Trumwyn, knight, for example, received the customary wage of 2s a day, double that of an 'esquire' or 'man-at-arms', in this case, who was remunerated at 12d per day.[20] The term *homines ad arma* is also recorded in the heading and one of the individual sub-headings of Lancaster's retinue roll.[21] In the first instance, it is used as a catch-all term for the broad category of men-at-arms, but in the second

---

[16] The esquire William Scargill, for example, held £40 of land in Yorkshire at the end of 1345, enough landed wealth for him to qualify as knight, while the wealth of Simon Simeon, another esquire of Henry of Lancaster, is reflected by the appointment of no fewer than four attorneys in 1344 to represent him in any legal affairs while he was overseas on campaign. C 47/1/12, m. 18 (Scargill); C 76/19, mm. 19, 22 (Simeon). For other examples of esquires who eschewed knighthood, see Chapter 9.

[17] The terms *armiger* and *scutifer* are used in the 'expenses' section of Lancaster's and Pembroke's formal accounts of service, respectively: E 372/191, m. 54d. The term *esquier* (Anglo-Norman equivalent) is used in Lancaster's indenture of service: E 159/123, m. 254.

[18] Peter Coss, *The Origins of the English Gentry* (Cambridge: Cambridge University Press, 2003), pp. 228–9. The sumptuary laws of the 1360s reflect the social mobility among esquires, which had no doubt increased as a result of the rewards of military service and the success of Edward III's armies during the first phase of the Hundred Years' War.

[19] E 101/24/20.

[20] That the terms 'man-at-arms' and 'esquire' were used interchangeably by clerks in the mid 1340s is epitomised by a writ of *liberate* relating to the service of Peter Gretheved in Aquitaine at the end of 1345, who received payment for the wages of his 'viginti homines ad arma et scutiferorum': C 62/122, m. 9.

[21] E 101/25/9, m. 3 (heading); E 101/35/2/10, m. 1 (sub-heading).

it refers to men of sub-knightly rank; and, indeed, the term retained its rather ambiguous function to denote both troop type and rank later in the fourteenth century.[22]

Other terms, such as *valettus*, *homines armati* and *serviens*, are also used by royal clerks to refer to men-at-arms of sub-knightly rank who served in Lancaster's army. Valet is problematic because it had both military and household connotations. For example, Richard de Stainton is described as a 'valettus' of Sir Nicholas de Rye in a request for a letter of royal protection, which indicates his inferior status to the knight.[23] The same term is used in another request for protection on behalf of a different knight, Sir Nicholas de Peyvre, but in this instance the latter is described by Lancaster's clerk as 'nostre bien ame vallet'.[24] In the case of Stainton, therefore, the term valet reflects his subordinate rank, as well as his association with Rye, but in the instance of Peyvre valet is indicative of his personal attachment to Lancaster and his place in the magnate's retinue.[25] It is also interesting to note that the Exchequer clerk William Farley, who was an important figure in administering the finance of the army, is described as a 'valet of the Treasurer'.[26] These few instances of the use of valet in the administrative records suggest that the term had evolved since the reign of Edward I, when it had been used generally to denote men-at-arms of sub-knightly rank.[27] By the mid 1340s, the term retained the same military connotations, but had become indicative more of an individual's relationship with a person, who was typically of superior status, than of his own military rank or social status. Indeed, the meaning of valet had evolved by the end of the fourteenth century to mean 'yeoman' in English, and was used to signify archer.[28]

'Armoured men, mounted and on foot' (*homines armati equitum et peditum*) appear in the bills of payment to the retinue leaders, sealed by the constable of Bordeaux.[29] In the absence of any reference to the wage rates of these 'armoured men' in the documents it is difficult to determine whether they belonged to the sub-knightly rank of man-at-arms, although we can be almost certain that the foot soldiers were of a lower status than

---

[22] In 1375, for example, *homines ad arma* is used as a catch-all term to denote the troop type in the heading of the muster roll for Edmund of Langley's expedition to Brittany, but is also used in the individual sub-headings to denote men of sub-knightly rank: Bell et al., *The Soldier in Later Medieval England*, pp. 100–1.

[23] C 81/1723/48.

[24] C 81/1724/58.

[25] Stainton is recorded as an esquire in Lancaster' retinue roll: E 101/35/2/10, m. 2.

[26] E 403/339, m. 44; E 404/501/336; E 404/501/338; E 404/501/339.

[27] Simpkin, *English Aristocracy at War*, pp. 94–5.

[28] Saul, *Knights and Esquires*, p. 18; Bell et al., *The Soldier in Later Medieval England*, p. 149.

[29] E 43/78: Walter Mauny; E 404/503/139: Ralph Stafford.

their mounted equivalents. Fortunately, an extant particulars of account relating to the expeditionary force led by Sir Thomas Ferrers, around the same time that Lancaster's fleet set out for Aquitaine, shows that 'armoured men' received 12d per day, as was customary for men of sub-knightly rank.[30] The clerk's decision to describe men in Ferrers' own retinue as 'armoured men', but others of the same rank on the expedition as 'men-at-arms', probably resulted from a personal whim. However, the term 'armoured man', like valet, evolved later in the fourteenth century, when it was used to refer to 'a separate class of soldier' who received a lower wage rate of 8d per day and served predominantly on naval expeditions in the 1370s and 1380s.[31]

Finally, a single reference is made to sergeants (*servientes*) in an entry in the Issue Rolls, which records a payment of wages for 'men-at-arms, archers and sergeants staying with Henry of Lancaster in Gascony'.[32] The term was used traditionally in England to describe armoured men on horseback who were below the rank of knight, but in this instance it seems more likely that *serviens* refers to the armed foot soldiers who served in the contingents of local Aquitanian lords, rather than men in the ranks of the English army.[33]

The evidence has shown that military nomenclature relating to men-at-arms in the mid 1340s was changing and could therefore be vague and imprecise at times. Of the different ranks which constituted the troop type of men-at-arms that of esquire was the most common. It seems feasible, therefore, that royals clerks considered *esquiers* to be ordinary (or 'other') men-at-arms, which might perhaps explain why they used the latter term synonymously to denote men of that rank.[34]

---

[30] E 101/25/6; the original rate of 12d per day has been struck through by the clerk and replaced by 6d. Interestingly, the rates of pay of all of the soldiers, including the knights and archers, were also reduced by half.

[31] David Simpkin, 'Keeping the Seas: England's Admirals, 1369–1389', in *Roles of the Sea in Medieval England*, ed. Richard Gorski (Woodbridge: Boydell, 2012), pp. 79–109 (p. 96). 'Armoured men' who were frequently employed by admirals in the 1370–80s received a daily wage of 8d, less than the 'men-at-arms' who were paid the customary wage of 12d per day. For other examples of *homines armati* who appear in the late fourteenth-century records as a troop type distinct from men-at-arms or archers, see Bell et al., *The Soldier in Later Medieval England*, pp. 181–3.

[32] E 403/339, m. 44.

[33] Prestwich, *Armies and Warfare*, p. 13.

[34] This view was shared by the sheriff of Lincolnshire in 1324 who listed the names of knights and the names of sixteen 'other men-at-arms' (*aliorum hominum ad arma*) of that county in a writ of return; the latter were also referred to as *armigeri* at the end of the writ. *The Parliamentary Writs and Writs of Military Summons*, ed. Sir Francis Palgrave, 2 vols (London: George Eyre and Andrew Strahan, 1827–34), II (1837), p. 645; Saul, *Knights and Esquires*, p. 11.

Archers

A second category of soldier that fought in Edwardian armies, and one which represents the largest group of combatants, was the archer. Traditionally, these troops belonged to the infantry divisions of a medieval army but the 1330s, or possibly an earlier period, witnessed the emergence of the 'mounted archer' whom J. E. Morris proclaims was 'the finest fighting man of the Middle Ages'.[35] These horsed archers served alongside men-at-arms in 'mixed retinues', which represented the most significant development in the organisation of English armies during the second quarter of the fourteenth century.[36] The recruitment of mounted archers who were better equipped, more skilled and fewer in number than their pedestrian equivalents facilitated the use of highly mobile retinue contingents that were used to great effect in lightning raids and chevauchées from the 1330s onwards.[37] In the administrative records for 1345 mounted archers appear simply as *sagittarii* (Latin), except for Lancaster's indenture with the king which records them as *archer a chival* (Anglo-Norman). The suffix 'pedites', however, is given as the Latin term to denote archers on foot who formed the companies of infantrymen.

Men who belonged to these two categories, or sub-types, of archers clearly did not derive from the same stratum of society. The archers who rode on horseback and dismounted during battle received wages of 6d per day – double the daily wage of those on foot – and would probably have been of yeoman stock, minor landholders, perhaps, and, as Maurice Keen describes, 'a cut above the ordinary peasant'.[38] The mounted archer must have had the financial resources needed to equip himself for warfare, including the costs of a harness and horse – which might typically have been a hackney worth around 20s (or forty days wages at 6d per day).[39] It would be misleading, however, to assume that all mounted archers shared the same social and economic origins, as recruitment into their ranks would have appealed to a wide range of individuals. The rate of remuneration surpassed that of most skilled workers in the fourteenth century up until the outbreak of the Black Death (1348) and therefore artisans and craftsmen

---

[35] J. E. Morris, 'Mounted Infantry in Medieval Warfare', *TRHS*, 3rd ser., 8 (1914), 77–102 (p. 78).

[36] Ayton, *Knights and Warhorses*, pp. 9–18; Morgan, *Medieval Cheshire*, pp. 37–49.

[37] Morgan, *Medieval Cheshire*, p. 41.

[38] Maurice Keen, *The Outlaws of Medieval Legend*, rev. edn (London: Routledge and Kegan Paul, 1977), p. xvii.

[39] Ayton, *Knights and Warhorses*, p. 15; Ayton, *The English Army at Crécy*, p. 221. In some instances men's equipment was supplied by their captain or sponsor: Andrew Ayton, 'Military Service and the Dynamics of Recruitment in Fourteenth-Century England', in *The Soldier Experience in the Fourteenth Century*, ed. Adrian R. Bell et al. (Woodbridge: Boydell, 2011), pp. 9–59, 40.

alike would have formed part of the pool of archers, while younger sons of gentry families, with little wealth and few career paths to pursue, would also have been keen to take up the horse and bow.[40] These men, whose standing in society is difficult to define, represent a heterogeneous group who effectively bridged the gap between the peasant foot soldiers and the genteel men-at-arms.[41] Clearly some individuals were of moderate wealth, but to what extent and what degree of men held this position we cannot be certain. The handful of mounted archers who are known to have taken out letters of protection later in the fourteenth century and presumably, therefore, held assets or property they deemed valuable enough to protect whilst on overseas campaigns, suggests that some men were of an equal footing to esquires and perhaps even some knights.[42] The men recruited into English armies fifty years earlier, however, belonged to a different society (gentry or peasantry) – new employment and career opportunities were yet to arise as a consequence of the Black Death and the intense period of warfare in the first phase of the Hundred Years' War.[43] There is, indeed, only one instance of an archer from Lancaster's retinue in 1345 who might have taken out royal protection prior to the expedition.[44]

It should also be borne in mind that the mounted archer was a recent phenomenon which had only been in existence for little more than a decade by the time of the expedition to Aquitaine. Comparisons with their later counterparts should therefore be made with caution. The two most useful sources that provide an insight of the men's social standing in the mid 1340s are the novel land-based military assessment of 1346 and the onomastic evidence of occupational names of archers in Lancaster's retinue in 1345. In accordance with the military assessment criteria, all men with 100s (or £5) worth of land were to serve as, or provide in their place, a mounted archer for service.[45] This land valuation provides a tangible, if somewhat general, indication of the social band to which these soldiers might have belonged

---

[40] Skilled building workers such as carpenters, for example, only earned around 3d. per day in the 1340s: Christopher Dyer, *Making a Living in the Middle Ages. The People of Britain 850–1520* (New Haven: Yale University Press, 2002), p. 293.

[41] Ayton, *Dynamics of Recruitment*, p. 40. Gary Baker, 'Investigating the Socio-Economic Origins of English Archers in the Second Half of the Fourteenth Century', *Journal of Medieval Military History*, 12 (2014), 173–216 (p. 214).

[42] For discussion of twenty archers who were granted royal protections whilst serving on overseas campaigns from 1369 to 1388, see Bell et al., *The Soldier in Later Medieval England*, pp. 154–5.

[43] For a brief outline of economic changes in agrarian society in the decades following the Black Death, see Gerald L. Harriss, *Shaping the Nation: England, 1360–1461* (Oxford: Clarendon Press, 2005), pp. 209–42.

[44] A William de Pemberton took out protection on 1 June 1345, and is listed 40th among the archers on Lancaster's 1345 retinue roll: C 76/20, m. 15; E 101/35/2/10, m. 3.

[45] *CPR, 1343–45*, p. 427.

and reinforces the notion that they were minor landowners. When it comes to the occupational names of archers, a handful of surnames provide a valuable, if only brief, glimpse of the men's trades and, by inference, their social milieu. Among the archers' names are a piper, a crier, a baker (but no candle stick maker!); harper, singer, cook, clerk, smith, and a 'flesh hewer' (i.e. butcher).[46] There are others with the names 'hunter', 'parker' and 'forester' who might be considered as the most skilled and sought-after bowmen. And the occurrence of a forester in Lancaster's army suggests that the yeoman archer described as 'a forster was he' by Chaucer in *The Canterbury Tales* had links with his forbears earlier in the century.[47] In all likelihood, however, the archer portrayed by Chaucer was not typical of the mounted archer in the 1340s.

When it comes to characterising the social composition of the English foot archers we are on more certain ground, as it is clear that they belonged to a lower social stratum than their mounted peers. The infantry ranks were filled by husbandmen, cottagers, landless labourers and men who lived on the margins of peasant society.[48] In spite of the gulf in status between the foot and mounted archer, both types of soldier would have been equipped with a bow, a quiver of arrows (each containing two dozen shafts), and typically a sword, or long knife.[49] Naturally, we would expect the weaponry of the mounted archers to have been of a better standard than those on foot, who were equipped for war by commissioners or by their communities in local counties. In addition, a thick padded tunic, perhaps something similar to an aketon, or jack, would have provided protection of the body. There is no evidence to suggest that helmets were commonly worn by archers in the mid 1340s, as was the case in the fifteenth century.[50]

Welsh Infantry

The Welsh infantry, or foot, represent a third category of soldier in English armies which by the 1330s typically comprised two sub-types: bowmen and spearmen (*homines ad lanceas*). With a daily wage of just 2d – the lowest rate of pay offered to soldiers in an Edwardian army – these troops natu-

---

[46] One might presume that Henry 'le Flesschere' probably worked in the butcher's trade. E 101/35/2/10, m. 1d.

[47] Chaucer, *Riverside Chaucer*, p. 25, line 117. *The Canterbury Tales* was written between *c.* 1387 and 1400.

[48] Ayton, *The English Army at Crécy*, pp. 220–1.

[49] Herbert J. Hewitt, *The Organization of War under Edward III, 1338–62* (Manchester: Manchester University Press, 1966), p. 40.

[50] Bell et al., *Soldier in Later Medieval England*, p. 146. In addition to a helmet, archers in the fifteenth century were expected to serve with both a dagger and a sword.

rally occupied the lowest status of all the combatants. The *Galeys a pie* (Anglo-Norman), or *Wallensii* (Latin) are known to have been more lightly equipped than their English counterparts, but there is no other evidence to suggest that there was any major difference between the weaponry of the English and Welsh foot archers. In addition to a bow or spear, a Welsh infantryman probably carried a long knife.[51] Men recruited from Wales for the expedition to Aquitaine in 1345, for example, were to be equipped 'with spears, bows and arrows and other suitable arms' (*lanceis et arcubus et sagittis et aliis armis competentibus*).[52] The vagueness of these 'other suitable arms' is dispelled by Jean Froissart, when he reports the devastating effects of the 'large knives' (*grandes coutilles*) used by the Welsh against the French during the mêlée at the battle of Crécy.[53] Almost fifty years earlier during Edward I's campaign in Flanders, the chronicler Lodewyk van Veltbem, reported that '[he] never saw them wearing armour ... they were running about bare-legged and wore a red robe'.[54] In 1314 at the battle of Bannockburn the contingent of Welshmen were apparently clothed in nothing but linen, and it was no doubt the absence of armour that enabled them to swim across the Scheldt in 1297 and plunder the homes of men in the Flemish town of Gent, who had reportedly started a confrontation with English soldiers in the town.[55]

In the plethora of royal writs pertaining to the recruitment of Welsh foot in 1337 there is no mention of armour, only that the men are 'to be clothed in a suit consisting of a tunic and cloak'.[56] Interestingly, there is also no reference to clothing in the writs ordering the recruitment of Welshmen for the expedition in 1345, but Lancaster's formal account of service shows that the Crown paid 5s *pro vestura* ('for clothing') each of the men recruited from South Wales who were part of the reinforcements sent to the duchy in

[51]   D. L. Evans claims that the Black Prince 'specified almost invariably' that one half of the Welshmen from the Principality were to be armed with 'pennoned lances' (*lanceae pencellatae*). In 1345, however, the writs of array relating to spearmen in Lancaster's army only mention 'lances'. D. L. Evans, 'Some Notes on the History of the Principality of Wales in the Time of the Black Prince', in *Transactions of the Honourable Society of Cymmrodorion*, session 1924–25 (London: Honourable Society of Cymmrodorion, 1927), 25–110 (p. 55).

[52]   C 76/20, m. 34.

[53]   *Oeuvres*, V, pp. 65–6. The English archers and men-at-arms are reported to have made way for the Welsh (and Cornish) who used 'long knives' to kill any wounded enemy they came upon.

[54]   Veltham is quoted in Evans, *Principality of Wales*, p. 46, n. 1.

[55]   John Barbour, *The Bruce*, ed. and trans. A. A. M. Duncan (Edinburgh: Canongate, 1997), pp. 500–1; Sir Thomas Gray, *Scalacronica, 1272–1363*, ed. and trans. and with an introduction by Andy King (Woodbridge: Boydell, 2005), p. 217.

[56]   C 61/49 m. 13.

the following year.[57] The use of uniforms had become commonplace among the companies of infantrymen recruited in England and Wales since the 1330s, and as a form of livery, often with a heraldic purpose, they became a potent symbol of a lord's power and authority.[58] In 1346, for example, the Welshmen raised on the lordships of Edward, prince of Wales, for service in Normandy each wore a green and white short coat with *un chaperon* ('a hood'). That green was the prince's choice of decor for his palace chamber at Westminster, as was the cloth used for his Exchequer in Chester, suggests that the colouring was indeed a symbolic manifestation.[59] The green and white uniforms may have been an innovation for the opening campaign of the prince's military career, and although it is possible that the Welsh reinforcements in Lancaster's army were supplied with the same clothing, we cannot be certain that it was of a uniform colour.

In conclusion, the terminology used to describe archers and Welsh infantry is simple in comparison to that of men-at-arms. However, the evidence does emphasise the problematic nature of defining a soldier solely by his troop type or his status. A Welsh spearman, for example, belonged to neither of the categories of man-at-arms or archer. It is only his modest wage of 2d per day, and the equipment that he bore that gives a clear sense of the 'type' of soldier he was. Therefore, a consideration of troop type, rank and a nuanced understanding of differences in status seems to provide the clearest means of defining a soldier during a period of change in the traditional order of the medieval world.

---

[57] E 372/191, m. 54d.

[58] As early as 1295 infantry from the Norfolk hundred of Launditch are known to have been clothed in white tunics (*blaunchecotes*), each worth 3s, and troops recruited from London (1321) and Wales (1342) wore uniforms made of green and yellow and red and white cloth, respectively, for service with Roger Mortimer of Wigmore and Richard Fitzalan, earl of Arundel. Morgan, *Medieval Cheshire*, pp. 104–5; Michael Prestwich, *War, Politics and Finance under Edward I* (London: Faber, 1972), p. 101. For a discussion on Prince Edward's use of uniforms to enhance his 'corporate image', see Adam Chapman, 'Wales, Welshmen and the Hundred Years War', in *The Hundred Years War (Part III): Further Considerations*, ed. L. J. Andrew Villalon and Donald J. Kagay (Leiden: Brill, 2013), pp. 217–29 (pp. 222–3).

[59] *BPR*, I, p. 14; Hewitt, *Organization of War*, pp. 39–40; Pryce Morgan, 'From Death to a View: The Hunt for a Welsh Past in the Romantic Period' in *The Invention of Tradition*, ed. Eric Hobsbawm and Terence Ranger (Cambridge: Cambridge University Press, 1992), pp. 43–100, (p. 90); Margaret Sharp, 'The Central Administrative System of Edward, The Black Prince', in *Chapters in the Medieval Administrative History of England*, ed. T. F. Tout, 6 vols (Manchester: Manchester University Press, 1920–33), V (1930) pp. 289–400 (p. 333–4); Morgan, *Medieval Cheshire*, p. 105. In 1343 Welsh troops were ordered to be arrayed in a uniform manner (*vestiri de una secta*), but it is likely that they never actually set out overseas: Evans, *Principality of Wales*, pp. 47–8.

3

Raising an Army:
Recruitment and Composition

Recruitment

The two principal methods of recruitment used by the Crown to raise armies during the first phase of the Hundred Years' War were the indenture system and the commission of array. Indentures, or contracts of service, were first used under Edward I, and then more frequently under Edward III during the Anglo-Scottish wars, until they became the predominant method of recruitment when an army was not led by the king in person and more specifically, when the royal Wardrobe was not present.[1] It was the use of short-term contracts between the king and his captains that allowed Edward III to pursue his highly successful strategy of fighting France on multiple fronts in the 1340s and 1350s. The indenture system essentially filled the vacuum created by the absence of the king and his Wardrobe clerks, who would ordinarily administer the army's finance, and became the most effective means of raising an expeditionary force, or several, if required, which were led overseas by the king's lieutenants.

The use of indentures resulted from the wider developments in military organisation during the first half of the fourteenth century, whereby the feudal elements of the English armies of Edward I and Edward II, based on the provision of compulsory and unpaid military service, were replaced by wholly paid armies. At the turn of the thirteenth century a royal host typically included a combination of feudal, voluntary unpaid and paid components, but by the time of Edward III's wars in Scotland all armies were paid. The system of contracts was used to raise 'mixed' retinues by indenture, which from the 1330s onwards consisted of approximately equal numbers of men-at-arms and mounted archers. These retinues could vary in size from a couple of soldiers to a more substantial force of several hundred men depending upon the rank and status of the captain under whose command

---

[1] Andrew Ayton, 'English Armies in the Fourteenth Century', in *Arms, Armies and Fortifications in the Hundred Years War*, ed. A. Curry and M. Hughes (Woodbridge: Boydell, 1994), pp. 21–38 (pp. 21–3).

they served. It was the retinue captain who was responsible for recruiting and leading his men in war.

The commission of array, by contrast, was the traditional means by which infantry divisions were raised from the local communities of England and Wales. The use of local officials who were commissioned to raise large numbers of foot soldiers for military service originated in Edward I's Welsh wars (1277, 1282), and remained the principal method of recruitment for the infantry of an army that continued to operate alongside the indenture system up to the Treaty of Brétigny in 1360.[2] After the resumption of the war in 1369, however, troops raised by commission of array rarely featured in English armies that embarked for the continent which, by now, were composed almost exclusively of indentured mixed retinues.[3]

Military Retinues

In 1345, half the military personnel that set out to Aquitaine were recruited into five separate mixed retinues of variable size, each composed of a roughly equal number of men-at-arms and mounted archers. By the terms of his indenture with the king, Henry of Lancaster agreed to recruit 250 men-at-arms and 250 mounted archers into his own retinue, and the other 250 men-at-arms and 250 mounted archers (as well as the remaining 500 English and 500 Welsh infantry) were to be provided by the king himself. In order to raise these retinue personnel, Edward III nominated four retinue captains who, like Lancaster, agreed to provide a specified number and rank of men for service. Four military retinues were thus raised by James, Lord Audley of Heighley, Laurence de Hastings, earl of Pembroke, Walter Mauny and Ralph, Lord Stafford, who also served as seneschal of Aquitaine during the course of the expedition.

Once an agreement had been made with the king, the retinue captains themselves presumably entered into contracts of service or informal agreements with men of lower rank and status who served under them. There is an abundance of evidence to suggest that this method of sub-contracting was prevalent after 1369, but the lack of such contracts around the time of Lancaster's expedition suggests that this system of 'second tier' recruitment was still at a nascent stage. That is not to say that this system of transferring the demands for soldiers on to subordinate captains was not practised in 1345. The retinue leaders enlisted men from their own affinities, who in turn brought their own followers for service. A leader of a large contingent also depended upon the recruiting power of his bannerets, or prominent knights bachelor, who served as sub-retinue captains and incorporated their own companies of men into the overall retinue. On occasion, esquires may have

---

[2] Prestwich, *Armies and Warfare*, pp. 123–5.
[3] Ayton, *English Army at Crécy*, p. 176; Ayton, *Armies and Military Communities*, pp. 215–39 (p. 219).

fulfilled a similar recruitment role but on a smaller scale. Other soldiers who had no previous connection to a particular captain may also have found themselves amongst the ranks of his retinue. The multiplicity of ways in which a captain attracted soldiers into his retinue when given an extraordinarily high manpower target is illustrated by a study of the formation and structure of Lancaster's own retinue, which is the subject of Chapter 7.

For men who served in Lancaster's retinue, then, the indenture represents the first step in the administrative process of military recruitment. We should therefore consider the terms of service embodied in the document, and investigate whether the same benefits and emoluments were offered by the Crown to the other four retinue captains in the earl's army. The original indenture made between Lancaster and the king on Sunday 13 March 1345 would have comprised two identical halves which set out the terms of contract, with both parties each retaining one half, but neither part of the document has survived. Fortunately, the terms of the indenture (written in Anglo-Norman) were enrolled in the king's remembrancer's memoranda rolls.[4] It states that Lancaster was to lead an army of 2000 men, composed of 500 men-at-arms, 500 Welsh infantry and 1000 archers (half mounted, half on foot). The earl's own retinue was to include 8 bannerets, 92 knights and 150 esquires, who were to be paid the customary daily rates of pay: 6s 8d for an earl, 4s for a banneret, 2s for a knight, 12d for an esquire and 6d 'for each archer on horseback' (*pour chescun archer de chival*). The earl's indenture is significant because it functioned not only as an indenture of war, which embodied the conditions and terms of service, but also as an appointment to the office of the king's lieutenant in Aquitaine. Such contracts between the king and the leaders of his campaigns abroad were unprecedented, but a similar indenture made between Edward III and the earl of Northampton over a month later, which appointed the earl as 'captain and guardian' (*chevetain et guardein*) in Brittany, suggests that the mid 1340s marked the beginning of a general royal policy whereby military indentures were used in addition for the appointment to a high political office.[5] Indeed, the administrative efficiency of such a policy was borne out ten years later by the Black Prince's indenture, wherein the prince was appointed the king's lieutenant in Aquitaine, with extensive powers, and engaged with his father to serve in the duchy with a retinue of 433 men-at-arms and 700 archers.[6]

Lancaster's highly detailed indenture of 1345 embodied all of the powers he was to have as the king's lieutenant, which essentially made him Edward's viceroy in Aquitaine. The first empowered him to seize into the king's hand

---

[4] E 159/123, m. 254; Appendix A. Also transcribed in Fowler, *King's Lieutenant*, pp. 230–2. Note that Lancaster received an advance payment of £3,333 6s 8d for *regard*, not £333 6s 8d as transcribed by Fowler.

[5] E 101/68/4, m. 72; *Feodera*, III, p. 37.

[6] E 36/278, fol. 88. Translated in *BPR*, IV, pp. 143–5.

any lands, tenements, towns, castles, franchises, customs, profits of mints and anything else in the duchy which he so desired. The second authorised him to make armistices and truces for the honour of the king and the safety of himself, his men and the duchy. The third charged him to scrutinise the work of all royal officials and replace any he deemed to be unsuitable, except for the seneschal and constable. The fourth empowered him to receive any rebels or contrarians into the king's peace and pardon them, or, in turn, banish any of the king's enemies.

The contract states that the truce of Malestroit (1343) was to end at a suitable time, and Lancaster would be informed of this before military operations got under way. He was to remain in the duchy for six months, initially, but if the king wished him to remain there for a further six then he was to do so on the same terms as the agreements made for the first half-year's service.

The indenture also gives some indication of how the intended campaign was to be financed. One clause stipulates the sources of revenue from which Lancaster was to receive two instalments of payment for the remuneration of his men: one was to be paid out of the clerical tenth, and the other out of the lay fifteenth and tenth. Both of these subsidies, which were forms of extraordinary direct taxation, had been granted by the Commons in the parliament of April–May in 1343, at which point the Lords and Commons had given their full support to the war with France.[7] The same parliament also authorised the extension of the wool subsidy, at the standard rate of £2 per sack, for a further three years.[8] As a result, the Crown received an annual payment of £53,500, on average, over the next eight years from the cartel of wool merchants who administered the subsidy, which provided the Crown with an important source of revenue to finance the military expeditions of the mid 1340s.[9]

In addition to wages, other forms of remuneration were given to Lancaster, such as *regard*, a bonus payment intended to contribute to the costs of preparing for war, and *restaurum equorum* (horse restoration), which were specified in the contract. The payments for wages and *regard* for six months' service, and the dates on which they were to be paid in instalments to the earl, are also recorded. The terms of the earl's indenture allowed him to have his mounts appraised at the port of embarkation as was usual or, if his men preferred to buy horses upon their arrival in the duchy, the process of horse appraisal was to be carried out there by the constable of Bordeaux. Again, as was usual, the costs of the return sea passage were to be met by the Crown. When it came to the division of war gains, however, Lancaster was

---

[7] *The Parliament Rolls of Medieval England*, ed. and trans. Chris Given-Wilson et al., 16 vols (Woodbridge: Boydell, 2005), IV, p. 331.

[8] *Parliament Rolls*, IV, pp. 327, 336–7; Ormrod, *Edward III*, p. 257.

[9] Ormrod, *Edward III*, pp. 257–8.

not obliged to hand over half of his profits to the king as was the custom of the time, and if any prisoners were captured he was to do with them as he wished.[10] He was therefore granted 'all other advantages of war' (*toutes autres avantages de guerre*), except for the towns, castles, lands, rents or homages, all of which would belong to the king; such a privilege was unprecedented in contracts of service and was not offered again by the Crown until the Black Prince led his expedition to Aquitaine in 1355.[11] Lancaster's powers in the duchy were augmented further on 10 May 1345, four days before the army's scheduled embarkation, when he was appointed as the king's captain-general and lieutenant in the duchy.[12] These two posts combined now gave him full and sole authority, whereby superior administrative and judicial powers, as well as military powers to summon and lead the army in Aquitaine, were committed to him.

The only other extant indenture of service made between the king and any of the other four retinue captains in Lancaster's army is that of the earl of Pembroke made on 10 April 1345.[13] The parchment is very badly damaged, but we can discern from the document that he was offered the same benefits of service as Lancaster for his retinue of 80 men-at-arms and 80 mounted archers, and he too was granted the privilege of choosing where his men's horses were to be appraised. It is impossible to establish, however, whether the same rights concerning captured prisoners and the ownership of war gains were granted to Pembroke.

In the instances of James Audley, Walter Mauny and Ralph Stafford there is no direct evidence that they were party to any contracts of war with the king in 1345. However, we can infer from the records produced in connection with their accounts of service that the three retinue captains received similar benefits of service to the two earls.[14] It is likely that Audley's indenture was submitted along with his particulars of account when the Staffordshire baron accounted for his service at the Exchequer, but the document has not

[10] In the first half of the fourteenth century it was customary practice on overseas field campaigns for a soldier to surrender half of his war gains to his retinue captain, half of which would then be given to the king. Later in the century the spoils of war were divided equally between the individual soldier, his captain and the king. Ayton, *Knights and Warhorses*, pp. 127–37; Denys Hay, 'The Division of the Spoils of War in Fourteenth-Century England', *TRHS*, 5th ser., 4 (1954), 91–109.

[11] E 36/278, fol. 88. Translated in *BPR*, IV, pp. 143–5. The prince was allowed to do as he wished with any prisoners 'except only the head of the war [i.e. king of France], and in his case the king will give a suitable reward'.

[12] C 61/57, m. 6.

[13] E 101/68/3/60.

[14] All three captains seem to have received the same benefits of service to Lancaster and Pembroke, such as wages, *regard*, horse restoration and cost of shipping paid by the Crown. For documentary references and a discussion of the variation in the rate of *regard* offered to Pembroke, see Chapter 4.

withstood the vagaries of time.[15] In the case of Walter Mauny, however, the absence of both an indenture of service and a particulars of account raises some doubt over whether he indented directly with the king. Indeed, none of the extant records relating to the service of Mauny's retinue, namely the payments recorded in the Issue Rolls and a sealed bill of the constable of Bordeaux, contain any reference to an indenture or contract of service.[16] The terms of service agreed between Edward III and Mauny, a trusted and loyal confidant of the king, may have been made verbally rather than embodied in a formal contract.

The absence of an indenture of war relating to the service of Ralph Stafford's retinue is not altogether surprising given that he was appointed seneschal of Aquitaine in February 1345.[17] Indeed, the chance reference to 'a certain indenture' (*quandam indenturam*) in a bill of payment to Stafford, sealed by the constable of Bordeaux, probably relates to his grant of that office.[18] The terms of the indenture made between the king and Stafford probably stipulated a fee, among other rewards, perhaps, as well as the size and composition of the retinue which he was expected to maintain during his term of office. It is also possible, however, that Stafford was party to a separate indenture of war with the king relating to the military service of his retinue over the course of the expedition. However, the use of two separate contracts – one relating to military service, and the other to the office of seneschal – would undermine the efficiency of the indenture system. Stafford's appointment as seneschal of the duchy was an integral part of Edward III's plans for the expedition in the south west of France, and the king intended him to lead his own war-time retinue when he was appointed seneschal.[19] It seems reasonable to suppose, therefore, that the terms of Stafford's service as retinue captain and as seneschal would have been covered by a single *indentura* for the purpose of administrative ease and efficiency when it came to accounting for service.

Frustratingly, the evidence does not reveal whether Walter Mauny deviated from the formalities of the bureaucratic system of recruitment, or whether the terms embodied in Stafford's indenture relating to the seneschalcy of the duchy were also sufficient for his retinue's service on the campaign. We can be certain, however, that the broad principles of recruitment still existed. The king essentially transferred the responsibility of recruitment to his captains, either through the use of indentures or by verbal agreement. Although the contract based system was centrally controlled through the Exchequer, the process of recruiting men-at-arms and mounted archers was decentralised

---

[15]   E 101/24/20.

[16]   E 43/78; E 403/336, mm. 14, 17, 22.

[17]   C 61/57, m. 8.

[18]   E 404/490/180.

[19]   C 61/57, m. 8.

as recruitment became the responsibility of the socially elevated men who served as retinue captains. The indenture system, therefore, was an innovative way for Edward III to tap into the recruitment pools and affinities of his nobility, who transferred their obligations of recruitment to the bannerets and leading knights of their own followings. The knights, in turn, would agree to provide a certain number of men-at-arms and archers for service. As a result the process of recruitment became decentralised, administration became more streamlined and the logistics involved in raising an expeditionary force of any size became more efficient.

Infantry Companies

The 500 English archers and 500 Welsh foot who served as infantrymen in Lancaster's army were raised by commission of array in 1345. This system of recruitment targeted all suitable males (between 16 and 60 years of age) who were obliged to serve the king when called upon. Typically, four local commissioners were ordered to 'choose, test and array' a prescribed number of men from a particular county. Commissioners served as local recruiting agents, tasked with weeding out the weakest and most unsuitable of the troops that turned up for inspection at the county's muster point. The commissioners were responsible for equipping, clothing and paying the wages of the men until they reached the county border; thereafter they would serve at the king's wages until their return.[20] The county levies were typically led to the port of embarkation or the army's point of muster by either a *centenar* or constable (officers responsible for a group of one hundred men) or an appointed leader (*ductor*).

In theory, the obligation to serve in arrayed companies of foot soldiers only existed for the defence of the realm when it was under threat of a foreign attack.[21] However, the notion that all men selected for service by commission of array were willing participants is spurious. That this crude method of recruitment was underpinned by elements of compulsion in the mid 1340s is illustrated by the example of Sir John Hyde, who was commissioned to choose and lead Cheshire archers in 1346. At the Cheshire trailbaston sessions – a court that tried cases of violence, oppression and extortion – in 1353, Hyde was found guilty of having taken bribes from soldiers when he had been commissioner of array six years earlier, 'so that he chose men in their place who were less suitable'.[22] The indictment against Hyde, therefore, and indeed the evidence of numerous other instances of arrayers who were found guilty of extortion in different counties during the

[20] Hewitt, *Organization of War*, pp. 36–45. Prince, *Army and Navy*, pp. 355–64.
[21] The obligation of military service for the defence of the realm was pursuant to the statute of Winchester in 1285.
[22] CHES 29/65, m. 3d. A forest eyre served effectively as a public hearing during which people could make complaint to their lord, who in this instance was the prince of Wales.

1330s and 1340s, demonstrates that commission of array was an institution open to abuse and, more importantly, was reliant upon obligatory service.[23]

For the expedition to Aquitaine English foot archers were raised from Cheshire, Derbyshire, Lancashire and Staffordshire, with each county expected to provide 125 men. The Welsh infantry were recruited from the principality of Wales, 250 men from the north and 250 from the south. It is no surprise that the English archers were recruited from the north Midlands and the north-west regions of England where the Lancastrian household had a tradition of influence based on land ownership, lordship, office-holding and military service. In all four of the northern counties that provided arrayed archers in 1345 Henry was the single greatest lord, and the earls of Lancaster had indeed been major landholders there for more than half a century.[24] Furthermore, that Cheshire archers had sought exemption from commission of array in 1342 on account of the minority of the prince of Wales,[25] but were recruited three years later for service in Aquitaine, with a commander other than the prince, is as much a testament to the exigencies of multi-front warfare in 1345 as to Lancaster's connection with that county.

The Cheshire archers and the Welsh foot were recruited slightly differently to the archers from the English shires. The Black Prince's independent governance of the earldom of Chester (which included the counties of Chester and Flint) and the principality of Wales meant that his administration functioned separately from the Crown's system of government.[26] The principality was divided into five counties in accordance with the Statute of Wales (1284) and had been granted to the prince by Edward III in 1343: Anglesey, Caernarvon and Merioneth formed the region of North Wales, while Cardigan and Carmarthen constituted the region of South Wales.[27] Each region was administered by a justiciar, although in practice it was often his deputy who performed the duties of his office. If the king, therefore, wanted to recruit soldiers from the royal lordships of Wales, or the palatinate of Chester, the writs had to be issued via the prince's administration rather than direct from the royal Chancery. Thus, the royal writs ordering Sir John de St Pierre, John de Legh, Peter de Ardern and Ralph de Oldyngton (sheriff of Chester) to recruit 125 archers for the expedition to Aquitaine were directed to the prince, rather than to the county sheriff.[28]

---

[23] For examples of corruption in the arraying process, see Prestwich, *Armies and Warfare*, pp. 124–5.

[24] Morgan, *War and Society*, p. 103; *Somerville*, pp. 1–48.

[25] C 47/2/34/11; Ormrod, *Edward III*, p. 251.

[26] Sharp, 'The Central Administrative System of The Black Prince', pp. 289–400.

[27] For a brief outline of the county divisions of the principality of Wales and the independent lordships of the march of Wales, see Adam Chapman, *Welsh Soldiers in the Later Middle Ages* (Woodbridge: Boydell, 2015), pp. 3–4.

[28] C 76/20, mm. 32, 34.

The prince's administration would then authorise orders to the same effect, and in the case of the Welsh troops, instructions would have been given to the justiciars of North and South Wales, respectively. It is interesting that the names of specific arrayers in Cheshire are mentioned in the king's writ, rather than leaving their appointment to the discretion of the prince, or his council, which shows the close level of organisation that was maintained centrally by the Crown.[29]

A more nuanced difference between the troops raised in the palatinate of Chester and those in the English shires concerns the role of the 'ductor' who took command of the men once they had mustered in their home county. The leader's role was distinct from that of the commissioner of array, but in the case of Sir John de St Pierre we find that he served in both capacities. At the end of February 1345 he was appointed as the designated 'ductor' and as one of the four commissioners of the Cheshire levy.[30] Interestingly, Sir John also served as a knight in the retinue of Henry of Lancaster, which no doubt strengthened the earl's connection with gentry society in the county and, perhaps, facilitated the recruitment of Cheshire archers.[31] It is difficult to determine how frequently commissioners of array in the English counties were also employed to lead the companies of men after they had been recruited. It seems logical that such practices would have created a stronger affiliation between the rank and file troops and their leader if the latter was personally involved in the recruitment process. The few instances of the Black Prince ordering knights (whether appointed as commissioners or retained by him), to 'choose *and* lead' Cheshire archers on overseas campaigns suggest that it may have been a practice more common among the Cheshire levies than with the infantry contingents from the English counties.[32]

---

[29] The naming of particular arrayers in royal writs may have only been practised during the minority of the prince, who was fifteen years of age in 1345.

[30] C 76/20, mm. 32, 34. The leadership of the Cheshire levy was reappointed to Peter de Ardern three months later, who, on 23 June, was ordered to repay the sum of 20 marks to the chamberlain which had previously been granted to Ardern for the expenses of the archers' journey to Southampton. Morgan, *War and Society*, p. 103; CHES 1/1, Part 1 (10). The repayment of the expenses for the archers' journey implies either that Ardern was not the person who led the troops, or that the archers never actually set out for Southampton in the first place.

[31] E 101/25/9, m. 3.

[32] For example, Sir Thomas Danyers was ordered to join the prince at Calais in 1347 and to 'choose and bring with him' 100 Cheshire archers. A separate writ relating to the payment of wages of three esquires in Danyers' retinue reveals that one of the esquires, rather than Danyers himself, had served as *centenar* of the archers. *BPR*, I, pp. 50, 63. It is possible that in the case of John de St Pierre, he too may have transferred the responsibility of leading the Cheshire archers to one of his esquires rather than assuming personal command of the troop.

In comparison, the responsibility of leading the Welsh foot down to Southampton was delegated not to a constable (who fulfilled a similar role to that of a *centenar* of English troops) but, according to Fowler, to two Englishmen named Richard Sholl and Geoffrey de Wrightington.[33] The two English *ductores* are listed as esquires in Lancaster's retinue roll but, interestingly, both men received the same rate of pay as a knight (2s per day) and presumably therefore were of that status.[34] It was often the case that a designated 'ductor' of Welsh infantry would be of superior rank to a constable, but the appointment of an esquire to lead 300 Welsh reinforcements to Aquitaine in 1346 suggests that leaders could also be of a status similar to a constable (both men received 12d per day).[35] Lancaster's account of service reveals that the esquire received a lump sum payment for the wages of the Welshmen and, therefore, fulfilled a similar role to the three English *centenars* who also served as leaders and paymasters of their own companies of men.[36] The examples of leaders, discussed above, who took charge of the various infantry divisions from Wales, Cheshire and the English counties prove that the duty of a *ductor* was fulfilled by men who held different levels of status in society. Clearly there is a difference of status between Sir John de St Pierre, knight, an esquire, and a *centenar* such as John de Lesyng, who only received 6d per day for leading the Staffordshire archers to Southampton.[37] All of these men, however, functioned as leaders in some capacity, but it should be borne in mind that the rank of *ductor* was not accompanied by a uniform social status.

The survival of correspondence from the officials of the administration of the prince of Wales throws further light on the recruitment and leadership of the Welsh foot. In an undated letter that was probably written shortly before the men from South Wales set off to Southampton, the deputy justiciar, Sir Richard Talbot, requested a 'patent for Gruffudd Dwn to lead three hundred and fifty Welshmen who are assigned to the earl of Derby'.[38] On the following day, or soon after (probably around 25 May), Richard's father Sir Gilbert Talbot, then justiciar of South Wales, confirmed that 'The two hundred and fifty Welshmen of Talbot's bailiwick are on their

---

[33] Fowler, *King's Lieutenant*, p. 222. On occasion constables are known to have commanded a greater number of troops than their English counterparts: Chapman, *Welsh Soldiers*, p. 187.

[34] E 372/190, m. 41d; E 101/35/2/10, m. 2.

[35] E 372/191, m. 54d.

[36] E 372/191, m. 54d. The lump sum payment was also intended to cover the costs of clothing and equipment for the 300 archers.

[37] E 372/190, m. 41.

[38] SC 1/42/118; *Cal. Anc. Corr.*, p. 193. In 1345 Sir Richard Talbot served as deputy justiciar and his father, Gilbert, as justiciar of South Wales. On Richard's career, see Scott L. Waugh, 'Talbot, Richard, Second Lord Talbot (c.1306–1356)', *ODNB*, Jan 2008 [accessed 3 March 2015].

way towards the Earl of Derby'.[39] The task of choosing and arraying the men from North Wales was given to Sir Roger Trumwyn, lieutenant of the justiciar of North Wales. In a letter to the prince confirming that 250 Welshmen had set off from Conway on 20 May 1345, Trumwyn advised that any future levies should be led by an Englishman, because 'the Welsh now chosen say that they were never led by a Welshman since the death of a certain Sir Gruffydd Llwyd'.[40] The soldiers were clearly disgruntled and their request for an English leader, based on the fact that they had not been led by a fellow countryman for the past decade, implies that it was indeed a Welshman who led the contingent from North Wales. Similarly, the soldiers from South Wales were supposed to have been led to Southampton by the Welshman Gruffudd Dwn and there is no reference to either Richard Sholl or Geoffrey de Wrightington in the correspondence. In the account of John de Watenhill, who was responsible for paying the wages of infantry at Southampton, the two Englishmen are described as *ductores* of the Welshmen, but they only received wages for thirty-seven days covering their period of stay at Southampton and their sea crossing to Aquitaine.[41] This suggests that Sholl and Wrightington were not appointed as leaders of the Welsh contingents until after they had arrived at the port.

In light of the evidence relating to the Welsh foot, it seems that they were not brought down to Southampton by English *ductores*, as was previously thought by Fowler, but were led by two Welshmen, one of whom was probably Gruffudd Dwn.[42] The latter originated from Lancaster's lordship of Kidwelly and served as an esquire in the earl's retinue on the ensuing expedition to Aquitaine.[43] Dwn, like St Pierre, is another example of Lancaster employing knights and esquires in his own retinue and service to array or

---

[39] SC 1/54/99; *Cal. Anc. Corr.*, p. 245. The discrepancy of the additional 100 Welshmen mentioned in Richard's letter was probably the result of a clerical error, or related to troops recruited for service on the king's intended overseas expedition in 1345. For further discussion on these additional Welshmen see the following section, 'Composition of the English Army'.

[40] SC 1/54/102; *Cal. Anc. Corr.*, pp. 247–8. Llwyd died *c.* 1335.

[41] E 372/190, m. 41d.

[42] Fowler did not consult the relevant letters relating to the recruitment of the Welsh foot located in the *Ancient Correspondence* series at the National Archives, Kew. His assertion that the Welsh foot were brought down to Southampton by Sholl and Wrightington is based solely on Watenhill's account: Fowler, *King's Lieutenant*, p. 222.

[43] Gruffudd Dwn is listed 57th among the esquires on Lancaster's retinue roll: E 101/35/2/10, m. 1. He was among the commissioners instructed to array men from South Wales and the March in 1338 and is probably a relative of the famous Sir Gruffudd Dwn of Kidwelly who reputedly fought at Agincourt.

lead companies of infantry to Southampton.[44] The appointment of these men whom he presumably trusted and considered to be competent leaders no doubt facilitated the efficient recruitment of soldiers. For the men of North Wales, however, it was not only the nationality of their 'leader' but also his social standing and military reputation that was clearly a matter of importance to them. Trumwyn's suggestion that any Welsh leaders chosen in future should be of baronial status 'in the said land, and not from among men of lesser estate', reflects the *mentalité* of the soldiers and the stark contrast in their attitudes to warfare in comparison to their English counterparts who seemed content to be led by a *centenar*.[45] Indeed, the appointment of Richard Sholl and Geoffrey de Wrightington as *ductores* may have been a response to the strong ideals surrounding the person under whom the Welsh served.

Pardon Recipients

One other means of military recruitment in 1345 was based on the grant of letters patent, or charters of pardon (*carte de perdonacione*). Outlaws, or men who might have sought royal clemency for other reasons, were offered pardons in return for military service based on the conditions that they serve for an entire year at their own expense and find sureties to guarantee their future good behaviour. On 10 March 1346, for example, Stephen Hykelot was pardoned for the death of Thomas Jun because of 'good service that he has done in Gascony, in the company of Henry, earl of Lancaster ... at his own cost, for one year'.[46] The incorporation of this conditional clause in charters at the beginning of the 1340s provided Edward III with additional manpower for his armies, and an innovative means of raising royal finance.[47] Of those pardon recipients who intended to serve with Lancaster in 1345, a large proportion discharged their obligation of service through the payment of a fine, which ranged from the nominal sum of one mark to the more

[44] Another of Lancaster's esquires, William de Whitton, led the Lancashire archers to Southampton in 1345. Similarly, one of Lancaster's bannerets, Sir Hugh Meynell, was appointed as commissioner of array in his home county of Derby in 1345. The examples of Dwn, Meynell and St Pierre suggest that Lancaster had some influence in the appointment of local officials who raised foot soldiers for service in his army. For further discussion on Meynell, see the section in this chapter, 'Military Preparations and Transport'.

[45] *Cal. Anc. Corr.*, pp. 247–8.

[46] C 61/58, m. 3. In addition, Hykelot had found two mainpernors, William Swyetng and John Atwater of Kent, in the Chancery to act as guarantors to the performance of service.

[47] Since 1294 conditional pardons had often stipulated that recipients were to provide a year's service, but the additional clause that men were to serve 'at their own costs' was first incorporated in pardons granted to men who intended to serve in Brittany in 1342. Ayton, *Knights and Warhorses*, pp. 144–5.

substantial amount of 50 marks.[48] In this way the Crown raised a total sum of £561; other financial benefits came in the form of sealing fees, which provided an important boost of cash, and the cost saving of a year's wages of those men who fulfilled their condition of service in Aquitaine.[49]

It is also important to distinguish between those pardon recipients who, on the one hand, served for a year at their own expense and, on the other hand, were paid royal wages and granted a charter of pardon as an incentive rather than a *reward* for service. Men such as Sir John de Norwich, for example, who served as one of Lancaster's bannerets, and was pardoned before the army embarked at Southampton as a privilege rather than a reward for his intended service. Indeed, the 'general' nature of his charter, which pardoned him 'for all homicides, felonies, larcenies and trespasses' suggests that some men sought pardons as a precautionary measure rather than for specific offences.[50]

The administrative records do not convey a clear sense of how pardon recipients were recruited into the ranks of Lancaster's army. However, the type of pardons that were granted to soldiers in 1345 and the date clause contained in the documents give some insight into how the charters were procured and, essentially, how the men were recruited.[51] The majority of patents granted before the expedition were 'general' pardons which excused men 'for all felonies and trespasses in England before 16 June'.[52] Considering the large number of pardons enrolled en bloc on the Patent Rolls, all of which contain the same date clause, it seems likely that Lancaster followed a procedure similar to Edward I in 1294.[53] A proclamation was probably made for all men wishing to acquire a pardon in return for service in Aquitaine to send a petition or make themselves known to Lancaster or his officials by 16 June 1345. These men may have been required to muster on a certain day

---

[48] For a detailed analysis of pardon recipients who intended to serve in Lancaster's army in 1345, see Gribit, 'Henry de Lancaster's Army in Aquitaine', University of Leeds, 2012), pp. 124–63.

[49] The importance of sealing fees (16s 4d per charter) is illustrated by Edward III's decision in 1347 to issue pardons during the siege of Calais in order to help pay the wages of his huge army: Ayton, *English Army at Crécy*, p. 195.

[50] *CPR, 1343–45*, p. 528.

[51] For an interesting discussion and contrasting views on the definitions of the different types of royal pardon in the mid-fourteenth century, see Gribit, 'Henry de Lancaster's Army in Aquitaine', pp. 126–32; Helen Lacey, *The Royal Pardon: Access to Mercy in Fourteenth-Century England* (York: York Medieval Press, 2009), pp. 19–20, 85–92; L. J. Andrew Villalon, '"Taking the King's Shilling" to Avoid "the Wages of Sin": English Royal Pardons for Military Malefactors during the Hundred Years War', in *The Hundred Years War (Part III)*, ed. Villalon and Kagay, pp. 357–435 (pp. 382–3).

[52] For example, see the long list of general pardons enrolled in the Patent Rolls: *CPR, 1343–45*, pp. 530–2.

[53] For an overview of the process of issuance in 1294, see Lacey, *The Royal Pardon*, pp. 100–2.

(probably on 16 June), at one or possibly more assembly points. Whether a review of these troops was as rigorous as that of the main army which had already assembled at Southampton seems unlikely considering that they were not in receipt of royal wages. The toponymic surnames of many of the pardon recipients suggest that a large proportion of the men resided in counties where the Lancastrian household had major landholdings. It seems logical to suppose, therefore, that a regional rather than a national proclamation was made.

The evidence is not direct on whether pardon recipients were recruited separately from the retinue-based contingents and infantry divisions of Lancaster's army, but the example of pardon recipients who were ordered to 'hurry to the port of embarkation [Portsmouth]' for Edward III's voyage to France in the following year implies that they had travelled to the army's point of muster independently from those troops raised by the indenture system or commission of array.[54] That this was the case for pardon recipients in 1345 who intended to serve in Lancaster's army is quite feasible.

Gascons

The military support of many of the Aquitanian lords who joined the Anglo-Gascon coalition forces in 1345 was secured through the grant of annuities and other financial privileges. It was the ducal administration operating under the seneschal and the king's lieutenants of the duchy that was responsible for the recruitment and military organization of indigenous forces in the region. With the recommencement of hostilities in 1337 the seneschal, Sir Oliver de Ingham, had been empowered to retain the military services of whatever lords he could and administer wages to them in line with the pay scale customary in English armies.[55] In the following year the joint appointment of Ingham and the leading Gascon noble, Bernat-Etz V, lord of Albret, as lieutenants of the duchy brought with it the support of the latter's affinity and no doubt induced other noblemen to join the English allegiance.[56] However, not all Aquitanians were brought into the English allegiance in this way; indeed, some noble families had remained loyal to the king-dukes during the tumult of the preceding decades, and had a tradition of service with the Plantagenet kings. Exemplary of such loyalty are the lords of Pommiers, whose service to the kings of England dated back more than a hundred years.[57]

---

[54] *Foedera*, III, pp. 57, 66.

[55] Fowler, *King's Lieutenant*, pp. 42–3.

[56] C 61/53, m. 3. For a detailed discussion of Albret and Ingham's appointment on 1 July 1338, see Jean Bernard Marquette, *Les Albrets: l'ascension d'un lignage gascon (XIe siècle – 1360)* (Bordeaux: Ausonius, 2010), pp. 258–61.

[57] Léo Drouyn, *La Guienne militaire … pendant la domination anglais*, 2 vols (Bordeaux: the author, 1865), I, pp. 58–60; Fowler, *King's Lieutenant*, p. 54.

Indentures of service were drawn up between the seneschal and Gascon lords during the early 1340s,[58] and it was probably by the same means that retinue captains from the duchy were recruited in 1345. The dearth of accounts of the constable and controller of Bordeaux from 1345 to 1347, which recorded payments made out of the ducal administration, casts doubt over the exact terms of service under which Gascon lords supported the English cause. However, a series of bills of payment to the lord of Albret for his retinue's service over the course of the expedition shows that he received the same standard rates of pay (in sterling) which operated in English armies, as well as horse restoration (in florins).[59] It is likely that other local lords who joined the coalition force were remunerated in the same way, while those Gascons who served in Lancaster's own retinue probably received the same benefits of service as their English comrades.

Composition of the English Army

The composition of the English armies that prosecuted the military campaigns of the Hundred Years' War has been a perennial source of interest to many historians. The size, structure and general character of the Plantagenet armies, in particular, have been well documented and the expeditionary force led by Henry of Lancaster in 1345 is no exception. Kenneth Fowler provides a detailed assessment of the various military components of the army that set out for Aquitaine under the command of Lancaster.[60] However, his survey of the army is limited somewhat because it only gives a sense of the number and types of troops that *intended* to serve in the duchy. If we are to understand the reasons for the success of the army, of the campaign as a whole and its wider implications then it is vital to determine the actual strength and composition of the army with as much certainty as possible. The range of documentary evidence produced largely by the royal administration, although patchy and often incomplete, lends itself to further analysis of the composition of the army which mobilised in England, and also of the indigenous forces that served under the command of local Aquitanian lords.

The composition of the overall army outlined in the king's indenture with Lancaster reveals that it was quintessentially a hybrid expeditionary force. It was not dominated by large numbers of infantry divisions as was characteristic of the armies that fought under Edward I and Edward II, nor was it dominated by 'mixed' retinue contingents consisting of approximately

---

[58] Fowler, *King's Lieutenant*, p. 42.
[59] E 404/508/130; E 404/508/132; E 404/508/133 (wages). E 404/508/131 (horse restoration).
[60] Fowler, *King's Lieutenant*, pp. 222–4.

equal numbers of men-at-arms and mounted archers. Instead, the force of
2000 men was equally balanced by the mounted and infantry elements of
the army: one half (500 men-at-arms and 500 mounted archers) belonged to
five retinue contingents of various sizes, and the other half (500 English foot
archers and 500 Welsh foot) belonged to infantry divisions. The contingent
of Welshmen was to comprise equal numbers of archers and spearmen.

Military Retinues

The largest of the retinue contingents was, as expected, to be led by
Lancaster himself, and constituted what Andrew Ayton refers to as a 'super
mixed retinue', a force that was in itself the size of a small army.[61] Indeed,
Lancaster's retinue of 250 men-at-arms and 250 mounted archers constituted no less than one quarter of the entire expeditionary force, and one
half of the army's retinue-based personnel. The second largest retinue, or
comitiva – a Latin term for 'company' used synonymously with retinue –
was to be led by the earl of Pembroke who by way of indenture with the
king had agreed to serve with 80 men-at-arms and 80 mounted archers.[62]
James Audley intended to lead a retinue of 40 men-at-arms and 40 mounted
archers and, according to Fowler, the remaining 130 men-at-arms and 130
mounted archers served in two retinues led by Walter Mauny and Ralph
Stafford.[63]

   This was the expeditionary force that Edward III envisaged would serve
in Aquitaine but, inevitably, it was at variance with the actual forces that
served under Lancaster's command. Can we extrapolate from the administrative records the size of the five retinues with greater accuracy, and is it
possible to discern the composition of the body of men-at-arms in each
contingent? Table 1 provides a breakdown of the estimated strength and
composition of the English retinues.

   According to the terms of Lancaster's indenture, the men-at-arms in his
own retinue were to comprise himself, 8 bannerets, 92 knights and 150
esquires.[64] However, two other administrative documents which relate to
Lancaster's military service – his particulars of account and attached retinue
roll, and his formal account of service enrolled in the Pipe Rolls after the
campaign – reveal that he did not in fact arrive at Southampton with these
numbers of men.[65] One of the anomalies concerns the number of bannerets
that served in his retinue. The expenses section of both accounts record
payments for the service of just seven bannerets, but the names of eight

[61] Ayton, *Dynamics of Recruitment*, p. 31.
[62] E 101/68/3/60.
[63] Fowler, *King's Lieutenant*, p. 222.
[64] E 159/123, m. 254.
[65] E 101/25/9; E 101/35/2/10; E 372/191, m. 54d.

Table 1. Estimated Composition of the English Retinue-Based Contingents

Retinue	Earls	Bannerets	Knights	Esquires	Mounted Archers	Total
Lancaster	1	8	106	228	269	612
Pembroke	1	2	21	56	80	160
Mauny	0	1	15	64	80	160
Stafford	0	1	16	33	50	100
Audley	0	0	1	39	40	80
Total	2	12	159	420	519	1112

Note: The estimated numbers of men of each rank in the retinues of Mauny and Stafford are based on the composition of their retinues in 1342, which comprised 113 men-at-arms (20% knights) and 74 men-at-arms (31% knights, including two bannerets) respectively. Ayton, *Knights and Warhorses*, p. 263. However, the fact that 34 of Stafford's men took out protections on 20 April 1345 suggests that 16 should be taken as the minimum number of knights in his retinue. C 61/57, mm. 15, 16. The estimated numbers of personnel in Lancaster's retinue do not include clerks or pardon recipients (the latter served at their own expense in return for a royal pardon).

bannerets are recorded in the retinue roll attached to the earl's particulars.[66] Interestingly, the last of the names listed under the subheading of *banneretti* in the roll, 'le Seign' de Pom's' (*the Lord of Pommiers*), appears to have been written over an erasure which suggests that the Gascon lord was included almost as an afterthought, or at least following some uncertainty as to whether his name should be included.[67] In the absence of a muster roll, which would have been drawn up by royal clerks following an inspection of the troops at the port of embarkation, we cannot be certain whether Lancaster's retinue included an eighth banneret when it arrived at Southampton. However, it seems logical that Pommiers and his retinue would have already been waiting in the duchy for Lancaster's arrival, rather than crossing from England with the earl, and the Exchequer's decision to allow wages for seven bannerets may be indicative of the number of bannerets whom Lancaster brought to the army's muster point.

The retinue roll also reveals some changes in the number of knights and esquires that served in Lancaster's *comitiva*. There are ninety-seven entries under the heading of *milites*, two of which read 'iij chivaliers de Frank de Hale' and 'iij chivaliers le seinior de Pom's'.[68] These six anonymous men – and five more men whose evidence of service can be found in other sources

[66] Prince and Rogers both assert that Lancaster's retinue included just 7 bannerets: Albert E. Prince, 'The Payment of Army Wages in Edward III's Reign', *Speculum*, 19 (1944), 137–60 (p. 153); Rogers, *Bergerac Campaign*, p. 94.

[67] E 101/25/9, m. 3.

[68] E 101/25/9, m. 3.

– show that Lancaster's retinue included 106 knights, and he had therefore exceeded the agreed quota by fourteen men.[69] However, if we consider that at least thirteen of these soldiers were Aquitanians, who no doubt joined the earl's retinue in the duchy, then it seems likely that 93 knights, just one more than was stipulated in the indenture, actually set out from England. When it comes to the esquires who served in Lancaster's retinue we find that a much greater number served than had originally been agreed. The retinue roll includes 187 entries, of which three include 'iij', 'viij' and 'xj' anonymous 'companions' of the same rank, and a further 22 men-at-arms can be shown to have served with the earl, which gives a total of 228 esquires in the retinue.[70] Of these men, possibly as many as 25 were Aquitanians which suggests that the earl's retinue comprised 203 esquires, 53 more than expected, when it mustered at Southampton. Finally, the roll reveals that Lancaster did not struggle to raise the required number of 250 mounted archers, and indeed, 269 names are recorded under the heading 'nomina sagittariorum' (*names of archers*).

Henry of Lancaster's ability to meet the recruiting target that he had agreed with the king was matched by the earl of Pembroke, who arrived at the point of muster with 2 bannerets, 21 knights, 56 esquires and 80 mounted archers.[71] Pembroke included himself among the retinue personnel and thus served as one of the 80 men-at-arms, although we cannot discern whether the ranks of his retinue were swollen by additional troops who served under his banner, as was the case with Lancaster, due to the absence of a retinue roll.[72] The particulars of account of James Audley reveals a particularly low number of knights in his retinue contingent; in fact, only John Trumwyn is recorded as a *miles* in the document.[73] Audley's retinue comprised one knight, 39 esquires and 40 mounted archers. Although the Staffordshire baron provided a substantial force in 1345, it seems that he did not take part in the expedition himself. The absence of any reference to Audley in a sealed bill attached to his particulars of account, which states that Trumwyn 'came on behalf of James Audley', indicates that the banneret did not lead his force as was intended. Subsequently Trumwyn served as Audley's proxy and led the retinue in the duchy. Indeed, Audley's failure to

---

[69] Names of knights not recorded on the retinue roll: Thomas Courtney, Andrew Luttrell, Constantine Mortimer, Hugh Trussebut and Edmund de Ufford.

[70] E 101/25/9, mm. 1, 3.

[71] E 372/191, m. 54d. Fowler confuses the number of knights with the number of esquires that served in the earl's retinue, and then accidentally omits any reference to the latter: 'Pembroke arrived ... with a retinue of 2 bannerets, 56 knights and 80 mounted archers'; Fowler, *King's Lieutenant*, p. 222.

[72] We cannot tell from the damaged indenture whether or not the earl was supposed to serve in addition to his retinue of 80 men-at-arms and 80 mounted archers.

[73] E 101/24/20. Trumwyn was probably a relative of the deputy justiciar of South Wales.

campaign overseas may be the reason for his summons to the king's council, which he failed to attend, and subsequently led to his arrest being sought in 1348.[74]

The size and composition of the retinues led by Walter Mauny and Ralph Stafford are more difficult to determine, owing to the absence of administrative documents, such as an indenture of service or particulars of account. If the king successfully secured the 500 men-at-arms and 500 mounted archers as he originally intended, then in theory the combined retinues of Mauny and Stafford must have totalled 130 men-at-arms and 130 mounted archers. The suggestion made by Fowler that Mauny's retinue was smaller than that led by the earl of Pembroke is tentative and based on incomplete pay records relating to the service of the two captains.[75] Fortunately, a more accurate estimate of the composition of Mauny's retinue can be derived from a payment of *regard*, or 'supplementary fee', recorded in the issue rolls.

The standard quarterly rate of *regard* offered by the Crown during the Hundred Years' War was calculated at 100 marks for 30 men-at-arms.[76] In 1345, however, Audley and Lancaster both received a higher quarterly rate of £100 for 30 men-at-arms (or £3 6s 8d per man-at-arms).[77] If we apply this same higher rate of remuneration to the payment of *regard* (£266 13s 4d) made to Walter Mauny, we can infer that 80 men-at-arms served under his banner during the expedition.[78] It seems reasonable, therefore, to surmise that Mauny's retinue comprised 80 men-at-arms and 80 mounted archers, based on the assumption that his retinue was equally balanced as were the three previous retinue contingents.

We can also infer from the size of Mauny's retinue that Ralph Stafford commanded a comparatively smaller contingent of 50 men-at-arms and 50 mounted archers. As seneschal of Aquitaine he would probably have been obliged to maintain a sizeable retinue in the duchy since his appointment to office on 25 February 1345.[79] Sir Thomas Cok, for example, who succeeded Stafford as seneschal in 1347, was required to maintain a retinue of 20 men-at-arms and 40 archers in times of peace, which increased to 60

---

[74] For an analysis of this account and the implications of Audley's decision not to serve on the expedition to Aquitaine, see Nicholas A. Gribit, 'Accounting for Service at War: The Case of Sir James Audley of Heighley', *Journal of Medieval Military History*, 7 (2009), 147–67 (p. 148).

[75] Fowler, 'Henry of Grosmont', I, p. 177, n. 3.

[76] Ayton, *Knights and Warhorses*, p. 110.

[77] Lancaster received a *regard* of £3,333 6s 8d for 250 men-at-arms for two quarter-years' service which is an exact proportional match for the £133 6s 8d received by Audley for a one-quarter term of service of 40 men-at-arms. E 159/123, m. 254 (Lancaster); Gribit, *Accounting for Service at War*, p. 152 (Audley).

[78] E 403/336, m. 22. A payment of *regard* for 80 men-at-arms based on the higher rate (of £100 for 30 men-at-arms for one quarter-year's service) is exactly £266 13s 4d.

[79] C 61/57, m. 8.

men-at-arms and 200 archers in times of war.[80] The enrolled royal household
and Wardrobe accounts – which have not previously been consulted by
historians for the purpose of establishing the composition of the 1345 army
– can be used to test the proposed size of Stafford's *comitiva*. The account
of Walter de Wetwang, keeper of the king's Wardrobe from 1344 to 1347,
records a payment of £2,464 17s 6d for the wages of Stafford's retinue for
one year's service in 'parts of the duchy of Gascony'. [81] The wages of one
banneret, 16 knights, 33 esquires and 50 mounted archers, based on the
customary rates of pay for one year's service, works out at £1720 4s, roughly
£744 less than the actual sum recorded in Wetwang's enrolled account.
However, the payment out of the Wardrobe may have included the fee of
£500 which Stafford would have received as seneschal, and it is possible that
his retinue would have grown in size over the course of the expedition with
the arrival of reinforcements. Therefore, the retinue composition proposed
above should be regarded as the minimum size of Stafford's *comitiva* based
on the evidence of the pay records.[82]

    Whatever the composition of Stafford's retinue, it is important to recog-
nise that it constituted part of the army outlined in Lancaster's indenture
with the king, despite having already served for several months in the duchy
when the army embarked at Southampton. Although it was customary
practice for the seneschal to maintain his own sizeable retinue in times of
war, the king's decision to include the seneschal's contingent amongst the
original expeditionary force was unprecedented and was a strategy not to
be repeated by Edward III.[83] In 1324, for example, Ralph Basset who was
seneschal of Aquitaine at that time had left his office in the duchy in order
to lead his own retinue as part of the expeditionary force that fought in the
War of Saint-Sardos.[84] The decision to incorporate a seneschal's retinue into
the overall structure and composition of an expeditionary force was not
taken until 1345 and, quite clearly, was an attempt to make army recruitment and organisation in general more efficient.

---

[80] C 61/ 59, m. 13; *CPR, 1348–50*, p. 26.

[81] E 361/2, m. 41. His account and term of office as keeper of the Wardrobe runs from
10 April 1344 to 24 November 1347.

[82] Interestingly, if the proposed number of 50 mounted archers in Stafford's retinue
doubled, and the composition of men-at-arms changed to include one banneret, 32
knights and 17 esquires, then the cost of the retinue's wages for one year's service works
out at £2470 10s. This is around £5 more than the payment recorded in Wetwang's
account.

[83] In 1355, for example, the retinue of the seneschal at that time was not included
among the retinue contingents which constituted the expeditionary force which the
prince of Wales led to Aquitaine: *BPR*, IV, pp. 143–5.

[84] BL, Additional MS 7967, fols 35v–36r.

Infantry Companies

Table 2 shows that the combined strength of the five retinue based contingents was matched, more or less, by the infantry divisions recruited from the English shires and the lordships of Wales. However, there are slight discrepancies between the array targets set by the Crown and the actual numbers of men raised by commission of array. Edward III was responsible for the recruitment of '500 [archers] on foot, and another 500 Welsh on foot' (*cink centz a pie, et outre cink centz Galeys a pie*).[85] The levies of archers raised in the English counties of Chester, Derby, Lancaster and Stafford were typically structured into groups of twenties and hundreds, each group being led by a *vintenar* and *centenar* respectively, who acted as officers. A *centenar* was often equipped with a warhorse and usually received a daily wage of 12d, and therefore probably belonged to the rank of esquire.[86] The lower status of a *vintenar*, who presumably belonged to the same social group as an ordinary foot archer, is reflected by his daily wage of 4d. A series of extant indentures of payment made between the Exchequer clerk, William Farley, and three *centenars* show that the latter each led a company of 6 *vintenars* and 118 foot archers; John Meynell led the Derbyshire contingent, John de Lesyng of Barton (alias John de Duffield) led the troops from Staffordshire and the Lancashire archers were led by William de Whitton.[87] However, the strength

Table 2. Composition of the Infantry Divisions

Infantry Division	Ductor	Centenar	Vintenar	Archers	Spearmen
Cheshire Archers	I	I	6	118	-
Derbyshire Archers	-	I	6	120	-
Lancashire Archers	-	I	6	119	-
Staffordshire Archers	-	I	6	118	-
Welsh Foot	2	6	24	238	238
Total	3	10	48	713	238

Note: The composition of the Cheshire officer corps is based on the customary command structure of one *centenar* for each group of 100 men and one *vintenar* for each group of 20 men. Although John de St Pierre was assigned to lead the Cheshire archers to Southampton, we cannot be certain if he served as their leader once the army disembarked in Aquitaine.

[85] E 159/123, m. 254.

[86] The Staffordshire *centenar*, John de Lesyng, received only half this rate, which suggests that he may have served with a non-armoured horse. David Bachrach has shown that a *centenar* who possessed an armoured horse during the Scottish wars of Edward I received 12d per day, but those who had a non-armoured horse were paid only 6d per day: David Bachrach, 'Edward I's Centurions: Professional Soldiers in an Era of Militia Armies', in *The Soldier Experience*, ed. Bell et al., pp. 109–28 (p. 11).

[87] E 404/501/336 (Staffordshire); E 404/501/338 (Lancashire); E 404/501/339 (Derbyshire).

of the county levies that arrived at the army's muster point is contradicted by the account of John de Watenhill, who acted as receiver of the sums of money for the wages of infantry and sailors at Southampton.[88] The account records payments for the wages of 120 Derbyshire archers and 119 Lancashire archers in addition to 6 *vintenars* in each company, which suggests that two of the companies were slightly larger than originally intended. The company of archers from Derbyshire, therefore, included two additional archers, and the company from Lancashire also exceeded its quota by one archer. The Staffordshire contingent totalled 125 men as had been intended. It is interesting to note that the Derbyshire contingent was able to set out at full strength despite the casualties sustained by them following an attack by 'malefactors and disturbers of the peace' at Derby, sometime before 30 March, which resulted in fatalities among the archers.[89]

In the absence of any pay records relating to the service of the Cheshire archers it is impossible to establish whether their contingent included the standard officer corps of *centenars* and *vintenars* commensurate with the size of the troop. A Cheshire knight, Sir John de St Pierre, was responsible for bringing the archers down to the port of embarkation, but we have no indication whether the quota of arrayed men was fulfilled.[90] Indeed, it may be, as Philip Morgan suggests, that archers from the county never ended up serving on Lancaster's expedition. We know that men from the lordship of Macclesfield refused to provide military service and other areas in the county may have been equally reluctant to meet the demands made of them.[91] It is interesting that in the following year the prince of Wales was to raise a smaller contingent of only 100 archers from the county for the expedition to Normandy, but that the arrayed levy may actually have comprised as few as 71 men.[92] It is tempting to think that this shortage of recruits in 1346 had resulted from a larger quota of archers having been raised for service in Aquitaine the year before or, perhaps, it reflected a general reluctance of men from the county to serve on overseas campaigns at a time when the prince had yet to establish his military prowess and the extent of the potential profits of war remained relatively unknown to the soldiers.

The Welsh infantry included a similar command structure to the English

---

The three indentures record payments for fifteen days' wages for one *centenar*, 6 *vintenars* and 118 archers from Staffordshire; for one *centenar*, 6 *vintenars* and 118 archers from Derbyshire; and for 6 vintenars and 118 archers from Lancashire. Note that wages were not paid for the *centenar* from Lancashire.

[88] E 372/190, m. 41d. Watenhill was appointed receiver of sums on 9 April 1345.

[89] *CCR, 1346–49*, p. 63; *CPR, 1343–45*, p. 513.

[90] C 76/20, m. 34.

[91] SC 1/54/100; Morgan, *War and Society*, p. 103.

[92] E 403/336, m. 42; Morgan, *War and Society*, p. 104.

county levies, although they seem to have been more heavily officered.[93] In February 1345 the king ordered the prince to raise 250 foot from North Wales and 250 foot from South Wales, of which half were to be archers and half were to be spearmen. Two writs sent from the prince's officials conflict over the strength of the contingent of Welshmen recruited from the south. In one writ Richard Talbot refers to 'three hundred and fifty Welsh' (*treys centz cynqant galeys*) being assigned to Lancaster, but in a subsequent writ, Talbot's father states that the agreed quota of 250 men from the southern counties were 'on their way towards the earl of Derby'.[94] J. Goronwy Edwards suggests that this discrepancy of 100 soldiers probably resulted from the recruitment of additional men from the neighbouring marcher lordships, situated on the border of the principality.[95] However, there is no evidence of service by these additional men in the pay records and it is more likely that men recruited from the March were supposed to serve with the prince on the king's intended expedition to France in 1345.

Fortunately, the account of John de Watenhill provides a detailed breakdown of the size and composition of the contingent of Welshmen who arrived at Southampton. The main body of the infantry was made up of 6 constables, 24 *vintenars* and 476 foot. In addition, there were two chaplains, two surgeons, two criers and six standard bearers.[96] On rare occasions an interpreter (*interperator*) is known to have been included among the Welsh officers, although it is likely that the chaplains, or perhaps Gruffudd Dwn, had the necessary linguistic skills to communicate between the Welshmen and English-speaking officers in Lancaster's army.[97] Considering that a constable commanded a group of 100 men, we would expect only five constables to have been given charge of 500 infantry. In spite of the additional officer, the ultimate responsibility of leadership did not rest with the constables because the entire contingent served under the overall command of the two *ductores* Geoffrey de Wrightington and Richard Sholl.

Although the writs of array stipulated that half of the Welshmen were to be spearmen 'and the other half of archers' (*et altera medietas de sagittariis*), no such distinction is made in Watenhill's account. It is impossible, therefore, to discern whether the 476 foot were in fact equally made up of

---

[93] Welshmen were typically divided into groups of twenties and hundreds in a similar fashion to the English infantry, but in 1343 the Welsh forces were unusually divided into groups of 83 men: Evans, *Principality of Wales*, p. 48.

[94] *Cal. Anc. Corr.*, p. 193 (Richard Talbot), pp. 245–6 (Gilbert Talbot).

[95] *Cal. Anc. Corr.*, p. 246.

[96] E 372/190, m. 41d.

[97] An entry in the Gascon Rolls for 1325 states that the Welsh 'request a priest who knows their own language', and in 1342 an individual explicitly called an 'interpreter' was among a Welsh contingent that intended to serve in Brittany. C 61/37, 2d. Adam Chapman, 'The Welsh Soldier, 1282–1422' (unpublished doctoral thesis, University of Reading, 2009), pp. 63–4.

archers and spearmen.[98] In reference to Edward III's Normandy campaign in 1346, D. L. Evans asserts that it is unlikely that half of the infantry arrayed from North Wales were bowmen. It is more likely, he suggests, that the arrayers aimed to recruit as many competent archers as possible 'to meet the demands of what was proving to be an archer's war'.[99] The same sentiment was probably shared by the arrayers of the Welsh infantry in 1345, as the need for archers in Aquitaine is reflected by the fact that they constituted such a large proportion (62.5%) of the expeditionary force. It makes sense, however, that a greater proportion of Welshmen recruited from the north of the principality would have been *lanceae*, given that the men from there were renowned for their use of the spear rather than the bow.[100] It is also possible that the levies of foot soldiers included men who tried to qualify as men-at-arms. In a letter sent to the Black Prince in 1345 concerning the recruitment of infantry from North Wales, Roger Trumwyn informs the prince that 'several of them claim to be men-at-arms'.[101] Although these troops were intended to serve with the prince and not Lancaster, it is possible that Trumwyn faced the same dilemma when it came to raising men for service in Aquitaine. Whatever the case, and in spite of what status certain Welshmen claimed, the Crown only paid the wages of 6 constables, 24 *vintenars* and 476 rank and file foot soldiers, in addition to the ancillary troops mentioned above.

Pardon Recipients

The number of military personnel in the army was increased by the group of soldiers who served on the expedition at their own expense in return for a royal pardon. There were at least seventy-two men who served in Lancaster's army 'at their own costs' (*a ses custages propres*) and who therefore do not appear in the pay records. These soldiers are often overlooked by historians because the task of distinguishing between these pardon recipients who were not paid wages and those who did receive wages for their service is difficult and laborious. It is complicated further by the need to identify the soldiers who actually went on to serve in the expedition as intended, and those men who discharged their obligation of service through the payment of a fine. It should also be borne in mind that the evidence of these 'additional troops' is largely understated because the majority of pardons were awarded

---

[98] C 76/20, m. 34; E 372/190, m. 41d.

[99] Evans, *Principality of Wales*, p. 55.

[100] Prestwich, *Armies and Warfare*, p. 127. In the twelfth century Gerald of Wales commented that men from Merioneth and Snowdon were accustomed to the use of the spear, 'nature's weapon for the poor and free men of the hills'; cited in Evans, *Principality of Wales*, p. 55.

[101] SC 1/54/101; *Cal. Anc. Corr.*, pp. 246–7. We cannot be certain whether the Welshmen who claimed to be men-at-arms served with the Black Prince or Henry of Lancaster.

for completed service and therefore do not stipulate the original condition of the pardon. Seventy-two, therefore, is the *minimum* number of soldiers that should be added to the total manpower of Lancaster's army.

How these troops fitted into the composition or structure of the army is unclear. Were they incorporated into the existing framework of the army, or did they operate as an independent contingent? The issue of royal writs ordering that all men in Lancashire and Staffordshire who had received pardons on the condition of serving the king were to be at Portsmouth by a certain date suggests that they were recruited separately from the main body of the army which invaded Normandy in 1346.[102] However, it is hard to imagine that these 'felons' of various status would have formed their own contingent, whether the theatre of war was in the north or the south-west of France. The idea of a mixed company of infantry and mounted troops operating independently of Lancaster's well-structured army, which was equally balanced by infantry divisions and wholly mounted contingents, seems unrealistic. It is more likely that the substantial number of unpaid troops were incorporated into the existing contingents. The notes of warrant in the letters patent of pardon provide nominal evidence of a variety of retinue leaders, and sub-retinue captains, who gave testimony to the completed service of men in Aquitaine.[103] This implies that the pardon recipient had served under the personal command of the person who gave this testimony and, therefore, was presumably attached to his retinue or company. For example, there is no evidence in the pay records of archers having served in John de Eltham, earl of Cornwall's, retinue of 135 men-at-arms in 1335, but the fact that fifty-one pardons granted to archers in the same year were warranted by the testimony of Cornwall suggests that these archers had served in the earl's retinue. More importantly, perhaps, it shows that pardon recipients were an integral part of retinue formation.[104]

Gascon Forces

The task of reconstructing the size and composition of the entire field army which Lancaster had at his disposal in Aquitaine is hampered severely by the uncertainty surrounding the size of the Gascon forces which augmented the English troops. The accounts of the constable of Bordeaux reveal the strength of the retinues commanded by local Gascons who were allied to Edward III and in receipt of royal pay, but unfortunately there is a *lacuna* in the accounts from 1345 to 1347. An analysis of the Gascon elements of

---

[102] *Foedera*, III, pp. 57 (28 August 1345), 66 (3 January 1346).

[103] The names of three men who served as bannerets in Lancaster's retinue are recorded in the notes of warrant of seven enrolled pardons: William, Lord Greystoke and John de Grey, *CPR, 1345–48*, p. 558; William la Zouche of Totnes, *CPR, 1345–48*, p. 557.

[104] Ayton suggests that the archers 'formed a special "felons company" serving at their own cost': Ayton, *Knights and Warhorses*, p. 146, n. 39.

the army, therefore, is dependent upon a few administrative documents and the narrative sources.

The principal lords from the duchy who formed a coalition with Lancaster were Bernat-Etz V, lord of Albret and *vicomte* of Tartas, and his younger brother Bérart, lord of Vayres; Johan III de Grailly, Captal de Buch; Pey de Grailly, *vicomte* of Benauge and Castillon-sur-Dordogne; Ramon VI, *vicomte* of Fronsac; Alixandre de Caumont, lord of Sainte-Bazeille; Arnaut and Bernat de Durfort; Guilhem-Sans III, lord of Pommiers; Bertran I de Barès, lord of Montferrand; Galhart de Saint-Symphorien, lord of Landiras; Bernat d'Escoussans, lord of Langoiran; Sénebrun V, lord of Lesparre; Arnaut-Guilhem de Béarn, lord of Lescun; Arnaut-Gassie du Foussat, lord of Thouras and Galhart d'Ornon, lord of Audenge.[105]

An indenture made on 10 September 1345 between Henry of Lancaster and the Albret brothers, Bernat-Etz and Bérart, stipulates that the latter were granted custody of the town of Bergerac following its capture within the first few weeks of the campaign in the duchy. The brothers had agreed to maintain a garrison force of 298 'armoured men on horses' and 1200 'foot sergeants, both crossbowmen or archers and spearmen with shields'.[106] The composition of the individual retinues of both captains can be reconstituted through two bills of payment for the wages of Bernat-Etz and his men, sealed by the constable of Bordeaux on 4 March and 9 November 1346.[107] The bills reveal that Albret was owed almost £4000 for the wages of 185 armoured men and 940 foot sergeants for 231 days of service undertaken in the previous year, including the period when he was joint keeper of Bergerac. From this retinue composition and the proposed garrison force outlined in the indenture, we can deduce that his brother Bérart led a comparatively smaller force of 113 armoured men and 260 foot sergeants. In stark contrast to the wholly mobile retinues of the English army, Albret's own retinue was predominately made up of infantry troops which outnumbered his cavalrymen by a ratio of five to one. As the leading nobleman in the duchy, his retinue was probably the largest of those led by the Gascon lords, and the high proportion of foot sergeants was no doubt characteristic of most military contingents raised in Aquitaine.

To reconstruct the composition or total strength of the Gascon forces that joined the English army is more problematic because we are reliant upon the reports of chroniclers writing around the time of the expedition rather than more reliable evidence such as pay records or accounts of service. However, Clifford Rogers has cleverly used the composition of the garrison force at Bergerac, namely the four-to-one ratio of infantry to men-at-arms,

---

[105] Fowler, *King's Lieutenant*, p. 54; Rogers, *Bergerac Campaign*, p. 95, n. 22. I owe thanks to Guilhem Pépin for his help in identifying the names of Aquitanian lords.
[106] BnF, MS Doat 189, fols 167–70; transcribed in Fowler, *King's Lieutenant*, p. 232.
[107] E 404/508/130; E 404/508/132.

and the figures given by the contemporary Florentine chronicler, Giovanni Villani, to provide an approximate size of the indigenous forces.[108] The chronicler reports that at the battle of Auberoche, which was fought in the month following the victory at Bergerac, Lancaster's force was made up of 1200 *cavalieri e arceri*, and 'innumerable men on foot'.[109] Assuming that Villani's figures are accurate and that the English retinues remained at full strength (500 men-at-arms and 500 mounted archers), Rogers implies that the Gascons contributed a total of 700 men-at-arms.[110] If the composition of the Gascon retinues in the field was equivalent to the garrison force at Bergerac, this would give an approximate total of 2800 foot sergeants, and a combined Anglo-Gascon force of '1,200 men-at-arms, 1,500 English archers and 2,800 Gascon sergeants, for a total of 5,500 men'.[111] However, as Rogers notes, this estimate is based on the assumption that a field army would have had the same ratio of infantry to men-at-arms as a garrison force, which seems unlikely. The mobility required for a campaign based on the chevauchée, and quick raids into enemy territory would have been hindered by a force that had four times as many foot soldiers as mounted troops. If we include the men at Bergerac, it seems plausible, therefore, that the Gascons had a maximum strength of approximately 1000 men-at-arms and 4000 sergeants. This suggests that Lancaster commanded a coalition force that totalled 1500 men-at-arms, 1000 English archers (half mounted, half foot), 500 Welsh foot and 4000 Gascon sergeants. The 2100 men-at-arms proposed by Jonathan Sumption seems too high, especially since he does not include the 300 men-at-arms at Bergerac, but his suggestion that they were accompanied by 'perhaps 4,000 to 6,000 foot soldiers and mounted archers' corresponds tolerably well with the estimate above (i.e. that the infantry comprised 500 English foot archers, 500 Welsh foot and 4000 Gascon sergeants).[112] Indeed, if the English fleet had stopped at Bayonne to

[108] Rogers, *Bergerac Campaign*, p. 95. Rogers mistakenly refers to 296, rather than 298 men-at-arms in the garrison force.

[109] Giovanni Villani, 'Cronica', in *Cronisti del trecento*, ed. Roberto Palmarocchi (Milan and Rome: Rizzoli, 1935), p. 384.

[110] Rogers' estimate is based on the assumption that Villani is only referring to 1200 cavalry, but this figure could also include archers. It is difficult to gauge the credibility of Villani's account because it is impossible to know how his information was obtained. Sumption suggests that the Florentine had 'good sources and was careful with statistics', however, Villani's erroneous assertion that Edward III ruined the Italian banking houses of Bardi and Peruzzi suggests that some of the chronicler's claims were prone to exaggeration. Sumption, *Trial by Battle*, p. 578.

[111] Rogers accidentally confuses the 500 Welsh foot with English archers: Rogers, *Bergerac Campaign*, p. 95, n. 23.

[112] Sumption, *Trial by Battle*, p. 467.

pick up a force of light infantry (*bidaults*) before it arrived at Bordeaux, as attested by some chroniclers, then it is quite possible that the number of infantry may have reached up to 6000 men.[113]

Military Preparations and Transport

A detailed itinerary of the troops' movements and an outline of the logistics of mobilising Lancaster's army can reveal how well oiled the Edwardian war machine was in 1345. Indeed, does an analysis of the administrative records substantiate the claim that '[t]he feat of organization had been staggering'?[114] It is perhaps surprising that few historians have looked at the military preparations of a single campaign in any detail.[115]

The designs of Edward III to launch an expedition to Aquitaine as part of a coordinated multi-pronged attack against the Valois forces came to fruition in the early months of 1345. At the end of February Ralph Stafford was appointed seneschal of Aquitaine, on the same day that the Chancery issued writs to local commissioners in Derbyshire, Lancashire and Staffordshire ordering them to levy 125 foot archers in each county.[116] A Derbyshire knight, Hugh Meynell, who served as a banneret in Lancaster's retinue, was one of the commissioners in his home county and William Trumwyn, a probable relative of both Audley's deputy and the lieutenant of the justiciar of North Wales, was among those appointed in Staffordshire.[117] The writs state that the archers are to serve with Henry of Lancaster, but no destination is given other than 'to parts overseas' (*ad partes transmarinas*), nor is there a specific date on which the men are to be ready. However, there can be little doubt that Edward had already decided on Aquitaine as the chosen theatre of war. The commissions of array made on the following day (26 February) ordered 125 Cheshire archers and 500 Welsh foot, equally divided between the north and south of the principality, to be equipped

---

[113] For references to chronicles see Chapter 5.

[114] Fowler, *King's Lieutenant*, p. 52.

[115] Unfortunately, Fowler's account of 'the assembling and financing' of Lancaster's expedition is limited to two and a half pages and incorporates some errors. Fowler, *King's Lieutenant*, pp. 222–4.

[116] C 61/57, m. 8 (Stafford's appointment). C 76/20, m. 34 (commissions of array dated 25 February 1345). Commissioners in Derbyshire: Hugh Meynell, Nicholas de Longford, Walter de Montgomery and James Coterel. Commissioners in Lancashire: Thomas de Lathum, John de Haveryngton, Gilbert de Haydock, Stephen de Irton. Commissioners in Staffordshire: James Stafford, John Stafford, Adam Peshale, William Trumwyn.

[117] Sumption, *Trial by Battle*, p. 486; Sumption describes Sir Hugh as a Leicestershire knight, but considering his longstanding involvement in shire administration in the county of Derby, and the fact that his family probably originated from Meynell in the same county, it seems more accurate to describe him as a Derbyshire knight.

and ready to set out on 10 April (*in quindena pasche*).[118] The army's point of muster and the destination are first mentioned in mandates issued two weeks later, ordering that all of the infantry contingents were to arrive at Southampton by 14 May (vigil of Pentecost).[119] This new date of muster was confirmed by the indenture made between Lancaster and the king on 13 March.[120] Meanwhile, orders had already been made for the requisition and fitting out of thirteen ships for Ralph Stafford's retinue.[121] The writs directed to Stafford as seneschal from 16 March onwards suggest that he had arrived in the duchy by this date, and was probably accompanied by his retinue.[122]

The earl of Pembroke was party to an indenture with Edward III on 10 April, almost one month after Lancaster had contracted to serve in the duchy as the king's lieutenant.[123] We cannot be certain on which date Pembroke had agreed to be at Southampton, due to the partial damage of his indenture, but we can deduce from the correspondence between the Black Prince and his officials that Trinity Sunday, which fell on 22 May in 1345, was set as the new date of muster sometime between 8 April and 15 May.[124]

The 250 Welshmen of North Wales set out for Southampton from their muster point at Conway on 20 May.[125] Their departure was delayed by one day due to the 'disobedient' men of Merioneth who refused to cross on the ferry and enter the Edwardian town, where troops from the other northern counties were inspected and arrayed. The Welshmen had previously mustered at Conway ferry on 1 May, but their departure was delayed on that occasion because no arrangements had been made for the delivery of the men's wages for their journey down to Southampton. There the troops disbanded following a three-day wait, only to be mustered again almost three weeks later. These events preliminary to the departure of the Welsh levy highlight

---

[118] C 76/20, m. 34. Note that the commissions of array made on 25 and 26 February ordered a total of 500 archers to be raised from Cheshire and the three other English counties, and not 600 archers as thought by Fowler and Morgan: Fowler, *King's Lieutenant*, p. 261, n. 46; Morgan, *War and Society*, p. 103.

[119] C 76/20, m. 32 (dated 12 March 1345).

[120] E 159/123, m. 254.

[121] *Foedera*, III, p. 32; E 101/24/18 (particulars of account of Robert Gyen and Walter de Hanley for fitting up ships for the passage of the seneschal of Aquitaine).

[122] C 61/57, m. 8 (writs to Stafford as seneschal). The bulk of the letters of protection granted to men intending to serve in Stafford's retinue were issued on, or around, 20 April: C 61/57, m. 5. It is possible that the letters could have been granted retrospectively once the retinue had arrived in the duchy, or Stafford's men may not have joined him until a couple of months after his appointment.

[123] E 101/68/3/60.

[124] A writ was issued on 8 April ordering the prince to have the contingent of Welshmen ready at Southampton on 14 May: C 76/20, m. 32. Roger Trumwyn refers to a letter received from the prince on 15 May, ordering that the Welsh foot from his bailiwick be at Southampton on Trinity Sunday: *Cal. Anc. Corr.*, pp. 247–8.

[125] *Cal. Anc. Corr.*, pp. 247–8.

two things. The first is the inefficiency of the prince's administration, whose failure to send an official to distribute the appropriate wages caused a delay in the contingent's departure and, as Trumwyn explicitly states, potential 'embarrassment' to the prince.[126] The second was the tensions that had arisen between the English and Welshmen which were no doubt exacerbated by the murder of Trumwyn's predecessor, Henry de Shaldeford, three months earlier.[127] Once the men of North Wales had mustered for a second time and their wages were paid to them, they are likely to have travelled along the coastal road towards Chester, and from there headed south via Shrewsbury and followed the Severn valley to Gloucester before turning south-eastwards, possibly at Salisbury, in order to reach Southampton.[128] For the contingent from South Wales, shipping would have been the best means of getting to the southern coast, but there is uncertainty as to how the levy travelled to Southampton.[129] After having probably mustered at Carmarthen, the great administrative centre in the south of the principality, the contingent set out on or around 24 May, four days after the men from the north had left Conway.[130]

An itinerary of the movement of troops levied from the earldom of Chester and the English shires is more difficult to reconstruct. The Staffordshire archers left Lichfield on 25 May and arrived at Southampton six days later, on the same day as the Derbyshire contingent.[131] Unfortunately, Fowler has misinterpreted the fifteen-day period recorded in the indentures of payment of wages made between William Farley, valet of the Treasurer, and the appointed *centenars* on 5 and 6 June.[132] It does not represent the duration of the archers' journey down to Southampton and therefore, contrary to Fowler, they did not arrive on 12 June.[133] The wages of the troops

---

[126] *Cal. Anc. Corr.*, pp. 246–7.

[127] Shaldeford was murdered on St Valentine's day (14 February 1345) by the brothers Hywel and Tudur ap Goronwy. *Cal. Anc. Corr.*, pp. 231–4.

[128] Hewitt proposes a similar route taken by the Cheshire archers who set out from Plymouth to Aquitaine in 1355, although in this instance the archers would have continued south to Exeter via Bristol, and then marched westwards to Plymouth: Hewitt, *The Black Prince's Expedition*, p. 17.

[129] Welsh infantry recruited for the Breton expedition in 1345 are known to have sailed from Carmarthen, but we cannot be certain whether they sailed to the army's port of embarkation on the southern coast of England or direct to the duchy. SC 6/1221/5 (Chamberlain's account for south Wales); Chapman, 'The Welsh Soldier', pp. 165–7. The convenience of transporting troops by ship from South Wales to the southern ports of England is reflected by Pembroke's decision to sail with his retinue from Tenby, presumably to Southampton, in 1345.

[130] *Cal. Anc. Corr.*, p. 245.

[131] E 372/191, m. 41; enrolled account of the sheriff of Staffordshire.

[132] E 404/501/336; E 404/501/338; E 403/501/339.

[133] Fowler, *King's Lieutenant*, p. 222; Fowler's assertion is based on Watenhill's account.

for their travel to the port had already been paid out of the issues of each sheriff's bailiwick and, moreover, the extraordinary length of time which Fowler proposes it took for the archers to reach the port is unprecedented.[134] It was customary practice for men raised by commission of array to receive the king's wages once they had arrived at the army's muster point; the period of pay recorded in the indentures must therefore be commensurate with the arrival of the archers, or rather, the day following their arrival at Southampton. The Derbyshire and Staffordshire contingents, for example, were paid royal wages from 31 May, which implies that they had arrived on the previous day.[135] Indeed, the arrival of the Staffordshire archers on 30 May is confirmed by the enrolled account of the county sheriff, John de Aston.[136] The foot archers from Lancashire were brought down to the rendezvous point three days earlier on 27 May.[137] It was probably sometime around the end of May when the Welsh foot joined the forces at Southampton. Unfortunately, none of the pay records reveal when, or indeed, whether, Sir John de St Pierre arrived at the port with the company of Cheshire archers.

The first of the indentured retinues arrived at Southampton on 21 May, led by Sir John Trumwyn on behalf of Sir James Audley.[138] They were joined on the following day by the larger retinues of Henry of Lancaster and the earl of Pembroke.[139] It seems that part, or perhaps all, of Pembroke's retinue had assembled at the port of Tenby before sailing along the coast to Southampton.[140] The king granted royal protection to the majority of men who sought legal security whilst they were absent overseas within one week of Lancaster's arrival at the port. The bulk of the letters of protection for Lancaster and his men were issued on 20 May and the protections for men in Pembroke's retinue were granted on 28 May.[141]

---

[134] See table showing the movements of archers in 1345 in Hewitt, *Organization of War*, p. 42.

[135] E 404/501/336; E 403/501/339.

[136] E 372/191, m. 41. The account states that the archers arrived on 30 May, which corresponds with the period of pay recorded in the indenture which commenced the following day on 31 May.

[137] E 404/501/338.

[138] E 101/24/20; the sealed bill attached to the particulars of account confirms that Trumwyn came on 'la veyle de la Trinite'. Fowler's claim that Audley's retinue arrived on 22 May, the same day as Lancaster and Pembroke, is incorrect: Fowler, *King's Lieutenant*, p. 222.

[139] E 101/25/9; E 372/191, m. 54d.

[140] E 372/191, m. 54d; payment is recorded for the 'freightage of the Earl, his men, horses and victuals from Southampton in England and the port of Tenby in Wales to the said parts of Gascony'. Presumably all of his retinue would have been present at Southampton for review by the Exchequer clerks, and therefore did not sail directly to Gascony from Tenby.

[141] C 76/20, mm. 15, 16.

An inspection of the fleet at Southampton was carried out personally by the king during the first week of June, around the same time as the last retinue to arrive, led by Walter Mauny, joined Lancaster's forces there.[142] The team of horse appraisers awaited Mauny's arrival on 8 June so that all of the men-at-arms in the different retinues were present with their mounts before beginning the process of horse valuation.[143] It has been argued that the horses of Lancaster's retinue were appraised after they had reached Bordeaux, and that the majority of the warhorses were purchased there.[144] However, a corresponding *restaurum equorum* account enrolled in the Pipe Rolls, which records the payment for horses either injured or killed over the course of the expedition, proves that the majority of horses lost by Lancaster's men were appraised at Southampton on the same day as Mauny's arrival.[145] Most of the horses belonging to the earl of Pembroke's retinue were also appraised at the southern port, and interestingly, eighteen 'great horses' had been shipped over from the island of Guernsey, which suggests that his men had difficulty in acquiring quality warhorses in England.[146] The entire process of valuing each man's principal warhorse could not have taken more than a few days because a royal writ made on 11 June records that 'the earl of Derby has shipped his horses for the most part at Southampton and is hastening to the said parts [Aquitaine]'.[147] The writ ordered the sheriffs of London to proclaim publicly that all men-at-arms and archers intending to serve in Gascony 'should hasten with all speed, upon pain of forfeiture' to the port of embarkation.[148] The soldiers residing in London are more likely to have belonged to the retinue based contingents than to the less disciplined infantry contingents raised by commission of array. Watenhill's account shows that the companies of archers were paid for 'staying in the port of Southampton', where presumably there would have been less opportunity for them to pillage or cause havoc than in the capital.[149]

---

[142] E 43/78. Ormrod, *Edward III*, p. 267.

[143] For a detailed assessment of the horse appraisal process for Lancaster's army, see Nicholas A. Gribit, 'Horse Restoration (*Restaurum Equorum*) in the Army of Henry of Grosmont, 1345: A Benefit of Military Service in the Hundred Years' War', *Journal of Medieval Military History*, 12 (2014), pp. 139–63.

[144] Ayton, *Knights and Warhorses*, p. 52.

[145] E 372/191, m. 55 (*restaurum equorum*); Lancaster received payment for the loss of 112 horses which had been appraised at Southampton, but his account of service reveals that he was compensated for the loss of 43 horses which had been appraised at Bordeaux. E 372/191, m. 54d.

[146] E 372/191, m. 54d. The *vadia* section of Pembroke's account of service includes the cost of £10 for shipping eighteen 'magni equi' from the island of Guernsey to England prior to his embarkation at Southampton.

[147] *CCR, 1343–46*, p. 573.

[148] *CCR, 1343–46*, p. 573.

[149] E 372/190, m. 41d.

The infantry divisions appear to have been the first components of the army to set out to Aquitaine, accompanied by the shipment of warhorses. Watenhill's account shows that the Welsh foot and the English archers were in receipt of wages from 8 and 12 June, respectively, up to 14 July, 'both for staying in the port of Southampton concerning their passage and for going overseas to the said parts' (*tam morando in dicto portu Suth' super passagio suo quam mare transfretando versus easdem partes*).[150] The foot soldiers, therefore, must have arrived in the duchy around mid July, more than one week before Lancaster's fleet was able to set sail from an English port due to adverse weather conditions. The twenty miners and four master miners who came down from the Peak District and the Forest of Dene to Southampton on 26 May were also part of this first sea crossing.[151] This made perfect strategic sense considering that siege warfare had already begun in the duchy and the English seneschal, therefore, would have had a greater need for infantrymen and miners than mounted retinue contingents.[152] Also, the early arrival of the horses in Aquitaine would have allowed the mounts ample time to recuperate after the long sea voyage.[153] This strategic decision to transport horses ahead of the retinue forces was largely determined by the army's destination. Obviously, it would have been futile to ship the horses in the first tranche if the fleet were to disembark at a port in hostile territory, but Bordeaux was in English hands and, therefore, the horses would be able to regain their legs, so to speak, in relative safety. Indeed, the same practice of transporting horses ahead of the main army was carried out during the expeditions to Aquitaine in 1355 and to Reims in 1359. The ports of destination on both occasions, namely Bordeaux and Calais, were held by the English.

On 16 June the majority of men who sought a royal pardon in return for their service on the expedition made themselves known to Lancaster's

---

[150] E 372/190, m. 41d.

[151] E 372/190, m. 41d. The miners were paid wages from 26 May to 14 July.

[152] Interestingly, a similar strategy was deployed during the English expedition to Brittany in 1342. On this occasion the earls of Gloucester and Pembroke decided to send the Welsh infantry to the duchy ahead of their retinue contingents, despite there being sufficient ships to transport both the infantry and retinue forces; a decision which may have arisen, perhaps, from the need for infantry in the garrison warfare which characterised the campaign in the duchy. I am grateful to Craig Lambert for this insight. For details of the transport fleet in 1342, see Craig L. Lambert, *Shipping the Medieval Military: English Maritime Logistics in the Fourteenth Century* (Woodbridge: Boydell, 2011), pp. 128–36.

[153] For a brief discussion of the adverse effects of sea travel on horses, such as mental stress and muscle wastage, see Ann Hyland, *The Medieval Warhorse from Byzantium to the Crusades* (Conshohocken, PA Combined Books, 1996), p. 148. Hyland asserts that horses need at least five days to recuperate fully following a short but rough one day crossing of the North Sea.

officials.[154] Priority was given to shipping the remaining troops to France, and on 21 June the mayors and bailiffs of the eastern and southern ports were ordered to allow only seaworthy vessels carrying men to France under the command of Lancaster or the king to leave England.[155] A letter sent from Lancaster to his clerk, Walter de Power, requesting that a protection be issued for one of his valets shows that he was at Faversham on the same day.[156] We can only surmise the reason why Lancaster was there on 21 June, but being a pious man it is possible that he had visited Canterbury cathedral, situated less than 16 kilometres away, in the hope of gaining more favourable weather after making the necessary oblations. Indeed, during the previous week Edward III had requested that the archbishops of Canterbury and York, and nineteen other bishops, pray for the success of his own intended expedition.[157] It is likely that Lancaster made a similar request for the archbishop's prayers at Canterbury in person.

After part of the fleet which transported the horses and infantry had set sail from Southampton, the remaining ships tacked along the southern coast of England and put in at Plymouth sometime during the third week of June.[158] It was not until over a month later, on 23 July, that a fleet of 252 ships finally set sail from Falmouth.[159] The king's sergeant-at-arms, Walter de Herewelle, was assigned to accompany Lancaster to Aquitaine to ensure that the ships returned to England once the army had disembarked at Bordeaux.[160] The appointment of Herewell is highly unusual and probably reflects Edward III's urgent need for further use of the ships in transporting his own expeditionary force to the continent in the summer of 1345. In addition to the horses and military personnel, victuals, munitions and enough boards and beams to build fifty bridges were transported to the duchy, which reflects good planning of the expedition.[161] It is significant,

---

[154] *CPR, 1343–45*, pp. 530–2.

[155] *CCR, 1343–46*, p. 588.

[156] C 81/1724/58; dated 21 June 1345. The place name written in the date clause is unclear, but with the aid of ultraviolet light, Faversham is almost certainly the place.

[157] *CCR, 1343–46*, p. 588.

[158] E 372/191, m. 54d. The Exchequer clerks, William Farley and Henry de Walton, were paid wages for an eleven-day return trip from Plymouth to Westminster. They collected £1000 at the Receipt of the Exchequer on 21 June, which implies that the clerks had set out from Plymouth on, or around, 16 June; this would allow five days for travel each way and one day to conduct their business at Westminster.

[159] E 101/25/9; E 372/191, m. 54d. Fowler, Sumption and Prestwich mistakenly claim that Lancaster's fleet comprised 152 ships: Fowler, *King's Lieutenant*, p. 50; Sumption, *Trial by Battle*, p. 457; Prestwich, *Armies and Warfare*, p. 275.

[160] E 372/191, m. 41d. Herewelle was involved in the process of ship requisition for military expeditions on numerous occasions in the 1340s and 1350s: Lambert, *Shipping the Medieval Military*, p. 31.

[161] Lambert, *Shipping the Medieval Military*, pp. 88–9.

perhaps, that in 1324 enough supplies were taken to Aquitaine to build just twenty bridges.[162] That Lancaster's expedition was better planned and better prepared may have resulted from the experience and knowledge of the duchy's topography which Lancaster and some of his bannerets possessed.

Thus, the expeditionary force took less than four months to mobilise, and as Jonathan Sumption asserts, was 'a masterpiece of careful preparation' delayed only by the vagaries of the weather. However, the view that Lancaster's army was ready 'by 22 May 1345, within a week of its appointed time', is only accurate with regard to three indentured retinues and it overlooks the late arrival of the army's infantry.[163] Although the original date of muster was 14 May, the Welsh foot and English archers levied from the north and the midlands arrived at Southampton more than two weeks later. Furthermore, the process of horse appraisal was delayed by Mauny, whose retinue did not join Lancaster's forces until the beginning of the second week of June. The strong south-west winds, therefore, were not the only reason for the fleet's delayed departure. Nevertheless, the efficiency of the military preparations and logistics which enabled the English Crown to deploy an army of around 2000 men within a period of less than four months is impressive.

The efficiency of military preparations is highlighted further by the comparatively longer period taken to mobilise the Black Prince's forces in 1355. Although the prince led a slightly larger army of around 2300 men to Aquitaine, it was not ready to embark until five months after preparations for the expedition had first began, and two months later than had originally been intended.[164] In 1359 the mobilisation of the king's army does not seem to have been any quicker; it took more than eight months to assemble a force with an approximate strength of 10,000 men, which was then delayed for a further two months.[165] Indeed, the feat of organisation in 1345 is even more impressive when we consider that other expeditionary forces were being mobilised simultaneously as part of the multi-front attack coordinated by Edward III. The army led by the earl of Northampton, destined for Brittany, had departed in the first week of June, as had a smaller force led by Thomas Ferrers. The largest force, under the king's own command, was ready in the last week of June.

---

[162] Lambert, *Shipping the Medieval Military*, p. 87.

[163] Sumption, *Trial by Battle*, p. 457.

[164] The first military preparations were made around mid April, with the date of embarkation set for the beginning of July; the prince did not set sail from Plymouth until 9 September: Ormrod, *Edward III*, pp. 341–2; Hewitt, *The Black Prince's Expedition*, pp. 14–42; Jonathan Sumption, *The Hundred Years War II: Trial by Fire* (London: Faber and Faber, 1999), pp. 154, 168.

[165] Ormrod suggests that the production of ovens and leather boots which were to be taken on the campaign had been a main cause of the delay: Ormrod, *Edward III*, pp. 397–9; Fowler, *King's Lieutenant*, p. 198.

Changes in Army Composition over the Course of the Expedition

The composition and general character of the English army in Aquitaine inevitably changed over the course of the expedition as events developed in the duchy. Apart from the inevitable loss of army personnel to the normal attritions of war, the size of Lancaster's forces was altered by the departure of individual knights and their companies, as well as entire retinue contingents which returned to England. However, this drop in military personnel was balanced by an influx of new arrivals and reinforcements in Aquitaine in 1346. Such changes to the strength and structure of the army, at an institutional level and at a lower retinue level, can elucidate certain aspects of the campaign – as well as the nature of warfare – and provide insights into military organisation. It is of great surprise, therefore, that changes in the composition of Lancaster's army have received so little attention from historians.[166]

The only retinue to withdraw from the expedition after an initial term of six months service was that of the absentee, Sir James Audley. His retinue returned to England under the command of Sir John Trumwyn on 30 November 1345, after having taken part in the famous victories at Bergerac and Auberoche.[167] The decision not to keep Audley's retinue in the field beyond half a year was probably made by Lancaster himself, and is of little surprise considering that the soldiers lacked the personal leadership of the banneret. Furthermore, that as many as half of the men in the retinue had been recruited from Audley's estates suggests that his absence may have had a particularly negative impact on the cohesion and morale of the retinue contingent.[168] The view that the earl of Pembroke's retinue also returned to England in the following month is based on a clerical error; the earl, in fact, remained in the duchy and later served as one of the captains of the garrison at Aiguillon during the unsuccessful siege of the town made by Jean, duke of Normandy.[169]

There were also changes in the military personnel of the retinues that remained in the duchy for the duration of the expedition. The movement of troops who left, or entered, the service of a retinue captain leaves little trace in the extant pay records. Indeed, Lancaster's retinue roll gives the impres-

---

[166] Fowler devotes a short paragraph to the subject, while Sumption's discussion of the changes in the army's composition is limited to a single sentence: Fowler, *King's Lieutenant*, p. 224; Sumption, *Trial by Battle*, p. 476. Ayton explains that 'we cannot be sure' how an esquire named Hugh Courson served in Aquitaine and then in Normandy the following year: Ayton, *English Army at Crécy*, p. 203.

[167] E 101/24/20.

[168] Morgan, *War and Society*, p. 76.

[169] Sumption's assertion that the earl's retinue returned to England at the end of 1345 is incorrect: Sumption, *Trial by Battle*, p. 476. E 372/191, m. 54d.

sion that the same men who mustered at Southampton returned to England in his retinue more than a year and a half later.[170] However, a comparison of the different types of nominal evidence of service of men in Lancaster's retinue shows that Sir Richard Fitzsimon, for example, was one of several soldiers who departed from the theatre of war in the south-west of France in time to take part in Edward III's great Normandy expedition in the summer of 1346. Among these returnees were men closely associated with the earl, such as his leading knights or trusted valets. These soldiers and the motivations for their departure from the duchy will be discussed in Chapter 8.

Perhaps the most significant departure from the duchy, which has evaded both chroniclers and historians, is that of Sir Walter Mauny's retinue. The Hainaulter is one of the most celebrated figures in Jean Froissart's account of the campaign, and his endeavours at Bergerac, Auberoche and in the capture of La Réole are well documented by other chroniclers.[171] Mauny's biographer and other scholars also give a comprehensive account of his accomplishments in the duchy, but they fail to mention his retinue's return at the beginning of 1346.[172] A personal dispatch of Henry of Lancaster refers to the capture of Mauny and his men at Saint-Jean-d'Angély, after they had been granted a passage of safe-conduct by the duke of Normandy during his siege of Aiguillon.[173] The military exploits of the Hainaulter during the siege are also attested by the narrative sources, so there can be little doubt, therefore, that Mauny took part in the defence of Aiguillon at some point during the siege. However, we cannot be certain if he was in the town when the duke of Normandy first began his assault of Aiguillon. A payment made to Walter Mauny at Bordeaux on 3 January 1346 for his men's wages and the cost of their sea passage *versus Angliam*, amongst other things, suggests that Mauny and his retinue returned to England at some point soon after the bill was sealed.[174] Although there is no evidence of further payments to Mauny for his service in Aquitaine beyond this date, the chroniclers' accounts and Lancaster's correspondence prove that he was at Aiguillon – possibly from as early as March – before heading northwards and his subsequent capture. Therefore, it seems that Mauny returned to England with his retinue at the end of the first campaign, marked by the capture of the citadel at La Réole, but he was back in the duchy by the following spring and had joined the garrison force at Aiguillon.

[170] E 101/25/9, m. 3; E 101/35/2/10.

[171] See chronicles referenced in the Bibliography below.

[172] Jonathan Sumption, 'Mauny, Sir Walter (c.1310–1372)', *ODNB*, Jan 2008 [accessed 12 March 2015]; Fowler; *King's Lieutenant*, pp. 53–74.

[173] Robert Avesbury, *De gestis mirabilibus regis Edwardi tertii*, ed. Edward Maunde Thompson (London: Eyre & Spottiswoode, 1889), pp. 372–4.

[174] E 43/78.

The decision to send reinforcements to Aquitaine was probably made in March 1346 around the time that the vanguard of the French forces pitched their tents outside the walls of Aiguillon. On 27 March the sheriffs of London were ordered to proclaim that all archers intending to go to Gascony were to assemble at Tothill, near Westminster, 'before the hour of prime' on the following day.[175] Although it is impossible to establish the number of archers that turned up, the sense of urgency in the mandate suggests that Edward III was aware that the duke of Normandy had entered the southern theatre of war in France, and possibly that the siege had already begun.[176] This wave of reinforcements was swollen by 300 Welsh archers (*Wallenses sagittarii*) who had been recruited from various parts of South Wales.[177] Some historians have considered these troops to be part of the original army which set out to Aquitaine in 1345, but there can be no doubt that they were raised in the following year.[178] A payment was made at the Receipt of the Exchequer on 10 April 1346 for their wages and other costs, although we cannot be sure when exactly the contingent set out from the port of Carmarthen.[179] It took three weeks for the two ships carrying the Welshmen and victuals to reach Bordeaux. One historian claims that 'a further four hundred foot left Portsmouth during May', but there is no indication that these troops were intended for service in Aquitaine.[180] It is interesting to note that the entire contingent of 300 Welshmen was made up exclusively of archers, rather than balanced proportions of archers and spearmen like the Welsh infantry that had set out in the previous year. This emphasis on the need for foot archers probably resulted from changes in the nature of warfare in the duchy, precipitated by the French offensive at the beginning of 1346. The fact that no indentured retinues consisting of wholly mounted troops were among the reinforcements sent from England in the

[175] C 76/22, m. 22d.

[176] If the proclamation was made in response to the siege then the French vanguard must have arrived outside Aiguillon by mid March at the latest.

[177] The fact that the 300 Welshmen were all archers supports the view that men from Gwent in South Wales were renowned for their use of the bow: Evans, *Principality of Wales*, p. 55.

[178] Rogers' erroneous assertion that Lancaster's retinue comprised 300 Welsh foot when it landed in Bordeaux in 1345 is based on Prince's assessment of the earl's retinue, which also fails to distinguish between troops that had served from the beginning of the expedition and those that arrived the following year. Rogers, *Bergerac Campaign*, p. 94; Prince, *Payment of Army Wages*, p. 153.

[179] E 372/191, m. 54d.

[180] Fowler, *King's Lieutenant*, p. 224. Although the troops were recruited from Lancaster's lordships of Carmarthen, Grosmont, Iscennen, Kidwelly, Monmouth and Whitecastle, there is no mention of Aquitaine in the mandate. *Foedera*, III, p. 79. The Welsh foot were almost certainly intended for service on the king's expedition to Normandy.

spring of 1346 suggests that Lancaster envisaged a more prominent role for siege warfare during the new campaigning season.

These changes in the character of the army reflect a growing importance of the infantry in the second half of the expedition and are typified by the changes in the composition of Ralph Stafford's retinue. All of the pay records relating to Stafford's first year of service record payments for the wages of 'men-at-arms and archers staying with him in parts of Gascony'.[181] However, a bill of the constable of Bordeaux made on 1 November 1346 records a payment to Stafford for his fee for half a year, and various other expenses, including the 'wages of his company of armed men, on horse and on foot'.[182] There is no reference to any archers and his retinue comprised both mounted troops and infantrymen. Furthermore, the bill states that his retinue's wages are for the time that 'he remained in the fortified town of Aiguillon (*Acuelo*), and also expedited the king's business around other parts of the duchy'.[183] It seems that the composition of Stafford's retinue altered commensurate with the change in the nature of warfare in the duchy. The battles of Auberoche and Bergerac and the intermittent raiding throughout the duchy during the first campaign required a wholly mounted and equally balanced retinue of men-at-arms and archers. However, the defence of the garrison town of Aiguillon favoured a different composition of soldiers. The armed men on foot (perhaps troops similar to Gascon sergeants), seem to have been more effective in a garrison force than the mounted archers.

The original retinue which Ralph Stafford recruited in 1345 had probably disbanded, in part at least, at some point during the winter months or the beginning of the new year.[184] A pardon granted to Sir John Hyde on 17 September 1345 suggests that his service in Stafford's retinue was completed by this date, and, therefore, he had probably returned to England.[185] His service in the Black Prince's retinue at Crécy the following year confirms that Hyde did not remain in Stafford's retinue for the entire expedition.[186] The case of Hyde, may have been an isolated instance; unfortunately there is no indication of how many soldiers from Stafford's original retinue remained in his service after he switched to a retinue that was more suited to siege warfare in 1346.

---

[181] E 361/2, m. 41.; E 403/337, m. 7.

[182] E 404/503/139.

[183] E 404/503/139.

[184] The caesura in hostilities during the winter months, around the time of Mauny's departure from the duchy, seems the most suitable time for men in Stafford's retinue to return to England.

[185] *CPR, 1343–45*, p. 549. Six months completed service up to this point implies that he had been in Stafford's service since March 1345.

[186] *BPR*, III, p . 413.

The administrative records reveal the significant changes in the strength of the English army, as well as the more nuanced changes in its general character over the course of the campaigns in 1345 and 1346. It is clear that the expeditionary force was a changing organism which responded to changes in the nature of warfare in the duchy, the unfolding of events during the expedition and, perhaps, the *mentalité* of the soldiers. The reasons for the departure of soldiers are interesting and will be explored later in the book. These endogenous and exogenous factors which influenced the changes in Lancaster's army have been largely overlooked by historians concerned with the expedition to Aquitaine, and indeed, there were probably further changes in the composition of the army that are not evidenced in the frustratingly patchy extant records.

4

Paying an Army:
Financial Administration

The financial system of the English government of the fourteenth century is a well-researched subject which has interested historians for more than a century. Consequently, there is an abundance of historiography based on the royal medieval administrative system.[1] T. F. Tout's impressive *Chapters in the Administrative History of Medieval England* marked the beginning of a plethora of important scholarly studies which have developed our understanding of the role of the state and of the king within the overall financial system, the evolution of the different departments of government and the working of the administration in practice.[2] It is no surprise, however, that comparatively little attention has been given to studying the financial administration of a single army or military expedition based firmly on the pay records, considering that the relevant documents are often widely dispersed among the administrative records and, in many respects, it remains a specialist subject of study.[3] An attempt to trace the expenditure of the Crown and military captains through the administrative records and to construct a schedule of payments which are itemised in the extant accounts has, up to now, yet to be undertaken.

This approach to the sources will enable us to understand some basic issues of financing an army. For example, how did the king's wages effectively reach the pockets of soldiers who served on expeditions overseas, and can we identify the individuals (both prominent and obscure) who were involved in the process? How did the 'money chain', so to speak, work in the mid 1340s – from which departments was funding issued, and what different methods of payment were used by the Crown? The details of payments to captains

---

[1]   See the Bibliography, particularly the publications of Edmund B. Fryde, Gerald L. Harriss, J. H. Johnson, Albert E. Prince and Thomas F. Tout.

[2]   T. F. Tout, *Chapters in the Administrative History of Medieval England: The Wardrobe, the Chamber and the Small Seals*, 6 vols (Manchester: Manchester University Press, 1920–33).

[3]   For an analysis of financing a naval campaign later in the fourteenth century, see Tony K. Moore, 'The Cost-Benefit Analysis of a Fourteenth-Century Naval Campaign: Margate/Cadzand, 1387', in *Roles of the Sea*, ed. Gorski, pp. 103–24.

can also be used to analyse the efficiency of the royal administrative system over the course of the expedition, and assess whether it was affected by the growing war effort following Edward III's great expedition to Normandy in 1346. A close scrutiny of the sources will help elucidate the various administrative procedures of accounting for service in Aquitaine, and provide valuable insight into how the financial system worked in wartime.

It was during the half century prior to Lancaster's expedition in 1345 that the English realm developed into a sophisticated 'fiscal state', whereby the Crown's traditional source of revenues based on the royal estates and the feudal and regalian rights which accompanied them was surpassed by a new system of general taxation.[4] The introduction of new revenue streams based on various forms of ordinary and extraordinary taxation provided the Edwardian kings with the financial means necessary to fight in costly and large-scale wars. A grant of extraordinary taxation could only be made with the consent of parliament and on the plea of necessity for the defence of the realm or the king.[5] In reality, the latter condition did not inhibit Edward III from prosecuting his more or less continual wars with France and Scotland. During the 1330s Edward devised a fiscal system that not only financed his own military enterprises but also those of his successors throughout the Hundred Years' War.[6] In general terms, the various financial schemes included the imposition of direct taxation of the clergy and the laity (known as the 'clerical tenth' and the lay 'fifteenth and tenth'), the imposition of indirect taxation in the form of subsidies on wool exports (over and above the standard customs rates) and the use of loans from international banking houses, English prelates and merchant cartels.[7] These fiscal demands were made possible because of the remarkable degree of support that Edward received from parliament between 1344 and 1360 for the French war – support that was vindicated by the spate of English military successes from the mid 1340s up to the Treaty of Brétigny. The parliamentary backing of war during this period resulted in a succession of grants of extraordinary taxation and it was, indeed, the lay subsidies of the 'fifteenth and tenth' which had been

---

[4]   W. Mark Ormrod, 'England in the Middle Ages', in *The Rise of the Fiscal State in Europe, c. 1200–1815*, ed. Richard Bonney (New York: Oxford University Press, 1999), pp. 19–52 (pp. 21–7).

[5]   Harriss, *King, Parliament and Public Finance*, pp. 314–20.

[6]   Ormrod, *Edward III*, p. 114.

[7]   Ormrod, *Edward III*, pp. 110–16; W. Mark Ormrod, *The Reign of Edward III: Crown and Political Society in England, 1327–1377* (New Haven, CT: Yale University Press, 1990), pp. 179–90; W. Mark Ormrod, 'The Western Monarchies in the Later Middle Ages', in *Economic Systems and State Finance*, ed. Richard Bonney (Oxford: Clarendon, 1995), pp. 123–60, (pp. 128–36); Edmund B. Fryde, *Studies in Medieval Trade and Finance* (London: Hambledon, 1983), chap. vii, pp. 1142–1216; chap. x, pp. 1–17; Edmund B. Fryde, 'Materials for the Study of Edward III's Credit Operations, 1327–48', *BIHR*, 22 (1949), 105–38.

granted by parliament in 1344 that largely financed Lancaster's army the following year.[8] Taxation, therefore, had become the principal source of war finance but of greater importance to this study is the question of how and, of course, how efficiently, the financial administration worked in practice.

English armies in the reign of Edward III were administered in a variety of different ways. The means through which payments were made to military captains often depended upon the commander of the army and the theatre of war; if an army were led by the king in person then the bulk of military expenditure was traditionally financed through the Wardrobe, the financial department of the royal household. This was sensible because if the king personally commanded an army he was still in effect leading 'the household in arms'.[9] The armies that set out to the Low Countries (1338), Brittany (1342), Normandy (1346) and France (1359), for example, were all under direct royal command and therefore administered by the Wardrobe (which functioned essentially as a war treasury), while the accounts of service for each campaign were recorded in the respective Wardrobe books. When the king appointed a captain to serve as his lieutenant and lead an army on campaign, however, it was the Exchequer that administered the finance of military operations. The medieval Exchequer, which had evolved since the twelfth century into a professional government department, controlled the expenditure of all public finance and effectively filled the administrative vacuum created by the absence of the Wardrobe clerks when the king did not take personal command of an army.[10] Thus, Henry of Lancaster's expedition to Aquitaine in 1345 and the smaller expeditions which set out overseas in the same year, led by Sir Thomas Ferrers and the earl of Northampton to the Channel Islands and Brittany, were the first of Edward III's reign to be financed directly by the Exchequer.[11] Moreover, the campaign in Aquitaine serves as a benchmark in the development of the newly adopted indenture system which had emerged from the Exchequer, and became the dominant method of recruitment used by the Crown for overseas campaigns that were not led by the king in person. It is for these reasons, not least, that the financial administration of Lancaster's army requires a more detailed assessment than has previously been attempted. Although the extant financial records relating to Lancaster's expeditionary force are patchy and incomplete, enough sources can be mined to demonstrate how, where and

[8] The stored subsidy of the fifteenth and tenth funded the bulk of expenditure for the wages and *regard* of retinue captains in Lancaster's army in 1345.

[9] Ayton, *Knights and Warhorses*, p. 11.

[10] For a detailed discussion of the major reforms of the Exchequer in the 1320s which gave the department greater authority and control over public finance, see Harriss, *King, Parliament and Public Finance*, pp. 208–11.

[11] For the role of the Wardrobe in financing the armies of Edward III up to 1345, see Prince, *Payment of Army Wages*, pp. 137–51.

when the finance of the army was administered. A prerequisite to any study of finance, however, is an understanding of the very items that were to be financed – thus, a brief assessment of the main benefits of service offered to Lancaster's army is needed.

Benefits of Service: Wages

In 1345 the Crown offered a variety of benefits of service to men-at-arms who served in the indentured retinues of an English army, all of which were embodied in a formal contract, or indenture of service. The three principal benefits of service were payments of wages, *regard* and horse restoration. All the men in Lancaster's army, except for the pardon recipients who served at their own expense, were in receipt of the king's wages based on what had become the customary rates of pay. Soldiers belonging to the troop type of men-at-arms were paid the following daily wage: 6s 8d for an earl, 4s for a banneret, 2s for a knight and 1s for an esquire (or ordinary man-at-arms).[12] A mounted archer received 6d per day. Naturally, the infantrymen found themselves at the bottom of the pay scale; the English foot archers received a daily wage of 3d and the Welsh foot received just 2d per day.[13] The *centenars*, constables and *vintenars* who made up the officer corps of the infantry divisions received pay rates commensurate with their rank; *vintenars* were paid a daily wage of 4d, while the *centenars* and constables were remunerated at 12d per day.[14]

These rates of pay had long been established as the 'accustomed wages of war' in English armies since the thirteenth century, and rarely fluctuated over the course of the Hundred Years' War.[15] A special inquiry held in 1337 to establish the appropriate rates of pay for service in Aquitaine confirmed that the Crown should offer the same rates as those that were offered for service in the duchy in 1294, and they became standard in all theatres of

---

[12] Hewitt, *Organization of War*, p. 36.

[13] Note that Welsh foot were generally paid the same rate as English foot soldiers in the reigns of Edward I and Edward II, but Welsh infantry who served in the armies of Edward III were typically remunerated at 2d per day. For an alternative view, namely that Welsh and English foot soldiers were remunerated at the same rate up to 1359, see Chapman, *Welsh Soldiers*, pp. 186–7.

[14] Prestwich, *Armies and Warfare*, pp. 84, 126.

[15] In 1212 Flemish mercenaries received the same customary wages for service in King John's army. Some instances of when the Crown deviated from its standard wage structure: Welsh archers were remunerated at the slightly higher rate of 3d per day during the final stages of the civil war of the 1260s; English foot archers received the reduced rate of 2d per day for service in Aquitaine in 1295. Prestwich, *Armies and Warfare*, p. 84. Prestwich, *Edward I*, p. 93.

war from the 1330s.[16] The pay records relating to Lancaster's expedition show that all the men serving in his army received these customary wages. The two Exchequer clerks, William Farley and Henry de Walton, who delivered an instalment of money to Lancaster in the duchy at the beginning of the expedition, received a daily wage of 2s, equivalent to that of a knight, and the bodyguards who accompanied them overseas were paid at the standard rate of pay for an esquire and mounted archers.[17] Further consistency in the wage rates is evinced by the retinue of Peter Gretheved, the king's clerk, which set out to Aquitaine at the end of 1345 and also received the standard levels of pay commensurate with their rank.[18]

The only time that the Crown deviated from its normal wage structure was in the period of service prior to the fleet's embarkation at Southampton, in connection with the wages paid to some of the officers of the English infantry. For example, John de Lesyng was paid just 6d per day, half of the usual wage of a *centenar*, for his journey from Staffordshire down to Southampton and for the initial two weeks that he remained at the port.[19] Also, the *vintenars* from the counties of Derby and Lancaster received wages at one and a half times the usual rate (6d per day) for the same two-week period at Southampton.[20] However, this fluctuation in the pay rates was only temporary. The account of John de Watenhill, king's receiver of money, shows that the officers' wages reverted to the customary levels on 12 June 1345.[21]

One interesting feature of Watenhill's account is the phraseology used in two entries concerning the wages of the English and Welsh infantry. On both occasions the rates stipulated by the king's receiver are followed by the phrase, 'just as wages of this type are allowed in the account of Richard de Ferriby of the Wardrobe' (*sicut huiusmodi vadia allocantur sicut in compoto Ricardi de Feriby de Garderoba*).[22] It seems odd that the clerk should make reference to 'wages of this type' which were offered by the Crown more than ten years earlier and, furthermore, why did he specifically refer to Richard de Ferriby's Wardrobe account? The clerk's attempt to prove that the same rates of pay offered to infantrymen in 1345 were also paid in 1334 may have resulted, perhaps, from the Crown's desire to establish, or at least reaffirm, these rates of pay as the customary wages of war. However, the reference to the Scottish expedition of 1334 is perplexing. Why did the clerk not refer to more recent Wardrobe accounts which covered the Scottish campaigns

---

[16] Ormrod, *Edward III*, p. 192, n. 63.
[17] E 372/190, m. 54d. The bodyguard comprised one esquire and ten mounted archers.
[18] C 76/122, m. 9.
[19] E 372/190, m. 41; E 404/501/336.
[20] E 404/501/338; E 404/501/339.
[21] E 372/191, m. 41d.
[22] E 372/191, m. 41d. The Wardrobe account of Richard de Ferriby was for 1334/5.

of the late 1330s, for example, or the expeditions that were undertaken at the beginning of the Hundred Years' War? Edward III had offered the same rates of pay to men who served in his armies from 1335 to 1345, with the exception of the Low Countries (1338) and the Sluys-Tournai (1340) campaigns; moreover, on these last two campaigns it was only men-at-arms who received double wages.[23]

It is possible, therefore, that the reference to Ferriby's account was made by chance, or the result of a clerical whim – indeed, the Scottish campaign of 1334 appears to be of little significance in terms of the infantry's rates of pay, or any other aspect of military organisation. However, two items in the 'expense' section of Lancaster's account of service for the expedition in 1345 throw further light on the matter.[24] Two separate payments of wages – one to Welsh archers, and one to sailors who manned the earl's fleet – are followed by exactly the same phrase, 'huiusmodi vadia allocantur in compoto...', that appears in Watenhill's account. In Lancaster's account, however, the clerk refers to the Wardrobe account (*compotus de Garderoba*) of William de Norwell, rather than Ferriby, who served as keeper of the Wardrobe during Edward III's campaign in the Low Countries from 1338 to 1340. The references to two separate Wardrobe accounts from the 1330s, therefore, confirm the clerks' intention to show that a precedent for the infantry's wages in 1345 had already been set on earlier campaigns. That the reference to previous campaigns was made in the accounts of both Lancaster and Watenhill implies that the Crown was making a concerted effort to confirm the customary rates of pay of soldiers (and sailors) who did not serve in retinues. It may be that the wages of the infantry were more susceptible to fluctuation than the wages of men-at-arms, as seems to have been the case during the thirteenth century, and therefore the standard rates needed to be confirmed by the Crown.[25]

Another reason may have been the officialdom of the Exchequer and its strict adherence to bureaucratic practices. The expedition of 1345 was one of the first of Edward III's reign to be financed directly by the Exchequer, and perhaps the Exchequer clerks had therefore been instructed to show that the department had administered the same wages to the infantry as had been traditionally administered by the Wardrobe on previous occasions. Such accounting practices reflect the importance that the entire administrative system placed on authenticity and precedence, and no doubt were a symptom of the development of the Exchequer as a professional institution. Not until more Exchequer accounts of service for infantrymen have been consulted can firmer conclusions about the clerical culture and practices

---

[23] Ayton, *Knights and Warhorses*, pp. 109–10.
[24] E 372/191, m. 54d.
[25] See above for examples of fluctuations of pay rates to infantrymen in the thirteenth century.

be made, but it is clearly the case that there is still much of interest and importance to be learnt from the royal administrative records.

The wages of war (*vadia guerre*) were intended primarily to meet the necessary expenditure of a soldier and sustain him for the duration of a campaign, rather than provide a reward for military service.[26] In the case of the Welsh infantry, for example, 'the pay was only a bare subsistence allowance',[27] and the real rewards of war were gained through pillaging and the sale of valuable prisoners of war to superior officers.[28] Although the basic wage rates of soldiers had remained largely unaltered for more than one hundred years, the Crown was able to increase the rewards of service to one troop type, that of men-at-arms, through the introduction of a new type of remuneration.

Benefits of Service: *Regard*

The payment of wages was supplemented by a fee, known as *regard*, which became part of the normal terms of service offered by the Crown to retinue captains from the mid 1340s onwards. 'Regard' was essentially a bonus payment designed to contribute towards the captains' growing costs of preparing for war, although men-at-arms may also have benefited from a share of their captain's fee. Later in the fourteenth century, however, the *regard* developed and was offered to men-at-arms as part of an improved package of terms of service following the abandonment of *restaurum equorum* (horse restoration) in the early 1370s.[29] There are a couple of examples of retinue leaders receiving *regard* in the decades preceding Lancaster's expedition to Aquitaine, but it was not until 1345 that this type of payment was offered to all of the retinue captains in an English army.[30] The accounts of service of Lancaster and Pembroke show that other terms were used synonymously with *regard* or 'reward' (*rewardum*), such as 'gift of the king' (*donum regis*), but it was the former expression which became widely used by royal clerks

[26] Prestwich, *Armies and Warfare*, p. 86.

[27] Evans, *Principality of Wales*, p. 52.

[28] That booty and prisoners were considered to be a more valuable source of profit than wages by other ranks of the army is borne out by the example of the Gascon troops who, in 1346, agreed to serve without wages for the initial four weeks of Lancaster's northern raid in Aquitaine in the hope of acquiring lucrative war gains. Sumption, *Trial by Battle*, p. 51.

[29] Ayton, *Knights and Warhorses*, pp. 110–27.

[30] The 'fee' paid to William Montague, earl of Salisbury, in 1338 almost certainly represents a *regard* payment and the £100 bonus promised to Thomas Berkeley in 1342 may also have been the same type of remuneration: Prince, *Payment of Army Wages*, p. 144; Prestwich, *Armies and Warfare*, p. 93.

during the fourteenth century.[31] Some military contracts relating to service in Edward III's expedition in the following year show that such payments were also termed 'fees' (*feoda*).[32]

A payment of 100 marks for thirty men-at-arms for a quarter-year's service (equivalent to £9 per man-at-arms for a year's service) became the standard rate of *regard* from around the mid 1340s onwards,[33] but the Crown offered a premium rate to Lancaster and the retinue captains who served under his command in 1345.[34] The king's lieutenant secured *regard* at one and half times the normal rate, while the two retinue captains Sir James Audley and Sir Walter Mauny also received this higher level of remuneration.[35] The earl of Pembroke, however, received a more lucrative quarterly rate of £112 10s for thirty men-at-arms, based on a payment 'for his reward ... £1200 per year' (*pro rewardo suo ... MCC li. per annum*) recorded in the *vadia* section of his enrolled account of service.[36] There are several examples of retinue leaders securing even greater *regards* throughout the fourteenth century,[37] but it was unusual for a retinue captain to be awarded more favourable terms than his commander, particularly in the case of Pembroke considering the pre-eminence and superior status of Lancaster.[38] One possible cause for the unusually high rate of reward granted exclusively to Pembroke in 1345 may lie in the fact that the young earl was one of the poorest of the retinue

---

[31] E 372/190, m. 54d.

[32] Ayton, *Knights and Warhorses*, p. 112.

[33] Albert E. Prince, 'The Indenture System under Edward III', in *Historical Essays in Honour of James Tait*, ed. J. G. Edwards, V. H. Galbraith and E. F. Jacob (Manchester: [n. pub.], 1933), p. 293. In 1345 the warrior-clerk, John Charnels, received 100 marks for himself, 7 knights and 22 esquires which set a precedent for what became the standard rate of *regard*.

[34] Ayton's assertion that Lancaster secured *regard* at three times the standard rate is based on his misinterpretation of the advance of £5000 to Lancaster from the Exchequer as a payment of *regard*, when in fact it was a payment for both *regard* and wages. Ayton, *Knights and Warhorses*, p. 112 and n. 148. E 159/123, m. 254.

[35] Lancaster's *regard* of £3333 6s 8d for 250 men-at-arms for six months service gives an exact remuneration rate of one and a half times the standard. E 159/123, m. 254; E 372/191, m. 54d. For calculation of Audley and Mauny's rate of *regard*, see Chapter 3.

[36] E 372/191, m. 54d.

[37] Double the standard rate of *regard* was awarded to John Chandos in 1362 and like terms were offered to John de Hastings in 1372: Prince, *Indenture System*, p. 293. The most exceptional case is that of Thomas Dagworth who received a *regard* of 100 marks for himself for just under a year's service in 1346: Ayton, *Knights and Warhorses*, pp. 113–14.

[38] The *regard* for Pembroke's third quarter-year's service delivered by Peter Gretheved in December 1345 works out at an even higher rate again, although this unexpectedly large sum may be the result of an overpayment. Pembroke received a payment of 1666 écus, equivalent to £333 4s (each écu valued at 4s): C 61/57, m. 1; C 62/122, m. 9. A payment of £333 6s 8d is recorded on the Issue Rolls: E 403/336, m. 22. The slight discrepancy is probably due to a clerical error.

captains in the English army.[39] He had previously led only one retinue contingent of notable size and Edward III, therefore, may have granted him a larger 'bonus' payment in order to help off-set the increased costs of raising a larger retinue force.[40]

Interestingly, none of the pay records relating to Ralph Stafford's service in the duchy stipulate payment for *regard*, but it is unlikely that he would not have been offered the same benefits of service as the other retinue captains in Lancaster's army. The payment of Stafford's wages and 'various other expenses' recorded in a bill sealed by the constable of Bordeaux on 1 November 1346 may have included his *regard*, although it is likely that the Crown intended the annual 'fee' which Stafford received as seneschal of Aquitaine to cover this type of payment.[41]

There is no evidence to suggest that *regard* was paid at one and half times the standard rate to any retinue captains who served on other military expeditions in 1345.[42] So why did the captains who served under Lancaster's command receive a 50% higher rate of *regard*, and on what other occasions did the Crown offer such favourable terms of service to retinue captains? William Montague, earl of Salisbury, received this generous rate during his command of the Scottish expedition from 1337 to 1338 (the only captain to do so), and as far as I am aware, the only other occasion up to the Treaty of Brétigny when the Crown employed these same terms was in 1356.[43] In that year John, Lord Beauchamp of Warwick, received a quarterly payment of

---

[39] An interesting comparison can be made with William de Bohun, earl of Northampton, who was among the six new earls created by Edward III in 1337. Interestingly, the largest of the annuities which accompanied the titles was granted to Northampton (£1000) not because he was especially favoured by the king but, as Chris Given-Wilson points out, because he was the poorest of the earls. Chris Given-Wilson, *The English Nobility in the Middle Ages: The Fourteenth-Century Political Community* (London: Routledge & Kegan Paul, 1987), p. 37.

[40] Pembroke had previously served on two overseas expeditions. In Flanders (1338) and Brittany (1342) he served with retinues which comprised 3 men-at-arms, and 64 men-at-arms and 100 mounted archers, respectively. Ayton, 'Hastings', *ODNB*.

[41] E 404/503/139. The seneschal of Aquitaine received an annual fee of £500: E. C. Lodge, 'The Constables of Bordeaux in the Reign of Edward III', *EHR*, 50 (1935), 225–41 (p. 229).

[42] The indenture made between Edward III and the earl of Northampton on 27 April 1345 does not contain details of any payments due to the king's lieutenant: *Foedera*, III, p. 37. On 9 December 1345 John Charnels was ordered to pay Northampton a *regard* of 3400 écus. Ayton, *Knights and Warhorses*, p. 112, n. 150. However, without knowing the size or composition of the earl's retinue it is impossible to calculate the rate of payment.

[43] Prince, *Payment of Army Wages*, p. 144; the earl's *regard* was paid at a quarterly rate of 150 marks for thirty men-at-arms from 7 December 1337 to 13 June 1338. After the resumption of the Hundred Years' War *regard* was paid to John of Gaunt (in 1369), and Robert Knolles (in 1370), at one and a half times the standard rate: Prince, *Indenture System*, p. 293.

£166 13s 4d for fifty men-at-arms for the garrison of Calais.[44] It seems, then, that the Crown seldom offered *regard* at one and a half times the normal rate and, furthermore, the evidence implies that neither the theatre of war nor the nature of warfare was a decisive factor that influenced such policy. From the late 1330s to the mid 1350s the premium rate was awarded to captains who had served on the Continent and in Scotland, who had comprised part of garrison forces and who had also served on field campaigns. On each occasion, therefore, the status of the captain and the characteristics of the military service for which *regard* was paid were variable. The only connection between Beauchamp, Lancaster and Salisbury is their close association with Edward III. The evidence does not reveal the extent to which a commander or captain was able to negotiate his own terms of service with the king, or if the latter simply dictated the rates of remuneration that were to be paid. A decisive factor, either way, in determining more favourable benefits of service would have been the captain's relationship with the king. All of the captains in Lancaster's army were closely associated with the monarch and they probably benefited all the more from serving under the command of Lancaster who had an intimate relationship with Edward III.

One uncertainty surrounding this type of remuneration, however, is whether it was intended as an incentive for the retinue captain alone or whether he divided the payment among the men-at-arms in his retinue. J. W. Sherborne argues that *regard* was paid to each man-at-arms in a retinue. Although there is evidence of this practice during the second phase of the Hundred Years' War, this does not seem to have been the case in 1345.[45] It is more likely that *regard* was intended to contribute to the retinue-raising costs of the captain, which had grown significantly with the emergence of mixed retinues and the emphasis on overseas expeditions from 1338 onwards. The enrolled accounts for Lancaster's and Pembroke's service in Aquitaine show that *regard* was calculated per capita, but no breakdown of payment for each man-at-arms is recorded in the expenses section, which suggests that the payment was intended for the captain.[46] Moreover, it seems that the Crown offered *regard* as a separate payment rather than simply increasing the basic rates of pay of soldiers, which implies that it was a financial benefit for the captain rather than his men.

The absence of any payments of *regard* to Ralph Stafford for his retinue's service in the duchy, mentioned above, implies that his 'fee' as seneschal

---

[44] C 76/34, m. 18d.

[45] Sherborne, *Indentured Retinues*, p. 743, n. 6.

[46] E 372/191, m. 54d. Pembroke's account is a rare example of a rate of *regard* being specified in an account, however, it does not stipulate the number of men for whom the '£1200 per year' was intended.

was intended to cover the 'bonus' payment.[47] It is reasonable to presume, therefore, that *regard* would have been paid to Stafford's men-at-arms at his own discretion. The sub-contract made between Stafford and Sir Hugh Fitz Simon on 16 March 1347, for example, demonstrates that the same rate of *regard* agreed between Stafford and the king was not passed on to his men-at-arms or sub-retinue captain.[48] Fitz Simon had agreed to serve in Stafford's retinue with twelve men-at-arms for one year, for which he was to receive a fee of 100 marks, equating to less than two thirds of the standard quarterly rate. The margin of profit which Stafford retained by offering this lower rate of remuneration suggests that the rate of *regard* was set at the captain's discretion and, furthermore, there is nothing to suggest that this practice was in contravention of the terms of service offered by the Crown.

An extrapolation of the evidence has shown that *regard* was paid to a retinue captain, and that it was his prerogative whether his men-at-arms received the same rate of remuneration, if any payment was made to them at all. However, it seems logical that a retinue leader would have passed this benefit of service on to his sub-retinue captains who might also have faced similar recruiting costs depending on the size of their own contingent. Henry of Lancaster, for example, would probably have paid *regard* to the bannerets who served as sub-captains in his own retinue, but whether the sub-captains paid a *regard* to the ordinary men-at-arms who served under their banners we cannot be sure. It seems, therefore, that the Crown introduced *regard* as an incentive for service for retinue captains rather than men-at-arms, although the latter might also have received the same benefit of service dependent upon the individual captain.

Benefits of Service: Horse Restoration

The third main benefit of service offered by the Crown to men-at-arms was horse restoration (*restaurum equorum*). This policy worked on the principle that one warhorse for each man-at-arms was valued during a formal appraisal process prior to a military campaign, and should the horse subsequently be lost in war, then restitution of the appraised cost was made by the king. The payment of compensation for horses lost, either killed or injured, during the course of a military campaign was a welcome benefit of service upon its introduction by the English Crown in the 1280s.[49] Horse

---

[47] Prince suggests *regard* was a 'bonus' payment for the retinue captain: Prince, *Indenture System*, pp. 293–4.

[48] Ayton, *Knights and Warhorses*, p. 113.

[49] We cannot be certain when the custom of horse restoration first began in England. The earliest extant documents produced in connection with the appraisal of warhorses date from 1282: Ayton, *Knights and Warhorses*, p. 50. Prestwich suggests that *restaurum*

restoration had originally also provided the Crown with a form of 'quality control' to check that men-at-arms were properly equipped, namely that they served with a warhorse of sufficient quality, but by the reign of Edward III the process no longer functioned in this way.[50] Although the policy of horse restoration continued to operate until the 1370s, its importance had grown commensurate with the development of the warhorse, which had reached its peak by the mid-fourteenth century.[51]

The task of horse appraisal was usually performed at the army's muster point, which for overseas expeditions was often the designated port of embarkation. Henry of Lancaster, however, was given the option of having his retinue's mounts appraised at Southampton 'in the customary manner' (*en manere acustumee*), or if his men preferred to buy their horses in Aquitaine, they would be appraised by the constable of Bordeaux.[52] Interestingly, similar terms which allowed the warhorses of a captain's retinue to be appraised in the duchy were also offered to the Black Prince (1355) and John of Gaunt (1369) later in the fourteenth century.[53] However, a horse restoration account relating to the service of Lancaster's retinue in 1345–46, and which has not been previously used by historians, reveals that the majority of horses lost by the earl's men, almost three quarters in fact (72.3%), were appraised at the port of Southampton (see Table 3).[54] The horses were valued there on

---

equorum might have been customary practice in the royal household from as early as the beginning of the twelfth century: Prestwich, *Armies and Warfare*, p. 96. An early example of compensation for the loss of horses occurred when the First Crusade was on the brink of starvation in January/February 1098 at the siege of Antioch. Because of the fear of losing their horses knights were refusing to escort foraging expeditions, and so Count Raymond of Toulouse set aside 500 marks to recompense any of his knights who suffered such a loss. This obliged the other crusader leaders to follow suit: John Hugh Hill and Laurita L. Hill, eds., *Le "Liber" de Raymond d'Aguilers* (Paris: Geuthner, 1969), pp. 54–5; translation by the editors of Raymond of Aguilers (or d'Agiles), *Historia Francorum qui ceperunt Iherusalem* (Philadelphia: American Philosophical Society, 1968), pp. 36–7: I owe this reference to Professor John France. The ad hoc decision by Tancred, prince of Antioch, to pay his knights compensation for any horses lost during their attack on the infantry of Shaizar in 1110 is an interesting example of horse restoration operating in a different military context, see *The Autobiography of Ousama*, ed. and trans. George Richard Potter (London: Routledge, 1929), p. 89.

[50] By the 1340s horse appraisal was no longer a prerequisite to the payment of wages. Ayton, *Knights and Warhorses*, pp. 84–103.

[51] Ayton, *Knights and Warhorses*, p. 37. The latest record of horse restoration was that offered to Thomas de Wennesley by John of Gaunt in 1384: Prestwich, *Armies and Warfare*, p. 97.

[52] E 159/123, m. 254.

[53] Gribit, *Horse Restoration in the Army of Henry of Grosmont*, p. 151.

[54] E 372/191, m. 55; transcribed and translated in Gribit, *Horse Restoration in the Army of Henry of Grosmont*, pp. 160–3.

Table 3. Number of Horses Lost in Aquitaine by Men in the Retinues of Henry of Lancaster and the Earl of Pembroke and the Place of Their Appraisal

Retinue	Bordeaux	Southampton	Total
Lancaster	43	112	155
Pembroke	5	19	24
Total	48	131	179

Source: E 372/191, mm. 54d, 55.

8 June 1345 by Master William Dalton, the controller, and Sir Thomas de Bourne, usher of the king's household.[55]

We cannot be sure whether Lancaster's choice of having his retinue's horses appraised at either Southampton or Bordeaux was offered to all the retinue captains in his army, although we can be certain that these favourable terms were also granted to the earl of Pembroke.[56] A payment for *restaurum equorum* recorded in Pembroke's account of service shows that nineteen horses lost by men in his retinue were valued at Southampton by the same usher and controller of the royal household who we know appraised the horses belonging to men in Lancaster's retinue.[57] Table 3 illustrates that these lost mounts represent almost four fifths (79.2%) of the total number of equestrian losses sustained by men in Pembroke's retinue and that roughly one fifth of the total number of horses lost by Pembroke's retinue – a smaller proportion than Lancaster's retinue – were appraised at Bordeaux.

There is no documentary evidence of the appraisal or the compensation of any of the horses owned by the men who served in the retinue of Sir James, Lord Audley. This, however, is of little surprise considering that the Staffordshire baron's force of 40 men-at-arms and 40 mounted archers represented the smallest of the mounted retinues, which also served for the shortest period of time.[58] The chances of suffering any warhorse casualties, therefore, must have been substantially reduced. An item of expenditure recorded in Audley's particulars of account for the 'passage and return passage' (*passagium et repassagium*) of 164 horses proves that the standard shipping allowance of four horses for a knight, three horses for an 'esquire'

[55] E 372/191, m. 55.

[56] Pembroke's indenture of service includes the clause: 'Et en cas que les uns des gentz darmes [ne se voilent monter des] chavalx decea la meer, mes faire lour pourveanceis es parties de dela la meer, que adonqes, meismes ceux chivalx ensi [...soient prisez illoeques par le conestable de Burdeux en la manere suisdite].' E 101/68/3/60 (indenture badly damaged).

[57] E 372/191, m. 54d.

[58] E 101/24/20; Audley's retinue served for a total of 239 days.

and one horse for each mounted archer was allowed by the Crown, but, more importantly, it implies that his retinue embarked with its full quota of horses and presumably, therefore, would not have needed to purchase mounts upon its arrival at Bordeaux.[59] Of course, not all of the horses taken overseas by men-at-arms would have been warhorses as men would have required horses for riding on the march or chevauchée, such as a palfrey or trotter, as well as packhorses (probably sumpters) to carry their baggage.[60] A mounted archer would probably have ridden a hackney, a horse more suitable for the march than for the battlefield.[61] When it comes to Ralph, Lord Stafford we know that his warhorse was valued at Bordeaux, but there is no surviving evidence which reveals whether any of his retinue's horses were also appraised in the duchy.[62] Similarly, the appraisal of the horses owned by men in Walter Mauny's retinue also remains unknown.

A retinue captain could wait months, often years, before he received full payment for the cost of his retinue's lost horses. Lancaster, for example, completed his service for the expedition in Aquitaine on 1 January 1347 and an account of his service was subsequently made at the Exchequer within one month.[63] A separate account for the restoration of his retinue's horses which were valued at Southampton, however, was not made until the following year at the end of June.[64] Ralph Stafford also had to wait more than a year

---

[59]   E 101/24/20; transcribed and translated in Gribit, *Accounting for Service at War*, pp. 163–7. In 1340 the English Crown had been willing to pay the costs of passage for the same number of horses for each rank of man-at-arms from Sluys to England: Ayton, *Knights and Warhorses*, p. 58. Although a much later comparison, it is interesting to note that the majority of the 39 men of unknown rank who served in the earl of Oxford's retinue on the Normandy expedition in 1415 took only one horse overseas, whilst only two men took four mounts. E 101/46/36. m. 2. Furthermore, three of the men whom James Ross has identified as esquires took only two horses each, rather than three horses as was customary practice in the mid 1340s: James Ross, 'The de Vere Earls of Oxford, 1400–1513' (unpublished doctoral thesis, Oxford University, 2004), pp. 218–21. Although it was conventional practice for the Crown to cover the cost of shipping one horse for each mounted archer on an overseas expedition, it was, as noted earlier, highly unusual for their horses to be valued during the appraisal process. Moreover, the administrative records provide little evidence of how a mounted archer was able to keep his mobility and, indeed, his status if his mount was injured or killed during a military expedition.

[60]   Charles Gladitz, *Horse Breeding in the Medieval World* (Dublin: Four Courts Press, 1997), pp. 155–7. The palfrey and the sumpter were complementary and often purchased and stabled together. The gait of the palfrey was the amble which enabled a more comfortable and faster paced ride than horses that trotted, while the speed and flexibility of the sumpter made it an invaluable pack horse in war.

[61]   Ayton, *Knights and Warhorses*, p. 57.

[62]   E 404/490/174.

[63]   E 372/191, m. 54d; on 30 January 1347 the king ordered the Treasurer, Barons and Chamberlain of the Exchequer to account for Lancaster's service.

[64]   The account was made on 26 June 1348 and payment was made on 5 July following:

before he received payment for the loss of his expensive warhorse. He was paid £142 on 13 December 1347,[65] although compensation had already been authorised by the constable of Bordeaux on 1 November 1346.[66] Similarly, an account was made with Stafford on 1 February 1347 for the restoration of horses lost by his retinue in Aquitaine, but no compensation payment was made until December of the following year.[67] Walter Mauny accounted for his men's horse restoration, amongst other benefits of service, on 3 January 1346, but the clause at the bottom of a sealed bill proves that he did not receive a payment of compensation until 1351.[68] Although these examples offer only a partial representation of the payments of *restaurum equorum* made to the men-at-arms who served in Aquitaine, it is clear that the great majority of soldiers or retinue captains, at least, received payments of compensation in arrears long after the dust of the campaign had settled.

Methods of Payment

In the absence of Edward III's personal command and with the predominant use of the indenture system in 1345, the finance of Lancaster's army which set out to Aquitaine was largely administered by the Exchequer. Thus, the retinue captains of Lancaster's army received the majority of payments for their *vadia guerre* and *regard* at the Receipt of the Exchequer (also known as the Lower Exchequer), and those captains who had indented directly with the king accounted for their service at the Exchequer of Accounts (or Upper Exchequer) after the campaign had ended. A clear schedule of payments made by the Crown to each captain can be reconstituted through the items recorded in the 'receipts' section of the particulars of account of James Audley and Henry of Lancaster, and the formal accounts of service of the earl of Pembroke and Lancaster.[69] Several types of information are recorded in these accounts including the item of receipt (such as wages, for example), the sum, the form of payment, and the place and date on which it was made. Sometimes not all of these details are recorded by the clerks and the accounts often leave little trace of the actual method of payment used by the Crown. Fortunately, the corresponding payments recorded in the Issue Rolls are more revealing.

E 372/191, m. 55; E 403/341, m. 19.

[65] E 403/340, m. 19.

[66] E 404/490/174.

[67] E 404/496/500.

[68] E 43/78.

[69] Particulars of account: E 101/24/20 (Audley); E 101/25/9 (Lancaster). Enrolled accounts of service: E 372/191, m. 54d.

There were two principal methods of payment used by the Exchequer in 1345; expenditure was either made in cash or by assignment. A classic example of the latter form of payment was the use of the tally system which Tout describes as an 'ingenious development' of the royal credit system during the reign of Edward I.[70] The tally system was originally used by the Exchequer as a form of receipt whereby a debtor of the Crown, such as a sheriff or collector of taxes, received a wooden tally once he had paid into the Exchequer the sum of money that was specified on it.[71] The new tally system, however, enabled the Crown to pledge its forthcoming royal revenue to creditors (such as military captains) who were owed money, and thus it was able to make payments of wages assigned on the local issues or duties of a certain county or port. If a retinue captain, for example, was paid by assignment then a common method was to issue a writ ordering the sheriff or collector addressed to pay a specified sum to the payee, or captain, and to receive a tally of the Exchequer from the captain for that amount.[72] Once the writ was issued the tally was cut and the sum was credited to the collector on the roll of receipt and debited to the captain on the roll of issue. The captain then took the tally to the sheriff or collector who exchanged the tally for the said sum of money.

The majority of assignments granted to the captains in Lancaster's army were made on the king's clerical and lay subsidies and it was not uncommon for them to be made on more than one subsidy depending upon the amount that was owed to the captain.[73] Lancaster, for example, was paid £4492 7s 4d 'by tallies levied on that day [4 November 1345] from the [lay] fifteenth in the counties of Wiltshire, Oxford, Berkshire and Buckingham and also from the [clerical] tenth in the dioceses of Salisbury, Coventry and Lichfield,

---

[70] Tout, *Chapters*, II, pp. 99–101. On the tally and assignment system, see William T. Baxter, 'Early Accounting: The Tally and the Checker-board', *The Accounting Historians Journal*, 16 (1989), 43–83; Harris, *King, Parliament and Public Finance*, pp. 219–20; C. Hilary Jenkinson, 'Exchequer Tallies', *Archaeologia*, 2nd ser., 62 (1911), 367–80; C. Hilary Jenkinson, 'Medieval Tallies, Public and Private', *Archaeologia*, 2nd ser., 74 (1925), 289–351; Anthony B. Steel, *The Receipt of the Exchequer, 1377–1485* (Cambridge: Cambridge University Press, 1954), pp. xxix–xxxviii.

[71] J. H. Johnson, 'The King's Wardrobe and Household', in *The English Government at Work*, ed. Willard et al., I, pp. 206–49 (p. 231). Johnson argues that the tally system was distinct from the conventional form of assignment because the writs authorising the payment were often made by the privy seal, rather than the Exchequer, which formed part of the royal household.

[72] William E. Lunt, 'The Collectors of Clerical Subsidies', in *The English Government at Work*, ed. Willard et al., II, pp. 227–80 (p. 258).

[73] These subsidies were the king's source of *extraordinary* taxation which had to be granted in parliament, unlike the customs duties. For an assessment of the 'fifteenth and tenth' lay subsidies granted from 1344 to 1360, see Harriss, *Public Finance in Medieval England*, pp. 313–55. The clerical subsidies were fixed at a rate of a tenth from the 1320s: Ormrod, *England in the Middle Ages*, p. 30.

and Hereford'.[74] When the royal officials and tax collectors next made their accounts at the Exchequer they would present the tallies they had received from Lancaster in exchange for cash, which was subsequently credited to their accounts. From the Crown's point of view this was an efficient method of payment because it removed the needless stage at the Exchequer of receiving and disbursing royal revenue by empowering creditors to collect the sums due to them directly from the sources of royal revenue. This credit system proved so convenient that '[i]t became as usual for the exchequer to pay the call on it by tallies as by solid coin' in the latter years of Edward I's reign and the tables of the captains' receipts demonstrate that this was still the case in the mid 1340s.[75] The retinue captains, however, would almost certainly have preferred payments in cash because they would have been disadvantaged by the use of 'wooden money'. For example, there was always a delay (and often a long one) between the grant of an assignment and the collection of cash from the subsidies. The delay of payment depended upon when the clerical and lay subsidies were due to be collected. Also, it was not uncommon for the Crown to grant too many assignments on the same source of income, which often fluctuated, especially in the case of customs revenues. Such instances could leave the claimant out of pocket.

The payments recorded on the Issue Rolls stipulate whether the money was assigned on local revenues, but unfortunately not all of the payments made to retinue captains were enrolled in this way. For some of the payments, therefore, it is impossible to establish the method of payment, but the tables of the retinue captains' receipts nevertheless show that a substantial proportion of the payments received by them were paid using the tally system. At least four of the ten payments to Lancaster were made in this way, as were three of the seven payments to Pembroke, two of the three payments to Mauny and at least one of the two payments made to Audley were assigned on the clerical and lay subsidies. The payments also reflect a seniority of credit amongst the retinue captains, whereby those who led the largest contingents received a greater proportion in cash.[76] The Exchequer's use of the tally system, therefore, was prevalent in 1345 and co-existed with the conventional method of issuing sums in cash. This dual method of payment must have provided some degree of flexibility to the Exchequer which could prioritise between those creditors who needed to be paid immediately in cash and those who could levy their payment against the collectors themselves. It also enabled the Crown to administer its finance without diminishing the royal coffers.

[74] E 403/336 m. 8; E 403/337, m. 9.
[75] Tout, *Chapters*, II, p. 101.
[76] Percentage of payments made in cash to four of the retinue captains: Lancaster, 19.6%; Pembroke, 20.4%; Mauny, 14.9%; Audley, 0%. These figures represent the minimum proportion of cash payments.

We have been able to assess the variety of methods used to pay retinue captains who accounted at the Exchequer, but how was finance administered to the different components of Lancaster's army over the course of the campaign? What was the process through which the king's wages reached the pockets of the soldiers and who were the individuals involved in the 'money chain'?

It was customary practice for the Crown to pay an advance of money to a captain for his men's wages before their period of military service began. This advance payment, known as a prest, was usually paid to captains following their agreement to provide service, whether embodied formally in an indenture or otherwise. The prest was set against the total due when the accounts were made once the service had been completed.[77] In 1345 the advance was also intended to cover *regard*, and thus James Audley, Henry of Lancaster and the earl of Pembroke were paid an advance of their wages and *regard* for the first six months of service. Similarly, the Black Prince also received a prest for half a year's service before he set out for Aquitaine in 1355, but by the fifteenth century it had become customary practice of the Crown to pay retinue captains a prest for only three months of service.[78] Although the administrative records do not reveal the form in which prests were paid, it is likely that it would have been cash so that the captains could in turn pay an advance to the men in their retinues before setting out overseas.[79] For some soldiers cash (or cash up front, more specifically) would probably have been a decisive factor in determining which retinue they joined. A prest therefore was an essential recruiting tool for captains, and might be considered a nascent form of what became known as the king's shilling in later centuries.

The prests of Audley and Pembroke were moderate enough to be made in a single payment; the former was paid on 16 April, nine days before his retinue departed from Heighley castle, and Pembroke received his prest on 11 April, the same day that his indenture with the king was sealed. The size of Lancaster's own retinue meant the wages and *regard* for a half-year's service had to be advanced to him in three instalments. Table 4 shows that the first instalment of £5000 was paid on 6 April and that an assignment of £1825 14s was made on 31 May during the second week of his arrival at Southampton.[80] The final instalment of £1000 was collected at Westminster on 21 June by two Exchequer clerks, Henry de Walton and William Farley,

---

[77] Prestwich, *Armies and Warfare*, p. 86.

[78] Hewitt, *The Black Prince's Expedition*, p. 20; Curry, *English Armies in the Fifteenth Century*, p. 42.

[79] Lancaster's indenture stipulated that the second and smaller instalment of his advance was to be paid by assignment: E 159/123, m. 254d.

[80] *Contra* to Fowler, who claims that £6825 14s had already been advanced to Lancaster by the time he arrived at Southampton: Fowler, *King's Lieutenant*, p. 223.

Table 4. Receipts of Wages and *Regard* of Henry of Lancaster

Date	Amount	Source (collected by)	Method of Payment	Note of Warrant
6 April 1345	£5000	Receipt of the Exchequer	--	--
31 May	£1825 14s	Rec. of Ex.	Assignment	--
21 June	£1000	Rec. of Ex. (William Farley, Henry de Walton)	Cash	--
4 November	£4492 7s 4d	Rec. of Ex. (John de Gynewell)	Assignment	PSW
20 November	£644 10s	constable of Bordeaux	Cash[a]	-
22 November	**Six Months of Service**			
20 December	£2400	Rec. of Ex. (Peter Gretheved)	Cash[b]	GSW
10 April 1346	£149 16s 10d	Rec. of Ex. (collected by John de Gynewell)	Cash	PSW
22 May	**Twelve Months of Service**			
29 May	£1333 6s 8d	Rec. of Ex.	-	
25 October	£2000	Rec. of Ex. (John de Gynewell)	Assignment	GSW
18 November	£2000	Rec. of Ex. (John de Gynewell)	Assignment	GSW
22 November	**Eighteen Months of Service**			

[a] Paid 3867 écus (1 écu = 3s 4d).
[b] Paid 12,000 écus (1 écu = 4s).
PSW = Privy Seal writ; GSW = Great Seal writ

who were accompanied by a bodyguard of an esquire and ten mounted archers.[81] Walter Mauny and Ralph Stafford do not appear to have received any advances, which implies that they did not enter into an indenture of service with Edward III.

The war expenses of the retinue captains in Lancaster's army were met by the English Exchequer and payments were made at the Receipt. The king had agreed to appoint deputies to take the equivalent wages and *regard* to Lancaster in the duchy of Aquitaine if he served beyond the initial period of six months.[82] Thus on 10 December 1345 Peter Gretheved, king's clerk, was ordered to take £10,200 to Aquitaine, of which £3000 was for the quarterly *regards* of Lancaster, Mauny and Pembroke while the residue was to be spent as Lancaster, the seneschal and the constable saw fit.[83] Although

[81] E 372/191, m. 54d. Fowler, *King's Lieutenant*, p. 223. Fowler's assertion that the clerks followed Lancaster to Aquitaine on 19 July is incorrect; Farley and Walton were already in Bordeaux (from 19 July to 6 August) before Lancaster had embarked on 23 July.
[82] E 159/123, m. 254.
[83] C 61/57, m. 1; C 62/122, m. 9.

we know that an indenture was made between Gretheved and the king, the document itself is now missing, therefore we can only hazard a guess at the purpose behind his visit to the duchy.[84] Gretheved's retinue of 19 men-at-arms and 100 foot archers were paid for one quarter-year's service (91 days), so using the date on which he was ordered to go to Aquitaine we can estimate that he remained in the duchy until around the beginning of March 1346.[85] This period of service coincides with the letter of protection granted to the king's clerk on 10 November 1345 which was valid until Easter (15 March 1346).[86] The transport of a large sum of money from the Exchequer in England to the theatre of war in the south west of France was clearly the main objective of Gretheved's mission, but the clerk was likely to have undertaken other administrative duties whilst in the duchy, hence his quarter-year term of service.[87] It also possible that Gretheved's troops were intended as reinforcements for Lancaster's army considering that they represented the composition and size of a war retinue.

On only two occasions, therefore, did the royal clerks transport actual specie from England to Aquitaine to make payments of wages and *regards* to men in Lancaster's army. These sums, however, only represent a fraction of the total amount paid to the retinue captains over the course of the campaign.[88] Once the army had embarked for Aquitaine the majority of the sums issued thereafter at the Receipt of the Exchequer were delivered to an attorney, or lieutenant, who had been appointed by a retinue captain to serve as their legal representative. John de Gynewell, for example, was Lancaster's treasurer in England and as such received wages and *regard* on behalf of Lancaster during his command in the duchy.[89] The corresponding entries in the Issue Rolls state that the sums were delivered to Lancaster

---

[84] An order to the constable of Bordeaux to appraise the horses of Gretheved's retinue states that Gretheved is 'to reside there [Aquitaine] according to indentures made between the king and him': C 61/57, m. 1.

[85] C 62/122, m. 9.

[86] C 61/57, m. 2.

[87] It is interesting to note that money was issued to Gretheved in écus (*florenis de scuto*) not in pounds sterling. One half of his retinue's wages was also paid in écus 'just as is current in Gascony' (*prout currit in Vasconie*), and the other half was paid in pounds sterling. Each écu was valued at 4s. In contrast, when Lancaster received 3867 écus from the constable of Bordeaux on 20 November , each écu was valued at the lower rate of 3s 4d. These different currency exchange rates might be explained by foreign exchange fluctuations in the market.

[88] The sums of money transported to the duchy by royal clerks totalled £11,200. Total sums of captains' receipts: Audley, £1085 2s 6d; Lancaster, £20,845 14s 10d; Mauny, £1795 10s; Pembroke, £5485 7s 10d; Stafford, £2464 17s 16d.

[89] E 403/336 m. 8; E 403/336, m. 49; E 403/338, m. 16; E 403/339, m. 13.

'by the hands' of Gynewell.[90] The earl of Pembroke's attorney, Robert de Elford, also served as his lieutenant, while Hugh de Walkan, chaplain, was the attorney who received the sums of money due to Walter Mauny.[91]

However, there is no way of knowing whether the sums received by the attorneys were taken to the duchy. If sums of money were not sent to Aquitaine then would the soldiers continue to be promptly paid out of their captains' own resources or would the captains have waited until they returned to England before disbursing money to their men? The fact that Robert de Elford was granted a letter of protection on 9 August 1346 for service in Pembroke's retinue 'until Christmas next' proves that at least one attorney intended to travel to the duchy during the campaign and we would expect him to have brought sums of money with him.[92] For those captains who only served in Aquitaine for the initial term of six months, such as James Audley's deputy, Sir John Trumwyn, or Walter Mauny who returned to England during the winter caesura of the campaign before heading back out to the duchy, it would not have been essential for them to have money sent over from England because neither captain was overseas for longer than roughly seven months at a time. And in Audley's case, his retinue's wages and *regard* for six months service were advanced to him before it set out, under Trumwyn's leadership, to Aquitaine. It is likely, however, that retinue captains such as Lancaster and Pembroke who served continuously in the duchy for the entire duration of the expedition would have required the sums issued at the Exchequer to have been sent out to them. The regular payments of wages and *regard* would have been vital for the soldiers' subsistence over the course of the campaign, and all the more considering that they remained 'in the field' for over eighteen months.

The retinue captains would have had their own household clerks with them in the duchy who acted as treasurers. The clerks would have been responsible for the receipt of any payments made to their lords whilst in Aquitaine, such as the money delivered by Peter Gretheved, and for the disbursement of wages and other sums due to men in their retinue. Peter de Wotton and John de Welbourne were the two men who served as Lancaster's treasurers in the duchy. The former clerk accompanied Lancaster to Brittany in 1342 and had since served as his chaplain, wardrober and receiver-general.[93] He is described as 'a clerk of the treasury of the Earl

[90] The £2000 issued to Lancaster on 25 October 1346, for example, was 'delivered by the hands of John de Gynewell, his treasurer' (*liberavit per manus Johannis Kynewell thesauri sui*): E 403/338, m. 16 ; E 403/339, m. 6.

[91] In issues of payment to Pembroke, Elford is referred to as 'the person holding his [Pembroke's] place' (*locum tenentis sui*): E 403/338, m. 16; E 403/339, m. 6. Walkan; E 403/336, mm. 14, 17.

[92] C 61/58, m. 1.

[93] C 76/17, mm. 22, 25 (Brittany); Fowler, *King's Lieutenant*, p. 224.

himself' from 1346 to 1347.[94] Wotton was appointed as Lancaster's attorney at some point before 30 January 1347 to render his account of service at the Exchequer, which suggests that it was he rather than Welbourne who recorded the daily expenses in Aquitaine.[95] John de Welbourne, who 'appears to have acted as paymaster of the troops' in the duchy in 1345, had served as Lancaster's chancellor and secretary on several occasions from the late 1340s to the mid 1350s.[96] It was probably in the latter capacity that he served on Lancaster's diplomatic mission in 1348 and he also served on Lancaster's second expedition to Aquitaine in 1349.[97] Welbourne was clearly a clerk of some repute and his status is reflected by the fact that he appointed no fewer than four attorneys on 30 August 1349, of whom Thomas de Welbourne was probably his brother.[98]

Unfortunately, the identities of the men who served as treasurers-of-war for the other retinue captains remain unknown. It was not only the retinue leaders, however, who required the services of a well-trained clerk. The leading knights and bannerets who brought their own companies, or sub-retinues, for military service would also have been in need of a financial administrator. It seems that Robert de Helpiston acted as a receiver of money for the banneret Sir John de Norwich, who brought his own *comitiva* for service in Lancaster's retinue.[99] A royal writ made on 20 April 1346, ordering the sheriff of Norfolk 'not to molest him [Helpiston] further while he is in the king's service', reveals that Helpiston had been placed in exigent (the preliminary step to outlawry) for not appearing before justices of the Bench to render account for the time that he was receiver of John Bardolf's moneys.[100] It was clearly for his administrative skills that Helpiston served in Norwich's company in Aquitaine, and it is likely that he fulfilled the same role of receiver for the banneret. That Helpiston is described as 'the king's clerk' in the writ is evidence that, in the course of their careers, the same clerks might serve the king as well as his close magnates. It is also possible that John Halden, 'le clerk', who served in the company of William, Lord Greystoke, acted as receiver for the young banneret.[101]

---

[94] C 76/25, m. 12d. (note of warrant for Andrew Luttrell's writ of exoneration); *CPP*, p. 111.

[95] E 159/123, m. 328 (appointment of attorney). Fowler only gives reference to Lancaster's account of service and Wotton's letter of protection as evidence that Wotton recorded the daily expenses: Fowler, *King's Lieutenant*, p. 224.

[96] Fowler, *King's Lieutenant*, pp. 185, 224.

[97] Fowler, *King's Lieutenant*, p. 185.

[98] C 76/27, m. 4.

[99] C 76/20, m. 20.

[100] *CCR, 1346–49*, p. 67.

[101] *CPR, 1345–48*, p. 558.

Infantrymen in Lancaster's army also received their wages in advance of service. The initial disbanding of the Welsh troops who had assembled for review at Conway ferry in May 1345 because 'no one from the prince came to pay them' highlights the importance of this customary practice of paying wages in advance.[102] The *vadia guerre* of the Welshmen for their journey to Southampton was paid out of the revenues of the Black Prince's administration in Wales, while payment to the English foot archers for travel from the muster point in their county down to the port of embarkation was made out of the issues of their sheriff's bailiwick.[103] It seems that a significant part of the financing of Lancaster's army was administered through William Farley who operated as paymaster of the infantry before they set out to Aquitaine and during their service in the duchy.[104] At the beginning of June 1345 he was resident at Winchester where he disbursed sums to the *centenars* who led the English foot archers.[105] However, it was John de Watenhill who paid wages to the English and Welsh infantry for their period of stay at Southampton and for their subsequent sea crossing. These payments from Watenhill were made 'by the testimony and advice of Philip de Whitton', the lieutenant of Richard, earl of Arundel, who had been given the responsibility for the disbursements connected with the naval preparations of the expedition.[106] We know that William Farley and Henry de Walton set out for Bordeaux ahead of Lancaster and remained in the city for six days from 19 July to 6 August, by which time the infantry divisions had already arrived in the duchy.[107] It seems likely, therefore, that Farley and Walton disbursed payments to the troops during this period as the infantry had only previously been paid by Watenhill for their service up to 14 July.[108] It is possible, as Fowler suggests, that Farley acted as treasurer-of-war to those troops who did not serve in retinues, but it is unlikely that he remained in the duchy for long periods of time.[109] Indeed, there is only one record of the Exchequer clerk having received money for the wages of troops once they had arrived in Aquitaine,[110] and the Issue Rolls show that he was involved in administrative affairs at Calais throughout the autumn and winter of 1346.[111]

---

[102] *Cal. Anc. Corr.*, pp. 246–7.

[103] C 76/20, m. 32.

[104] Fowler, *King's Lieutenant*, p. 223.

[105] E 404/501/336; E 404/501/338; E 404/501/339.

[106] E 372/190, m. 41d.

[107] E 372/190, m. 41d; E 372/191, m. 54d.

[108] E 372/190, m. 41d.

[109] Fowler, *King's Lieutenant*, p. 223.

[110] E 403/339, m. 44; Farley paid £666 13s 4d in wages to 'men-at-arms, archers and sergeants', but it is not clear to which retinue or military contingent they belonged.

[111] E 403/339, mm. 2, 13, 32.

Table 5. Receipts of Wages and *Regard* of Walter de Mauny

Date	Amount	Source (collected by)	Method of Payment	Note of Warrant
24 November 1345	£1057 18s 5d	Receipt of the Exchequer (Hugh de Walkan)	Assignment	PSW
7 December	£470 18s 3d	Rec. of Ex. (Hugh de Walkan)	Assignment	PSW
8 December	**Six Months Service**			
20 December	£266 13s 4d	Rec. of Ex. (Peter Gretheved)	Cash 1333 écus (1 écu = 4s)	GSW

The pay records, therefore, do not fully illuminate the role of William Farley in Aquitaine. Although we know that he received sums of money from both the Exchequer in England and the administration in Gascony, it is impossible to determine the number of visits that Farley made to the duchy or the length of time that he remained there. We know that he was accompanied to Aquitaine by Henry de Walton on at least one occasion and the annuity of £16 granted to William de Kelsey 'for good service by himself both in the duchy of Aquitaine and in parts of Ireland' suggests that other clerks were also involved in financing the army over the course of the campaign.[112] Indeed, the clerks in the Gascon administration might also have been involved. The task of distributing wages to the rank and file infantry was probably given to the *centenars* or constables who were responsible for leading their own companies of men. A series of extant sealed writs states that three of the English *centenars* were assigned 'to receive the wages of the archers' (*de Resceyvre les gages de les archiers*) and indentures of payment were subsequently made between themselves and William Farley at Winchester in June 1345.[113] The *centenars* no doubt continued to perform their duty as receivers of wages over the course of the expedition and each leader of 100 Welshmen probably acted in the same capacity.

Accounting for Service and War Expenses

The finance of the three retinue captains – Audley, Pembroke and Lancaster – who indented with Edward III was administered and accounted through conventional means. Advance payments of wages and *regard* and the subsequent sums for their military service in Aquitaine were issued out of

[112] C 62/124, m. 1; E 403/336, m. 26.
[113] E 404/501/335; E 404/501/337; E 404/501/unnumbered, filed between 338 and 339.

the Receipt of the Exchequer on royal authority via writs of the Great Seal and Privy Seal. In the case of Peter Gretheved, the Chancery issued a writ of *liberate*, ordering the Exchequer to pay the Wardrobe clerk a sum of £10,200.[114] The only instance when money was not issued at the Receipt in England is the sum of £644 10s paid to Lancaster by the constable of Bordeaux on 20 November.[115] The sums issued at the Exchequer were either delivered to royal clerks assigned to the duty of transporting the money to Aquitaine, or to the retinue captains' attorneys who would deliver the sums to the captains in the duchy if they were required to do so. Once the captain had completed his military service an account was made at the Exchequer for his receipts and expenses and a balance was struck. Any debt or overpayment was to be paid thereafter.

When it comes to the retinue captains Walter Mauny and Ralph Stafford, the pay records reveal that their military service was accounted for in a different manner from that of the other captains in Lancaster's army. It has already been noted that neither captain was in receipt of a prest or, in all likelihood, had entered into a formal indenture of war with Edward III. There are no formal accounts of service enrolled in the Pipe Rolls relating to Mauny or Stafford because they accounted for their service with Master John de Wawayne, constable of Bordeaux, in the duchy rather than at the Exchequer in England. The bills of payment for their service were sealed by the constable of Bordeaux after an account had been made upon receipt of a mandate from Lancaster. The account of Mauny's service, for example, was made 'by mandate of the eminent man lord Henry … by his letters patent' (*mandato egregii viri domini Henrici...per suas patentes litteras*), and the account of Stafford's horse restoration was made 'by virtue of warrant of the Lord Earl of Lancaster' (*virtute garenti domini Comitis Lancastrie*).[116] The accounts themselves have not survived, but fortunately there are several extant corresponding bills which served as warrants and were presented at the Exchequer at a later date by the accountant/captain where the sum due was issued to him. These bills of the constable essentially functioned in the same way as a promissory bill of the Wardrobe, except it was the Gascon administration rather than the *garderoba* which had pledged money of the Exchequer to its creditors. Once the payment had been made in full to the captain, which could often take several years or even decades, the bill was signed 'persolvitur' (*it is paid in full*) and retained by the Exchequer as receipt of payment.

Although the service of both Mauny and Stafford was accounted for in the same way at Bordeaux, the financing of their retinues had been administered

---

[114] C 62/122, m. 9; the note of warrant in the writ of liberate reads 'by the King himself and his council and bill of the Treasurer'.

[115] E 372/190, m. 54d.

[116] Mauny: E 43/78. Stafford: E 404/490/174.

differently up to that point. Table 5 shows that all of the money paid to Mauny was issued at the Receipt of the Exchequer.

In Stafford's case, however, the only evidence of money paid to him directly out of the Exchequer is an entry in the Issue Rolls which records a payment of £991 18s assigned on the clerical and lay subsidies for his retinue's wages in Aquitaine.[117] Strangely, the phrase 'To Walter de Wetwang, keeper of the wardrobe of the lord King, by the hands...' (*Waltero de Wetewang' custodi garderobe domini Regis per manus*) is written above the first line of the entry in a different hand which indicates that it was done after the payment was first recorded. Furthermore, the original name of the payee written in the margin, which has been erased and replaced with Walter de Wetwang, was almost certainly that of Stafford.

Wetwang's enrolled account as keeper of the Wardrobe from 1344 to 1347 throws further light on this clerical anomaly.[118] It records a payment of £2464 17s 6d to Stafford for his retinue's wages for one year's service in Aquitaine, which suggests that the sum (£991 18s) issued at the Exchequer was in fact part of a repayment to the Wardrobe for wages already paid to Stafford. The wages, however, may not have been issued in cash by the Wardrobe but rather by a 'bill of the keeper' which Stafford could then have presented to the Exchequer for payment.[119] That the Wardrobe had pledged Exchequer credit to cover the entire sum of Stafford's wages seems unlikely given that there is no evidence in the Issue Rolls of further payments which relate to the remaining £1472 19s 6d, or Stafford's wages for one year of service. It seems very likely, therefore, that the remaining sum of money was issued out of the Wardrobe and that the £991 18s instalment was issued at the Exchequer.

The payments issued out of the Exchequer and the Wardrobe departments, whether it was by bills or in cash, highlight the flexibility of the royal administrative system during war-time. They also reveal that Stafford's retinue was financed differently from those of the other captains. That Stafford accounted for his service in Aquitaine with the constable of Bordeaux can be understood by the fact that he did not indent with the king. However, none of the other retinue captains were paid money out of the Wardrobe including Walter Mauny, who also did not enter into an indenture of service. Moreover, all of the captains except for Stafford had payments of *regard* delivered to them in the duchy by Peter Gretheved during the winter of 1345.[120] One plausible explanation for these differences

---

[117] E 403/337, m. 7. Payment was made on 3 November 1345.

[118] E 361/2, m. 41.

[119] Harriss, *Public Finance in Medieval England*, pp. 219–20. Tout, *Chapters*, IV, p. 118; Tout suggests that many of the sums recorded as Wardrobe issues, such as wages, were not paid directly by the Wardrobe.

[120] C 61/57, m. 1; C 62/122, m. 9.

in the administration of Stafford's retinue is his appointment as seneschal of Aquitaine. The constable's bill relating to Stafford's account made on 14 November 1346 refers to a 'certain indenture made between the king and the said seneschal in England'.[121] This indenture probably embodied the terms of holding the office of seneschal as well as the benefits of service offered by the Crown for his retinue's service during the forthcoming campaign. In addition, the contract would have stipulated the sums of money, the dates on which they were to be paid, and the department from which they were to be issued had it been as detailed as that of Henry of Lancaster. The retinue that Stafford was required to maintain as seneschal of Aquitaine was therefore distinct from other retinues in Lancaster's army in terms of the way it was financially administered and, like Mauny's retinue, the way in which its captain accounted for service.

Accounting for service at the Exchequer rather than with the constable at Bordeaux was a natural consequence of the Crown's use of the indenture system. Hence, those captains who indented with the king had to submit after their service various documents at the Exchequer such as their half of the indenture and their particulars of account, for example, so that an account could be made. The subsequent accounts enrolled in the Pipe Rolls for the service of Lancaster and Pembroke provide a clear breakdown of the captains' expenses and receipts over the course of the expedition. It was not necessary to enrol a formal account of James Audley in the Pipe Rolls because the initial prest covered his retinue's expenses for their entire period of service.[122] The enrolled accounts, therefore, enable us to assess the efficiency of the royal administration for the expedition in 1345 and how well the army was financed as the campaign progressed.

Table 4 shows that Lancaster's advance of £7825 14s (£4492 7s 4d wages and £3333 6s 8d *regard*) for the first six months of service was paid in three instalments, the last one being paid on 21 June 1345, almost five months earlier than the date stipulated in his indenture with the king (15 November).[123] The sum of wages for Lancaster's next term of six months service was paid by assignment to his attorney on 4 November, more than two weeks before the start of the next period of service. A *regard* payment of £2400 was delivered by Peter Gretheved at the end of 1345 and the final instalment of £1333 6s 8d was paid on 29 May following. The Crown, therefore, had paid Lancaster in full for his retinue's twelve months of service one week

[121] E 404/490/180.

[122] E 101/24/20. The assignment delivered to John Bulneys on 17 November 1345 for the wages of Audley's retinue must have been for their second term of six months service, and presumably therefore, the Crown was not aware that Trumwyn would return to England with Audley's retinue within the following two weeks: E 403/336, m. 11; E 403/337, m. 11.

[123] E 159/123, m. 254.

Table 6. Receipts of Wages and *Regard* of James Audley

Date	Amount	Source (collected by)	Method of Payment	Note of Warrant
16 April 1345	£443 12s 6d (£576 19s)	Receipt of the Exchequer	--	--
17 November	£591 10s	Rec. of Ex. (John Bulneys)	Assignment	PSW
21 November	**Six Months Service**			

after that period ended. However, for the final half-year's term of service Lancaster only received two further assignments of £2000 each, which meant he was still owed £3825 14s by the Crown for wages and *regard* for the third term of service and the remuneration for his retinue's additional forty-three days of service.[124]

Two receipts which do not relate to the remuneration of Lancaster's retinue are the payments made by the constable of Bordeaux on 20 November 1345 and by the Exchequer on 10 April 1346. The latter payment of £149 16s 10d was for the clothing, equipment and wages of 300 Welsh reinforcements. Lancaster had been responsible for the recruitment and payment of wages for the Welshmen's initial period of service, but any future financing after their disembarkation at Bordeaux was probably administered in the same manner as the other infantry divisions. The other 'foreign' receipt in Lancaster's account is a sum of £644 10s paid in écus by the constable of Bordeaux.[125] Although the account stipulates that it was for the wages of Lancaster's men, the sum does not fit with the schedule of payments made at the Exchequer. The receipt seems all the more ambiguous considering that Lancaster had already received his advance of wages for the second term of six months service on 4 November. It is possible that the latter payment did not reach Lancaster in the duchy and that a shortage of cash precipitated the constable's payment in November, but an item in the expenses section of Lancaster's account implies another explanation. A sum of £645 15s 9d was paid by Lancaster to the sailors of his fleet because 'they refused to sail until their wages were satisfied in full' (*vadiis suis satisfieret penitus exire recusarunt*).[126] It seems that the commander was forced to pay the sailors' wages which would normally have been issued by the Crown because they refused to set sail from England until they had received sufficient payment. It is possible, therefore, that the payment of £644 10s made by the constable represents the cost of the army's outward sea passage from Falmouth to

---

[124] E 372/191, m. 54d; Lancaster's account states that he served for one year and a half and forty-three days.

[125] Each écu valued at 3s 4d.

[126] E 372/191, m. 54d. Note that the clerk's omission of 'nisi' is a scribal error.

Bordeaux, and although the account describes the payment as 'wages of war' it was actually a reimbursement for Lancaster's unexpected outlay.[127]

Table 7 demonstrates a similar pattern for the financing of the earl of Pembroke's retinue. The earl was also promptly in receipt of a prest (£1389 5s 4d wages and £600 *regard*) for his initial half-year's service, after having been paid £1989 5s 4d on the same day that he indented with Edward III. Similarly to Lancaster, the wages for Pembroke's second term of six months service were advanced at the beginning of November, followed

Table 7. Receipts of Wages and *Regard* of Laurence de Hastings

Date	Amount	Source (collected by)	Method of Payment	Note of Warrant
11 April 1345	£1989 5s 4d	Receipt of the Exchequer	-	-
5 November	£1389 5s 4d	Rec. of Ex.	Assignment	PSW
23 November	**Six Months of Service**			
20 December	£333 6s 8d	Rec. of Ex. (Peter Gretheved)	Cash 1666 écus (1 écu = 4s)	GSW
23 May	**Twelve Months of Service**			
29 July 1346	£300	Rec. of Ex.	Cash	--
24 October	£500	Rec. of Ex. (Robert de Elford)	Assignment	GSW
6 November	£488 4s.10d	Rec. of Ex. (Robert de Elford)	Assignment	GSW
23 November	**Eighteen Months of Service**			
6 March 1347	£485 5s 7d	Rec. of Ex. (Robert de Elford)	Cash	GSW

by two payments of *regard* on 20 December and 29 July following.[128] The remuneration of Pembroke's retinue for one year of service in Aquitaine, therefore, was not paid in full until the midsummer of 1346, more than two months after they had completed twelve months of service. The sums issued for his retinue's third term of six months service were comparatively smaller than previous payments; Robert de Elford received assignments of £500 and £488 4s 10d on behalf of Pembroke in the autumn of 1346 and a final sum of £485 5s 7d was issued to him on 6 March 1347. Thus, the third term of Pembroke's service was not fully financed because he was still owed £515 14s

---

[127] The difference of £1 5s 9d may be a clerical error.

[128] One quarter-year's *regard* paid at the higher rate of £1200 per annum offered to Pembroke works out at £300; the additional £33 6s paid on 20 December 1345 may represent an even higher rate of *regard* (see above), or the additional sum may be an overpayment.

11d for his retinue's wages and *regard* up to eighteen months as well as their remuneration for the remaining twenty-nine days service in the duchy.[129]

The evidence of the accounts of service of both captains shows that they were adequately financed by the Crown over the first twelve months of the campaign. By the spring of 1346, however, preparations for Edward III's forthcoming invasion of Normandy were well under way and the strain that the king's expedition placed upon the royal administrative system can be detected in the financing of Lancaster's army. The payments made to Lancaster out of the Exchequer became more sporadic with just two instalments paid to him during his third term of service rather than the usual three. In addition, the size of the sums issued to both of the captains after twelve months became drastically smaller in comparison to earlier payments. Although the Exchequer failed to pay either of the retinue captains in full for their third term of service and the remaining days of service before their return to England, the Crown's debts were not particularly large; Lancaster was owed around half of the remuneration his retinue would have received for six months service and Pembroke was owed an even smaller proportion.[130]

At the end of January 1347, within one month of Lancaster's return to England, the king ordered that a formal account of his lieutenant's service be made at the Exchequer, while the earl of Pembroke's account was made on 7 May. The total sum of money received by the captain was set against the expenses incurred over the duration of the expedition, such as costs of horse restoration or shipping, for example, in addition to the remuneration of wages and *regard*. After the balance had been struck it was found that Lancaster had an overspend (*superplusagium*) of £17,728 8s 10½d and Pembroke too was owed money by the Crown but for the much smaller sum of £1359 12s 1d. Subsequently, a king's writ was delivered to the treasurer and chamberlains of the Exchequer on 2 July 1349 ordering that the sum owed to Pembroke be issued at the Receipt and the debt satisfied.[131] However, the young earl never received the payment of arrears in his lifetime since he died at Abergavenny near the end of August 1348.[132]

In the case of Lancaster it is more difficult to establish when the Crown's debt was satisfied and repaid in full because the payments recorded in the Issue Rolls which relate to his service in Aquitaine are often aggregated with other payments. When an entry in the rolls states that a particular sum is 'owed to him [Lancaster] by the account of expenses made with him at the exchequer for his service in Gascony', there can be no doubt

---

[129] Based on the payment of £1989 5s 4d for six months service.

[130] In the third term of six months service Lancaster received £4000 instead of the usual £7825 14s and Pembroke received £1473 10s 5d of the usual £1989 5s 4d.

[131] E 372/191, m. 54d.

[132] Ayton, 'Hastings', *ODNB*.

that it is a payment in arrears for the expedition in the duchy.[133] However, there were numerous cases when the Crown, probably for the sake of administrative ease, consolidated different debts to the same creditor into a single payment. The sum of £3057 7s 2d issued on 5 July 1348, for example, was both for Lancaster's sale of wool and for his wages and expenses in Aquitaine. The £3026 6s 7d issued on the same day was for Lancaster's *regard* and for recompense from Queen Philippa for the castle and honour of Pontefract.

Another payment made on 5 July was that of £8727 7d to Walter de Wetwang for money owed in the Wardrobe for the wages of Lancaster's retinue 'for staying with him *in parts of France*'.[134] The clerk does not explicitly refer to the duchy of Aquitaine in this last entry and therefore it is possible that the sum relates to Lancaster's service during the siege of Calais. However, it is unlikely that Lancaster's wages would have amounted to such a large sum because he did not cross the Channel to join the king at Calais until the end of May in 1347, roughly two months before the siege ended.[135] Furthermore, the payments made to Lancaster from 1349 onwards which explicitly state that they are for his service in Aquitaine are also problematic because he led a second expedition in the duchy from 1349 to 1350. In addition to the problem of overlapping payments relating to different expeditions in Aquitaine is the fact that not all of the money paid at the Receipt of the Exchequer was recorded in the Issue Rolls. Indeed, the only evidence of the £352 assignment issued to Lancaster on 27 April 1347 is a copy of a royal writ addressed to the abbot of Milton who was the collector of clerical subsidies in the counties of Dorset and Salisbury from which the payment by tallies was to be made.[136]

Although the problems associated with tracing the repayments of Lancaster's expenses prevent us from establishing when exactly the money owed to him was fully repaid by the Crown, nevertheless, it is clear from the payments recorded in the Exchequer rolls that most of the debt was paid to Lancaster in January and July of 1348.[137] When James Audley accounted for his service at the Exchequer it was found that he was in debt rather than in credit with the Crown on account of his decision to send a deputy

[133] E 403/341, m. 19.

[134] E 403/341, m. 19.

[135] John Montgomery, Admiral to the West, was instructed on 19 May 1347 to prepare shipping for Lancaster and his 'huge number' (*ingenti numero*) of men: *Foedera*, III, p. 121.

[136] E 159/123, m. 379d.

[137] For his service in Aquitaine Lancaster received separate payments of £1000 and £5317 19d in January, and £3026 6s 7d and £8727 7d in July; E 403/340, m. 25; E 403/341, m. 19.

to serve as his proxy on the campaign.[138] The other retine captains did not have to wait long for their arrears of pay. One of the advantages for captains who accounted for their service in Bordeaux rather than in England was that they were able to avoid any delay in the account being drawn up. The constable could immediately make account with the captain in the duchy and authorise any payment owed to him via a bill once his service had been completed. The clause written in a different hand at the foot of the constable's bill beginning 'persolvitur...' indicates the date on which the money was issued out of the Exchequer and the payment can be verified by the corresponding entries in the Issue Rolls. Thus, the bills sealed by John de Wawayne on 1 and 14 November 1346 record payments for Ralph Stafford's expenses, such as horse restoration, shipping and wages, amongst other things which were subsequently paid out of the Exchequer over the next twenty months.[139] The largest sum of £2072 12d was paid to Stafford in two instalments of £1041 18s 11d on 13 December 1347 and £1660 2s 1d on 4 July following.[140] The account which took the longest to settle was that of Walter Mauny, who accounted for his service with Wawayne on 3 January 1346, but he had to wait until 10 June 1350 before the sum of £3248 14s 2d was issued to him.[141]

All of the accounts of the retine captains, with the exception of James Audley, were therefore settled within five years of them completing their service in the duchy and most of the captains' expenses had been repaid by the summer of 1348.[142] It was not uncommon for the Crown to owe much larger sums to captains at the end of their service on account of poor financing over the duration of a campaign and there are numerous examples of royal debts to men dragging on through the decades of the fourteenth century.[143] The efficiency with which royal debts were paid to retine captains for service in Aquitaine seems even more impressive considering that the Exchequer would have been inundated with accounts relating to

---

[138] Gribit, *Accounting for Service at War*, p. 148. However, if Audley's assignment of £591 10s represents a payment of wages for his retinue's second six-month term of service in the duchy, then this may have been the cause of Audley's debt. The entire sum would have had to have been paid back to the Exchequer considering that his retinue returned to England at the end of November, although it is possible that the cash was not collected from the subsidies on which it was assigned.

[139] E 404/490/174; E 404/503/139; E 404/490/180.

[140] E 403/340, m. 19; E 403/341, m. 19.

[141] E 43/78.

[142] Gribit, *Accounting for Service at War*, pp. 148–9; it was no less than seventeen years before Audley's account was finally settled with the Exchequer because of the retine captain's dispute over his debt.

[143] Prestwich claims, 'It was common for men to have to wait at least ten years for payment, and payment was often made only because men acquired the right degree of political influence': Prestwich, *Armies and Warfare*, pp. 87–8.

other English campaigns of the mid 1340s, and the plethora of payments that the department would have been required to make in arrears. Moreover, the tabulated evidence of captains' payments in Lancaster's army reinforces Mark Ormrod's view, namely that war finance became better managed by the Crown after 1341, and especially after 1344, when finance was organised according to the principles of the Walton Ordinance (1338). The ordinances upheld the principle that Edward III's 'military needs had absolute priority over all other forms of crown expenditure', and thus observed the priorities of the king and central government by putting warfare at the top of the demands on ordinary and, more particularly, extraordinary revenue.[144] Warfare now sat firmly at the top of the agenda in parliament and Edward's increasing control in the management of war finances enabled the king to realise his own military designs.

Conclusion

The most striking feature of the finance of Lancaster's army is the efficiency with which it was administered. In 1345 finance was predominantly administered by the Exchequer, which assumed responsibility for all royal expenditure, but for the war in Aquitaine administration involved a multitude of departments, offices and individuals, all of whom were responsible for the disbursement of payments to the army. The efficiency of the administration was facilitated by the Crown's use of the indenture system, but ultimately it was the flexibility of the royal administrative system that ensured that financial operations ran smoothly.

The versatility of Exchequer clerks is evinced by the roles of Farley and Watenhill prior to the fleet's embarkation. In spite of each clerk being assigned the specific task of disbursing sums to different components of the army, both men paid wages to the English infantry. This temporary operation of two paymasters ensured that wages were promptly paid to the rank and file foot soldiers who might otherwise have been tempted to cause havoc during their wait at the port. Such flexible practices, however, offered the potential for administrative oversights such as the overlap of payment from 12 to 14 June when the Staffordshire archers were in receipt of pay from both clerks.[145]

---

[144] Ormrod, *Edward III*, pp. 198–200.

[145] Farley paid wages to the English foot archers on the day they arrived at the muster point for a set fifteen-day period and from 12 June onwards they were in receipt of wages from Watenhill for a further thirty-three days. The county levies did not all arrive on the same day and therefore the Staffordshire archers, who arrived at Southampton on 31 May, were paid wages by Farley up to 14 June: E 404/501/336. The Derbyshire archers

Another example of the fluidity of payments to ensure the smooth running of military operations is the prest of £10,855 18s 6d delivered by Lancaster to the constable of Bordeaux.[146] That the constable was in need of such a large prest, which was probably drawn from Lancaster's own resources, reflects the importance of a military commander who, if required, was capable of contributing large sums of cash to the war effort. Interestingly, the sum of the prest in Lancaster's account is followed by the word 'debet' which has been written over an erasure after the account was initially made. The corresponding sum is recorded in the Pipe Rolls of the following year, but surprisingly there is a blank space where 'debet' should appear to indicate that the sum is owed by the constable.[147] Clearly the fluidity of payments in and out of the ducal administration brought its own complexities and on this occasion even the Exchequer clerks were themselves confused as to how to account for this item of Lancaster's expenditure.

The issues and receipts of the royal Wardrobe relating to war expenses in Aquitaine show that the administrative practices of the department and those of the Exchequer complemented one another. The Wardrobe fulfilled an important role in administering the wages of Ralph Stafford's men, while much larger sums were issued later on at the Exchequer to the keeper of the Wardrobe, for payments which had previously been assigned to Lancaster for his service in the duchy.[148] That the keeper's payments were made by assignment suggests that the department, at least in this instance, fulfilled an accounting role rather than serving as a depository which dispensed large sums of cash. Nevertheless, the Wardrobe was an integral part of the war administration, even when the king did not lead an army in person.

In the absence of the constable of Bordeaux's account book it is impossible to determine to what extent the administration at Bordeaux financed, and administered the finance of, the army over the course of the campaign. The constable's spurious payment of *vadia guerre* recorded in Lancaster's account offers a glimpse of its potential role in paying the army, but we can be certain that it was the flexibility of the administrative system overall that enabled captains to account for service either in the duchy or in England. The importance of Lancaster himself in keeping the army efficiently financed should also not be overlooked, not only in respect of his personal financial resources, but also of his intimate relationship with

were also in receipt of pay from both clerks on 12 June because they had arrived on 29 May: E 404/501/339.

[146] E 372/191, m. 54d. The prest was intended to cover costs of the earl's return sea passage and other business in the duchy.

[147] E 372/192, m. 21.

[148] E 403/341, m. 19. £8727 7d was issued to Walter de Wetwang on 5 July 1348 for money he had assigned to Lancaster as payment in arrears for his service in Aquitaine.

the king. Royal favour and patronage were indeed useful tools which often helped the administrative system run smoothly.

It should be borne in mind that the formal accounts of service do not always fully represent the financing of an army and the administrative records can often hide the different and sometimes complex administrative processes at work. However, a close scrutiny of the financial accounts has revealed clerical anomalies which have furthered our understanding of accounting practices and procedures in the mid 1340s. The schedule of payments to captains, officers and clerks suggests that Lancaster's army was supported by a flexible, professional and well-oiled administrative system.

II

The English Expedition to Aquitaine, 1345–46

5

The Twin Victories:
The First Campaign, 1345

When Lancaster's fleet sailed up the Gironde estuary and disembarked at Bordeaux on 9 August 1345 the duchy of Aquitaine was only a pale shadow of what it had once been.[1] The territories under English control were limited to the southern coastal towns of Bayonne and Bordeaux, Saint-Sever and the maritime strip of land which joined them. There were no towns deeper inland which had remained loyal to Edward III, as French forces had advanced as close as Libourne, to the east/north-east of Bordeaux, and to Langon in the south.[2] The principal aim of the expedition was simply to recapture the key fortifications that had fallen to the French, and to regain control of areas that had been gradually encroached upon since Philippe VI had declared the duchy confiscate in May 1337. The grant of extensive administrative, judicial and military powers to the king's lieutenant suggests, as Jonathan Sumption points out, that 'his military objectives were left entirely to his own discretion'.[3] It is unlikely that Lancaster had any preconceived plans of attack before landing in Aquitaine, and the openness of his objectives

---

[1] E 372/191, m. 54d. The fleet may have initially landed at Bayonne, where one chronicler reports 'decem milia Bayonenses collegerunt secum', and another claims that a force of light infantry was added to the English army: *Chronographia regum Francorum*, ed. H. Moranvillé, 3 vols (Paris: Librairie Renouard, 1891–97), II (1893), pp. 210–11; *Istore et croniques de Flandres, d'après les textes de divers manuscrits*, ed. Kervyn de Lettonhove, 2 vols (Brussels: [n. pub.], 1879–80), II (1880), p. 12. A stop at the southern port is certainly feasible considering that Lancaster was at sea for a total of seventeen days, and in 1355 the Black Prince's voyage from Portsmouth to Bordeaux took only one week. Guilhem Pépin, 'La collégiale Saint-Seurin de Bordeaux aux XIIIe-XIVe siècles et son elaboration d'une historiographie et d'une idéologie du duché d'Aquitaine anglo-gascon', *Le Moyen Âge*, 117 (2011), 43–66, (p. 56). Alfred H. Burne's assertion that Lancaster initially landed at Bayonne and remained there for one week in order to refresh his men and horses before marching to Bordeaux makes no sense considering that the coastal town is situated over 240 km further down the coast from the duchy's capital: Burne, *Crécy War*, p. 102.

[2] Fowler, *King's Lieutenant*, pp. 41–53.

[3] Sumption, *Trial by Battle*, p. 455. For a summary of the four commissions granted to Lancaster in his indenture of service with Edward III, see Fowler, *King's Lieutenant*, pp. 50–1.

is reflected by the lack of precision in his indenture with the king, which simply states that 'if there is war … to do the best he can' (*si guerre soit, et a faire le bien q'il poet*).[4]

The first acts of warfare in the duchy had begun in the regions surrounding Bordeaux two months prior to the arrival of Lancaster. Local Gascon lords allied to the English conducted raids in Agenais, Périgord and Saintonge, which resulted in the capture of Montravel and several other formidable castles along the Dordogne river.[5] It was in the second half of June, however, that the official offensive began when the English seneschal, Ralph, Lord Stafford laid siege to Blaye.[6] This garrison town lies roughly 40 kilometres north of Bordeaux and seems to have been an obvious choice of attack given its proximity to the provincial capital and its strategic position on the north bank of the Gironde. Stafford then doubled back and marched up the Garonne valley and laid siege to Langon, having left part of the Gascon forces behind at Blaye. The besieging forces were probably augmented by the infantry troops who arrived in the duchy a few weeks in advance of the main fleet. The seneschal's strategy of retaking lost lands through methodical sieges was 'briskly repudiated' by Lancaster, according to Sumption, upon his arrival in the duchy.[7] The earl did not want to allow the opposition time to consolidate their forces given his late arrival in the southern theatre of war – six weeks after Thomas Ferrers and the earl of Northampton had already landed at their destinations – nor did he want to lose the initiative by engaging in time consuming and indecisive siege warfare.

The French forces in the south were divided into four armies, the largest of which was led by Bertrand Jourdain, count of l'Isle, who according to Froissart, 'was at the time like a king in Gascony' (*pour le temps d'adont estoit en Gascongne comme rois*).[8] The count's force was further divided; the largest part was commanded by him at the town of Bergerac and the other, led by Henri de Montigny, laid siege to Montcuq, a strong castle belonging to Bernat-Etz, lord of Albret, which was located a few kilometres south-east across the Dordogne river. The remaining three field armies active in the duchy were led by Jean, count of Armagnac, who was besieging Mouchan outside Condom, the seneschal of Agenais, Robert de Houdetot, who was laying siege to Casseneuil in Agenais, and Jean de Marigny, bishop of Beauvais, who was with Louis of Poitiers attempting to keep in check the Gascon forces laying siege to Blaye in Saintonge.[9] Such a division and spread of

---

[4]   E 159/123, m. 254.
[5]   Other captured places included Ans, Monbreton and Nontron: Sumption, *Trial by Battle*, pp. 457–8.
[6]   *Chronographia*, II, p. 214.
[7]   Sumption, *Trial by Battle*, p. 463.
[8]   *Oeuvres*, IV, p. 221.
[9]   Sumption, *Trial by Battle*, p. 458.

the French forces provided Lancaster with a happy chance, in furnishing what Clifford Rogers describes as 'a textbook case of how *not* to conduct an operation'.[10] The Anglo-Gascon forces at Bordeaux and Langon occupied a central position in the field, whereas the French contingents were further apart from one another than the opposition. A military engagement between the opposing sides, therefore, could easily have been concluded before French reinforcements could arrive.

The Capture of Bergerac

Once the English army disembarked at Bordeaux, Lancaster acted swiftly upon learning of the disposition of the French forces. He remained in the capital for only a few days before making a local truce with the castellan of Blaye, Miles de Hauteroche, and recalling the besiegers to Bordeaux.[11] The *Chronique de Bazas* notes Saint-Macaire, a town located in the Garonne valley south-east of Bordeaux, as the rendezvous where the Anglo-Gascon forces united with Stafford's contingent which had remained occupied with the siege of Langon.[12] It was due to this latter enterprise that Lancaster upbraided the English seneschal, whom he deemed to have wasted valuable time and resources on such an insignificant place. From here the king's lieutenant advanced eastwards marching at double speed 'by day and night' (*de die et de nochte*) towards Montaut which was almost half way between

[10] For a detailed discussion of the strategic advantage of the 'interior lines' occupied by the Anglo-Gascon forces, see Rogers, *Bergerac Campaign*, p. 96.

[11] *Chronique normande du XIVe siècle: publiée pour la Société de l'histoire de France*, ed. A. and E. Molinier (Paris: Renouard, 1882), p. 65. The castellan is also described as 'Milo de Altaruppe, burgensis Tholose', see *Chronographia*, II, p. 214. Contrary to Froissart's report that Lancaster stayed in Bordeaux for about fifteen days, it would have been impossible for him to have remained in the capital for more than a few days given that Bergerac capitulated on 24 August 1345 – fifteen days after his arrival in Bordeaux. *Oeuvres*, IV, p. 232.

[12] 'Chronique de Bazas, 1299–1355', ed. M. E. Piganeau, in *Archives historiques du département de la Gironde*, 58 vols (Paris: Aubry, 1859–1932), XV (1874), pp. 15–84 (p. 43). In a deposition given during the heraldic dispute between John Lovel and Thomas Morley in 1385, Hugh Courson, an esquire who served in the *comitiva* of John de Norwich, claims to have been present at the siege of Langon: C 47/6/1, no. 99. If his testimony is to be taken literally, then it seems that Norwich, who served as one of Lancaster's bannerets, had broken away from the earl's retinue at Saint-Macaire and supported Stafford at Langon. It is also possible that Lancaster led his entire force to Langon, situated less than 4 km from Saint-Macaire on the opposite side of the Garonne river, but this would make little sense considering that he intended to head northwards as soon as possible. Burne states that Lancaster's army assembled at Libourne before following the Dordogne river up to the south bank of Bergerac: Burne, *Crécy War*, p. 102. His view of events does not account for the siege of Langon which is well attested by the narrative and administrative sources.

the two French forces at Bergerac/Montcuq and Casseneuil.[13] Either of these sites would have been feasible targets for Lancaster's army and we cannot be certain which one he intended to attack. The natural obstacles of the river Dropt and hilly terrain of the surrounding area no doubt afforded the moving army partial cover from the enemy; indeed, if the French were aware of Lancaster's movements they too could not have been certain of his intended place of attack. Along the way the Anglo-Gascon forces were probably swollen further by the retinue of Guilhem-Sans III, lord of Pommiers, whose formidable castle of Saint-Félix was located around 15 kilometres north east of Saint-Macaire.[14] At Montaut the decision was made to attack Bergerac. The choice was probably based on the town's strategic importance and not, as Burne suggests, because Lancaster had learned of the count of l'Isle's concentration of forces there.[15] Bergerac was the major garrison town in Périgord and it provided an excellent base from which further expeditions into French-held territory could be launched, and the town's location on low-lying ground and inadequate fortification of the castle rendered it the ideal place to attack.[16]

The exact chronology of events that led to the capture of Bergerac is not entirely clear, as the sources disagree and there is little consensus among historians.[17] Fortunately, the recently rediscovered *Saint-Omer Chronicle* has thrown new light on the unfolding of events before Bergerac.[18] According to Rogers, Lancaster set an ambush of men-at-arms and foot archers on a small area of open grassland between two copses near the town, before luring the count of l'Isle's men with a show of plundered cattle and French prisoners driven by 250 cavalrymen before the castle walls.[19] Such an affront provoked the desired response, as the *Chronographia regum Francorum* claims that

---

[13] *Chronique de Bazas*, p. 43. Rogers claims that Montaut was a predetermined rendezvous point for Lancaster's forces and other Gascon detachments: Rogers, *Bergerac Campaign*, p. 98. Several places in Agenais and Périgord share the name of Montaut, but the site suggested by Rogers seems most likely given its location equidistant between the opposing forces.

[14] Rogers, *Bergerac Campaign*, p. 97. Alternatively, the Gascon's contingent may have mustered at the main commune of Saint-Sulpice-de-Pommiers, situated a couple of kilometres north of Saint-Félix.

[15] Burne, *Crécy War*, p. 102. The lord of Albret may also have held some sway in the decision considering that his besieged castle of Montcuq was in close proximity to Bergerac and his old enemy, the count of Périgord, was foremost among the attackers: Sumption, *Trial by Battle*, p. 463.

[16] Sumption, *Trial by Battle*, pp. 463–5; the stone bridge of the eleventh-century castle was also the principal crossing of the Dordogne river.

[17] For a discussion of existing historiography of events at the battle of Bergerac, see Rogers, *Bergerac Campaign*, pp. 90–4.

[18] *Saint-Omer*, fols 206–33.

[19] Rogers, *Bergerac Campaign*, pp. 99–102.

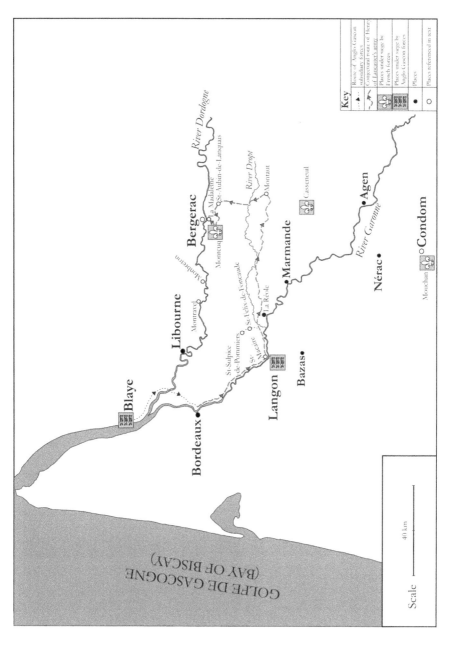

Map 2. The Bergerac
Campaign, August 1345

Key

	Route of Anglo-Gascon subsidiary forces
	Conjectural route of Henry of Lancaster's army
	Places under siege by French forces
	Places under siege by Anglo-Gascon forces
•	Places
○	Places referenced in text

GOLFE DE GASCOGNE
(BAY OF BISCAY)

Scale —————— 40 km

Blaye
Bordeaux
Libourne
Montravel
Montbreton
Bergerac
La Madeleine
St-Aubin-de-Lanquais
River Dordogne
Montcuq
St-Sulpice-de-Pommiers
St-Macaire
St-Felix-de-Foncaude
La Réole
River Dropt
Montaut
Casseneuil
Marmande
River Garonne
Agen
Langon
Bazas
Nérac
Mouchan
Condom

'about 1600 men came forth' (*exierunt quasi mille et sexcenti viri*).[20] This large mounted contingent probably outnumbered the English and Gascon men-at-arms who were arrayed in a novel manner in front of the archers, waiting for the French approach. As the opposing forces of cavalry charged they passed through each other as Lancaster's men opened their formation. Once the French had passed through the first line of men-at-arms they were met by the arrows of the archers positioned at the rear flanks of Lancaster's position. Almost all the French were either killed or captured. Henri de Montigny, who was engaged in the siege of Montcuq about 5 kilometres from Bergerac, was probably brought news of the rout by those who had fled. Panic spread and fighting ensued as the English and Gascons caught up with Montigny's retreating army at La Madeleine, the suburb located on the south bank of the Dordogne.

Froissart reports that it was Sir Walter Mauny, one of the marshals of the army, who pushed through the barbican gate on the southern end of the stone bridge that joined with Bergerac on the opposite side of the river.[21] Many of the retreating French were killed on the narrow causeway after becoming trapped between the relief force, which sallied out of the castle, and the advancing enemy. In the fierce engagement that ensued, the English and Gascon men-at-arms, led by Mauny, were able to push their way up to the main entrance of the castle after a fallen horse had become trapped beneath the portcullis of the tower mid-way along the bridge, which would otherwise have dropped and halted the English advance at that point. In spite of the threat from Genoese crossbowmen positioned on the battlements, the defences were breached after the main gate was set alight and eventually knocked down. The archers on the south bank wreaked havoc firing beyond their army lines, and continued 'to shoot with great quickness causing great mischief' (*à traire sus yaus à grant randon et à mettre en grant mischief*).[22] It was probably growing dark by the time the town was taken by storm in the initial assault.[23]

---

[20] *Chronographia*, II, p. 215.

[21] *Oeuvres*, IV, pp. 226–7. Froissart refers to Mauny and, on another occasion, Frank van Halen as marshals of the army but it was in fact Thomas Cok who was appointed to serve in that capacity. Cok is described as 'Marescallus exercitus': E 372/191, m. 54d.

[22] *Oeuvres*, IV, p. 227.

[23] The firmest evidence that the town was taken by assault rather than surrendered is the deposition of Hugh Courson mentioned earlier. He specifically testifies that he fought 'al Gayne de Brigerak', which translates as at the 'capture' or the 'winning' of Bergerac: C 47/6/1, no. 99. The fact that the Albret brothers, subsequent captains of Bergerac, were empowered to pardon the citizens of the town implies that it was taken by storm rather than by a prolonged attack and negotiated surrender: Rogers, *Bergerac*, p. 103. This view is supported by several narrative sources: *Chronique de Bazas*, p. 44; 'Chronique de Guyenne', ed. H. Brackhausen, in *Archives municipales de Bordeaux*, 12 vols (Bordeaux: Gounouilhou, 1867–96), V (1890), p. 400; Henry Knighton, *Knighton's*

The capture of Bergerac was a significant event in Lancaster's expedition. Such an early and important victory not only lifted the morale of the Anglo-Gascon forces but it also put the French on the back foot in the south-west. Lancaster had successfully captured the headquarters of the largest French army in Aquitaine at that time, and he now effectively commanded all movement in the Dordogne valley due to its strategic position. Adam Murimuth states that ten lords were taken prisoner and Robert of Avesbury records the capture of Henri de Montigny, Jean de Galard and nine other lords.[24] The haul of prisoners, however, did not include the count of l'Isle who managed to escape to La Réole before the town's capitulation and form a small force from those who had escaped southward, while other survivors who made their way out of Bergerac to the north headed towards Périgueux.[25] The count of Armagnac took command of this latter force. Upon learning of the defeat at Bergerac the French gave priority to the southern theatre over the other fronts in Brittany and northern France. Pierre, the duke of Bourbon, took up his lieutenancy in the Languedoc in September and immediately began intensive recruitment in the southern seneschalcies; the assembled forces were augmented by an army led by Louis of Poitiers which had been operating in the Saintonge.[26] These various forces mustered in the north of the duchy, with their headquarters at Angoulême. Overall command was given to the king's son, Jean, duke of Normandy, who arrived there in the first half of September.[27]

Chronicle 1337–1396, ed. and trans. G. H. Martin (Oxford: Clarendon Press, 1995), pp. 52–3; *Chronique normande*, p. 67; Avesbury, *Edwardi tertii*, p. 356. Burne and Fowler both follow Froissart's earlier redactions which claim reinforcements were brought up on boats from Bordeaux and the town was defended for several days: Burne, *Crécy War*, p. 104; *Oeuvres*, IV, p. 229.

[24] Adam Murimuth, *Continuatio chronicarum*, ed. Edward Maunde Thompson (London: Eyre & Spottiswoode, 1889) , p. 251; Avesbury, *Edwardi tertii*, p. 356. Galard received a royal grant of 100,000 gold *écus* in order to pay his ransom: AN, JJ 68, no. 601, no. 662.

[25] AL, Livre velu de Libourne, fol. 133v; Raymond Guinodie, *Histoire de Libourne et des autres villes et bourgs de son arrondissement…*, 3 vols, 2nd edn (Paris: chez l'Auteur, 1876), I, p. 49; Burne, *Crécy War*, pp. 104–5.

[26] The duke of Bourbon was appointed the king's lieutenant in Aquitaine and Languedoc at Sablé on 8 August, the day before Lancaster had disembarked at Bordeaux, but did not arrive in the region until the following month. Fowler, *King's Lieutenant*, p. 59; Sumption, *Trial by Battle*, p. 466.

[27] Sumption, *Trial by Battle*, pp. 465–8; Duke Jean later established his headquarters at Limoges.

The Battle of Auberoche

Lancaster's army remained at Bergerac for just over two weeks, using the town as a base from which his forces could regain control of the small fortifications and *bastides* within southern Périgord.[28] These conquests included Lamonzie, Lalinde, Laforce, Lunas, Beaumont, Montagrier, Pellegrue and Monségur; the latter town was captured with the aid of a siege engine apparently transported from Bordeaux.[29] A large Gascon force of almost 300 men-at-arms and 1200 infantry remained in Bergerac under the command of Bernat-Etz and Bérart Albret; the two brothers had been appointed captains of the town by Lancaster on 10 September and agreed to remain so, initially, for one month during which time they were to maintain the garrison and undertake any necessary improvements to the town's defences.[30] Meanwhile, the main field army marched north-north-west to Mussidan, before continuing eastwards to Périgueux, securing the course of the lower Isle through the recapture of numerous places along the way.[31]

The provincial capital would have probably capitulated to the raiding army but for the timely arrival of the count of Armagnac and his men who, after fleeing from Bergerac, managed to defend its walls. It was apparent to Lancaster that the city could not be taken without a concerted effort, and so the earl decided to withdraw leaving garrisons in nearby strongholds, which included Auberoche, in order to maintain a loose blockade thereby cutting off supplies to the town.[32] Numerous places of importance in Agenais and

[28] A *bastide* was a small settlement that had no evident military function, but they were important centres of local administration, trade and exchange. Vale, *Origins of the Hundred Years War*, pp. 152–60.

[29] Fowler, *King's Lieutenant*, p. 57; *Chronique de Bazas*, p. 43.

[30] The Albret brothers were contracted to maintain a garrison of 298 cavalry and 1200 infantry: BnF, MS Doat 189, fols 167–70 (indenture), for a transcription of the indenture see Fowler, *King's Lieutenant*, pp. 232–3.

[31] The towns of Maurens, Saint-Jean-d'Eyraud and Les Leches were taken along the way from Bergerac to Mussidan, followed by the capture of Saint-Louis, Saint-Astier, Lisle and Montagrier en route to Périgueux: Fowler, *King's Lieutenant*, pp. 57–8; Avesbury, *Edwardi tertii*, 356; *Chronique de Bazas*, p. 44, Murimuth, *Continuatio*, 251; *Oeuvres*, IV, p. 234–39. C 61/60, mm. 6, 9, 14; C 61/63, m. 9. It is during this period of military operations that Froissart describes the capture of the earl of Oxford during a midnight raid by 200 French lances who sallied out of Périgueux. However, this report is completely fictitious because Oxford was in England at the time and any similar events involving the capture of another nobleman are unsubstantiated by other narrative sources: *Oeuvres*, IV, p. 238.

[32] AN, JJ 68/157; JJ 80/699. Lancaster moved eastwards and began to arc back around, taking first Bonneval and then Auberoche which was immediately surrendered by one of the petty lords of Périgord to whom it belonged and not, as Froissart claims, by the archbishop of Toulouse: *Oeuvres*, IV, p. 237–45; Sumption, *Trial by Battle*, p. 468. We cannot be certain of the exact chronology of the capture of the various towns and castles

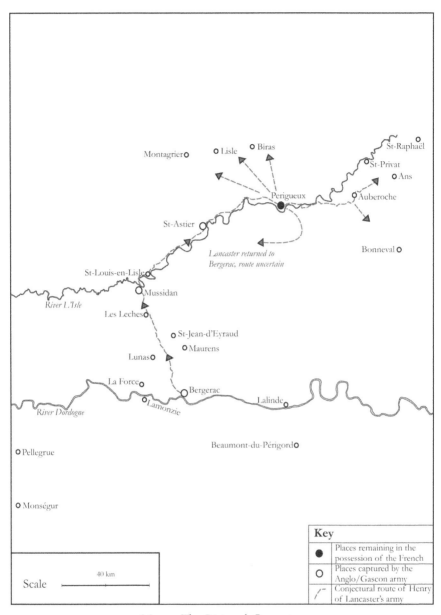

St-Raphaël

St-Privat

Ans

Biras

Lisle

Montagrier

Auberoche

Perigueux

St-Astier

Bonneval

Lancaster returned to
Bergerac, route uncertain

St-Louis-en-Lisle

Mussidan

River L'Isle

Les Leches

St-Jean-d'Eyraud

Maurens

Lunas

La Force

Bergerac

Lalinde

Lamonzie

River Dordogne

Beaumont-du-Périgord

Pellegrue

Monségur

Key	
●	Places remaining in the possession of the French
○	Places captured by the Anglo/Gascon army
⌐	Conjectural route of Henry of Lancaster's army

Scale 40 km

Map 3. The Périgord Campaign

Périgord had been recovered; some had willingly joined the English allegiance, others were taken by force. The attack on Bonneval, for example,
was reported to have been particularly violent 'and many men were killed
and wounded within [the town]' (*et plusieurs homes bleciés dedens et dehors*),
although we should not presume it to be typical of the manner in which
places came under English control.[33] Avesbury records that four *villas magnas*
and a further forty-six lesser towns under Philippe VI's allegiance were taken
at a time when, one chronicler poignantly notes, 'the Englishmen went on
robbing and despoiling the lands of Agenais and Guienne' (*Et ensi alerent li
engles reubant et essillant le paiis d'Aginois et de Ghyenne*).[34]

The sequence of events becomes obscure from this point up to the famous
battle at Auberoche a couple of weeks later. After Lancaster withdrew from
the lands of Périgord we cannot be certain whether the earl returned to
Bordeaux or to Libourne, 'a large and strong town' (*une bonne ville et
grosse*) roughly 30 kilometres from the duchy's capital.[35] The *Saint-Omer
Chronicle* states that he returned to Bordeaux, but the chronicler seems to
have conflated the events after Bergerac with the events following the later
battle of Auberoche.[36] Froissart accounts that the earl retreated to Bordeaux
after leaving a sufficient garrison at Auberoche under the command of his
Brabantine banneret, Sir Frank van Halen. His command was shared with
'Sir Alain de Sinefroide' and the English knight, Sir John de Lovedale.
The chronicler also reports that Libourne surrendered to the English after
a brief siege, before the earl's return to Bordeaux.[37] The possibility that
Lancaster headed north into the Limousin and then Quercy after leaving
Périgord seems unlikely considering the proximity of the French forces.[38]
An expedition further north or eastwards would have led the Anglo-Gascon
army deeper into enemy territory with the potentially dangerous prospect

in Périgord, but it was probably in the weeks following Lancaster's arrival at Périgueux
that Ans, Biras, Saint-Privat and Saint-Raphaël came under English control. Avesbury,
Edwardi tertii, p. 356; Murimuth, *Continuatio*, 251, Sumption, *Trial by Battle*, p. 468,
n. 20.

[33] *Oeuvres*, IV, p. 243.

[34] Avesbury, *Edwardi tertii*, p. 356; *Saint Omer*, fol. 210.

[35] *Oeuvres*, IV, p. 239.

[36] *Saint-Omer*, fol. 210v.

[37] *Oeuvres*, IV, pp. 239–40.

[38] Fowler's suggestion of an advance northwards is based on a petition from Bertran de
Pommiers, brother of Guilhem-Sans III, to the English king which states that the castle
of 'Maureuxs' (possibly 'Maurens', north of Bergerac) had been granted to Bertran by
Lancaster following the count of Périgueux's rebellion. The document is dated in 1347
and, therefore, it could have been retaken by the Anglo-Gascon forces at any time
between 1345 and 1347. SC 8/243/12138; Fowler, *King's Lieutenant*, p. 58. C 61/60, mm.
6, 14.

of having its line of retreat back to Bordeaux cut off. These operations were probably undertaken by the earl later in the expedition.

The English and Gascon withdrawal from Périgueux had been forced by the arrival of a substantial French force led by Louis of Poitiers at the beginning of October. His detachment of 3000 men-at-arms and a very large number of foot soldiers included the count of l'Isle who had left La Réole to join the duke of Normandy, whose headquarters had now moved from Angoulême to Limoges. Louis relieved the siege of Périgueux and followed the conventional French military practice of a slow and methodical reconquest of the surrounding area, a stratagem not too dissimilar to that deployed by Stafford earlier in the summer.[39] Meanwhile, the duke of Bourbon had moved his troops to Gourdon on the frontier of Périgord and Quercy and, as Fowler points out, if Normandy had co-ordinated the movement of his forces more effectively, so as to surround Lancaster's army, then perhaps the earl might have been forced to give up on Auberoche altogether and retreat along the valleys of the Donne and the Isle.[40] As it was, the old seigniorial fortress of Auberoche, 16 kilometres east of the provincial capital, was besieged by Poitiers' army around mid-October.

How Lancaster learnt of the French siege is impossible to know; the movements of Poitiers' large army would not have been difficult for a scouting party to spot or, perhaps, word had emerged from the besieged camp. Interestingly, the report that a messenger had escaped from Auberoche with secret correspondence intended for Lancaster should not be dismissed out of hand. The daring escapist had initially been able to pass freely through the enemy camp because he was able to speak the local Gascon dialect, but he was subsequently captured and returned hastily over the castle walls via a catapult with the letters tied around his neck.[41] This dramatic case of 'shooting the messenger' may seem to have a semblance of exaggeration but the manner in which the garrison intended to send word of its plight, at least, should be given credence. Once the siege became known to Lancaster he marched towards Auberoche and awaited reinforcements from Laurence de Hastings, earl of Pembroke, who, according to Froissart, had returned with his retinue to Bergerac. Although the young earl had intended to rendezvous with the main army at Libourne, en route to Auberoche, he did not join Lancaster's army until the morning after the battle. The Anglo-Gascon forces were augmented by the military contingent attached to the garrison at Libourne which included Ralph Stafford, Sir Stephen de

---

[39] Sumption, *Trial by Battle*, p. 468.

[40] For movement of French forces in September and October 1345, see Fowler, *King's Lieutenant*, pp. 59–60; Sumption, *Trial by Battle*, p. 468.

[41] *Oeuvres*, IV, pp. 259–61. According to Froissart the messenger was a valet of Sir Frank van Halen.

Gumby and Sir Alexander Auncel, the latter two being part of Lancaster's own retinue.[42]

After travelling along back roads to Auberoche, as part of a covert night approach, Lancaster's army secreted itself in nearby woods. The main body of the French army which totalled between 7000 and 10,000 men was camped before the castle in a meadow on the banks of the river Auvezere less than 300 metres from the English troops.[43] The castle itself stands on a rocky prominence overlooking the river and the small hamlet of Auberoche, and to the north a smaller French force was camped within the proximity of the castle's entrance. After riding throughout the night Lancaster's force of around 1200 men, which faced an enemy at least six times its strength, waited in vain for several hours for the arrival of Pembroke. The entire morning and most of the afternoon had passed when a council of war was held between Lancaster and his principal knights. The earl's decision to attack immediately was a justified conclusion considering that the army's supplies which had been brought from Bergerac by pack-horses were severely diminished and had little chance of being replenished as foraging was forbidden. Of greater significance, perhaps, was the danger of being discovered by the enemy and losing the element of surprise, the prospect of which grew stronger as the day wore on. An attack was now imminent and a personal reconnaissance by Lancaster himself found the enemy host relaxed and unprepared for battle. The earl's tactics were simple but effective: the archers were to crawl to the edge of the wood and, upon Lancaster's signal, continuously shoot on the French camp opposite while the mounted men-at-arms charged the enemy from the rear. Of course, the simplicity of the plan does not mean it was easy to execute – timing was crucial to its success. According to Froissart, it was about 'the hour of supper' (*l'eure dou souper*) when Lancaster's forces were in position and ready to launch their surprise attack – the archers were in place and the men-at-arms had quietly made their way to the level ground at the beginning of the meadow.[44]

On the evening of 21 October 1345, exactly two months after the assault on Bergerac, Lancaster's army broke from its hiding place and charged the unsuspecting siege camp.[45] The French were taken completely by surprise

---

[42] *Oeuvres*, IV, pp. 246–56.

[43] For a detailed treatment of the battle, an assessment of the topography of the valley in which Auberoche is situated and sketch maps of the positions of the opposing forces, see Burne, *Crécy War*, pp. 106–12.

[44] *Oeuvres*, IV, p. 262. Villani's report that the battle started in the morning and continued up to around midday is plausible, but does not fit with the notion that Lancaster's force had travelled through the night and were awaiting Pembroke's arrival. Villani, *Cronica*, pp. 383–4. Note that the long days in the summer months in Aquitaine meant that it would have been feasible to launch an attack in the early evening with the hope of securing victory before dark.

[45] AL, Livre velu, fol. 133r; Guinodie, *Libourne*, I, p. 51; *Chronique de Bazas*, p. 43.

and suffered heavy casualties from the English arrows, no doubt a result of not having time to don their armour.[46] The archery barrage was accompanied by cries of 'Derby! Guyenne!', and as the cavalry tore through the enemy lines a few Frenchmen at the furthest end of the camp who had managed to rally themselves for battle became new targets for the English archers.[47] In the pandemonium that ensued hundreds of French were killed, either cut down or pierced by arrows. Despite their numerical advantage the French were overcome, and the timely *coup de grâce* was delivered by Sir Frank van Halen. The captain of Auberoche, who had witnessed the events unfold before him, sortied from the castle with a small retinue of men-at-arms and charged into the mêlée.[48] The small French camp occupied with blocking an escape route for the besieged broke up, and those who were able to escape the onslaught joined their comrades in flight from the battlefield.

The victory at Auberoche signified the 'greatest single achievement of Lancaster's entire military career', and was matched by the rewards of war.[49] On this occasion the count of l'Isle, who was the principal French commander in the south, was among the captives, as was Louis of Poitiers, who later died of his wounds, along with one other count, seven viscounts, three barons, fourteen bannerets 'and many others were captured in that very place' (*et multibus et aliis ibidem captis*).[50] The assessment of the battle by one historian as 'breath-taking in its audacity and dazzling in its brilliance' is justifiable considering the superior size of the French forces.[51] The purpose of the expedition was given more momentum by these twin victories at Bergerac and Auberoche as they effectively undermined French resistance in the south-west. On the day of the battle the duke of Normandy was reported to have been no more than ten leagues (55 kilometres) from Auberoche, but upon learning of the French defeat he withdrew to Angloulême where his army disbanded.[52] Consequently, no French forces were left in the field to oppose Lancaster's advances until the return of the duke's huge army in the following spring.

After the battle of Auberoche the earl of Lancaster (as he became upon his father's death in September 1345)[53] did not return to Bordeaux, as several chronicles reported, but instead moved southwards to expand the territory

---

[46] Kelly DeVries, *Infantry Warfare in the Early Fourteenth Century: Discipline, Tactics and Technology* (Woodbridge: Boydell, 1996), p. 189. Murimuth's estimate of more than a thousand casualties is probably gross exaggeration: *Continuatio chronicarum*, p. 190.

[47] *Oeuvres*, IV, p. 255.

[48] Sumption, *Trial by Battle*, pp. 468–9.

[49] Fowler, *King's Lieutenant*, pp. 58–9.

[50] Avesbury, *Edwardi tertii*, pp. 356–7.

[51] Burne, *Crécy War*, pp. 112–13.

[52] Villani, *Cronica*, p. 383.

[53] Henry, third earl of Lancaster and Leicester, died on 22 September 1345: Scott

under his control and fulfil what must now have been his principal objective of securing the Garonne valley.[54] The capture of fortified places in the surrounding area of the Garonne, combined with his existing control of the Dordogne valley, would secure all routes to Bordeaux and provide a gateway for further expansion inland. The two principal castles that remained under French control in this area were Aiguillon and La Réole, but the latter was of greater importance owing to its strategic position on the river Garonne and its formidable thirteenth-century castle which had been rebuilt by Henry III and Edward I after 1254. The castle is situated on the western edge of the town and stands on a rocky outcrop overlooking the river – its broad corner towers (three of which are still standing) were encompassed by the walls of the town.[55] The capture of La Réole now became the principal objective of Lancaster, and after taking the *bastides* of Pellegrue and Monségur he arrived there on 2 November.[56] An initial assault upon the town's walls with catapults and giant belfries (large moveable towers) seems possible, but we can be certain that the leading citizens of La Réole granted Lancaster access to the town through one of the gates.[57] Among the chief architects of the plan to surrender La Réole voluntarily were the powerful Piis family who, in the words of the town's jurats (councillors), 'worked more than anybody

L. Waugh, 'Henry of Lancaster, Third Earl of Lancaster and Third Earl of Leicester (c.1280–1345)', *ODNB*, May 2006 [accessed 09 March 2015].

[54] Froissart claims that Lancaster returned to Bordeaux and remained there throughout the winter, while the *Saint-Omer* chronicle describes a brief stay at Bordeaux before the earl headed to La Réole: *Oeuvres*, IV, p. 281; *Saint-Omer*, fol. 210v. The *Chronique normande* reports that Lancaster took the towns of Sainte-Foy, Sauveterre, Montpezat, Loury and Castelmoron after the battle of Auberoche. The description of the ambush that led to the capture of Loury and Castelmoron, however, is similar to the tactics used to lure the French from Bergerac a couple of months earlier, which implies that the chronicler has conflated the two events. He describes how the English 'set up an ambush, and sent a large amount of booty to pass within the view of the castle and the town. Those of the town sallied out in order to seize the plunder, but the Englishmen who were set in ambush surprised them, so that most of them were killed or captured, and the town and the castle were taken.': Clifford J. Rogers, *The Wars of Edward III: Sources and Interpretations* (Woodbridge: Boydell, 1999), pp. 116–17; *Chronique normande*, pp. 67–9.

[55] For a map of the castle and town of La Réole, see Sumption, *Trial by Battle*, pp. 475.

[56] E 159/123, m. 327. Avesbury, *Edwardi tertii*, p. 356; Sumption, *Trial by Battle*, p. 474. Froissart claims that the towns of Sainte-Bazeille, Roce-Millon, Aiguillon and Segrat also came under English control before Lancaster arrived at La Réole: *Oeuvres*, IV, pp. 274–83.

[57] Burne, *Crécy War*, pp. 114–15; Burne mistakenly asserts that the town's walls were taken by assault. A grant of taxation by Edward III to the burgesses of La Réole in 1346 for the 'fortification and enclosure of the town [with a wall]' suggests that the town's walls had been damaged during Lancaster's initial assault in the previous year. C 61/59, m. 10.

else in this world' so that it came under English obedience.[58] The grant of an anuuity of 100 *livres bordelais* made on 2 December 1345 by the earl to a burgess of the town named Guilhem Mirail 'for his great service to the king [of England] in the present Gascon war, most especially for his part in the return of the town of La Réole', proves that the bourgeois of the town had colluded with the English.[59] Moreover, the besiegers had entered the town within a month of their arrival there.

The French garrison under the command of Agout des Baux retreated to the citadel of the town, where they remained under siege for eight or nine weeks.[60] Intensive mining works were immediately undertaken during which the earl himself is reported to have worked in the tunnels, but the castellan soon negotiated a truce with Lancaster after the citadel had been partly undermined. The earl granted Baux five weeks grace in order to seek help from the duke of Normandy.[61] But none was forthcoming and, despite the efforts of the duke of Bourbon to raise some sort of relief force, the response to his proclamation of the *arrière-ban* was poor.[62] Interestingly, it was during this intervening period that Walter Mauny is reported to have discovered the burial place of his father somewhere in the town, after a local inhabitant informed him of its whereabouts.[63]

At some point early in January 1346, the garrison commander of La Réole agreed a conditional surrender with Lancaster after no attempt was made to relieve the besieged castle.[64] La Réole was given into the custody of the lord of Pommiers.[65] The English success of the previous months had a dramatic impact on the political allegiances of Gascon lords in Agenais,

[58] In a petition to Edward III in 1347 the jurats of La Réole claimed that, 'les quex ont plus trayte et mis affin qe la dite ville venist a vostre oubeyssance qe nul autres au monde': SC 8/243/12134, no. 15. Cited in Guilhem Pépin, 'Introduction: 21 Edward III (1347–48)', *Gascon Rolls*; www.gasconrolls.org

[59] C 61/59, m. 10. Another grant made on 26 January 1346 states that the issues of the corn tax (*bladaria*) should remain in the hands of the jurats and community of La Réole because it 'was in their hands when the town surrendered'.

[60] One chronicle records that the siege lasted for eight weeks, while another reports that 'nine weeks passed before the town was taken': *Chronique de Bazas*, p. 44; *Récits d'un bourgeois de Valenciennes (XIVè siècle)*, ed. Kervyn de Lettenhove (Louvain: P. et J. Lefever, 1877), p. 195.

[61] *Chronique normande*, p. 70; *Saint-Omer*, fol. 211r.

[62] The *arriére-ban* was an institution used to recruit soldiers in times of dire necessity, see Allmand, *Hundred Years War*, pp. 92–6.

[63] *Oeuvres*, IV, pp. 292–8. Mauny's father was murdered while returning from his pilgrimage to St James of Compostella.

[64] Although Fowler dismisses the long siege reported by Froissart, it is clear that, despite the town's capture at the beginning of November, it was not until at least two months later that the citadel surrendered to the earl: Fowler, *King's Lieutenant*, p. 61; *Oeuvres*, IV, p. 285.

[65] C 61/60, m. 14.

the majority of whom quickly pledged their support to Edward III. Most of Agenais succumbed to English control through the combination of force and economic incentives. The turn of the tide of Gascon support in the favour of the English is typified by the powerful Durfort family, whose loyalty to the English prompted the support of other local lords and the defection of many places in Agenais.[66]

It was during the siege of La Réole (the period between the initial surrender of the town and the final capitulation of the citadel) that Lancaster led a raid into Agenais and Quercy, in an attempt to capitalise on the political impact of the twin victories at Bergerac and Auberoche.[67] The *Saint-Omer Chronicle* reports the capture of Castelsarrasin, which is not mentioned in any other source, 'Mouron' (Castelmayran), the castle of 'la Pereuse' (Laspeyres) and Castelsagrat. It was probably during this period of the campaign when Lancaster's forces failed to capture the castle of Clairac after a prior (possibly Jean de Nanteuil, the Hospitaller grand prior of Aquitaine) had deceived the attackers by reinforcing the castle's defences during an eight-day truce.[68] These raids were conducted in the months of November and December by separate forces which operated independently of one another, and as a part of the same operations Ralph Stafford received the submission of the town of Aiguillon sometime at the beginning of December 1345, after the inhabitants led a coup and killed the French soldiers there.[69] Through the acquisition of Aiguillon the English now had a second garrison in Agenais, the other being at Casseneuil.[70]

It was during the succeeding winter months that the English gained control of more than a dozen other places in Agenais and southern Périgord, including Monclar, Villeréal, Bajamont, Beauville, Montignac, Réalville, Mirabel and Montpezat.[71] One raid deep into French territory in the north

---

[66] Fowler, *King's Lieutenant*, pp. 62–3.

[67] Noted by Clifford Rogers in his transcription of the *Saint-Omer* chronicle.

[68] *Saint-Omer*, fol. 210v. In December 1345 Nanteuil was sovereign captain in Saintonge, and by 1346 was Admiral of the Sea: Philippe Contamine, *Guerre, état et société à la fin du moyen âge: études sur les armées des rois de France 1337–1494* (Paris: Mouton, 1972), p. 173, n. 95.

[69] *Chronique normande*, p. 67. Aiguillon was back in English hands sometime before 10 December and, as with La Réole, it had been captured during the War of Saint-Sardos. For a detailed discussion of the town's surrender, see Fowler, *King's Lieutenant*, pp. 63–4.

[70] Jean le Bel claims that Sainte-Bazeille, Roce-Millon (probably Madaillan) and Montsegur (probably Monségur), were all taken around the same time as Aiguillon: Jean le Bel, 'Chronique de Jean le Bel', ed. E. Déprez and J. Vivard, 2 vols (Paris: [n. pub.], 1904–5), II (1905), p. 41.

[71] Other places: Duras, Saint-Sardos, Puch, Montclar, Villefranche, Villeneuve-sur-Lot, Puyguilhem and Puymirol. *Chronique normande*, pp. 68–9; Bel, *Chronique*, II, pp. 42–3; Murimuth, *Continuatio*, p. 251; *Oeuvres*, IV, pp. 302–10. Fowler, *King's Lieutenant*, p. 61; Sumption, *Trial by Battle*, p. 479.

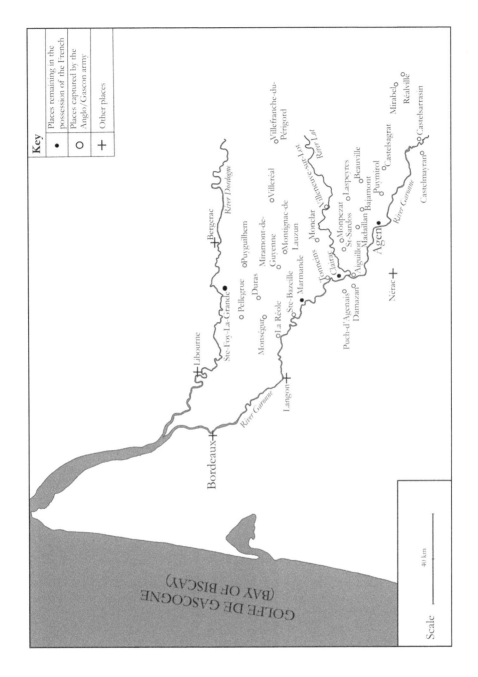

Map 4. The Winter
Campaign, 1345–46

Key

•	Places remaining in the possession of the French
○	Places captured by the Anglo/Gascon army
+	Other places

GOLFE DE GASCOGNE
(BAY OF BISCAY)

Scale ⎯⎯⎯⎯ 40 km

Bordeaux +

Libourne +

Ste-Foy-La-Grande

Langon +

River Garonne

Pellegrue

Duras

Monségur

La Réole

Ste-Bazeille

Marmande

Bergerac +

River Dordogne

Puyguilhem

Miramont-de-Guyenne

Montignac-de-Lauzun

Villeréal

Villefranche-du-Périgord

Tonneins

Clairac

Puch-d'Agenais

Damazan

Auguillon

Monclar

Monpezat

St-Sardos

Madaillan

Bajamont

Villeneuve-sur-Lot

River Lot

Laspeyres

Beauville

Puymirol

Castelsagrat

Mirabel

Realville

Castelsarrasin

Castelmayran

Agen

River Garonne

Nérac +

resulted in the capture of Angoulême. It seems likely that John de Norwich had conducted an audacious attack on the capital of the Angoumois considering that he was later made governor of the town, although we cannot be sure whether its inhabitants had surrendered after a brief siege, or whether the principal townsmen had entered into Lancaster's allegiance following a month-long truce. The town was held for only a short period, until February 1346, when French forces regained possession.[72] Also around this time the *vaillant chevalier*, Thomas Cok, was reportedly made governor of Villefranche after the town was taken 'par engine aussy et par soubtilleté'.[73] Thereafter the castle of Montpouillan was captured before Lancaster's army continued to the town of Miramont which surrendered after a four-day siege.[74]

The appointment of captains and castellans such as Cok or Norwich, for example, reveals the subtle changes in the composition of Lancaster's retinue once it was active in the field. Although the English retinues in 1345 were primarily formed from groups of soldiers that were recruited together, or at least assembled and travelled to the theatre of war together, and served under the same banner, it is difficult to imagine that the retinue maintained its exact composition and size once the campaign was under way, besides the inevitable effects of attrition and fatalities. Individuals who were given command of castles could not have continued with the main army's campaign and we might expect their companions and brothers-in-arms, as well as their own companies of men, to have remained at their side. Sir Frank van Halen, for example, was detached from the main Anglo-Gascon force during his command of Auberoche and he could not have rejoined Lancaster's retinue until the French siege was raised.[75] Interestingly, the sources reveal that men of more modest rank in Lancaster's retinue such as the esquires John Briscoe and Thomas of Lancaster were also given charge of recently conquered places and at times, therefore, served independently of the earl rather than under his immediate command.[76]

---

[72] *Chronique normande*, pp. 70–1; Bel, *Chronique*, II, pp. 43–4, 50–4; *Oeuvres*, IV, pp. 307–8. There is a consensus among the narrative sources that Angoulême was surrendered, but not of the manner in which it was done. Froissart reports that twenty-four of the town's citizens swore homage and fealty to van Halen and Mauny, after being detained at Bordeaux for one month, whereas the *Chronique normande* suggests that the town surrendered after a pusillanimous resistance.

[73] Bel, *Chronique*, II, p. 43.

[74] Froissart also describes the capture of Tonniens and Damazan after the surrender of La Réole: *Oeuvres*, IV, pp. 303–7.

[75] The three anonymous knights of 'Frank de Hale' that served in Lancaster's retinue probably remained with their lord at Auberoche: E 101/25/9, m. 3.

[76] Briscoe was given command of Miramont: Bel, *Chronique*, II, p. 43; *Oeuvres*, IV, p. 332. John Briscoe is possibly a corrupt form of John de Bickerton, whose name appears 167th among the list of esquires in Lancaster's retinue roll: E 101/35/2/10, m. 3.

Henry of Lancaster set up his winter quarters at La Réole where he oversaw the appointments of officers, grants of land and other executive matters that resulted from the newly expanded administration following the acquisition of territory in the first campaign of the expedition.[77] Some elements of the Anglo-Gascon army disbanded during the winter months. The Aquitanian lords and their retainers, as Jonathan Sumption points out, probably did return to their homes until the new campaigning season began in the following spring, but his assertion that the earl of Pembroke's retinue returned to England is inaccurate.[78] The *vadia* section in Pembroke's enrolled account of service proves that the earl remained in the field for the entire duration of the expedition.[79] Two retinues which *did* return to England during the winter caesura, however, were those led by Sir James Audley's deputy, Sir John Trumwyn, and Sir Walter Mauny.[80] The departure of the latter retinue leader from Aquitaine at the beginning of January in 1346 has surprisingly passed unnoticed by other historians.[81] It is also possible that some of Lancaster's own men who are known to have returned to England during the expedition might have departed from the duchy in the winter.[82]

At the conclusion of the first campaign, Henry of Lancaster must have considered the preceding events of the expedition to have been nothing short of a complete success. The significance of the twin victories at Bergerac and Auberoche should not be underestimated. The military success not only dented the French flower of chivalry in the southern theatre of war, but the infliction of a double defeat over superior forces gave a massive boost of morale to the Anglo-Gascon army. Indeed, the psychological impact of the successive victories against the French would have been even greater

According to Froissart, Thomas of Lancaster was 'a squire of his [Henry of Lancaster] own', and made captain of Montpouillan with 20 archers under his command. Jean Froissart, *Chronicles of England, France, Spain and the Adjoining Countries: from the Latter Part of the Reign of Edward II to the Coronation of Henry IV*, ed. and trans. Thomas Johnes, 2 vols (London: Bradbury and Evans, 1839), I (1839), p. 140.

[77] Fowler, *King's Lieutenant*, p. 65. For numerous instances of grants and confirmations of offices and other privileges, see C 61/59, mm. 7–10, 12; C 61/60, mm. 3, 5, 19, 29, 32, 34.

[78] Sumption, *Trial by Battle*, p. 476

[79] E 372/191, m. 54d. Although the heading of Pembroke's account states that his retinue set out to *Vasconie* in 1345 and 'returned from there' in the same year, the corresponding payment in the *vadia* section proves that his wages had been reckoned for 577 days from 23 May 1345 (1346 is recorded) to 20 December 1346. The incorrect regnal years recorded in both sections of the account are a clerical error.

[80] For an analysis of retinues which departed from Aquitaine over the course of the expedition, see subsection 'Changes in Army Composition' in Chapter 3.

[81] E 43/78; a bill of payment sealed by the constable of Bordeaux includes the cost of wages for Mauny's service from 8 June 1345 to 3 January 1346 and the cost for shipping his retinue and their horses back to England.

[82] This corpus of men is discussed in Chapter 8.

due to the short period in which they occurred. Furthermore, Auberoche represented the first decisive land battle in the kingdom of France since the beginning of the Hundred Years' War – and the English had drawn first blood, much of which, it should be added, was blue in colour.

The capture of a significant number of the French nobility and the rewards of war amassed after the battles must have also had a profound impact on the *mentalité* of soldiers and their attitudes to warfare, and particularly to campaigning overseas. At Bergerac, the booty gained from the defeated army and the town and the ransoms generated from the captives produced profits of war unprecedented for either side up to that point of the Anglo-French conflict. The 52,000 marks (equivalent to £34,667) that Lancaster reportedly amassed in profits were spent on building his Savoy palace in London.[83] The amount accrued by ransoms following the 'extraordinary victory' (*mirabilis victoria*) at Auberoche is reported to have been £50,000.[84] The military engagements, therefore, would have revealed for the first time the huge potential for financial reward from military success during the French war. It is likely that such rewards would have benefited the ordinary man-at-arms, as well as the rank and file infantry who must have found ample opportunity to pillage during the havoc which ensued the capture of towns and castles over the course of the expedition. At Bergerac, in particular, foot soldiers probably profited greatly considering it was a large commercial centre of some importance and as Thomas Walsingham explains, albeit with a degree of exaggeration, 'when a town was sacked, he [Lancaster] took little or nothing for himself'.[85] It was perhaps the profits and glory of war earned during this first campaign which renewed soldiers' enthusiasm for warfare, and may have caused some of Lancaster's own knights to return home after the initial success in the duchy in order to find service in other theatres of war, namely Edward III's great expedition to Normandy.

---

[83] Knighton, *Chronicle*, p. 188.

[84] Villani, *Cronica*, p. 384. Froissart gives a total of 300,000 écus, equivalent to £60,000 according to the current English exchange rate in 1345: Rogers, *Bergerac Campaign*, p. 90, n. 7.

[85] Thomas Walsingham, *Historia Anglicana*, ed. Henry Thomas Riley, 2 vols (London: Longman, Green, Longman, Roberts, and Green, 1863–64), I, p. 265.

6

Siege and Conquest by Sword: The Second Campaign, 1346

The Siege of Aiguillon

At the beginning of 1346, the French army in Aquitaine and the surrounding regions was in disarray following the English acquisition of territory, and by March its possessions were restricted to a few major strongholds.[1] In response to Lancaster's military success and territorial gains the French raised an army of an unprecedented size for the southern theatre of war. The army that Philippe VI provided for his son, Jean, duke of Normandy, was the result of a period of intense military recruitment financed by papal loans and taxation of the communities in the south. Soldiers were recruited from various regions in France and crossbowmen were hired from Aragon and Genoa.[2] It is difficult to determine the size or composition of the entire French army; from among the vast range of numbers given by the chroniclers, it seems reasonable to estimate that the army numbered somewhere between the 10,000 given by Robert Avesbury and the 30,000 recorded in the *Récits d'un bourgeois de Valenciennes*.[3] This huge force was led by no fewer than twenty-one counts and another thirty-one noblemen.[4]

The main army under Normandy's command comprised an array of northern lords, including Pierre, duke of Bourbon, Eudes IV, duke of Burgundy, and Gautier of Brienne, duke of Athens, as well as Jean, count

[1] The French strongholds on the Garonne included Port-Sainte-Marie, Agen and Moissac.

[2] On the finance and recruitment of the French forces, see Sumption, *Trial by Battle*, pp. 480–4.

[3] Avesbury, *Edwardi tertii* , p. 357; *Récits*, p. 196. Geoffrey Baker notes that the duke of Normandy and other lords came 'with a great many young knights' (*cum magna multitudine iuvenum militum*); Geoffrey Baker, *Chronicon Galfridi le Baker de Swynebroke, 1303–56*, ed. Edward Maunde Thompson (Oxford: Clarendon Press, 1889), p. 78. The estimates of 80,000 men-at-arms and 100,000 men given in the *Chronographia* and by Froissart are a gross exaggeration: *Chronographia*, p. 218; *Oeuvres*, IV, p. 356.

[4] For a nominal list of the nobility who served in the French army, see Murimuth, *Continuatio*, p. 250.

of Boulogne, Bouchard, count of Vendôme and Charles, count of Joigny.[5] They were augmented by the military officers of the royal household: Raoul II, constable of France and count of Eu, and both marshals and the master of the Royal Archers.[6] A second army assembled at Toulouse at the instance of Jean de Marigny, bishop of Beauvais, which included nobility drawn from the southern seneschalcies, such as Jean, count of Armagnac, Pierre-Ramond, count of Comminges, and Gaston Fébus, count of Foix.[7] The French force which mustered in the south brought with it a train of siege equipment, including five cannons;[8] considering the weight and size of such equipment it made logistical sense for it to be brought by the southern army which was located closer to the intended theatre of war than its northern counterpart.

The largest force, which was under Normandy, departed from Châtillon-sur-Indre in the centre of France at the beginning of February and moved south to Cahors, where the army was arrayed and organised into battle formations around mid-March.[9] It was probably during this southward march that some of the places which had been retaken by the English during the winter months were quickly overwhelmed by the French forces. Froissart relates how most of the defenders at Miramont and Villefranche were killed. The latter stronghold, however, soon returned into English hands because four of the most trusted knights of Lancaster's retinue, Sir Stephen de Gumby, Sir Ralph de Hastings, Sir Richard de Hebden and Sir Norman de Swinford, were able to retake the town after it had been left 'unprotected' (*sans garde et sans abatre*).[10] The cunning of Sir John de Norwich is also portrayed by the chronicler who recounts the negotiation for a one-day truce between the English captain and Normandy at the castle gates of Angoulême, which secured the safe departure of Norwich and his companions.[11]

From Cahors Duke Jean headed to Agen and then travelled up the east bank of the Garonne to Port-Sainte-Marie, before approaching Aiguillon

---

[5] *Saint-Omer*, fol. 211v.

[6] The *Saint-Omer* chronicler's claim that the count of Eu and the bishop of Beauvais were jointly responsible for assembling the 'barons of Languedoc' is probably erroneous. An extant pay record shows that Eu maintained a large retinue of men-at-arms under the command of the duke of Normandy in 1346 from 2 February to 10 July: BnF, MS français 32510, fols 185–7.

[7] The counts are named in *Saint-Omer*, fol. 211v.

[8] Sumption, *Trial by Battle*, p. 484.

[9] *Saint-Omer*, fol. 212. The duke of Normandy's letters are dated at Châtillon-sur-Indre on 1 February 1346, and at Cahors on 13 March 1346: AN, JJ 76, no. 398; Fowler, *King's Lieutenant*, p. 264, n. 48.

[10] *Oeuvres*, IV, pp. 335, 336–40. Bel, *Chronique*, II, pp. 48–9.

[11] *Oeuvres*, IV, pp. 348–55. Froissart claims that Norwich departed from Angoulême on Candlemas day (2 February), but the duke of Normandy had only recently left Châtillon-sur-Indre by this date.

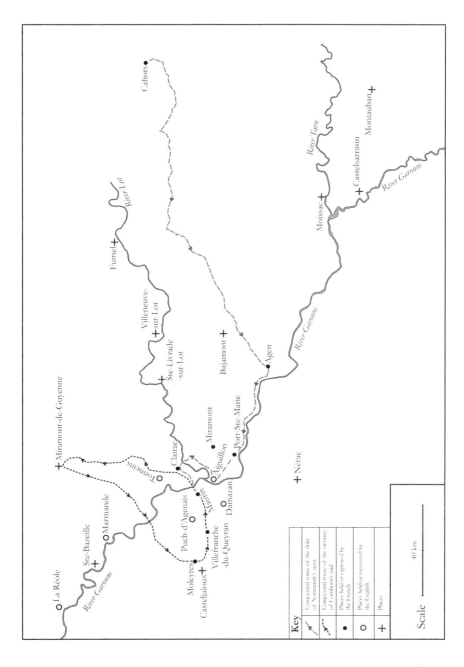

Map 5. The Siege of
Aiguillon, 1346

Places shown on map:

Cahors

River Tarn

Castelsarrasin
Montauban

River Lot

Moissac

Fumel

River Garonne

Villeneuve-
-sur-Lot

Ste-Livrade
-sur-Lot

Bajamont

Agen

Miramont-de-Guyenne

Miramont

Port-Ste-Marie

Clairac

Tonneins

Aiguillon

Nérac

Marmande

Ste-Bazeille

River Garonne

Nicole

Damazan

Puch-d'Agenais

Moleyres

Villefranche
-du-Queyran

Casteljaloux

La Réole

River Garonne

from the south.[12] Meanwhile, the bishop of Beauvais led the van of the French army – comprising the comparatively smaller force raised in the south – before the walls of Aiguillon, and encamped before the town on the western bank of the Garonne around mid-Lent Sunday (26 March 1346).[13] The principal aim of Normandy's expedition was the recapture of La Réole, but control of Aiguillon was a vital prerequisite to fulfilling this objective due to its strategic position on the confluence of the rivers Garonne and Lot. The duke, therefore, laid siege to Aiguillon which lasted throughout the entire summer of 1346.

The defence of the town was organised by some of the leading captains of the English army serving under the overall command of Ralph, Lord Stafford, Walter Mauny, the earl of Pembroke, and the Gascon lord, Alixandre de Caumont.[14] In addition to these well-known retinue captains was a Derbyshire knight named Hugh Meynell.[15] This seasoned war veteran was a banneret in Lancaster's retinue and was clearly a soldier of some repute.[16] The town consisted of two *faubourgs* (Lunac and Le Fossat) that were surrounded by a rectangular perimeter wall. The latter was a recent construction, but in 1346 it remained unfinished and, according to Henry Knighton, gaps in the wall had to be filled with wine casks packed with stones.[17] Further defensive preparations were carried out by Meynell who demolished a nearby monastery in order to utilise its stone, and the town was 'enclosed with a good palisade and deep ditches'.[18] Aiguillon was located on a corner of land that jutted out between the Garonne and the Lot; thus

---

[12] The duke of Normandy's letters are dated at Agen on 5, 7 and 10 April 1346: Fowler, *King's Lieutenant*, p. 264, n. 48. The *Saint-Omer* chronicle reports that the duke pitched his tents at Port-Sainte-Marie before arriving at Aiguillon, which is situated roughly 10 kilometres downstream from the port. *Saint-Omer*, fol. 212.

[13] *Saint-Omer*, fol. 211v.

[14] E 404/503/139; a payment of wages to Stafford made on 1 November 1346 for his retinue's half a year of service in the town of 'Aculeo', confirms that he was at Aiguillon from 1 May to 1 November 1346. The *Saint-Omer* chronicle describes how Lancaster 'set a very good garrison inside [Aiguillon], namely the lord of Stafford, the lord of Buscare [possibly the Captal de Buch], Sir Bérart d'Albret, Sir Alixandre de Caumont, Sir Walter Mauny and many other valiant men': *Saint-Omer*, fol. 211.

[15] Fowler, *King's Lieutenant*, p. 184; Sumption, *Trial by Battle*, p. 486. Martin Bertrandy-Lacabane, *Étude sur les Chroniques de Froissart: Guerre de Guienne, 1345–1346* (Bordeaux : Impr. centrale A. de Lanefranque, 1870), pp. 151, 354.

[16] See discussion of Meynell in Chapter 7.

[17] Knighton, *Chronicle*, pp. 65–7. At parts of the unprotected wall Stafford 'made a barricade … of wine-barrels, drained and filled with stones'.

[18] Meynell demolished a Carmelite monastery on the edge of the town causing damage estimated at 2234 *livres tournois*: Bertrandy, *Chroniques de Froissart*, p. 355, n. 1. The palisade and ditches described in the *Saint-Omer* chronicle relates to the defence efforts of the English following the town's initial capture in 1345, but it seems more likely that these preparations were undertaken later in the spring of 1346: *Saint-Omer*, fol. 211.

two sides were protected by water and the northern side was only accessible by a fortified bridge which ended with a barbican on the northern bank of the Lot.[19] It took some time for the French to occupy the ground beyond both of the rivers and because they struggled to maintain a closed siege, it was possible for the English to gain access to the besieged town. In this way Sir Thomas Cok and three other knights from Lancaster's retinue – Sir Frank van Halen, Sir Robert de Neville and Sir Richard de Rawcliffe – entered Aiguillon during the early stages of the siege accompanied by 40 *chevaliers*, 140 esquires and 500 archers. If Froissart's report that the town's garrison consisted of 120 'good companions' (*bons compaignons*) is accurate, and the additional reinforcements led by Cok are taken into account, we can infer that the Anglo-Gascons had a total defence force of 300 men-at-arms and 500 archers.[20]

An initial assault on the town with twelve large engines that cast stones 'by day and by night into the castle' (*nuit et jour tout dedens le castiel*), was countered by catapults which the defenders had constructed themselves.[21] The besiegers also faced a constant threat of attack from the English who had strong garrisons at Damazan to the west of Aiguillon, and at Tonneins to the north. To combat this problem the duke of Normandy attempted to bridge the Garonne, thus moving his main army onto the ground west of the confluence of the rivers and within closer proximity to Damazan. The *Saint-Omer Chronicle* reports that the duke ordered plenty of timber and carpenters to be brought, but the French attempts to build a wooden bridge over the Garonne were met by frequent sorties led by the defenders of Aiguillon.[22] In spite of the protection afforded by a large escort of Genoese crossbowmen, the bridge was broken up twice as the English launched daily assaults, first on land and then from boats on the river. The feat of engineering could not be achieved due to the beleaguered position of the carpenters, and after several weeks Duke Jean decided to move his army to the north of Aiguillon where the barbican gate of the town stood.[23] He

---

[19] Jacques Gardelles, *Les châteaux du Moyen Age dans la France du Sud-Ouest: La Gascogne anglaise de 1216 à 1327* (Genève: Droz, 1972), pp. 83–4. For a map of the defences of Aiguillon, see Sumption, *Trial by Battle*, p. 486.

[20] Other knights among the reinforcements named by Froissart include Sir John Touchet, Sir Richard de Beauvais, Sir Philip Radcliff and Sir Thomas Bisset. *Oeuvres*, IV, p. 337. Jean le Bel suggests a slightly larger garrison of 300 men-at-arms and 600 archers: Bel, *Chronique*, II, p. 62.

[21] *Oeuvres*, IV, p. 358.

[22] *Saint-Omer*, fol. 212: 'sailors and carpenters came in great abundance' (*Marien et carpentiers fist venir a grant fuison*).

[23] Contrary to the account in the *Saint-Omer Chronicle*, Sumption asserts that the French completed the bridge by the end of May and were able to stretch a chain across the Garonne to stop supplies and reinforcements entering the town from the west: Sumption, *Trial by Battle*, 486.

crossed the river Lot by a bridge at Clairac, which is situated less than 10 kilometres north-east of Aiguillon, and remained there for several days.[24] Shortly before 18 June the duke moved from Clairac and pitched his tents on the east bank of the Garonne between Tonneins and Aiguillon, while the bishop of Beauvais, the prior of Aquitaine (Jean de Nanteuil, the Hospitaller *grand prieur d'Aquitaine*) and the master of crossbowmen encamped on the opposite side of the river.[25]

The duke of Bourbon and the count of Armagnac were assigned to secure the mountain situated between Aiguillon and Tonneins, from which the English caused 'much trouble' (*moult de destourbier*) for their enemy.[26] The French, however, were harassed day and night by the garrison at Tonneins, to the point that the French were unable to enclose the castle and prevent the English from entering or leaving 'at their pleasure' (*a leur plaisir*).[27] Further assaults were made on the castle but even with the support of Normandy's *engiens* the assailants had little success.

The French siege engines also had little effect on the walls of Aiguillon and attacks from the opposing sides became a daily occurrence.[28] The most notable fighting, however, took place on 15 June when the English successfully captured two large barges containing provisions brought up from Toulouse.[29] We cannot be certain whether this audacious attack was carried out in response to a skirmish between men-at-arms from Tonneins and a Genoese patrol, or was part of a planned offensive by the garrison at Aiguillon to capture the barges laden with supplies.[30] Whatever the cause, Alixandre de Caumont charged out of Aiguillon and across the Lot bridge

---

[24] *Saint-Omer*, fol. 212.

[25] *Saint-Omer*, fol. 212. After 18 June 1346 the duke of Normandy's letters are dated 'in our tents between Tonneins and Aiguillon' (*en noz tentes ent Tonnis' et Aguillon*): AN, JJ 68, no. 286.

[26] *Saint-Omer*, fol. 212: 'from this mountain the English could cause much trouble for the enemy' (*de la quele montaigne li engles pooient faire moult de destourbier al ost*).

[27] *Saint-Omer*, fol. 212.

[28] *Oeuvres*, IV, p. 359.

[29] Sumption, *Trial by Battle*, p. 488. There is no mention of any barges transporting goods from Toulouse in the *Saint-Omer* chronicle, although it does give a detailed account of the intense fighting on the bridge at Aiguillon on the feast of Corpus Christi (15 June 1346). *Saint-Omer*, fol. 212.

[30] There is no consensus on the cause of the attack. Sumption claims it was a planned coordinated assault with the aim of capturing the French supplies: Sumption, *Trial by Battle*, p. 488. The *Saint-Omer* chronicle, however, describes how the garrison at Aiguillon were impelled to attack the French upon hearing the news of an early morning skirmish between part of the garrison at Tonneins and a Genoese patrol, which escalated into a larger engagement and left eleven knights from Tonneins dead. *Saint-Omer*, fol. 212v. Froissart does not mention any attempt by the Anglo-Gascon forces to capture French cargo, but he does describe the French use of barges during the battle of the bridge of Aiguillon: *Oeuvres*, IV, p. 359.

with 100 men-at-arms in an attempt to break through the enemy lines on the opposite bank. The French proved resolute and forced the Anglo-Gascons to retreat onto the bridge; a long and bloody hand-to-hand fight 'with sword and dagger' (*d'espees et de couteaus*) ensued, as the portcullis at the main gate was dropped and men became trapped on the bridge.[31] Meanwhile, a second sortie party launched an amphibious assault from boats, and captured the barges before bringing them into the castle.[32] The fighting continued until nightfall, by which time the barbican gate and Alixandre de Caumont had been captured. All the boats of the castle, which had been utilised to great effect against the French since the siege began, were reportedly burnt by the Genoese and both sides suffered heavy losses. It was the English garrison, however, that sustained the greatest casualties, and despite the speedy delivery of Caumont from his captors following a hefty ransom payment, the besiegers no doubt received an important boost of morale for their military endeavours.[33]

On realising that Aiguillon would not capitulate without a protracted siege, the duke of Normandy detached military contingents from his main army, and sought to capture strongholds in the surrounding territory and regain control of areas which had fallen into English hands. A 'Monsieur Muchart de Conbon' (probably the viscount of Comborn) led a large party of men-at-arms north to the castle of Miramont, where he negotiated a surrender with the castellan.[34] From there Comborn headed south-west to Moleyres before travelling 10 kilometres east to Villefranche, both of which surrendered in a similar fashion.[35] Upon his return to Aiguillon, Comborn's men came to the town of Maurin which lies a short distance north of Damazan.[36] The garrison at Maurin, however, did not surrender as other places taken over the course of the expedition had done, and so it was

---

[31] *Saint-Omer*, fol. 212v. *Oeuvres*, IV, p. 359–60. Froissart recounts that the bridge of the town was taken during the assault, but the French were unable to capture the main gate and it cost them a great number of lives, 'more than it was worth' (*plus qu'il ne vaulsist*).

[32] Sumption, *Trial by Battle*, p. 488.

[33] Most of the huge ransom of Caumont was funded by Henry of Lancaster: Bertrandy, *Chroniques de Froissart*, pp. 326–7.

[34] *Saint-Omer*, fols 212v–213. The *Saint-Omer* chronicle is the only narrative source to mention the chevauchée of Comborn. Miramont-de-Guyenne is 40 km directly north of Aiguillon. It is also possible that Comborn may have headed to Miramont in Lagarrigue, which is situated 5 km east of Aiguillon.

[35] Moleyres is approximately 45 km south-west of Miramont-de-Guyenne. Presumably, the *Saint-Omer* chronicler is referring to Villefranche-du-Queyran, although it is plausible that Comborn may have headed east and taken Villefranche-du-Périgord. Rogers proposes an alternative and longer route of Miramont-de-Guyenne, Moleyres in southern Périgord (55 km north-east), Villefranche-du-Périgord (45 km south) and Castelmoron (70 km south-west) taken by Comborn.

[36] Maurin is 5 km due north of Damazan.

immediately besieged by the French. The *Saint-Omer* chronicler describes how Comborn's men were deceived by Henry of Lancaster, who used 'a great dirty trick' (*un grand malice*).[37] Purportedly the 'pages' of Lancaster's army were mounted at dawn on a nearby hillside overlooking the town, arrayed in the arms and banners of his knights.[38] In the early morning sun, the French perceived the English banners as part of a substantial relief force which caused confusion and panic in the camp; everyone took flight and the men of Maurin sallied out to seize the pavilions and other plunder which had been left behind. Apart from the setback at Maurin, the strategic military operations of Comborn had essentially created a protective curtain to the north and west of Aiguillon. The French benefited from his expedition in two ways: first, by expanding the area under their control, and thus opening lines for communication or supplies, and second, by reducing the risk of an English attack on the French forces camped on the west bank of the Garonne.

Around one month after the battle of the bridge at Aiguillon it was the turn of the French to suffer defeat, on this occasion outside the walls of Bajamont.[39] The latter was a stronghold from which the English ally, Archdeacon Galhart de Durfort, lord of Duras, had launched numerous attacks on the provincial capital of Agen. To combat this threat and to nullify Durfort's attacks on the short stretch of the river Garonne between Moissac and Aiguillon, which was a principal supply route for the besieging army, the seneschal of Agenais, Robert de Houdetot, had deployed several hundred men to besiege Bajamont, but with little success. On 18 July the duke of Normandy detached a substantial force of at least 2000 men to support the seneschal, who was ordered to enclose the castle with defensive earthworks and pursue the time-consuming strategy of starving the town into submission. Such measures were theoretical, however, as before they had begun the garrison of Bajamont attacked and inflicted a humiliating defeat upon the French forces, in which Houdetot himself was captured.[40] This marked the last significant engagement of the duke's army during the siege.

The prospect of a successful outcome for the duke of Normandy rapidly diminished as the siege continued well into the summer of 1346, and the low morale in the French camp was exacerbated by the problems of dysentery and food shortages. The misfortunes of war had reached all ranks of the army, as evidenced by the death of Philippe, son of the duke of Burgundy,

---

[37] *Saint-Omer*, fol. 212.

[38] Rogers suggests that the English 'pages' had come from Damazan, and were mounted on a hillside near Puch d'Agenais, separated from Maurin by 3 km of low ground. 'Pages' were men-at-arms of a similar rank to an esquire.

[39] Bajamont is situated approximately 40 km east of Aiguillon.

[40] Sumption, *Trial by Battle*, p. 513.

who was fatally injured in a riding accident after his horse fell on him in a ditch.[41] In spite of the lack of progress at Aiguillon, the 'young and high-spirited' Duke Jean, as described by Knighton, had sworn an oath not to raise the siege until the town had fallen, but it was an oath he could not fulfil.[42] His decision to invest the majority of his manpower at Aiguillon for such a protracted period, rather than to leave a smaller besieging force there while prosecuting the campaign elsewhere, highlights the shortcomings of the duke of Normandy. Indeed, Froissart portrays him as an inept commander who had no reserve plan of attack after the French failed to breach the town's defences during an assault of the northern citadel.[43] The topography of the region immediately surrounding Aiguillon afforded the town a natural defence, and the presence of English garrisons within the vicinity of the town made its capture more difficult. However, it was the fact that the French were never able to fully enclose the town and establish a closed siege which proved insurmountable for Normandy. For the duke, it seems that the capture of Aiguillon had become an obsession beyond its strategic purpose to fulfil the principal objective of his mission, which was the capture of La Réole, and other strategically important strongholds in Aquitaine.

At the beginning of the siege of Aiguillon Henry of Lancaster was probably in Bordeaux, but he had returned to La Réole by 1 May where he remained for the most part of the siege.[44] From here he directed the defence and running of supplies to the besieged town, and was able to keep in check the movements of any French forces that were held up in castles or itinerant in the duchy. On 12 August the earl set out to Bergerac where he held a council of war, and curtly refused an offer of truce made by Duke Jean, knowing that his cousin, the king of England, had already landed at Saint-Vaast-la-Hougue on the Cotentin peninsula in Normandy.[45] Edward III's original plan to attack the French on three fronts during the previous

---

[41] Philippe, who was also count of Boulogne and Auvergne, is reported to have died a few days after the accident. *Oeuvres*, V, p. 89; *Saint-Omer*, fol. 213.

[42] Knighton, *Chronicle*, pp. 66–7; 'iuuenis et elatus erat'.

[43] Froissart, *Chronicles of England*, I, p. 150; Duke Jean 'was at a loss what plan to follow … for he had vowed he would never quit the place [Aiguillon] until he was master of it and the garrison, unless the king, his father ordered otherwise'.

[44] Fowler, *King's Lieutenant*, p. 66. The notes of warrant of Lancaster's correspondence are dated at Bordeaux on 2 and 22 April 1346: C 61/59, mm. 6, 7; C 61/60, m. 41. Other letters are dated at La Réole on 1 and 16 May 1346; E 43/741; C 47/24/7, no. 3. They are also dated at La Réole in the following months from June to August: E 404/508/47 (23 June); C 61/59, m. 10 (3 July); C 61/57, m. 5 (26 July); C 61/60, m. 25, *CPR, 1348–50*, p. 24 (7 August 1346).

[45] In a dispatch Lancaster claims that he already knew of Edward's landing in Normandy when the offer of peace was made: Avesbury, *Edwardi tertii*, pp. 372–4; also translated in Rogers, *The Wars of Edward III*, pp. 135–7.

year had now come to fruition as the English armies that were operating in Aquitaine and Brittany were joined by a large army in the north of France.[46] On Philippe VI's orders, but with great reluctance, the duke of Normandy raised the siege on 20 August and hastened to the north with his army in the hope of aiding his father against Edward III.[47] In a personal dispatch Lancaster describes how his enemies 'departed there very dishonourably' as some of the men from Aiguillon successfully captured a large portion of the duke's baggage train, including his chapel and jewels.[48] The French withdrawal was disorganised and frantic to the point that troops became jammed in the bottle-neck on the bridge at Clairac, where many soldiers drowned. Subsequently, the army doubled back and retreated in the direction of Tonneins, before crossing the Garonne and heading south to Agen.[49] From there the duke's army began the long march northwards to Ponthieu.

To Poitiers and Back

In the wake of the duke of Normandy's departure Lancaster immediately led a short chevauchée from Bergerac into Agenais where he reported taking 'a good town of the [French] king' called Villeréal, and other strongholds in the vicinity. He then moved quickly to secure Tonneins and Aiguillon by strengthening the towns' defences and garrisons, before returning to La Réole where he remained for more than a week. Another war council was held upon Lancaster's return, whereby the decision was made to divide

[46] Edward's army in the north was supplemented by the small contingent commanded by Hugh Hastings, which landed in Flanders around 21 July 1346: Sumption, *Trial by Battle*, p. 503.

[47] AL, Livre velu, fol. 133r. Guinodie, *Libourne*, I, p. 52. Jean le Bel claims that the duke argued with his military advisers over the matter of raising the siege honourably: Bel, *Chronique*, II, pp. 63–4. The *Saint-Omer* chronicler and Froissart both state that Normandy raised the siege on his father's orders after the French defeat at Crécy, but the battle did not take place until 26 August, six days after the siege was raised. *Saint-Omer*, fol. 220v; *Oeuvres*, V, pp. 97–8.

[48] Avesbury, *Edwardi tertii*, p. 374. *Saint-Omer*, fol. 221. Baker describes how after 'having burnt his tents and pavilions, [the duke] began a concealed flight in the darkness of the night'. These acts would certainly have been considered dishonourable by Lancaster, but the earl makes no mention of a night time retreat by the duke of Normandy. Baker claims that Stafford and the lord of Albret's son, presumably Arnaut-Amanieu, cut off the rear of the French army and were 'enriched by the tents they were able to save from the fire', as well as the capture of horses and prisoners. Geoffrey Baker, *The Chronicle of Geoffrey le Baker of Swinbrook*, trans. by David Preest with introduction and notes by Richard Barber (Woodbridge: Boydell, 2012), p. 69. Knighton also reports that the English 'killed many [French] as they ran' and captured horses, supplies, tents and other valuables: Knighton, *Chronicle*, pp. 66–7.

[49] *Saint-Omer*, fols 220v–21.

the Anglo-Gascon forces into three field armies, probably with the aim of bringing those places in Agenais and Bazadais that had eluded earlier campaigns securely under English control.[50] Two of the armies were led by Gascons; the Albret brothers and Alixandre de Caumont led one force into Bazadais, while Galhart de Durfort and other lords from Agenais operated around the Garonne valley. The earl of Lancaster commanded a third army of 1000 men-at-arms and an unknown number of infantry, which embarked on a seven-week raid into Saintonge and Poitou.[51]

Lancaster's principal objectives were to recover parts of Saintonge, and to undermine the authority of Philippe VI in the south-west through the conquest of towns further north which had a tradition of loyalty to the French king. A raid into the northern provinces was an obvious but calculated choice for the earl, knowing that many places in the region lacked either strong defences or garrisons. More significantly, perhaps, he knew that the political impact of such an enterprise would be more profound following the recent capture of the count of Eu at Caen, whose principal lands were in Saintonge.[52]

On 12 September Lancaster left La Réole and headed on the northern road to Sauveterre, which duly surrendered to him on the same day. After having spent the night at Sauveterre the earl took homage of the town's inhabitants and continued north, covering 140 kilometres in eight days, crossing the Dordogne, Isle and Dronne rivers but avoiding any towns or castles along the way, until he reached Châteauneuf-sur-Charente. In an attempt to slow the advance of the Anglo-Gascons, the French had broken the bridge north of the town, but with no other suitable river crossings nearby, it was quickly repaired. On 21 September Lancaster crossed the Charente, but deviated from his course upon learning of the plight of Sir Walter Mauny, who had been imprisoned at Saint-Jean-d'Angély despite

---

[50] Principal places still under French control at this time included, amongst others, Agen, Bazas, Marmande and Port-Sainte-Marie.

[51] Avesbury, *Edwardi tertii*, pp. 372–4. This group of men-at-arms probably consisted largely of Gascons, and included the retinues of Lancaster, Pembroke and Stafford. In his dispatch, Lancaster only mentions men-at-arms, but infantry forces were left to garrison some of the towns that would be taken in the forthcoming raid. Mounted archers belonging to the English retinues would also have taken part in the campaign.

[52] Eu had been recalled from the siege of Aiguillon early in the summer and was amongst the defenders of Caen during Edward III's invasion of Normandy. He was captured on 26 July 1346 when the town was sacked by the English and, as Graham St John points out, an attack on the count's lands by Lancaster would have created further pressure which Edward could exert on his most important prisoner. Graham E. St John, 'War, the Church and English Men-at-Arms', in *Fourteenth Century England, VI*, ed. Chris Given-Wilson (Woodbridge: Boydell, 2012), pp. 73–93 (pp. 89–90).

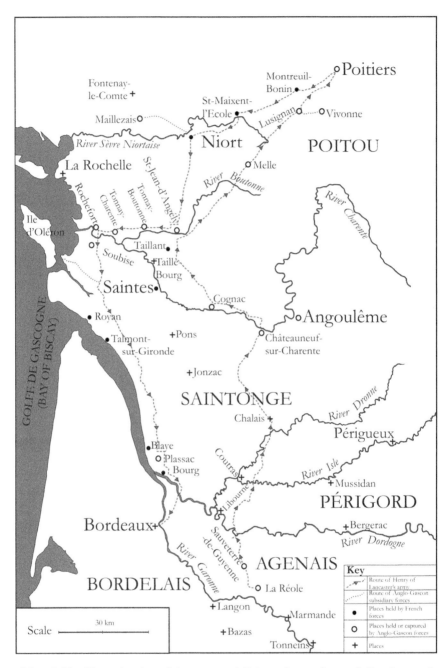

Map 6. The Campaign into Saintonge and Poitou, September and October 1346

having been previously granted a safe-conduct from the duke of Normandy to join Edward III's army in northern France.[53]

The men of that town clearly did not hold to the same chivalric values as Duke Jean, or at least, were not prepared to accept the validity of the document, but the famous Hainaulter managed to escape with three of his companions nonetheless. The remaining prisoners of Mauny's retinue were released (and presumably joined the earl's army) upon the capture of the town.[54] Lancaster himself reports that he took Saint-Jean-d'Angély by force, and that its inhabitants 'became English' after paying him homage and agreeing to strict terms, whereby they were to maintain a garrison of 200 men-at-arms and 600 infantry for the duration of the war.[55] Many of the townsmen were taken prisoner and ransomed, others were stripped of their lands and vineyards.[56] Among the dispossessed were Master Andriu Moirusson and Jean Serchemont; their property was granted to two of the earl's esquires, William Nichol and Henry Rose, respectively, on condition that the latter served as captains in the town's garrison.[57] The invading force remained for eight days, during which time all the religious houses were looted and stripped bare, including the Benedictine abbey whose famous relic of St John the Baptist's head made it an important stopping point for pilgrims on the road to Compostella.[58] The scale of such sacrilege caused Pope Clement VI to write to Lancaster in the following month, ordering him to return to the abbey all of the 'things, privileges, perpetual letters, books, chalices, crosses, relics … and all ornaments and apparel' stolen by

[53] Mauny obtained a pass of safe-conduct in exchange for the release of one of the duke of Normandy's relatives, who had been captured in a skirmish during the siege of Aiguillon. Mauny only proceeded north as far as Saint-Jean-d'Angély before he was ambushed and incarcerated in the town: *Oeuvres*, V, pp. 97–108; Sumption, *Trial by Battle*, p. 542.

[54] Mauny's retinue consisted of 20 men-at-arms: *Oeuvres*, V, p. 97. Saint-Jean-d'Angély surrendered on around 24 September.

[55] Avesbury, *Edwardi tertii*, pp. 372–4. In times of peace the town's inhabitants agreed to pay an annual rent 4000 écus higher than that paid to the French Crown. The *Saint-Omer* chronicle reports that the wisest men of Saint-Jean-d'Angély negotiated a surrender with Lancaster, which may have been the case following an initial assault on the town. *Saint-Omer*, fols 221–221v.

[56] On 3 October 1347 Lancaster was granted the 'lands, vineyards and other goods' of the prisoners of the town, who had entered into French obedience after swearing an oath of allegiance to the earl. *CPR, 1345–48*, p. 562.

[57] C 61/60, mm. 7, 19, 20.

[58] Avesbury, *Edwardi tertii*, pp. 372–4. Other religious houses in the town included Dominican and Franciscan friaries, and three churches: St John, *English Men-at-Arms*, p. 90; 'Registres de l'échevinage de Saint-Jean-d'Angély, 1332–1496', ed. Denys d'Aussy, in *Les Archives historiques de la Saintonge et de l'Aunis*, 50 vols (Paris: [n. pub.], 1874–1967), XXIV (1895), pp. 134–6. For a plan of Saint-Jean-d'Angély see p. xxv.

his men.[59] Such atonement, however, was not forthcoming. It was probably around the time of the of the earl's sojourn at the town that a detachment of the army, or perhaps part of the recently installed garrison, laid siege to the nearby town of Taillant. The assailants, however, were unsuccessful owing to the strength of the town's defences.[60]

On 30 September Lancaster took the road to Poitiers, and after marching at high speed for three days, reached the small town of Lusignan.[61] The townsmen capitulated after a perfunctory resistance, and the castle, which the earl considered to be 'one of the noblest and strongest … in all of France or Gascony', was surrendered to him on 3 October.[62] It had probably not been Lancaster's intention to spend time or resources on besieging such a formidable place, which had become the principal refuge for the inhabitants of the region.[63] Indeed, one chronicler describes how the earl was 'quite astonished' when he was greeted by two knights who presented him with its keys.[64] In a similar measure taken to protect the town captured previously, a garrison of 100 men-at-arms and a number of infantry remained at Lusignan under the command of Bertran, lord of Montferrand.[65]

On the following day Lancaster's troops arrived at Poitiers – the principal destination of their northern raid. After the leaders of the city refused to surrender, an assault was made and by Lancaster's own admission, 'all those in the city were taken or slain'.[66] The bishop and four of the barons responsible for the keeping of the city fled during the violence and destruction

---

[59] *Calendar of Entries in the Papal Registers Relating to Great Britain and Ireland: Papal Letters*, ed. W. H. Bliss and C. Johnson, 18 vols (London: HMSO, 1893–1989), III (1897), p. 29. *Clément VI (1342–1352): Lettres closes, patentes et curiales: publiées ou analysées d'après les registres du Vatican*, ed. E. Dèprez, J. Glénisson and G. Mollat, 3 vols (Paris: E. de Boccard, 1925–59), II (1958), no. 2901, p. 261.

[60] *Saint-Omer*, fol. 221v. Taillant is situated 10 km from Saint-Jean-d'Angély in the opposite direction to Poitiers, and is of no strategic significance.

[61] It was probably on the road to Lusignan, which lies approximately 80 km north-east of Saint-Jean-d'Angély, that the towns of Melle and Vivonne voluntarily surrendered to the English. Lancaster arrived at Lusignan on 2 October, and assaulted the town on the following day: Avesbury, *Edwardi tertii*, pp. 372–4.

[62] Avesbury, *Edwardi tertii*, pp. 372–4. Knighton notes that Lusignan was 'reputed the strongest castle in France', while the *Saint-Omer* chronicler claims it was 'so strong and noble, and of such great fame'. Knighton, *Chronicle*, pp. 74–5; *Saint-Omer*, fol. 221v.

[63] The castle was reportedly 'very well stocked with supplies', and 'a great many local knights had come, along with their wives and their children': *Saint-Omer*, fols 221v–222.

[64] *Saint-Omer*, fols 221v–222.

[65] C 61/60, m. 36. Avesbury, *Edwardi tertii*, pp. 372–4. *Chronique de Maillezias*, pp. 166–7. The *Saint-Omer* chronicle claims that the garrison included archers and crossbowmen: *Saint-Omer*, fol. 222. Montferrand was among the Aquitanians who served in Lancaster's own retinue over the course of the entire expedition in Aquitaine from 1345 to 1346.

[66] Avesbury, *Edwardi tertii*, pp. 372–4. Poitiers was taken by storm on 4 October.

which ensued: carnage enveloped the streets and many areas were set on fire, including parts of the royal palace.[67] About 600 people died in the attack, many of whom were labourers or petty tradesmen, such as vintners and butchers, while those of any worth were put to ransom.[68] Poitiers suffered the same fate as Saint-Jean-d'Angély, although the booty and plunder seized by its captors was even greater. Lancaster remained in Poitou's capital for what seems like his usual eight-day period, during which time his men 'coursed through the town, robbing and destroying everything they found' (*par toute la ville coururent reubant et essillant quanques il trouverent*).[69] Knighton states how the troops killed at their will and 'carried off gold, and silver, and treasure of all manner of reckoning'.[70] The abbot of Charroux lost the monastery's entire treasury after he had brought it within the assumed safety of the city walls. Several years later the cathedral chapter lamented the loss of its 'ornaments, sacred vessels, copes, crucifixes, and everything comprised of gold or silver'.[71]

Lancaster had no intention to occupy Poitiers, and so no garrison was left in the town when he departed on around 12 October. It was the northern-most point of the raid, more than 250 kilometres distant from where it originally began, and the earl now started his return south by way of Montreuil-Bonin, Saint-Maixent and Niort. Unsuccessful assaults were made on all three castles, of which the first two were reportedly burned and the walls of Montreuil-Bonin were defended fiercely by 200 moneyers from the royal mint, many of whom lost their lives.[72] At some point along the way the town of Maillezais voluntarily surrendered to Lancaster at the decision of the bishop of the town, and by 19 October the earl was once again at Saint-Jean-d'Angély, where his dispatch was written.[73] Over the course of

[67] Heinrich Suso Denifle, *La Guerre de cent ans et la désolation des églises, monastères & hôpitaux en France*, 2 vols (Paris: A. Picard et fils, 1899), I, p. 30.

[68] Sumption, *Trial by Battle*, p. 545. 'Recueil des documents concernant la commune et la ville de Poitiers', ed. E. Adouin, II, 1328–80, in *Archives historiques du Poitou*, 61 vols (Poitiers: Société des Archives Historiques du Poitou, 1872–1982) XLVI (1928), pp. 116–17, n. 1.

[69] *Saint-Omer*, fol. 222. It is interesting that Lancaster remained at both Lusignan and Poitiers for eight days before departing the towns.

[70] Knighton, *Chronicle*, pp. 74–5.

[71] Denifle, *La Guerre de cent ans et la désolation des églises*, I, pp. 30–1. Some of the wealthier inhabitants of Poitiers allegedly moved their valuables to Châtelleraut and Chauvigny, situated north and east of the capital, but were recovered by the attackers.

[72] 'Fragments inédits d'une chronique de Maillezais', ed. Paul Marchegay, *Bibliothèque de l'École de Chartes* (1840–41), 148–68 (pp. 166–7); *Oeuvres*, V, pp. 112–14. Froissart claims Montreuil-Bonin was captured by Lancaster.

[73] Avesbury, *Edwardi tertii*, pp. 372–4. On details of the nature of the surrender of Maillezais and the subsequent trial of the bishop, see Sumption, *Trial by Battle*, 545–6; 'Recueil des documents concernant le Poitou contenus dans les registres de la chancellerie de France', ed. Paul Guérin, II, 1334–8, in *Archives historiques du Poitou*, in *Archives*

the second half of October the English were able to extend their control in Saintonge through the acquisition of several towns and castles to the west of Saint-Jean-d'Angély, including Tonnay-Boutonne, Tonnay-Charente and Soubise, as well as the harbour of Rochefort and the island of Oléron.[74] Lancaster's men probably returned south along the coast, thus avoiding any French troops which the earl suspected were operating in the region, and possibly took Cognac along the way. By 30 October he had reached Plassac, and on the following day he was in Bordeaux.[75]

The nature of the campaign in 1346 differed from the one conducted in the previous year. Fowler asserts that 'burning and bloodshed' had replaced the policy of 'negotiations and reward' as towns in the hostile territory north of upper Gascony had stronger allegiances to the French crown and were less likely, therefore, to defect through the bribery that had caused places in Gascony and the surrounding regions to join the English side.[76] The purpose of the raid had not been to establish English control in Poitou, but to expand English territory in Saintonge and capture places of strategic importance, whereby future attacks could be launched further north. In this sense the earl fulfilled his objective. From Lusignan, the English were able to harry the French over the following four years, during which time the lord of Montferrand and his two brothers terrorised the inhabitants of the surrounding region. They are reported to have desolated large parts of Poitou, and in the process destroyed no fewer than fifty-two parish churches and ten monasteries, including the Augustinian house of Fontenay-le-Comte.[77]

The success of the chevauchée was largely due to the speed with which it was conducted; the entire operation was accomplished in seven weeks. Lancaster, therefore, was able to capitalise on the weak defences of towns whose inhabitants were ill-prepared for an attack, and before any substantial force could oppose him. It is no coincidence that those places which had recently repaired their towns' walls were the very places which avoided capture by the Anglo-Gascons.[78] Indeed, the only substantial force in the duchy at the time was operating in Agenais under the lieutenancy of the

---

historiques du Poitou, 61 vols (Poitiers: Société des Archives Historiques du Poitou, 1872–1982), XIII (1883), pp. xxx–xxxvi. The dilemma faced by the inhabitants of Maillezais would have been shared by many towns in the region.

[74] Knighton, *Chronicle*, pp. 74–5. Soubise and Tonnay-Charente surrendered to Lancaster, and Taillebourg may also have surrendered around this time: Fowler, *King's Lieutenant*, pp. 68–9.

[75] Fowler, *King's Lieutenant*, p. 68. We cannot be certain whether Lancaster returned to Bordeaux directly from Saint-Jean-d'Angély, or from Rochefort down the west of Saintonge.

[76] Fowler, *King's Lieutenant*, pp. 64–5.

[77] Denifle, *La Guerre de cent ans et la désolation des églises*, I, p. 31; *Chronique de Maillezais*, p. 167.

[78] In September 1346 the seneschal of Poitou was instructed by Philippe VI to repair

count of Armagnac.[79] The acquisition of new territory in Saintonge brought with it the profits of war as well as new responsibilities. In this way Sir Frank van Halen was granted the castle of Rochefort, which guarded the entry to the river Charente. The famous Brabantine, like Montferrand, was also rewarded by a grant of privileges during his castellany.[80] Other towns, such as Saint-Jean-d'Angély and Tonnay-Charente, were placed in the custody of loyal Gascons.[81] The spoils amassed over the course of the campaign were enormous and, according to Froissart, when the earl returned to Bordeaux his troops were 'altogether rich and burdened with good things' (*tout rice et trousé de bonnes coses*).[82] The French still had possession of several key places in Saintonge but nevertheless Lancaster had successfully inflicted another political blow on Philippe VI in the south-west, boosted the morale of the Anglo-Gascons and fortified Plantagenet rule in Aquitaine.[83]

The earl of Lancaster and his army entered Bordeaux on 30 October, where he remained throughout the month of November. In December he set sail for England, but his fleet was caught in a violent storm during the sea voyage.[84] The earl of Pembroke's retinue arrived home on 20 December 1346, and although it is likely that Pembroke had taken part in Lancaster's northern raid into Poitou, his exact movements remain obscure.[85] Lancas-

---

the walls of the towns of Niort, Saint-Maixent and Fontenay-le-Comte, so as to serve as refuge centres for the local inhabitants. Sumption, *Trial by Battle*, p. 545 .

[79] Armagnac threatened to resign within three months of his appointment as royal lieutenant in the south-west because of his lack of troops and money, and countermands from the king. The forces that Armagnac raised in the Languedoc were occupied with keeping in check the raiding party led by Durfort, which culminated in the French siege and subsequent surrender of the town of Tulle. Sumption, *Trial by Battle*, pp. 541, 549–50.

[80] Van Halen was granted the right to receive £6 during the king's pleasure on every tun of wine brought within the district of the castle, one half of which was given to the king, the other was kept for himself: *CPR, 1345–48*, p. 560. Montferrand was granted the rights to all revenues and profits of the castellany of Lusignan: C 61/60, m. 36. The revenues and profits of the priory of Saint-Agnant were granted to Guilhem de Monségur: Fowler, *King's Lieutenant*, pp. 69–70; C 61/60, mm. 7, 17.

[81] Galhart, lord of Agassac, was appointed captain and marshal of Saint-Jean-d'Angély; C 61/60, m. 39. Tonnay-Charente was granted to Hélias de Saint-Symphorien: C 61/60, mm. 1, 3.

[82] *Oeuvres*, V, p. 118.

[83] French possessions included the provincial capital, Saintes, Blaye, Bourg, Talmont and Royan.

[84] Knighton's report of a huge storm on 7 December 1346 is corroborated by Lancaster's formal account of service, which records a 'magnam tempestatem' during the homeward voyage. Knighton, *Chronicle*, pp. 76–7; E 372/191, m. 54d.

[85] The *Saint-Omer* chronicle is the only source which mentions Pembroke's involvement. He is reported to have been given charge of Saint-Jean-d'Angély, but the chronicler's claim that Pembroke was still in charge of the town when Lancaster set sail for England is erroneous: *Saint-Omer*, fols 221v–222.

ter's fleet returned safely to England on New Year's Day in 1347, and he was released from the office of captain and lieutenant in Aquitaine at the beginning of February.[86] By 1 June he had joined Edward III's army at the siege of Calais where he was given command of the English force at Nieulay.[87]

Conclusion

The remarkable achievements of Lancaster's expedition in Aquitaine are even more significant when regarded in the wider context of the Anglo-French conflict from 1345 to 1347. The course of events of the campaigns in the south-western duchy had a direct impact on military operations in the north of France. Edward III's original strategy of a co-ordinated multi-front attack on France had been negated by an uprising in the Low Countries in 1345, which jeopardised the king's alliance with Flanders and caused him to visit the county that summer.[88] However, his overall designs to divide the French forces and engage his opponent in different theatres of war had come to fruition at the time of his landing in Normandy the following year. The early success of Lancaster's first campaign drew a considerable proportion of the French forces into the south and forced the duke of Normandy to take the offensive in a region where the French had previously adopted a holding operation in order to concentrate their forces elsewhere. By the time the orders had reached Duke Jean to join his father in the north, it was too late, and less than a week later the English had won a resounding victory at Crécy which reverberated throughout all Christendom. The dominant position of the English was strengthened further by their victory against the Scots at Neville's Cross in October 1346, which resulted in the capture of the French ally King David II. This series of victories was followed up by the successful siege of Calais in 1347 which concluded an outstanding series of military successes for Edward III.

The astute generalship of Lancaster underpinned the success of the entire expedition, and the campaigns that he led in the duchy are characterised by the speed in which they were conducted. The earl demonstrated an excellent military acumen; indeed, his intentions were evident from the moment his army disembarked in the duchy. The decision to reject the traditional strategy of a slow and methodical outward siege of the towns and castles surrounding Bordeaux, and his desire to seek out the enemy upon learning of their tactically flawed positions in the field, highlight his excellent understanding and knowledge of how to conduct military affairs. Such foresight

---

[86] E 372/191, m. 54d.
[87] Fowler, *King's Lieutenant*, pp. 70–1.
[88] Sumption, *Trial by Battle*, pp. 459–63.

and judgement probably derived from the experience of leading his own retinues during previous campaigns on the Continent and in Scotland. He also demonstrated important skills as an administrator and diplomat during the course of the campaigns through negotiating surrenders and rewarding those who came back into English allegiance with grants of privileges and concessions.

The division of the Anglo-Gascon forces into smaller military contingents which operated independently from one another was an effective method of regaining control of a large number of strongholds within a short space of time. It also enabled Lancaster to capitalise on the political impact of his earlier success by conducting simultaneous raids in different regions. This highlights the importance of his sub-captains, such as Sir Frank van Halen and Sir John de Norwich, and the retinue leaders of his army who were given the charge of small expeditionary forces or castles. Indeed, the earl's highly effective strategy of deploying small mounted task forces under experienced commanders was adopted by the seneschal of the duchy four years later.[89] The events of the campaigns in 1345 and 1346 also reflect the cohesion and fluidity of Lancaster's own retinue composition throughout the expedition. Apart from excellent leadership, it was the structure and composition of the earl's retinue that enabled some components to break away and reform depending on the nature of events which unfolded in the duchy.

A contemporary chronicler who described Lancaster as a man 'who is so successful in war' provides a simple but accurate assessment of a general whose talents in the art of warfare not only turned the tide of war in favour of the English in the duchy of Aquitaine – his extraordinary achievements were also a precursor for the wave of military success that enabled England to dominate the first phase of the Hundred Years' War.[90]

[89] In 1349 Sir Thomas Cok, then seneschal of Aquitaine, and Sir Stephen de Cosington led small task forces around the Dordogne valley which resulted in military success against the opposing Poitevins and the capture of Taillebourg. Both men had experienced Lancaster's use of this strategy in the duchy when they served in the earl's retinue four years earlier. Sumption, *Trial by Fire*, pp. 49–50.

[90] *Saint-Omer*, fol. 221v.

III

Military Service and the
Earl's Retinue for War

7

Lancaster's War Retinue in 1345: Formation and Structure

If 'the size and splendour of a magnate's retinue signalised his importance in the [medieval] world', then Henry of Lancaster must have been considered one of the most important men of his time.[1] The *comitiva* (retinue) which Lancaster assembled for war in 1345 was not only the largest of the retinue contingents which set out to Aquitaine in that year, but the largest ever to be mobilised for any military expedition up to that date. It was a harbinger of the 'super-retinues' which characterised the structural composition of the English armies of the second half of the fourteenth century and more importantly, from a historian's point of view, it remains the most fully documented of the retinue contingents in Lancaster's army.

The subject of the military retinue has received much scholarly attention over recent decades, but an in-depth study of a single English retinue which campaigned in France up to the Treaty of Brétigny (1360) has rarely been undertaken.[2] As a result of the recent rediscovery of the missing portion of Lancaster's 1345 retinue roll, the men who served under his banner in Aquitaine now can be seen to represent the largest military retinue of the first half of the fourteenth century for which there is full nominal evidence of the entire troop, that is to say, the identities of all of the men are known to us. This provides a unique opportunity to investigate the formation and structure of a war retinue of exceptional size based firmly on prosopographical evidence of the individuals who took up the sword (or indeed the bow) with Lancaster. Such an approach can modify Kenneth Fowler's earlier assessment of the earl's *comitiva*, and further our understanding of the means by

---

[1] Maddicott, *Thomas of Lancaster*, p. 40.

[2] Andrew Ayton's focused studies of the retinues led by the earl of Warwick and Thomas Ughtred are the only examples of such studies: Ayton, *Dynamics of Recruitment*, pp. 11–25; Andrew Ayton, 'Sir Thomas Ughtred and the Edwardian Military Revolution', in *The Age of Edward III*, ed. James S. Bothwell (York: York Medieval Press, 2001), pp. 107–32. For broader studies of military retinues in the thirteenth and fourteenth centuries see the Bibliography, particularly publications by Ayton, Adrian Bell, David Simpkin and Andrew Spencer.

which a magnate could raise a retinue of unprecedented magnitude in the mid 1340s.[3]

To understand Lancaster's war retinue in 1345 we must endeavour to answer the basic but fundamental question: how was Lancaster able to assemble a military contingent which itself was the size of a small army? By what means did he go about the task of recruiting such a sizable troop? Did they differ from the methods used to raise retinues of a more conventional size? And what factors enabled him to accomplish such a feat? In its broadest sense the retinue of Henry of Lancaster encompassed men who provided him with different types of service. These men included administrators, household and estate officials, as well as other men and officers who were part of the household and attended to the earl's personal affairs. In this study, however, our primary concern is with the men who provided him with military service in 1345. By exploring what Andrew Ayton terms 'the mechanics of retinue formation' we can, as far as the sources permit, reveal the internal structure and temporal identity of this group of men. In turn, the process of distinguishing between the contributions of manpower made by the individuals and the different groups of men which comprised the military retinue can provide a nuanced understanding of retinue formation, and elucidate the relationships between the various military components upon which it was based.

Retainers, Knights and Esquires

When assembling his military retinue Lancaster presumably turned first to those men who had a direct attachment to him and could be relied upon to provide military service. Men such as his retainers – individuals formally bound to the earl's service – and loyal knights, esquires and archers attached to his household or associated with him through frequent service represented the earl's most dependable and personal sources of manpower. Some of these men would have served individually, but others would have brought their own small following or company of men into the service of their retinue captain. To what extent, then, can the followings of such individuals be reconstructed and what contribution did they make to the total manpower of the retinue?

Of the known indentured retainers who contracted to serve with Lancaster in times of war and peace, only three men, Sir Ralph de Hastings, Sir

---

[3]   Fowler offers a brief analysis of the formation and structure of Lancaster's retinue in 1345, which is limited to the followings of three bannerets and based on only two types of source: captains' bills of request for letters of royal protection and the subsequent enrolment of the letters in the Chancery rolls. Fowler, 'Henry of Grosmont', I, pp. 719–20.

Norman de Swinford and Sir Edmund de Ufford, provided their lord with military service.[4] We know that Hastings and Ufford were both retained for life for an annual fee of 40 marks each assigned on the Yorkshire manor of Pickering and the manor of Higham Ferrers in Northamptonshire, respectively.[5] Unfortunately, the latter's indenture of retainer is the only extant contract but it is likely that the other two retainers were also party to similar terms. If this was the case, then Hastings and Swinford would have served Lancaster with a specified number of men-at-arms (reduced during peace time), each of whom would have worn Lancaster's livery and whose maintenance (wages and food) would have been the responsibility of the retainer. Thus Ufford was to serve with three men-at-arms, as well as ten horses and nine pages to attend them and a chamberlain dining in Lancaster's hall in time of war. The chamberlain probably acted as Ufford's financial officer, and the fact that the retainer was accompanied on campaign by his servants is a poignant reminder of the importance of ancillary personnel in the military retinue and warfare in general.[6] Moreover, it demonstrates how the military retinue often overlapped with the domestic establishment and was swollen in size by its non-combatant members.

With only three men-at-arms under his command, the company of Edmund de Ufford seems small compared with those led several decades earlier by the retainers of Henry's uncle, Thomas of Lancaster. The contrast in the size of the retainers' followings, however, is to be expected considering Thomas' extensive landholdings and his need of a large military retinue during the tumultuous period of the barons' rebellion against Edward II.[7] In

---

[4] William Bracebridge and the London carpenter, Richard Felstede, were also indentured retainers of Lancaster, but there is no evidence of their military service: Fowler, *King's Lieutenant*, p. 181. Jonathan Sumption's claim that Sir Thomas Uvedale and Sir Thomas Fogg were retainers of Lancaster cannot be substantiated by documentary evidence. Sumption, *Trial by Fire*, p. 274.

[5] William Dugdale, *The Baronage of England*, 2 vols (London: Tho. Newcomb, 1675–1676), I (1675), p. 579 (Hastings). DL 27/155 (Ufford's indenture); transcribed in Fowler, *King's Lieutenant*, p. 234.

[6] In the day-book of the Black Prince's controller, John Henxteworth, relating to the expedition to Aquitaine in 1355–56, there are numerous instances of payments made to the chamberlains of the prince's retainers. For examples of money that was paid to a retainer 'by the hands of his [i.e. the retainer] chamberlain', see payments to John Sharnesfeld, Sir Thomas Despencer, Alan Cheyne and John Ripon: Duchy of Cornwall Office, Journal (*Jornale*) of John de Henxteworth, fols 7v, 8, 11. There are also instances of payments made to the retainers' esquires: Henxteworth, fols. 10v (Sir Neil Loring), 11 (Sir Stephen de Cosington).

[7] Sir William Latimer was contracted to serve Thomas for life in peace and war with forty men-at-arms, Sir John Eure and Sir Adam de Swillington both with ten men-at-arms: Maddicott, *Thomas of Lancaster*, pp. 41–2; George A. Holmes, *The Estates of the Higher Nobility in Fourteenth-Century England* (Cambridge: Cambridge University Press, 1957), pp. 122–3 (Latimer); 'Private Indentures for Life Service in Peace and War,

the first half of the fourteenth century it seems to have been the norm for a knight who was part of a lord's affinity to lead a small company comprising between one and three men-at-arms, but there were exceptions.[8] Sir Robert Herle, for example, who was retained for life in 1339 by Thomas Beauchamp, earl of Warwick, was contracted to serve in times of war with four men-at-arms, and of the eight knights who served in Lancaster's retinue in 1344 two were accompanied by at least four and five men-at-arms respectively.[9] The size of each knightly company would vary slightly, commensurate with the knight's status and the nature of his relationship with the retinue captain. In terms of military manpower, the three men-at-arms whom Ufford probably brought into the field represent just 2% of the total number of esquires that Lancaster was contracted to provide.[10] It seems very unlikely, therefore, that the men-at-arms raised by indentured retainers would have contributed more than a small proportion of the military personnel in Lancaster's retinue.

In reconstituting the followings of Lancaster's retainers our conclusions need to be regarded as likelihoods rather than certainties due to the patchiness of the documentary evidence. For example, we cannot be sure whether Ufford actually served in Aquitaine with the number of men-at-arms stipulated in his indenture because the contract was not made until 1 March 1347, exactly two months after Lancaster's retinue had returned from the duchy.[11] In the case of Sir Norman de Swinford it is impossible to determine the size of his company, due to the absence of an indenture, or even whether he was retained for life or for the duration of a single campaign. We can infer from a letter of appeal against the seizure of Swinford's property, sent by Lancaster to the chancellor in 1347, that the knight had been formally retained over the course of the recent expedition. The supplication states that Swinford had been in the earl's service 'according to certain conditions drawn between them',[12] which implies that an indenture had indeed been

---

1278–1476', ed. Michael Jones and Simon Walker, *Camden Miscellany XXXII*, Camden Fifth Series, 3 (1994), pp. 58–9 (Swillington), pp. 60–1 (Eure). Thomas also contracted two retainers to provide smaller companies proportionate in size to that led by Ufford: Sir Hugh Meynell agreed to serve with three men-at-arms and Sir Thomas Lovel with two men-at-arms. Jones and Walker, *Private Indentures*, pp. 59–60 (Meynell); pp. 56–8 (Lovel).

[8] In 1325, for example, the force provided by twelve of the earl of Warenne's knights totalled thirty-six men-at-arms: Ayton, *Dynamics of Recruitment*, p. 19. Of the knights bachelor who served in Lancaster's retinue in 1344 half served with one man-at-arms and a quarter with two men-at-arms: C 81/1724/49. David Simpkin has shown that a knight bachelor was accompanied by two to four men during the English expeditions to Scotland in 1297, 1300, 1301 and 1303: Simpkin, *English Aristocracy at War*, p. 62.

[9] C 81/1724/49.

[10] Lancaster's indenture stipulated that his retinue was to include 150 esquires.

[11] Fowler, *King's Lieutenant*, p. 234 (indenture).

[12] Fowler, 'Henry of Grosmont', I, p. 677; SC 1/42/64.

made, but without the evidence of a grant of annuity or fee it seems likely that Lancaster had retained Swinford's services for the short term rather than for life.[13]

Another intractable problem is that the identities of the men whom Swinford brought into Lancaster's retinue remain unknown. Probably a relative of Norman, Edmund de Swinford is the only man-at-arms who can be identified as having possibly served in the knight's company. Although Edmund's name does not appear on the 1345 retinue roll, a royal writ exonerating him from providing military service on the expedition to Normandy in 1346 states that he had served in Lancaster's retinue in Aquitaine. The writ is enrolled in the Treaty Rolls immediately beneath that of Norman, and the military careers of both men reveal further connections between them besides kinship.[14] In 1342 they served together in Brittany in the retinue of Hugh Audley, earl of Gloucester, and they probably served in the same retinue during the king's expedition to the Low Countries four years earlier.[15] Moreover, the two men were associated through their landholdings in Leicestershire in the mid 1340s, and sometime during the following decade Norman granted the manor of Herlaston in the same county to Edmund.[16] The latter was probably an esquire at the time of the expedition to Aquitaine, and no doubt was among the men-at-arms who comprised Norman's company. In the following of Lancaster's other retainer, Sir Ralph de Hastings, it is tempting to place his cousin William and his anonymous companion, particularly as both men appear near the bottom of the list of *milites* on Lancaster's retinue roll and therefore were probably of a lower status than Ralph.[17] Likewise William de Hastings, who is listed as an esquire in the same document, might also be included.[18]

The use of indentured retainers, and the followings that accompanied them, was one of the ways in which Lancaster built up his retinue in 1345. Other individuals who had a personal attachment to Lancaster, such as Sir John Blount, Sir Nicholas de Peyvre and Simon Simeon who are described as his valets, would have provided additional manpower.[19] Similarly, the earl relied upon the service of his loyal knights, men who had served repeatedly

---

[13] Fowler, *King's Lieutenant*, p. 180. Fowler's claim that Swinford received a fee tied to a specific manor in return for military service is incorrect.

[14] C 76/24, m. 8d. The writ is abbreviated and recorded beneath the writ of Norman de Swinford, which is written in full.

[15] *Treaty Rolls*, II, p. 317 (1338); C 76/17, m. 25 (1342).

[16] *CIPM*, X, pp. 192–3.

[17] E 101/25/9, m. 3. 'Le Compaignon' of Ralph is 89th in the nominal list of knights and Sir William de Hastings' name is listed three entries below.

[18] E 101/35/2/10, m. 1.

[19] Fowler mistakenly includes John de Aldewyncle, another valet of Lancaster, among the men who served in 1345: Fowler, 'Henry of Grosmont', II, p. 244.

under his banner and who also brought small groups of combatants into his retinue. An example of such knights who served under Lancaster's command is Sir Nicholas de Rye. He was a native of Gosberton (Lincolnshire) who was recruited into Lancaster's retinue in 1340 and served with the earl on two further military campaigns overseas prior to the expedition to Aquitaine.[20] In spite of the lack of evidence that he was an annuitant of Lancaster there is a clear connection between the two men based on continuity of service. The parlous task of identifying him as a company leader and delineating his group of men is more problematic owing to the fact that none of the documentary evidence relating to Rye's service in 1345 – letters of protection, retinue roll, writ of exoneration – indicates that he led his own company of men on the campaign. However, a bill of request for protections produced in connection with Lancaster's expedition to Aquitaine, Spain and Avignon in the preceding year shows that Rye intended to serve 'with two men-at-arms' (od deux homes darmes).[21] It seems reasonable to presume, therefore, that the Lincolnshire knight maintained a company of similar strength when he served with Lancaster in 1345.

Furthermore, by drawing on prosopographical evidence relating to Rye we can be almost certain of the identity of one of the two men-at-arms who probably accompanied him to Aquitaine. An esquire named Richard de Stainton, whose name appears in Lancaster's 1345 retinue roll, is described as a 'valettus' of Sir Nicholas de Rye in an undated request for protection for service 'in the company of the Lord Earl of Derby'.[22] Stainton also appears in a bill of request for royal protections along with Thomas Gilling and William de Pemberton, which corresponds to the protections enrolled in 1345.[23] This suggests that either two separate requests for protection were made on behalf of Stainton in 1345 or, more likely, the individual request for the 'valettus' was made in 1344. We can therefore deduce that Stainton had twice served in Lancaster's retinue as Rye's valet and more importantly, for our purposes, was part of the knight's company. That Rye was directly responsible for bringing additional men-at-arms into Lancaster's war retinue, who had no previous connection with the earl, is demonstrated by the fact that Rye and Stainton had previously served together in John Wiloughby's retinue in the Low Countries in 1338.[24] Thus, when Rye entered into the service of Henry of Lancaster in 1340 he also brought with him

---

[20] C 76/15, m. 18 (1340); C 76/17, mm. 25, 39 (1342); C 76/19, m. 19, C 81/1724/49 (1344).

[21] C 81/1724/49.

[22] C 81/1724/48.

[23] C 81/1724/38; C 76/20, m. 15 (enrolled protections).

[24] C 76/12, mm. 3, 4 (Rye); C 76/12, m. 6 (Stainton).

the service of his valet.[25] The close relationship between Rye and Stainton is also reflected by the appointment of Gilbert de Gosberkirk, clerk, as the general attorney who represented both men in 1344 and 1345.[26] Although there is no evidence linking others to Rye's company in 1345 we might also attribute Thomas de Rye, esquire, to this small group of men. As a likely relative of the Lincolnshire knight and with the position of his name immediately above that of Stainton in the retinue roll, it seems we may well have identified the second man-at-arms of Rye's company.[27]

As we have seen in the case of Rye, royal letters of protection and, indeed, the initial requests for letters are an important type of source which can help to elucidate the links between individuals and expose the internal structure of a following of a particular knight. It should be borne in mind, however, that protections were usually nearly always issued to men before they set out on an expedition and therefore only provide evidence of intended service.[28] The system of providing legal protection to a recipient during a period of military service was open to abuse on occasion, but in all likelihood most men who were issued protections did in fact go on to serve on a military campaign.[29] Other sources such as a retinue roll – which was submitted to the Exchequer together with other documents such as an indenture, or particulars of account, when a captain accounted for his service – or a writ of exoneration were drawn up either during or after service had been completed and therefore represent firmer evidence of military service.

Lancaster's war retinue also comprised small knightly companies which

[25] There is no evidence that Stainton served in Lancaster's retinue before 1344 but it seems likely that he would also have served with Rye in Lancaster's retinue in 1340 and 1342. Rye's service with Lancaster: C 76/15, m. 18 (1340); C 76/17, mm. 25, 39 (1342).

[26] C 76/19, m. 22; C 76/20, m. 15.

[27] E 101/35/2/10, m. 2. Thomas de Rye's name is listed 118th and followed immediately by that of Stainton.

[28] Protections issued to men over the course of a campaign often reflect a continuance of service, although sometimes they might indicate service which started after an expedition had begun. One of Lancaster's knights, Sir Thomas de Verdon, for example, was issued two protections over the course of the expedition in Aquitaine; the first was issued on 10 July 1345 before the army set out overseas and was valid 'for one year' (*per unum annum*), and the second was subsequently issued just over a year later on 12 July 1346 on account of his continuous service in the duchy. Thomas Mountjoy, on the other hand, was issued his first and only protection for service in Lancaster's retinue on 1 February 1346, which suggests that he had arrived in the duchy and entered into the earl's service half way through the expedition. Furthermore, that Mountjoy's protection was only valid 'until 24 June next' implies that he intended to fight in Aquitaine for a relatively short period. Verdon: C 76/20, m. 5 (1345); C 61/58, m. 2 (1346). Mountjoy: C 61/58, m. 3; C 81/1730/26.

[29] For a detailed assessment of the limitations of the use of letters of protection and other types of sources as evidence of military service, see Ayton, *Knights and Warhorses*, pp. 138–93; Gribit, 'Henry de Lancaster's Army in Aquitaine', pp. 10–40.

had no attachment to the retinue leader. Sir Thomas Courtney, for example, does not seem to have had any connection with Lancaster prior to the expedition in 1345, and the Devonshire knight had originally intended to serve under the earl of Pembroke's banner before switching to Lancaster's retinue.[30] Courtney's name is not recorded on the 1345 retinue roll but a royal writ of exoneration for service in 1346 proves that he served on the expedition in Aquitaine. The same writ also exonerates a Robert Chippelegh because he had served 'with' Thomas Courtney in Lancaster's retinue, which suggests that Chippelegh was part of the latter's following.[31] If Chippelegh was an esquire, as we might infer from the absence of a title attributed to him in the writ, then he was certainly one of moderate wealth. Indeed, Courtney can be shown to have owed Chippelegh the not inconsiderable sum of 50 marks in 1344.[32] No other men can be linked to Courtney, but the partial reconstruction of his military following reaffirms that it was common practice for knights to be accompanied by a small number of men-at-arms who were typically of lower rank.[33] Sir John de Chetewynde is a case in point. He had intended to set out to Aquitaine as part of Lancaster's retinue but on account of him being 'weak and incapable' (*languidus et impotens*), Chetewynde sent three men-at-arms to serve in his place.[34] A retinue leader would have expected many of the knights in his service to bring a company of this size into his *comitiva*. The anonymous 'companions' of four knights listed in the 'milites' section of Lancaster's retinue roll show that leaders of knightly companies sometimes included men of equal rank, although on the whole these small groups of men-at-arms comprised esquires.[35] And with the emergence of mixed retinues in the 1330s, we would expect such companies to have had an attachment of one or two mounted archers.[36]

It is frustrating that the names of more men who served in the 'micro' companies led by retainers or other knights of Henry of Lancaster cannot be recovered. The few examples of knights who led their own companies

[30] C 76/20, m. 16. Courtney took out a letter of protection on 28 May 1345 for service in the earl of Pembroke's retinue.

[31] *Crécy and Calais*, p. 172; E 372/196 (Somerset).

[32] *CCR, 1343–46*, p. 366.

[33] In 1323, for example, Sir Robert de Shirland became an indentured retainer of Hugh Despenser the Younger and agreed to serve him in times of peace and war with two men-at-arms: Nigel Saul, 'An Early Private Indenture of Retainer: The Agreement Between Hugh Despenser the Younger and Sir Robert de Shirland', *EHR*, 128 (2013), 519–34, (p. 526).

[34] C 76/24, m. 3d. Although Chetewynde was 'incapable' of providing military service, it is possible that the three men-at-arms who served as his proxy would have accompanied Chetewynde had he been able to serve himself.

[35] E 101/25/9, m. 3; 'Le compaignon[s]' of Arnaut de Durfort, the mayor of Bordeaux, Ralph de Hastings and Andrew Luttrell are recorded in the nominal list of knights.

[36] Ayton, *Armies and Military Communities*, p. 232.

of one, two or three men-at-arms demonstrate one of the means by which Lancaster formed his military retinue, although it is impossible to determine the exact contribution of manpower they made to the retinue. Nevertheless, the fact that a quarter (26.4%) of the 'English' knights known to have served in Lancaster's retinue either were, or became, annuitants of the earl gives some indication of the number of companies that may have been raised in this way.[37] An annuitant such as Sir Thomas de Verdon, for example, who is described as 'his [Lancaster's] knight' in a petition sent to the pope by Lancaster in 1348 would almost certainly have served with his own following in 1345.[38] Similarly, as the example of Nicholas de Rye illustrates, men who had previously served under Lancaster with some regularity before 1345, but for whom there is no evidence of a grant of land or fee, should also be considered as potential company leaders.

The size of each knight's following, as mentioned earlier, would have been commensurate with his status. Sir Thomas Cok, for example, whose prominence is reflected by his position as marshal of the army (and whose name was recorded first in the retinue roll) would probably have led a larger contingent than the average small knightly company which consisted of only a few men-at-arms.[39] In addition, the number of esquires who served in Lancaster's retinue would have been augmented by men drawn from the earl's own pool of esquires. It is difficult to distinguish between esquires who, on the one hand, served in Lancaster's retinue as part of a knight's following and, on the other hand, had a personal attachment to Lancaster and therefore were directly recruited by him. Among the men who might be considered 'household esquires' of the earl are individuals who are described as his 'donzels' (*domicelli*) or valets, or were granted an annuity by him. Of the esquires listed in the 1345 retinue roll, five can be identified as Lancaster's valets and eleven were annuitants.[40] However, it would be misleading to consider this entire group of men to be the earl's 'own' esquires at the time of the expedition to Aquitaine. Only in the instance of Simon Simeon can we be certain of his attachment to Lancaster's household prior to 1345; others such as Thomas de Burton and Thomas de la Mare are not described as valets of the earl until the 1350s, and all five men are described as his

---

[37] Of the 87 'English' knights (excluding the 11 anonymous or 8 Aquitanian knights), 23 were annuitants. For a list of annuitants, see Fowler, 'Henry of Grosmont', II, pp. 313–20. Simon Walker notes that Avery de Sulny was also an annuitant: Walker, *The Lancastrian Affinity*, p. 28, n. 85.

[38] *CPP*, p. 133.

[39] E 101/25/9, m. 3.

[40] Valets: Thomas de Burton, Thomas Florak (donzel), Thomas de la Mare, Philip de Popham and Simon Simeon. Annuitants: Walter de Bintree, Edmund de Bulstrode, Thomas de Burton, John de Elmsall, Thomas Florak, Payn de Mohun, John de Newmarch, Philip de Popham, Thomas de la Ryvere, Henry Rose, Simon Simeon.

donzels in the foundation charter of Newarke College in Leicester, which they attested too in 1356.[41] In most instances, therefore, we cannot be certain when the esquires became valets of Lancaster, or at what point their close relationship with him developed. Similarly, the majority of the annuities were granted to esquires in the 1350s, and only in the case of John de Elmsall can we be certain that he was in receipt of an annuity before setting out to Aquitaine.[42]

Therefore both types of evidence pertaining to the status of valet and the grants of annuity, with the exceptions of Elmsall and Simeon, have their own interpretative complexities. The evidence of repeated military service in Lancaster's retinue before 1345, however, might be more indicative of their close association with the retinue leader. Of the eleven annuitants only six can be shown to have previously served under Lancaster's banner. Two men had served only once, but four men – Edmund de Bulstrode, Payn de Mohun, Thomas de la Ryvere and Simon Simeon, mentioned above – had served with Lancaster on at least three previous occasions.[43] Moreover, at least three of these esquires had either served or belonged to families who had served previous earls of Lancaster and therefore had a tradition of service with the noble household.[44] It is likely that these four men were very much Lancaster's 'own' esquires and their place among the first ten esquires

[41] In 1344 Simeon was Lancaster's household esquire: *CPP*, p. 46. References were made to Burton and Mare as the earl's valets in 1354 and 1353, respectively: E 403/373, m. 22 (Burton); E 403/368, m. 11 (Mare). Charter witnesses: Alexander Hamilton Thompson, *The History of the Hospital and New College of the Annunciation of St Mary in the Newarke, Leicester* (Leicester: E. Backus, 1937), p. 30.

[42] Elmsall was granted an annuity of 10 marks assigned on the manor of West Derby (Lancashire) on 1 May 1345: *John of Gaunt's Register, Part I*, ed. Sydney Armitage-Smith, 2 vols, Camden Society, 3rd series, XX–XXI (London: Offices of the Society, 1911), I, pp. 236–7. For the various dates by which annuities were granted to the esquires see Fowler, 'Henry of Grosmont', II, pp. 313–20.

[43] Bulstrode: E 101/15/12 (1336); C 76/12, m. 8, E 36/203, fol. 125v (1338); C 76/17, m. 25 (1342). Mohun: E 101/15/12 (1336); C 76/12, m. 7, E 36/203, fol. 125v. (1338); C 76/17, m. 25, C 76/17, m. 29 (1342); C 81/1724/49, C 76/19, m. 19 (1344). Ryvere: C 76/12, m. 8 (1338); C 76/17, m. 25 (1342); C 76/19, mm. 19, 22, C 81/1724/49 (1344). Simeon: C 76/12, m. 8; E 101/15/12 (1336); C 76/12, m. 8; E 36/203, fol. 125v (1338); C 76/15, m. 20 (1340); C 76/17, mm. 25, 30 (1342); C 76/19, mm. 19, 22; C 81/1724, m. 49 (1344). Elmsall and Walter de Bintree had served on one previous expedition with Lancaster, although Bintree's service on expeditions to Brittany (1342) and the Low Countries (1338) in Sir Walter Mauny's retinue suggests that he was an experienced soldier who did not become established in Lancaster's household until after the mid 1340s. Elmsall: C 76/12, m. 8. Bintree: *CPR, 1334–38*, p. 533 (1338); E 36/204, fol. 87r (1342); C 76/19, m. 19; C 81/1724/49 (1344).

[44] Mohun's father was a close supporter of Earl Thomas; *CPR, 1313–17*, p. 23. Ryvere's father was a knight of Earl Henry, and was his steward at Kidwelly at various times from 1308 to 1332: John Roland Seymour Phillips, *Aymer de Valence, Earl of Pembroke, 1307–1324: Baronial Politics in the Reign of Edward II* (Oxford: Clarendon Press, 1972),

in the retinue roll is no doubt a reflection of their prominence within the war retinue.[45]

It was not always by way of personal attachment to the earl, or as part of a knight's following, that an esquire found service in Lancaster's retinue. There is one instance of an esquire, John Musard, leading his own company of men-at-arms in 1345. A nominal entry on Lancaster's retinue roll shows that Musard led a company of eleven unnamed men who were of equal rank to himself, and which surpassed the typical size of a knight's 'micro' company.[46] How exactly this company leader came into the Lancaster's service, or where his men fitted in to the retinue structure is not altogether clear. John was a relative (and probably the son) of the notorious gentry criminal, Malcolm Musard, who was twice pardoned as an adherent of Thomas, earl of Lancaster, during the reign of Edward II.[47] In spite of his family's association with the previous earl, there is no apparent connection between John and Henry of Lancaster in 1345 or evidence of further service by him in the earl's retinue after the expedition to Aquitaine. It is possible that John Musard and his company were brought into Lancaster's service through one of the earl's leading knights such as Robert de la Mare, for example, owing to the predominance of both families in the same county of Gloucester, or perhaps they formed part of a larger sub-retinue led by one of Lancaster's bannerets.[48] Another possibility is that Musard and his companions represent a 'specialist' company of esquires, or self-standing troop, which was independent of the other followings or groups of men that comprised Lancaster's *comitiva*. However this 'comradeship group' fitted into the structure of the earl's retinue, its importance in terms of manpower contribution is borne out by the fact that the men constituted 8% of the esquires that Lancaster had contracted to provide. This rare example of an esquire leading his own company in the 1340s demonstrates another means by which Lancaster was able to boost the number of esquires who served under his banner.[49]

pp. 256–7. Simeon is described as a yeoman of Grosmont's father in 1329: *CPR, 1327–30*, p. 442.

[45] E 101/35/2/10, m. 1. Positions in the nominal list of esquires on the 1345 retinue roll: Mohun, 1st; Simeon, 2nd; Ryvere, 3rd; Bulstrode, 9th. Elmsall's previous service with Lancaster and his grant of annuity before 1345 suggests that he too should be considered one of the earl's household esquires.

[46] E 101/35/2/10, m. 1. The entry immediately below that of John Musard, who is listed 62nd among the esquires, reads 'xj companions of the said John'.

[47] Malcom was pardoned as an adherent of Thomas of Lancaster in 1318 and 1326: *CPR, 1317–21*, p. 233; *CPR, 1340–43*, p. 304. For a brief overview of his felonies, see John Hunt, 'Musard family (*per. c.*1070–*c.*1330)', *ODNB*, Jan 2008 [accessed 9 March 2015].

[48] For office-holdings and property of the families in Gloucestershire, see Chapter 9 (Mare) and Hunt, 'Musard family', *ODNB* (Musard).

[49] Another example of an esquire leading his own retinue in the first half of the

Bannerets

In order to assemble such a formidable retinue for war Henry of Lancaster relied on his knights banneret to raise and lead their own sub-retinues of men-at-arms and archers, which were much larger than the small knightly companies discussed above. As the *élite* of society, bannerets had the financial resources to provide their own sizeable contingents for warfare, and established their own social networks within various military communities throughout England based on landholding, kinship and a history of service, amongst other things. It was these networks that Lancaster exploited in order to gain access to a substantial pool of manpower which might otherwise have remained out of his reach. In this sense the bannerets served as recruiting middle men or, as Ayton puts it, 'a team of sub-contractors', who provided the retinue leader with preformed groups of combatants.[50] All eight of Lancaster's bannerets in 1345, with the exception of the youthful William, Lord Greystoke, had extensive military experience and brought their own personal followings into the earl's service.[51] Indeed, most of these elite knights were contemporaries of Lancaster, and retinue leaders in their own right.[52] The exact size and composition of the bannerets' followings remain unknown due to the paucity of sources such as captains' bills of requests for protections or horse inventories which can often distinguish such groups, but a partial reconstitution of the sub-retinues can be made based on an array of prosopographical evidence.[53]

There is no evidence to suggest that any of Lancaster's bannerets were formally retained by him, but at least five had an attachment to the earl based on previous experience of campaigning in his retinue.[54] The most prominent war captain amongst this group of men was undoubtedly Sir John de Norwich. Since beginning his military career in Scotland in the 1320s Norwich had served in numerous theatres of war, and on at least

---

fourteenth century is John de Houton, who served in Scotland in 1336. BL Cotton MS Nero C VIII fol. 44r; cited in Gary Baker, 'The English Way of War, 1360–1399' (unpublished doctoral thesis, University of Hull, 2011), p. 144.

[50] Ayton, *Dynamics of Recruitment*, p. 19.

[51] E 101/25/9, m. 3. Bannerets: Adam de Everingham of Laxton, John de Grey of Codnor, William, Lord Greystoke, Frank van Halen, Hugh Meynell, John de Norwich, Guilhem-Sans III, lord of Pommiers, and William la Zouche of Totnes.

[52] The six English bannerets had an average age of thirty-five years.

[53] Simpkin has shown that bannerets served on average with twelve to thirteen men-at-arms during the Scottish expeditions from 1297 to 1303, but it is likely that the contingents in 1345 were larger given that retinues grew in size under Edward III: Simpkin, *English Aristocracy at War*, p. 62.

[54] Only Lord Grey of Codnor, Greystoke and van Halen had not previously served with Lancaster.

two occasions his retinue is known to have exceeded 25 men-at-arms.[55] In 1345 the banneret's following was probably of a similar strength, but we can be certain of the identities of only six men. A group of enrolled letters of protection reveals that Henry de Caldecotes, knight, John son of Alan Sesoul and Robert de Helpiston intended to serve in Norwich's *comitiva* in 1345.[56] The service of the two former men is confirmed by Lancaster's retinue roll, which lists Sesoul among the esquires, and a royal writ made in 1346 shows that Helpiston was a clerk.[57] In addition, John de Brigham and Geoffrey Vernoun can be identified as having served with Norwich based on their writs of exoneration and we can also add the esquire Hugh Courson of Carleton to the sub-retinue.[58] The latter testified at the Court of Chivalry (1386) that at the age of nineteen he had fought with the Norfolk banneret at Langon, Bergerac and Auberoche during the expedition in Aquitaine.[59]

In spite of the small number of men who are known to have served in Norwich's sub-retinue in 1345, there are several others who can be identi-fied as likely members of his following. For example, three of the knights who intended to serve with Norwich in Scotland a decade earlier – Richard Fitzsimon, Robert de Greasley and Constantine Mortimer – also served in Lancaster's retinue in Aquitaine and, therefore, may well have been part of Norwich's *comitiva*.[60] That Fitzsimon was a knight of some standing is reflected by his position as sixth among the nominal list of *milites* on Lancaster's retinue roll, and his own company in 1345 probably exceeded the

[55] In 1335 Norwich served in Scotland first alongside the earl of Suffolk, and then Edward Balliol with 26 men-at-arms: BL Cotton MS Nero C VIII, fol. 237. In 1337 he led a retinue to Aquitaine which potentially comprised 13 knights and 28 esquires: C 81/1750/33 (request for letters of protection). That twelve protections requested on behalf of Norwich's men were never enrolled in the Gascon Rolls suggests that almost a third (29.3%) of his men-at-arms never actually served on the campaign. Ayton, *Knights and Warhorses*, p. 160, n. 113; C 61/49, m. 17. We can deduce from the sum of £1818 13s owed to Norwich by the Crown that his retinue included approximately 10 knights, 21 esquires and 60 foot soldiers – wages for a retinue of this composition for the full term of service come to within £5 of the sum owed to Norwich. I am grateful to Andrew Ayton for this calculation.

[56] C 76/19, m. 20.

[57] E 101/25/9, m. 3 (Caldecotes); E 101/35/2/10, m. 2 (Sesoul); *CCR, 1346–49*, p. 67 (Helpiston).

[58] C 76/22, m. 16d. (Brigham). E 159/123, m. 172; E 372/191 (Vernoun). C 47/6/1, no. 99; C 76/22, m. 7d. (Courson). Brigham is recorded as an esquire in 1337 and Vernoun was probably of the same rank owing to his small landholding in Norfolk: C 81/1750/33 (Brigham); see note above (Vernoun).

[59] C 47/6/1, no. 99 (Courson).

[60] Service in 1335: C 81/1735/39 (Fitzsimon and Greasley); C 71/15, m. 28 (Fitzsimon, Greasley and Mortimer). Service in 1345: C 81/322/18663 (Mortimer); E 101/25/9, m. 3 (Fitzsimon and Greasley); C 76/20, m. 15; C 81/1724/42 (Fitzsimon).

five men-at-arms whom he led on campaign in the previous year.[61] It was possibly through his connection with Norwich that Fitzsimon first entered into Lancaster's service in 1344, and the knight's company of men illustrates one of the means by which the banneret built up his own sub-retinue.[62]

A further three men from Lancaster's retinue in 1345 – Robert de Shelton, knight, Hugh Cressy and Richard de Walkefare – as well John de Brigham and Robert de Greasley (mentioned above), had intended to serve on a previous expedition in the retinue of the Norfolk banneret in 1337.[63] All these men are likely to have comprised Norwich's sub-retinue in 1345, and none more than Greasley, who had served under Norwich's captaincy on at least two occasions during the 1330s. Furthermore, two men who took out protections for service with Norwich in 1337 share their surnames with two men in Lancaster's retinue in 1345, although without firmer evidence of these individuals we cannot attribute them to Norwich's following.[64] The Norfolk esquire, Thomas Gerbergh, whose eponymous nephew had a tenurial connection with Hugh Courson, is another soldier who belongs to the group of men likely to have formed Norwich's company, although whether he too was a military novice like Courson is uncertain.[65] Thomas' name is listed among the esquires in Lancaster's retinue roll immediately below that of John Gerbergh, who also may have served under the same banner as his kinsman in the mid 1340s.[66]

Sir William la Zouche of Totnes is another of Lancaster's bannerets in

[61] E 101/25/9, m. 3. C 81/1724/49: a bill of request for protections corresponding to Lancaster's diplomatic expedition in 1344 shows that Fitzsimon intended to serve with at least five men-at-arms.

[62] Fitzsimon and Norwich both served in Lancaster's retinue for the first time in 1344.

[63] The men's names are listed on a bill of request for protections pertaining to service in Norwich's retinue in Aquitaine in 1337: C 81/1750/33.

[64] Sir William Rose, knight, and Simon de Hedersete, esquire, who are listed in a bill of request for protections in 1337 may be relatives of Henry Rose and Esmund de Hedersete, esquires, who served in Lancaster's retinue in 1345. C 81/1750/33 (1337); C 81/1750/33 (1345).

[65] Courson and Thomas Gerbergh's nephew and namesake were both tenants of Thomas, Lord Morley in 1386. That the younger Thomas was involved in land transactions relating to the estates of his older relative suggests that the latter may also have been a tenant of the same lord. Philip Caudrey, 'War, Chivalry and Regional Society: East Anglia's Warrior Gentry Before the Court of Chivalry', in *Fourteenth Century England, VIII*, ed. Hamilton, pp. 119–45 (p. 128, n. 64). *The History of Parliament. The House of Commons, 1386–1421*, ed. John Smith Roskell, Linda Clark and Carole Rawcliffe, 4 vols (Stroud: Sutton, 1992), III, pp. 179–80.

[66] E 101/35/2/10, m. 2: John is listed 131st among the esquires and Thomas is 130th. Interestingly, the names of Thomas de Astley, Richard de Illey and Baudry de Taverham – all of whom can be identified as Norfolk gentry – are interspersed on the 1345 retinue roll between those of Sesoul, Gerbergh and Courson. It is therefore tempting to view this entire group of esquires as John de Norwich's men.

1345 who, like Norwich, had served on the earl's diplomatic mission in the previous year. On this last expedition Zouche served with eight men-at-arms, and he certainly would not have struggled to raise and lead a much larger contingent for the expedition to Aquitaine considering that he was the most extensive landholder of the bannerets.[67] It is not clear whether Zouche was a replacement for his grandfather, who was discharged from service in Lancaster's retinue 'as a special favour' because the young banneret was setting out to Aquitaine with the earl.[68] However, the latter's service with Lancaster twelve months earlier suggests that he had been an original choice from the outset. Only six individuals can be identified as having served in Zouche's *comitiva* in 1345. Five of these men were granted military pardons, but the subsequent enrolments give no indication of the rank or status which they held.[69] The other person known to have served under the same banner is a Leicestershire knight, Sir Robert Burdet of Huncote, who was granted a letter of protection prior to the expedition.[70] It would be no surprise, however, to discover that the banneret's relatives Sir Richard la Zouche and Sir William la Zouche of Lubbesthorpe (who also resided in Leicestershire) were amongst the personnel of his company.[71] It was typical for captains, or sub-captains, to rely on family members to provide them with military service, although without evidence of a stronger connection between the two knights and the banneret, their place in his following remains a tentative suggestion.[72]

Sir Adam de Everingham of Laxton and Sir Hugh Meynell are the bannerets who had served Lancaster the most prior to 1345. Frustratingly, it is the followings of these two captains which can be reconstituted to the least extent. In the instance of Meynell, only Sir William Meynell, who was probably his son, and two esquires who share his surname can be considered

---

[67] C 81/1724/49 (1344). *CIPM*, XV, pp. 259–63 (landholdings).

[68] C 81/304/16839; *CPR, 1343–45*, p. 467. On 16 May 1345 Sir William la Zouche of Harringworth was granted a discharge of service 'as a special favour' because his grandson was going to serve in Lancaster's retinue in Aquitaine.

[69] Pardon recipients: John de Bolewyk, John Caynell, John del Howes, John Kelyng, Matthew Kelyng. *CPR, 1345–48*, p. 557.

[70] C 76/20, mm. 15, 16. Burdet was actually issued two protections in 1345, one on 20 May and another on 28 May. The first was granted to 'Robert son of Robert' on the testimony of Lancaster and the second was granted to 'Robert' for service in the *comitiva* of, and on the testimony of, William la Zouche. The second protection was probably requested in the name of his synonym for added legal protection.

[71] William of Lubbesthorpe belonged to the Leicestershire branch of the Zouche family, but it is unclear in what way Richard was related to the banneret. The names of both men are listed on Lancaster's retinue roll: E 101/25/9, m. 3.

[72] Another speculative choice of soldier to place in Zouche's sub-retinue is William de Quinton. He is listed among the esquires on the 1345 retinue roll but, interestingly, a knight of the same name is known to have taken out a protection for service in Zouche's retinue ten years later. E 101/35/2/10, m. 2 (1345); C 76/33, m. 5 (1355).

as men likely to have served under his banner.[73] To Everingham's following we can attribute the service of Sir John Paynel and John Bozoun of Claxton, although a Sir Ralph Paynel and a Gilbert Paynel, esquire, whose names are recorded on the 1345 retinue roll might also have served in the same company.[74] Similarly, John de Everingham and Robert de Everingham who are listed next to one another on the retinue roll probably served under their kinsman's banner, and Sir Philip de Lymbury is another knight who is likely to have formed part of the sub-retinue.[75]

It is significant that no more than two men-at-arms are known to have served in the companies of Everingham and Meynell who carried a banner for the first time in 1345. The rise to banneret was certainly a recent promotion for both men who had served as knights bachelor in Lancaster's retinue in 1344; the former with two men-at-arms and the latter with only one *homme d'arme*.[76] Moreover, the conventional practice for a knight to receive a grant of land or annual fee from his patron in order to maintain his newly acquired status of banneret does not seem to have occurred at any point.[77] It is plausible, therefore, that Henry of Lancaster may have promoted Everingham and Meynell – both of whom were closely connected to the house of Lancaster – prior to the campaign in order to fulfil his recruitment target of eight bannerets. In the absence of any grant of annuity to support the new rank, we might expect the followings of both men to have been comparatively smaller than those of more experienced and wealthy bannerets such as John de Norwich.[78] We can surmise that the sub-retinues of Everingham and Meynell might have constituted between 10 and 15%

---

[73] E 101/25/9, m. 3 (William Meynell, knight). E 101/35/2/10, mm. 1, 2 (John and Richard Meynell, esquires).

[74] John Paynel: C 76/20, m. 16 (protection). John Bozoun: C 76/20, m. 21 (protection). Ralph Paynel: E 101/25/9, m. 3. Gilbert Paynel: E 101/35/2/10, m. 2. Bozoun may be the same person as Sir John Boson who served in the *comitiva* of William, Lord Greystoke.

[75] John and Robert de Everingham: E 101/35/2/10, m. 3. Philip de Lymbury had not served in Lancaster's retinue before 1344, and a letter close made in the same year which permitted Everingham and Lymbury to leave the port of Dover with their horses and equipment implies that both men set out on the expedition together. *CCR, 1343–46*, p. 361. On Lymbury's career, see Chapter 9 and Ayton, *Knights and Warhorses*, pp. 237–9, and n. 202.

[76] C 81/1724/49.

[77] There is no evidence that either man was granted a fee or land by Lancaster during his lifetime.

[78] The modest wealth of Meynell, for example, is reflected by the low valuation of his warhorse at 20 marks in 1340, which was of equivalent value to the horse lost by the esquire, Edmund de Bulstrode. E 36/203, fol. 126. Similarly, the warhorse that Everingham took on campaign to Scotland in 1337 had a modest value of 25 marks. Ayton, *Knights and Warhorses*, p. 79; E 101/35/3, m. 1.

of Norwich's *comitiva* in 1345, based on the proportional difference of the number of men-at-arms they had served with on the previous campaign.[79]

The banneret whose *comitiva* can be reconstituted in greatest detail is Sir John de Grey of Codnor. An extant bill of request for protections made by Grey on behalf of his men in 1345 reveals the identities of nine men, of whom Roger Beler and Gervase de Clifton are noted as knights.[80] All these men, except for Richard de Strolley, are listed on Lancaster's retinue roll, which confirms that two more of them were ranked as knights – William Favell and Simon Secre – and four as esquires.[81] In addition, two pardon recipients are known to have served in the same company.[82] It is difficult to estimate the size of Grey's following in 1345, particularly as there is no evidence pertaining to companies which he had previously led. Indeed, despite his wealth of military experience the expedition to Aquitaine was the first on which he served as a banneret.[83] However, Grey, like other bannerets, would have relied on his most prominent knights to provide him with substantial manpower, while individuals who had a direct attachment to the banneret would have further augmented the number of combatants at his disposal.[84]

The only banneret in Lancaster's retinue who was indigenous to the duchy of Aquitaine was Guilhem-Sans III, lord of Pommiers. The family of Pommiers had been loyal supporters of the kings of England throughout the

[79] In 1344 Norwich intended to serve with five times more men-at-arms than Everingham, and ten times more than Meynell. C 81/1724/49.

[80] C 81/1727/60 (request); C 76/20, m. 16 (enrolment). Robert de Clifton, William Favell, John de Sandwich, Simon Secre, Hugh de Shirfield, Richard de Strolley, and Peter de Wokendon are listed without title. Interestingly, a Gervase de Clifton, along with an esquire named Thomas de Clifton, served in Scotland from 1337 to 1338 as a *centenar* at the head of a company of mounted archers from Lincolnshire. E 101/20/25, m. 14; I owe this reference to Andrew Ayton.

[81] E 101/25/9, m. 3; E 101/35/2/10, mm. 1, 3. Knights: Beler, Clifton, Favell and Secre. Esquires: Clifton, Sandwich, Shirfeld and Wokendon. The esquires are roughly grouped together and positioned 156th, 157th, 160th and 163rd on the retinue roll. The names of Thomas de Cockfield, William de Misterton, Nicholas Percy and John de Stacey are interspersed within the group.

[82] *CPR, 1345–48*, p. 558. The pardons were granted to John son of John Halden and his cousin, John 'le clerc', on the testimony of the Lord of Greystoke and John de Grey. We might presume that the pardon recipients served in the latter's retinue considering that they were both from Stanton on the Wold in Nottinghamshire, a county in which Grey had landholdings, in contrast to Greystoke who held no property in the county.

[83] Simon Walker, 'Grey, John, third Baron Grey of Codnor (1305×11?–1392)', *ODNB*, 2004 [accessed 18 March 2015]. Grey had served on numerous campaigns in Scotland during the 1330s and was with Edward III in the Low Countries between 1338 and 1340.

[84] Men like Peter de Wokendon, for example, who had served on previous expeditions with Grey before he was elevated to banneret, which suggests the two men shared a close association: C 76/14, m. 7 (1340); C 71/21, m. 3 (1341).

fourteenth century, and Guilhem-Sans had taken part in Lancaster's expedition in 1344. Two entries on the 1345 retinue roll show that his following comprised at least three knights and three esquires, although their identities are unknown because the phrases 'iij milites' and 'iij esquiers' are recorded in place of the men's names.[85] This anonymous group of men-at-arms probably represents the core of the banneret's company – men who were his loyal followers and who had a personal attachment to the lord. We would also expect some of his kin to have swollen the ranks of his company further. The two esquires named Amaniu de Pommiers, for example, are likely to have served under their family's banner.[86] The two brothers of the lord of Pommiers, Hélias and Guilhem, may also have formed part of his sub-retinue, but as a former canon of Bazas and retainer of Edward III, Hélias, at least, would probably have maintained his own distinct personal following during the expedition.[87] It is, of course, possible that the brothers' retinues and perhaps the other Aquitanian knights in Lancaster's *comitiva* may have merged under the banner of the lord of Pommiers.

All the bannerets discussed above have been shown to have had a history of service with Henry of Lancaster. In the cases of Sir William, Lord Greystoke and Sir Frank van Halen, however, there is no evidence of any association between the men and the earl prior to 1345. The expedition to Aquitaine was only the second military campaign of Greystoke's career – on coming of age in 1342 he had served in the retinue of William de Bohun, earl of Northampton.[88] Furthermore, the nominal evidence of service linking men to the sub-retinues of either captain is scarce. A John Boson, knight, is known to have served under Greystoke's banner in Aquitaine and afterwards at the siege of Calais, while in the instance of van Halen only three anonymous knights are known to have served under his banner.[89] The Brabantine was clearly a captain of some repute, and his contribution to the army's success in the duchy is reflected by the favourable appointments and grants he received as rewards for his service.[90] If, as Kenneth Fowler suggests, van Halen was a retainer of Lancaster, then it was a bond that was forged in

---

[85] E 101/25/9, m. 3 (knights); E 101/35/2/10, m. 3 (esquires).

[86] E 101/35/2/10, mm. 1, 2.

[87] E 101/25/9, m. 3; Hélias and William are listed as knights on the 1345 retinue roll. Hélias was retained by Edward III before 1340, and was canon of Bazas by 1344 at the latest. C 61/52, m. 21 (retainer); C 61/56, m. 12 (canon).

[88] C 76/17, m. 8; E 36/204, fol. 83r.

[89] Boson: C 76/25, m. 15d. (writ of exoneration); E 101/25/9, m. 3 (retinue roll). The close association between Boson and Greystoke is reflected by his appointment as the banneret's attorney in 1349 and 1351: C 76/27, mm. 4, 5; *CPR, 1350–54*, p. 172. The entry for van Halen's anonymous knights is identical to that of Pommiers, which is positioned two places above the Brabantine's men on the retinue roll. E 101/25/9, m. 3.

[90] He was granted the castle of Rochefort on the bank of the Charente in 1346, and was appointed seneschal of the duchy in 1350. *CPR, 1345–48*, p. 580; C 61/61, m. 5.

later years.[91] The only campaign on which both Lancaster and van Halen had served up to 1345 was Edward III's expedition to the Low Countries in 1340. Thus, it was in the theatre of war and at the king's court that the two men had no doubt become acquainted.

The sub-retinues of Greystoke and van Halen might be considered independent or 'off-the-peg' companies, which some retinue leaders are known to have relied upon when faced with the task of expanding their existing retinue or raising a new contingent for the first time.[92] The start of the baron's military career coincided with Lancaster's need for substantial manpower, and the Brabantine would also have been a recruit welcomed into the elite ranks of the earl's retinue. Such men with whom Lancaster had no, or only a loose, association provided another avenue through which his retinue could be built. The majority of the bannerets, however, had some sort of attachment to Lancaster or his household. That at least half of these men were serving as bannerets for the first time on the expedition shows that Lancaster had forged a new crop of elite knights who were capable of providing him with a sufficient number of men for warfare. These recent promotions, albeit on a smaller scale, echo Edward III's creation of six new earldoms on the eve of the Hundred Years' War because Lancaster, like the king, was now able to exploit the social networks of his subordinate captains for the purpose of military recruitment.[93] It is impossible to determine the exact contribution of manpower which the eight bannerets made to the war retinue in 1345, but we can surmise that they provided around two thirds of the men-at-arms and archers who were expected to serve with the earl.[94]

[91] Fowler, *King's Lieutenant*, p. 101.

[92] Ayton, *English Army at Crécy*, p. 208.

[93] It is unclear exactly when Everingham, Grey of Codnor, Greystoke, Meynell and van Halen were made bannerets, but in the instances of Everingham and Meynell the promotion was made within twelve months of the expedition to Aquitaine and Lancaster would almost certainly have been influential in securing their newly acquired rank. On the creation of the earldoms in 1337, see Andrew Ayton, 'Edward III and the English Aristocracy at the Beginning of the Hundred Years War', in *Armies, Chivalry and Warfare in Medieval Britain and France: Proceedings of the 1995 Harlaxton Symposium*, ed. Matthew Strickland, Harlaxton Medieval Studies, n.s., 7 (Stamford: Paul Watkins, 1998), pp. 172–207.

[94] If the sub-retinues on average comprised 20 men-at-arms and 20 mounted archers, the total contribution would represent 64% of the 250 men-at-arms and 250 mounted archers which Lancaster had contracted to provide for service. Inevitably, there would have been some variance in the size of each sub-retinue, but the large followings of men such as John de Norwich, who is known to have served with 40 men-at-arms on previous expeditions, would probably have compensated for the smaller sub-retinues. In the first half of the fourteenth century a retained banneret was expected to lead a company of 20 to 40 men-at-arms: Ayton, *Dynamics of Recruitment*, p. 20.

Royal Knights and Valets

One of the other means by which Henry of Lancaster expanded his war retinue in 1345 was through the attachment of royal knights and valets. Sir Frank van Halen, for example, who had no history of service with Lancaster prior to 1345, was retained by Edward III during his expeditions to the Low Countries between 1338 and 1340. This banneret belonged to a prominent family of Lombard money lenders that had settled in Brabant, and after coming over to England with Philippa of Hainault (Edward III's future wife) in the 1320s he established himself successfully in the royal household.[95] Van Halen was knighted at a tournament in London in 1331 and a decade later was granted a substantial annuity of £90 by the king for 'retention' (*retentione*), although it is not clear whether he was retained for pleasure or for life at this point in time.[96] His close relationship with Edward III is also evident in the gift of a silver bowl with ewers which he personally received 'for bringing secret business to the king', although the ultimate manifestation of their intimacy was the creation of van Halen as a founding knight of the Order of the Garter.[97] It seems, therefore, that Lancaster had recruited him from Edward III's established network of knights. Indeed, Aymer de Valence, earl of Pembroke, had utilised a similar strategy in 1314 to 'top up' the knights in his retinue.[98] For our purpose of determining the formation and structural character of Lancaster's retinue, it is important to establish the extent to which the earl depended upon the king's men. Who else, therefore, can be identified in Lancaster's retinue as belonging to the king's affinity?

The firmest and most obvious evidence of a soldier's connection to

---

[95] Van Halen's original family name was Mirabello and his father, Jean de Mirabello, became receiver general of the duke of Brabant in the period 1321–33. David Kusman, 'Jean de Mirabello, dit van Halen (*c.* 1280–1333). Haute finance et lombards en Brabant dans le premier tiers du XIVe siècle', *Revue belge de philologie et d'histoire*, 77 (1999), 843–931; David Kusman, 'Entre noblesse, ville et clergé. Les financiers lombards dans les anciens Pays-Bas aux XIVe-XVe siècles: un état de la question', in *Rencontres d'Asti-Chambéry (24 au 27 septembre 1998): Crédit et société : les sources, les techniques et les hommes (XIVe-XVIe s.). Actes*, ed. Jean-Marie Cauchies (Neuchâtel: '[n. pub]', 1999), pp. 113–32.

[96] E 101/389/8, m. 9. A part of a counter-roll relating to the king's foreign expenses in 1340 records that van Halen was granted the annuity of £90 'for maintaining an armed retinue'. In 1347 he became a life retainer of Edward III and was granted an annuity of £150 for his liege homage, which increased to £300 in 1352. *CPR, 1345–48*, p. 560; *CPR, 1350–54*, p. 239. For details on van Halen's later career, see Richard Barber, *Edward III and the Triumph of England* (London: Penguin, 2013), p. 516.

[97] E 36/204, fol. 81r. Van Halen is incorrectly referred to as a knight from Flanders in the royal Wardrobe book.

[98] Phillips, *Aymer de Valence*, pp. 254–5. John de Kingston and Nicholas de la Beche were both royal knights attached to Pembroke's retinue for a single campaign in 1314.

Edward III was his place in the royal household. Also indicative of royal association is the description of an individual as 'king's yeoman', or 'king's valet' in the royal administrative records. However, this status alone is not firm evidence that a soldier served predominantly with the king because it was not uncommon for men to move from royal service into the service of a magnate household. Simon Simeon, for instance, is described as a king's yeoman in 1335 but we know that it was during his career in the Lancastrian household that he was raised to prominence.[99] A grant of annuity from the king, usually as reward for good service, represents firmer evidence of royal association. Moreover, there is greater certainty that men had been recruited from the king's team of knights when they can be shown to have had no previous association or history of service with Lancaster.

Of the knights in Lancaster's retinue at least seven can be shown to have had a strong association with Edward III.[100] Two of these men – Robert Boseville and Oliver de Bordeaux – are described as the king's valet or yeoman, and neither of them had previously served with Lancaster.[101] Three of the men, including John de Dalton and Neil Loring, were granted royal annuities before 1345, while three others became annuitants of the king thereafter.[102] Only Neil Loring and Oliver de Bordeaux, however, appear on the standard royal household 'membership' lists of men who received fees, robes, footwear and so forth.[103] In the case of the latter, Lancaster had acquired the services of a faithful servant of the Crown, whose family had loyally served all three Edwardian kings.[104] The importance of Oliver's service to the royal household is reflected by the extensive grants of office

---

[99] Fowler, *King's Lieutenant*, p. 176.

[100] These seven men were: Oliver de Bordeaux, Robert Boseville, John de Dalton, Vasco-mede Despaigne, Edmund Everard, Neil Loring and Richard la Zouche. It is possible that the two royal household knights, Edmund and Robert de Ufford, may be the persons who served in Lancaster's retinue in 1345. However, we cannot be certain due to problems of homonymity.

[101] Boseville and Bordeaux do not appear to have been knighted, but both men clearly had enough wealth to be elevated to the order of knighthood. Oliver Bordeaux is only ever referred to as the 'king's valet' in the administrative records.

[102] Royal annuitants before 1345: *CPR, 1317–21*, p. 27 (Bordeaux); *CPR, 1338–40*, p. 396 (Dalton); E 403/339, m. 29 (Loring). Royal annuitants after 1345: Boseville (1364), Everard (1369), and Zouche (1349).

[103] Caroline Shenton lists Loring as a chamber squire from 1334 to 1338 and as a knight in 1340: BL Cotton MS Nero C III, fols 225r–227r; E 101/388/5, mm. 17–19 (squire); *CPR, 1338–40*, p. 397 (knight). Bordeaux is listed as a squire from 1328 to 1330: E 101/383/10 (1328); E 101/385/4 (1330). Caroline Shenton, 'The English Court and the Restoration of Royal Prestige, 1327–1345' (unpublished doctoral thesis, University of Oxford, 1995), pp. 253–65.

[104] C 61/33, m. 13d; Oliver's brother, Lop-Bernugh, appears to have been in the service of Edward I.

and land which he received from both Edward II and Edward III.[105] In 1322, for example, he was granted the custody of the castle of Bayonne and served as the city's prévôt, an office he held for at least twenty years. In addition, many grants of land and economic privileges in England were also made to him.[106]

In contrast, royal knights of more obscure origins and comparatively low status were also recruited by Lancaster.[107] Sir Vascomede Despaigne can be shown to have had no connection with the earl before serving in his retinue, and the only reference to the Spaniard in the administrative records is a payment of £8 6s 8d made to him for 'coming to the king on an embassy' (*venienti ad Regem in nuncio*).[108] It was probably from his role as envoy to Edward III that he developed a close association with the king and became part of Lancaster's retinue. The Spaniard's inclusion in the earl's *comitiva* would also have been advantageous to the king, who no doubt benefited from having such a trusted confidante who operated within close proximity of the military commander.

This group of men, therefore, represents a small but significant proportion of the knights who served with Lancaster in 1345, amongst whom were experienced and talented soldiers such as Neil de Loring (who later became a founding member of the Order of the Garter) and other men whose families had a tradition of service with successive kings of England. The earl relied upon such royal knights as van Halen to bring military experience and their own companies of men into his retinue. Interestingly, the service of a Gascon esquire named Arnaut Micol, who was described as Edward III's butler in 1331, shows that Lancaster also recruited men of modest rank from the king's affinity.[109] Ultimately, it was the earl's complicit and intimate relationship with Edward III which allowed him access to the 'king's men', and provided another means by which he could assemble an extraordinarily large military retinue.

---

[105] Many of the financial rewards granted to him by Edward II were later confirmed by Edward III. For example, his exemption for life 'from tenths, twelfths and any other quota of movables': *CPR, 1327–30*, p. 196; *CCR, 1343–46*, p. 298.

[106] C 61/49, m. 40. He held lands in Berkshire, Buckinghamshire, Cheshire, Leicestershire, Norfolk and Surrey.

[107] E 101/25/9, m. 3; Vascomede is positioned 95th, at the bottom of the nominal list of knights on the 1345 retinue roll.

[108] E 403/340, m. 30 (14 February 1348).

[109] E 101/35/2/10, m. 3; C 61/43, mm. 9, 10, 16 (Butler). A pardon issued to Micol in 1322 as an adherent of Thomas, earl of Lancaster, shows that the Gascon also had a connection with the noble household. *CPR, 1321–24*, p. 139.

Aquitanians

One of the most striking features of Lancaster's retinue is the number of Aquitanians who served as men-at-arms. At least 14 of the 100 knights (bachelor and banneret) and 25 of the 150 esquires that Lancaster was contracted to provide for war were native to the duchy of Aquitaine. Among these men were lords who had served with Lancaster on previous occasions, such as the lord of Pommiers, and others whose families had remained loyal to the English king-dukes during the previous decades of fighting in the duchy.[110] Other notable lords included Johan de Grailly, or Captal de Buch as he was more commonly known, who distinguished himself at the battle of Poitiers in 1356 and belonged to a family which had consistently served the English Crown over several generations.[111]

The inclusion of such noble and prominent knights in Lancaster's *comitiva* would have been mutually beneficial to the retinue leader and to the Aquitanians themselves. The latter's service under Lancaster's banner would have enabled the earl to exercise greater control over some of the Gascon forces which augmented the English army, based on the political clout and reputation of the men. It is interesting to note that the knights' lordships were spread across much of the duchy, which would inevitably have brought their own spheres of influence directly under Lancaster's control.[112] Among the rank of esquire were men who also belonged to families of prominence such as Johan de Lamothe, Ponset de Lalande and Johan d'Escoussans who

---

[110] The family of Pommiers had been in the service of the king-dukes since the beginning of the fourteenth century: Françoise Bériac and Eric Ruault, 'Guillaume-Sanche, Elie de Pommiers et leurs frères vers 1340-1360', *Journal of Medieval and Humanistic Studies*, 1 (1996), 207–27, p. 208. Other Aquitanians who were long-standing supporters of the English crown include Arnaut de Durfort III, lord of Frespech, who had loyally served Edward I, II and III. His father, Arnaut de Durfort II had been a household banneret and knight of Edward III in the 1320s and 1330s. For a royal writ acknowledging the loyalty of the Durfort family to the English kings, see C 61/36, m. 24. For Durfort's service as a royal household knight, see Shenton, 'Restoration of Royal Prestige', pp. 253–6.

[111] Malcolm Vale, 'Grailly, Jean (III) de (*d.* 1377)', *ODNB*, Jan. 2008 [accessed 18 March 2015]. For the names of all of the Aquitanian lords in Lancaster's retinue see Chapter 3.

[112] The lord of Tartas and Poyanne, for example, held lands in the southern seneschalcy of Landais, the lord of Montferrand and the Captal de Buch had estates in Bordelais and the stronghold of the lord of Pommiers was in Bazadais. The lord of Durfort's power base was in the eastern seneschalcy of Agenais, while Fergaunt d'Estissac originated from the north-eastern seneschalcy of Périgord. I am extremely grateful to Guilhem Pépin for his insight on the lineages and various landholdings of the Aquitanians in Lancaster's retinue. For the geographical location of the seneschalcies that constituted the duchy of Aquitaine see Map 1.

brought a further concentration of power under the earl's banner.[113] From
the Aquitanians' perspective it was probably considered a privilege to serve
in the retinue of such a prominent noble. Their close proximity to the centre
of command would have brought its own advantages when it came to the
distribution of the spoils of war, or to grant of the custody of strongholds
captured over the course of the expedition. In 1347, for example, Bertran
de Montferrand was made captain of Lusignan, and the lord of Pommiers
was granted custody of the castle of La Réole following its capture in the
previous year.[114] Indeed, it is no surprise that some of the most prominent
commands were granted to Aquitanians to whom the Crown was indebted
for the retinues they had maintained in the duchy since the outbreak of the
Hundred Years' War.[115]

In 1345 the 'indigenous elements' of Lancaster's retinue represented more
than 15% of the total number of men-at-arms who were expected to serve
under the earl's banner. They formed an integral part of the war retinue,
and by acquiring the services of these Aquitanians Lancaster had not only
increased the number of personnel under his immediate command but
had also, quite cleverly, strengthened his wider control of command over
the entire Anglo-Gascon coalition forces. Furthermore, the proportion of
Aquitanians and their places among all three ranks of banneret, knight and
esquire in Lancaster's retinue gives the contingent a distinct and collective
cosmopolitan identity.

Archers and Attendants

The 1345 retinue roll provides a full list of names of the mounted archers
who served alongside men-at-arms in Lancaster's retinue. However, the
source material which can often illuminate the internal structure of a retinue
or reveal the connections between a captain and his men seldom relates
to archers, mounted or foot, due to their comparatively low economic

---

[113] The lords of Roquetaillade belonged to the family of Lamothe, the lords of La Brède
and Lalande (now the isle of la Lande on the river Garonne) were of the family of
Lalande, and Escoussans was related to the lords of Langoiran.

[114] C 61/60, m. 36 (Montferrand); C 61/60, m. 14 (Pommiers). Another example of the
earl's patronage to Aquitanians in his retinue is the grant of the toll of Saint-Macaire
to Arnaut de Durfort in 1352, which had previously been held by Neil Loring. C 61/64,
m. 2.

[115] Fowler asserts that by 1341 Pey de Grailly was owed £13,850 and the lord of Pommiers
was owed £6488, based on the accounts of the constables and controllers of Bordeaux:
Fowler, *King's Lieutenant*, p. 44, n. 13.

standing.[116] It is therefore impossible to establish what proportion of the retinue-based archers was provided, on the one hand, by the leaders of sub-retinues and small knightly companies and, on the other hand, by Lancaster himself.

In spite of this intractable problem an extrapolation of two types of evidence can provide an insight, albeit a limited one, into how these men fitted into the formation and structure of the *comitiva*. We have already located a handful of men, for example, within the followings of Grey and Zouche based on the evidence of letters of pardon, and in all likelihood these men were mounted archers.[117] The notes of warrant which follow the enrolled letters indicate that the bannerets had certified the pardons, and confirm the place of the recipients within the respective sub-retinues. Only in the case of Thomas Natrel 'archer', however, can we be certain of his troop type, although there still remains some doubt as to whether Natrel served in Lancaster's retinue or in one of the other four principal war reti-nues of the army.[118] Moreover, none of the names of the pardon recipients who set out for Aquitaine in 1345 appear on the earl's retinue roll, which implies that any men who served in Lancaster's *comitiva* with a pardon were not only additional troops attached to his retinue, but also that they served without pay.[119]

The other useful source which can be utilised to gain a sense of how the mounted archers fitted into the retinue's formation is the evidence of the men's surnames. By establishing the regional origins of archers we can make a tentative connection with the banneret or knight under whom they might have served because, as Ayton asserts, 'we would expect to find captains recruiting their mounted archers from the areas in which their landholdings lay'.[120] William Spink and John Payn, for example, who are listed among the archers on the 1345 retinue roll and known to have resided in Norfolk, are likely to have been part of John de Norwich's sub-retinue, considering the

---

[116] Sources such as horse appraisal lists, royal protections (requests and enrolments) and writs of exoneration relating to land assessment very rarely include nominal evidence of mounted archers.

[117] For names of pardon recipients see above.

[118] *CPR, 1345–48*, p. 218 (Natrel). Although Natrel's pardon was certified by Lancaster, the fact that the overwhelming majority of pardons were also certified by him suggests that the earl testified to the service of pardon recipients on behalf of other retinue leaders in the army, as well as sub-captains in his own retinue. It should also be borne in mind that some pardon recipients would have been foot archers, but in the absence of testimony from a constable or leader of the infantry in the notes of warrant, there is no way of establishing which pardon recipients belonged to this category of soldier.

[119] For a discussion of pardon recipients serving at their own expense, see Chapter 3.

[120] Ayton, *English Army at Crécy*, p. 218.

banneret's influence and extensive social networks in that county.[121] Similarly, we might expect to find William de Roos among the archers who served in the *comitiva* of Adam de Everingham based on the predominance of the Roos family in the banneret's home territories of Nottingham and Yorkshire.[122]

Perhaps the most striking feature of the toponymic evidence of surnames is the predominance of archers who originated from Cheshire and Lancashire. That such a large proportion of men resided in counties where the Lancastrian household had most exerted its influence and power over previous decades is no surprise. It reinforces the point that captains had a penchant to recruit mounted archers from their own regions of influence and, furthermore, the high number of Cheshire and Lancashire archers in Lancaster's retinue suggests that Henry may have used a county array-style method of recruitment to obtain their services.[123] It was possibly by this means that eleven mounted archers from the Lancashire manor of Wolfall were recruited into the earl's retinue. This example of a large comrade group of archers probably represents a preformed fighting unit similar to those identified among the higher ranks of the army, and provides a rare insight into the patterns of recruitment at the level of mounted archer. Whether it was by systematic selection at county level or through an attachment to the earl that these men joined the retinue is unclear, but it is safe to presume that their recruitment, probably like many of the mounted archers, was a direct result of Lancaster's influence rather than that of his bannerets.[124]

In addition to military personnel, Lancaster's retinue would have included household servants and staff who served the earl's needs in times of peace and war. Interestingly, forty-two names recorded on the dorse of the first membrane of Lancaster's retinue roll are listed without a heading. It is possible that these 'heading-less' and 'title-less' individuals were mounted archers, but the occupational names of several of the men imply that they were attached to Lancaster's central household rather than being retinue-based combatants. The surnames 'of the Butlery' (*de la Buttlere*), 'the

[121] I am delighted to thank Philip Caudrey for his help in identifying the names of Norfolk esquires and archers in Lancaster's retinue.

[122] Early in the fifteenth century the Roos family succeeded to the manor of Laxton which had formerly been held by Adam Everingham. Robert Thoroton, *History of Nottinghamshire*, ed. John Throsby, 3 vols (London: B. and J. White; J. Walker, 1796), III, p. 209.

[123] William de Bohun, earl of Northampton operated a similar method to select and recruit mounted archers from his home county of Essex in 1346. Ayton, *English Army at Crécy*, p. 221; C 81/1735, no. 2.

[124] The manor of Wolfall was located within Huyton township which formed part of the hundred of West Derby. This hundred was part of the earldom of Lancaster. *The Victoria History of the County of Lancaster*, ed. William Farrer and J. Brownbill, 8 vols (London: Constable, 1906–1914), III (1907), pp. 172–4.

Carpenter' (*le Carponter*), 'the Cook' (*le Keu*), 'the Tailor' (*le Taillour*) and 'of the Chamber' (*de la Chambre*) suggest that they were personal attendants of the retinue leader, and the fact that Hugh 'the Cook' was granted an annuity by Lancaster implies that these were important men on whom he depended.[125] There is evidence that some magnates relied on their attendants and other members of the household to serve as archers during a campaign, whereby they would double up as both household servants and mounted archers.[126] However, it is difficult to imagine that Lancaster would have risked his choice cook or carpenter on the battlefield; and without linking these men to other nominal evidence of service it seems prudent to discount them as mounted archers.

Conclusion

Henry of Lancaster assembled his war retinue in a multitude of ways in 1345. The prosopographical evidence of individuals and groups of men has allowed us to reconstitute to some extent the various military components that formed Lancaster's retinue, and expose some of the internal structures on which it was built. As was typical of the time, Lancaster's *comitiva* included retainers and loyal followers, small knightly companies and sub-retinues of bannerets on which he depended to provide the greatest proportion of manpower. In addition, the rare examples of preformed groups of esquires and mounted archers reveal the internal small-scale companies among the lower military ranks which are often untraceable in the administrative records.

Above all else it was Lancaster's estimable reputation as a retinue captain and the relationships he had forged with individuals at home and abroad over the previous decade which enabled him to raise a retinue of unprecedented size. The earl's intimate relationship with Edward III and his strong affiliation with some of the nobility in Aquitaine were privileged attributes of a retinue leader, and central to the recruitment of a significant proportion of men who served under his banner. Indeed, Lancaster's extensive recruiting reach, which stretched across the Channel, was unique and unparalleled within the English nobility. The inclusion of Aquitanians and such men as

---

[125] Sometime before 1352 Hugh was granted an annuity of one mark in the manor of Shelton in Staffordshire, and the right of lands and pasture: *CIPM*, XI, p. 93; Fowler, 'Henry of Grosmont', II, pp. 319–20.

[126] For example when John Mowbray, earl Marshal, assembled his retinue in 1413, 'men, such as the earl's baker, came along simply in their own right as archers': Anne Curry, 'Personal Links and the Nature of the English War Retinue: A Case Study of John Mowbray', in *Liens personnels, réseaux et solidarités*, ed. E. Anceau, V. Gazeau and F. J. Riggin (Paris: Publications de la Sorbonne, 2006), pp. 153–68 (p. 166).

Sir Vascomede from the king's affinity also brought a continental dimension to the collective identity of the troop. It was by traditional methods of exploiting the spheres of influence and social networks of prominent knights that Lancaster raised large numbers of men but, ultimately, it was his own networks at the royal court and in the duchy which provided him with the wherewithal to raise such a formidable war retinue.

8

Lancaster's War Retinue in 1345: Cohesion and Stability

An investigation of the extent to which Henry of Lancaster's war retinue was a cohesive force, and an assessment of the stability of its composition, are prerequisites to understanding why it was such a formidable fighting contingent in 1345. The strength and cohesion of the retinue were fundamental to establishing efficient networks of command and communication, discipline and tactical capability, all of which were vital to its 'operational effectiveness' and no doubt contributed to the overall success of the expedition in the duchy.[1] A feeling of camaraderie based on previous experience of fighting alongside one another, of serving under the same captain or campaigning in the same theatre of war, would have helped forge a collective identity among the troop and enhanced their effectiveness and efficiency as a team of combatants. An insight into the *esprit de corps* which had developed among Lancaster's retinue can be gained by analysing the men's histories of service: including how often they had taken up arms together on earlier occasions and the proportion who had previously served under Lancaster's command. Moreover, evidence of continuity of military service with Lancaster on campaigns undertaken either side of the expedition to Aquitaine can be used to establish the stability of his military personnel in the mid 1340s. The level of stability of the composition of Lancaster's retinue can also be compared with that of retinues led by other captains around that time, as well as those led by noblemen at the end of the thirteenth and later in the fourteenth centuries, in order to determine whether the size of his *comitiva*, and the means by which it had been assembled, affected the overall stability of his troop in 1345.

In addition to a shared campaigning experience prior to 1345, the cohesion and unity of Lancaster's retinue derived from a wide range of personal connections which existed, on the one hand, between the retinue leader and his men (at-arms or archers) and, on the other, between the men themselves based, among other things, on family and friends, comradeship, lordship,

---

[1] Ayton discusses the benefits of cohesion and the stability of retinue composition in the context of the earl of Northampton's retinue in 1346: Ayton, *English Army at Crécy*, pp. 205–10.

tenure and a shared locality. The prosopographical evidence of Lancaster's men can be used to elucidate the pre-existing ties and personal relationships between individuals and groups of men who served under the earl's banner. Such 'horizontal' ties among the military personnel would have provided greater impetus to the sentiment of camaraderie and, in many ways, can reveal the complex social networks which often underpinned a war retinue. The corpus of men who left Lancaster's service in the duchy and returned to England during the course of the expedition will also be considered with a view to understanding the mentality of these soldiers, and gain a further insight into the retinue's cohesion.

Continuity of Service and Retinue Stability

A detailed study of Henry of Lancaster's retinue undertaken by Kenneth Fowler more than half a century ago elucidated many of the relationships between the earl and his men, and identified those individuals who served repeatedly under his banner.[2] Fowler's conclusion that the men who served Lancaster on military campaigns with some consistency 'amounted to no more than a small proportion of the troop' implies, as Ayton points out, a limited continuity of military personnel and a low level of stability among the retinue.[3] However, the analysis upon which this conclusion is based poses several interpretative problems. First, Fowler's conclusions are based on the service of 538 men who served with Lancaster throughout his military career, rather than on a single campaign, and therefore do not allow for the fluctuation in size of the war retinues which the earl led on different expeditions.[4] The size of Lancaster's *comitive* would have varied depending upon the stage that he had reached in his career as well as various other factors, such as the theatre of war, military developments, the nature of the expedition, the overall size of the army and his position within its command structure. It would be inaccurate, therefore, to apply such general analysis to the retinue which set out to Aquitaine in 1345. Second, Fowler's sample is superficially high because it includes individuals whose service has been counted twice due to problems of homonymity; moreover, clerks and household attendants have been mistakenly included among the corpus of men-at-arms who served in 1345.[5] Any proportional analysis based on Fowler's

[2]   Fowler, *King's Lieutenant*, pp. 175–86.
[3]   Fowler, *King's Lieutenant*, p. 183. Ayton, *English Army at Crécy*, p. 204, n. 223.
[4]   For the nominal list of 538 men who served in Lancaster's retinue on military and diplomatic expeditions throughout the earl's career, see Fowler, 'Henry of Grosmont', II, pp. 240–63.
[5]   For example, Fowler regards the two letters of protection granted to William son of Roger de Pemberton and to his alias, William son and heir of Roger de Pemberton, in

current sample, therefore, would be relatively diminished and skewed. This invites a more comprehensive study of the continuity of service in Lancaster's retinue to be undertaken and, more importantly, one that is based firmly on prosopographical evidence of individuals who served him in 1345.

The fresh analysis of military service in this study of Lancaster's war retinue is based on a sample of 661 men who served or who intended to serve with the earl in 1345. The lengthy retinue roll originally attached to Lancaster's particulars of account provides the identities of 588 individuals. In addition, the names of a further 35 men have been recovered from an array of administrative and narrative sources which predominantly comprise letters patent of pardon, royal protections and writs of exoneration produced in connection with the military-based land assessment of the mid 1340s.[6]

Table 8. Service in Lancaster's Retinue before 1345: Whole Retinue

Number of expeditions	0	1	2	3	4	5	Total
Number of men (% of sample)	600 (90.8)	32 (4.8)	14 (2.1)	8 (1.2)	4 (0.6)	3 (0.5)	661 (100%)

In order to assess the stability of the retinue's composition in 1345 we must first establish how many of Lancaster's men had served with him before the expedition to Aquitaine. What proportion of the troop had fought together under the earl's banner and were accustomed to or at least had some experience of his tactical command? Table 8 suggests that the great majority of men (90.8%) from the sample were serving in Lancaster's retinue for the first time in 1345 and that sixty-one men (9.2%) had already served with him at least once. The evidence implies that Lancaster had recruited heavily from outside the nucleus of his retinue, or perhaps that his retinue was still in its infancy during the mid 1340s. Furthermore, that only twenty-nine men had served with him on two or more previous expeditions seems to support Fowler's conclusion that only a small proportion of men served regularly with Lancaster.

1345 as pertaining to different people. Conversely, his nominal roll includes five men whose service in 1345 cannot be substantiated by the cited documentary sources: John de Aldewyncle; Jankyn Bushy; Richard Ronolme; John son and heir of John St Philbert (arrested in Pisa) and Thomas Uvedale. Fowler, 'Henry of Grosmont', II, p. 257; C 76/20, m. 15; C 81/1724/38. The 173 men-at-arms identified by Fowler as having served in 1345 include clerks and likely attendants of Lancaster, whose names are recorded on the dorse of the first membrane of the retinue roll. Fowler, *King's Lieutenant*, p. 229.

[6] The discrepancy between the sample (661) and the number of named men (623) has resulted from the inclusion of 38 anonymous knights and esquires.

However, the sample of 661 men does include several groups of men whose presence skews the evidence for previous service in Lancaster's retinue. First, there is the problem of anonymity. In total there are thirty-eight individuals among the ranks of knight and esquire whose identity remains unknown. The companion of Andrew Luttrell, for example, has provided valuable evidence relating to the formation and structure of Lancaster's war retinue, but without the name of Luttrell's companion it is impossible to reconstruct his history of service. Similarly, the careers of men who belonged to the anonymous groups of esquires led by Henry de Lalande and John Musard cannot be reconstituted. Second, we need to consider the Aquitanian contingent whose service with Lancaster was directly linked to the proximity of warfare in 1345.[7] These men are not likely to have fought in the theatres of war in which Lancaster had previously led retinues, namely Scotland, Brittany and the Low Countries, or, indeed, taken part in other fighting that was far removed from the proximity of the duchy.[8] And, although Lancaster had spent time in Aquitaine in 1344 he was yet to lead a war retinue in the duchy prior to 1345.[9] It seems unrealistic, therefore, to include men in the sample who had had no real opportunity of previous service in the earl's retinue.

The third and largest group which skews the evidence of prior service is that consisting of mounted archers. The careers of these soldiers (and, to a lesser extent, esquires) are the most difficult to reconstitute due to the nature of the administrative sources, biased as they are towards men of higher rank and status. Indeed, the only extant retinue roll – one of the principal sources of nominal evidence of archers' service – which relates to prior service with Lancaster is that for the Scottish expedition in 1336 but, frustratingly, it lacks archers' names.[10] Consequently, it is almost impossible to determine whether any of the archers at all in 1345 had previously served

---

[7]   The known Aquitanians in Lancaster's retinue comprised one banneret, 8 knights and 12 esquires.

[8]   It was fairly common for relatively humble 'Gascons' to serve in the English armies which campaigned in Scotland during the reigns of Edward I and Edward II, but there is no evidence that any of the Aquitanians in Lancaster's retinue had served in Scotland. David Simpkin, 'The King's Sergeants-at-Arms and the War in Scotland, 1296–1322', in *England and Scotland at War, c. 1296–c. 1513*, ed. Andy King and David Simpkin (Leiden: Brill, 2012), pp. 77–117 (pp. 82–4).

[9]   The appointment of the lord of Pommiers by Lancaster to negotiate with Alfonso XI of Castile in 1344 suggests that the Gascon lord, and perhaps the same company of knights and esquires who accompanied him in 1345, had taken part in the diplomatic mission to Avignon and Spain, although we cannot be certain whether Pommiers was actually part of the earl's retinue.

[10]   E 101/15/12. Strictly speaking the document is a muster roll, which was drawn up as part of the muster process, rather than a retinue roll which would have been produced at a later date and presented for account at the Exchequer. The roll is attached to a truncated list of warhorses lost by Lancaster's retinue on the expedition.

with the earl. The final corpus of men who should be removed from the sample is the probable attendants and personal servants of Lancaster, whose names are recorded on the dorse of the retinue roll attached to the earl's particulars of account. In all likelihood, these men were not retinue-based combatants and therefore should be discounted in our analysis of the continuity of military personnel.

The removal of these four groups from the original sample gives us a smaller, and more realistic, sample of 295 men, whose history of prior service with Lancaster is presented in Table 9 below. The table shows that the service history of esquires is almost identical to the evidence presented in Table 8, while the results for men belonging to the 'Others' category – which comprises clergymen, clerks and pardon recipients – also generally reflects those of the main sample.[11] That only one in ten of the esquires are known to have taken up arms with Lancaster on a previous occasion is no surprise owing to the paucity of records, such as muster rolls or retinue rolls, which represent men of this rank. Conversely, the results of the 'bannerets' and 'knights' categories show a completely different pattern of previous service, which is somewhat expected given that both categories represent the best documented groups of men in Lancaster's retinue.

Six of the bannerets (75%) had served in Lancaster's retinue at least once before 1345, and half of them had fought with him at least twice. Amongst these men were experienced war captains such as Adam de Everingham and Hugh Meynell who had already served with their retinue leader on three and four previous occasions, respectively. Both men had fought in the main theatres of war since the 1330s, and possibly earlier. The latter's venture on the celebrated raids in Scotland (1336) and Cadzand (1337) no doubt provided invaluable experience for the chevauchée which characterised much of the expedition in Aquitaine, while the former banneret had experienced fierce fighting and the deployment of 'new' combined tactics involving the use of dismounted men-at-arms and longbowmen at the battle of Halidon Hill (1333). And among those who had served Lancaster once we find John de Norwich – the most prominent of the sub-captains who led an expeditionary force to Aquitaine in 1337. His previous command and experience of warfare in the duchy must have been a significant factor to the success of the strategies utilised by Lancaster over the course of the expedition in 1345. The collective experience of the earl's sub-captains was underpinned by a high level of continuity of military personnel, but the *bannereti* constitute the smallest group in Lancaster's retinue and therefore are not representative of the entire contingent.

---

[11]   The majority of the 'Others' have no prior service with Lancaster, and the high proportion (25%) of men who had twice served the earl can be understood by the relatively small size of the group and the diversity of its subjects' status.

Table 9. Service in Lancaster's Retinue before 1345: 295 Selected Men

	Number of Expeditions						Total in 1345 retinue	Total with prior service (%)
	0	1	2	3	4	5		
Bannerets (%)	2 (25.0)	3ª (37.5)	1 (12.5)	1 (12.5)	1 (12.5)	0 (0.0)	8 (100)	6 (75)
Knights (%)	55 (63.2)	14 (16.1)	9 (10.3)	5 (5.7)	2 (2.3)	2 (2.3)	87 (99.9)	32 (36.8)
Esquires (%)	169 (89.4)	12 (6.3)	4 (2.1)	2 (1.1)	1 (0.5)	1 (0.5)	189 (99.9)	20 (10.6)
Others (%)	8 (72.7)	0 (0.0)	3 (25.0)	0 (0.0)	0 (0.0)	0 (0.0)	11 (100)	3 (27.3)
Total							295	61 (20.7)

Note: The sample of 295 does not include the 269 archers, 39 attendants, 38 anonymous men-at-arms and 20 Aquitanian men-at-arms who served in Lancaster's retinue in 1345.
ª Includes Lord Pommiers.

To make a wider assessment of the stability of retinue composition in 1345 we must turn our attention to Lancaster's knights. Table 9 shows that 32 out of 87 knights (36.8%) had already served with Lancaster at least once before the expedition to Aquitaine: five of these had served on at least three expeditions, two on at least four expeditions, and two on at least five expeditions. That more than a third of the men had served previously with Lancaster suggests a moderate degree of stability within the knight's rank, but how does the evidence compare with the continuity of service in other comital retinues of the mid 1340s? Ayton's study of the English army at Crécy (1346) has shown that a much larger proportion of knights in the retinues of Thomas Beauchamp, earl of Warwick, and John de Bohun, earl of Northampton, had fought with their respective captains on previous campaigns. In the case of Warwick, 85% of men had previously served the earl, and a similar proportion of knights returned to take up arms under Northampton's banner again.[12] It should be borne in mind, however, that the retinues of Northampton and Warwick were small compared with that led by Lancaster in 1345: the former comprised only 48 knights, of whom the names of 12 are missing, and the latter may have included as few as 29 knights.[13] When we consider the extraordinary size of Lancaster's *comitiva*, which included more than double the number of knights in Northampton's retinue, and four times as many in Warwick's, the figure of 36.8% seems to reflect a greater stability among the knightly class than initially might be thought the case. Moreover, this stability is all the more impressive considering how the earl's retinue had greatly expanded over the course of the previous decade. The *comitive* that Lancaster led to Scotland (1336) and to the Low Countries (1338, 1340), for example, comprised less than half the number of men-at-arms that served with him in 1345, while the proportion of knights that served under his banner in Aquitaine was almost double that which he led to Brittany in 1342.[14] Quite clearly Lancaster's extended or 'super' retinue in 1345 was distinct in size from the 'standard' retinues which

---

[12] Out of 20 knights, 17 (85%) and 29 out of 36 knights (81%) had previously served Warwick and Northampton, respectively. The evidence of prior service in Warwick's retinue is based on 20 knights listed in a bill of request, but other administrative records provide the identities of another 9 knights. C 81/1742/26; Ayton, *Dynamics of Recruitment*, p. 16; Ayton, *English Army at Crécy*, p. 207.

[13] The precise size and composition of either retinue is unknown, but Ayton's extrapolation of the administrative records suggests Northampton led approximately 161 men-at-arms and 141 mounted archers, and Warwick around 150 men-at-arms and 150 mounted archers. Ayton, *English Army at Crécy*, p. 205; Ayton, *Dynamics of Recruitment*, pp. 12–13.

[14] Number of men-at-arms (of which knights banneret or bachelor) in Lancaster's retinues: 1336, 100 (18); 1338, 70 (18); 1340, 115 (32); 1342; 182 (40); 1345, 250 (100). E 101/15/12 (1336); Fowler, 'Henry of Grosmont', I, p. 34, n. 1 (1338); Fowler, 'Henry of Grosmont', I, p. 36, n. 2 (1340); Ayton, *Knights and Warhorses*, p. 263 (1342); Appendix A (1345). Note that the proportion of knights and the overall size of Lancaster's retinue

he had led on earlier campaigns and, indeed, from those led by North-ampton and Warwick on Edward III's Normandy expedition. The level of continuity, therefore, has to have been distorted by the relative growth of Lancaster's retinue and his reliance upon the indirect recruitment of an unusually large number of men through the use of sub-captains, which inevitably had a negative impact on the levels of perceived continuity.

Table 10. Number of Lancaster's Men in 1345 Who Served in 1344 and 1347

	No. of men in 1345	No. of men in 1345 who served in 1344	No. of men in 1345 who served in 1347
Bannerets and Knights	95	20 (21.1%)	31 (32.6%)

Perhaps a more accurate indication of the stability of military personnel in Lancaster's retinue is the rates of service of the same men on campaigns undertaken by the earl immediately before and after the expedition to Aqui-taine. The evidence presented in Table 10, which excludes the service of esquires and mounted archers, shows that a greater proportion of bannerets and knights in 1345 continued to serve with Lancaster at Calais (1347) than had served previously with him in the Iberian peninsula (1344). This differ-ence in retinue stability is to be expected considering that Henry would probably have maintained a smaller retinue for the latter expedition which was diplomatic in nature. Nevertheless, that only a third (32.6%) of the bannerets and knights from the retinue of 1345 continued to serve with their retinue leader in 1347 is comparable to the diminished rates of re-service evident among the retinues raised later in the fourteenth century.[15] Of the knights in the *comitive* of the earl of Arundel and John of Gaunt in the 1370s and 1380s, for example, around one in three were returning campaigners, and the rates of re-service among non-comital retinues seem to have been similar.[16] Apart from the usual caveats which often accompany interpretative

---

fluctuated from 1338 to 1339 on account of the arrival of reinforcements and seven esquires who became newly created knights: *Norwell*, p. xcviii.

[15] It is also interesting to note that that in the case of Northampton's retinue in 1346, if we focus on military service over consecutive campaigns, we find that just 43% of his retinue at Crécy had served with him on the preceding expedition to Brittany in 1345. Ayton, *English Army at Crécy*, p. 206.

[16] In 1388 35% of knights in the earl of Arundel's retinue had also served with him during the expedition of the previous year, and a similar rate of re-service is evident amongst most of the retinues led by John of Gaunt. Ayton, *Dynamics of Recruitment*, p. 24, n. 58; Walker, *Lancastrian Affinity*, p. 51. In the 1370s the proportion of men-at-arms in the retinues of Guy, Lord Brian, who returned to his service from the previous campaign never exceeded one third, and, a similar rate of returning men-at-arms is evident among William de Windsor's retinues which campaigned in Ireland in the 1360s: Ayton, *Dynamics of Recruitment*, p. 24; Baker, 'The English Way of War', p. 143.

analysis of military service, namely that the evidence is largely understated due to the unevenness in quality of the extant records, the rate of re-service among Lancaster's men in 1347 should also be considered in light of the nuances in retinue formation for the expedition two years earlier.

In 1345 we know that Lancaster relied, more than usual, upon 'off-the-peg' companies and the recruitment of knights with whom he had little or no personal connection, which probably resulted in a large number of men departing from the earl's service once the campaign had ended. The need for a smaller retinue in 1347 would have caused a natural break-up of some of the previous 'super' retinue's components, such as followings of bannerets and small knightly companies, which led to an inevitable fall in the number of men returning into Lancaster's service. The two bannerets John de Norwich and John de Grey of Codnor, for example, resumed their roles as retinue leaders in their own right, and served at Calais independently of Lancaster with their personal followings.[17] A drop in the number of returning knights in 1347 can also be accounted for, albeit in a small way, by those *milites* who remained in the duchy of Aquitaine after Lancaster had returned to England. Sir Thomas Cok, for instance, who had served Lancaster on four previous occasions and, as marshal of the army, was the earl's right-hand man, would almost certainly have served again under the same banner had he not been appointed seneschal of the duchy on 22 March 1347.[18] The absence of Cok, therefore, and possibly other regular followers of Lancaster who remained in Aquitaine due to military practicalities or for other reasons unknown, had a negative effect on the rate of re-service.

If, then, we adopt a similar analytical approach to that of Andrew Ayton and view the evidence of military service from the past and look forward to the expedition in 1345, perhaps we can get a clearer sense of the level of stability in Lancaster's retinue which set out for Aquitaine.[19] The retinue which Lancaster had led to the Iberian peninsula in 1344 probably consisted of eighty men-at-arms (of whom forty can be identified based on the evidence of letters of protection) and, more than likely, an unknown number of mounted archers.[20] An extant bill of request for protections reveals the identity of twenty-six men and their names are grouped in such a way as to

[17] On 14 May 1347 Grey and Norwich were ordered along with thirty other magnates, including Lancaster himself, to join the king at Calais. The summons also included Sir John de Verdon who was another knight who served in Lancaster's retinue in 1345. C 76/24, m. 10.

[18] C 61/59, m. 13; appointment to office of seneschal.

[19] Ayton, *English Army at Crécy*, p. 207; Ayton, *Dynamics of Recruitment*, pp. 16–17.

[20] The bill of request for protections indicates that the prominent knights of the retinue brought a combined force of thirty-six unknown men-at-arms: C 81/1724/49. Note that the esquires who took out protections may have been included amongst the men-at-arms who served in the knightly companies, therefore eighty men-at-arms (including Lancaster himself) should be taken as a maximum number.

indicate the military rank of each man.[21] The names of a further two knights and twelve esquires are provided by the enrolled letters of protection.[22]

Table 11. Number of Men in Lancaster's Retinue of 1344 Who also Served in 1345

	No. who served in 1344	No. who re-served in 1345
Bannerets	2	2 (100%)
Knights	18	14 (77.8%)
Esquires	20	13 (65%)

Table 11 shows a high level of continuity of service among the military personnel who had served with Lancaster in 1344 – almost three quarters of the men-at-arms served with the earl again the following year, including both bannerets, 14 out of 18 knights (77.8%) and 13 out of 20 esquires (65%). Such high rates of re-service are equivalent to the levels of stability which existed among Northampton and Warwick's men at Crécy, or, indeed, the retinues led by Henry, Lord Percy and Ralph, Lord Neville in the previous decade.[23] Interestingly, the level of stability evident in the composition of Lancaster's retinue was also characteristic of the retinue contingents led by earls of Edward I, and a similar degree of continuity existed in the retinue contingents which fought in the Scottish wars during the reign of Edward II.[24] Retinues of a relatively stable composition, therefore, had been a common feature of English armies for more than half a century, and the figures presented in Table 11 suggest that the majority of men who served with Lancaster in 1344 represent a core group of soldiers who brought an important element of cohesion to his troop that set out to Aquitaine in the following year.[25]

[21] C 81/1724/49.

[22] C 76/19, mm. 19, 22, 23.

[23] Less than 70% of Warwick's retinue in 1345 returned in 1346: Ayton, *Dynamics of Recruitment*, p. 17. Of the fifty-six men-at-arms who accompanied Percy to Scotland in 1336, 73% returned to his service in the following year, while the rate of re-service in Neville's retinue was approximately 60%: Ayton, *Armies and Military Communities*, p. 233 and n. 75. Note that the rates of re-service among the retinues of Northampton and Warwick would probably increase if we had corresponding extant and complete retinue rolls for service in 1346.

[24] Andrew Spencer has demonstrated that 56% of men-at-arms who served in the *comitiva* of Edmund of Lancaster during the Welsh campaign of 1294 returned to serve with the earl again in 1296, and similar patterns of continuity are also evident among the earls of Lincoln and Surrey. Andrew Spencer, 'The Comital Military Retinue in the Reign of Edward I', *Historical Research*, 83 (2008), 46–59 (pp. 54–8). In a sample of fifty retinues in the English army at Falkirk (1298), around 50% of knights served on consecutive campaigns with the same captain: Simpkin, *English Aristocracy at War*, p. 129.

[25] Of the four non-returning knights in 1345, two – James Audley and John Lovel – had relatives in Lancaster's retinue in that year, which reinforces the point that the knights

Furthermore, much of the retinue's stability in 1345 had been built up over the previous decade. The retinue roll for Lancaster's service in Scotland in 1336 shows that more than a third of the knights and around one in five esquires went on to serve with Lancaster in Aquitaine.[26] This implies that many of the stable elements of the earl's retinue in 1345, those soldiers who served him with some consistency, had been established earlier in his military career. Conversely, the evolution of Lancaster's *comitiva* and the very nature of the 'dynamics of recruitment' meant there was a natural flux in the personnel who repeatedly served under his banner – indeed, the extent to which his core group of followers could either change or expand over one generation is reflected by the fact that only a quarter of the men-at-arms in 1344 had also served, or shared the same surname, with men who had served with him in 1336.[27] Inevitably, the stability of his retinue in 1345 was reduced by the influx of a swathe of new faces due to the extraordinarily high recruitment target for retinue-based manpower. Soldiers who were taking up arms for the first time on the expedition, such as Hugh Courson, would not have been an exception, nor would men like Sir Philip de Waure, whose service in the duchy appears to have been part of a one-off campaign in an otherwise non-existent martial career.[28] However, there can be no doubt that those men who served with Lancaster for the first time were joining a settled team of experienced warriors. The knights Thomas Cok and Hugh Meynell, and the veteran esquires Edmund de Bulstrode and Payn de Mohun, are but a few of many examples of long-standing comrades-in-arms who had campaigned in Lancaster's retinue for almost decade. The prosopographical evidence has revealed a much greater continuity of service in Lancaster's retinue than was previously thought to have been the case, and one that was typical of other retinues of the mid 1340s and, indeed, of the five previous decades.

---

who served the earl in 1344 represented his 'core group' of men. Indeed, the only reason Audley did not serve again the following year was because he intended to lead his own retinue force separate from Lancaster's on the 1345 expedition.

[26] E 101/15/12. Six out of 16 knights (37.5%) and 15 out of 77 known esquires (19.5%) went on to serve with Lancaster in 1345. If we include men who shared the same surname as others in 1345, then the proportion of returning esquires increases to almost a half. Note that the continuity of service between the two campaigns would probably have been much higher but for the absence of Sir Nicholas Cantilupe ('Kauntelon') on the latter expedition, who had served as Lancaster's banneret in 1336 and was part of the earl's retinue in 1338 and 1342. The Twyford family, who had regularly contributed to Lancaster's retinue manpower throughout the 1330s, also appear to have left the earl's service at the beginning of the 1340s.

[27] Surnames of men who served, or whose relatives served in 1336 and 1344: Cok, Hastings, Meynell, Mohun, Norwich, Seaton, Simeon, Walkington.

[28] It is surprising that no records of military service for Waure can be found relating to other campaigns, particularly as he is named 5th in the nominal list of knights on the 1345 retinue roll and was therefore clearly a knight of some standing.

Among the soldiers who served in Lancaster's retinue in 1345 are a handful of individuals whose families had also provided the earl's father, and namesake, with military service. At least twelve knights and six esquires share their surnames with men who are known to have served the elder Earl Henry, and all of whom must have acted as a strengthening and stabilising force on the war retinue in 1345.[29] Indeed, more than forty of Lancaster's men in 1345 belonged to families whose members had either served with or militarily supported his uncle, Thomas, earl of Lancaster.[30] The prevalence of the families' tradition of service across several generations with the same noble household is also evident in the retinues raised by Edmund, first earl of Lancaster, near the end of the thirteenth century and those led by his successor in the subsequent decades.[31] And in the cases of Cuilly and Meynell, we find different generations of the same family having served all four successive earls up to the mid-fourteenth century.[32] Such longstanding supporters of the house of Lancaster reveal the extent to which continuity of service underpinned the martial tradition of particular families, and a not insignificant proportion of military personnel who set out for Aquitaine in 1345.[33]

[29] Surnames: Blount, Burdet, Dalton, Darcy, Ferrers, Grey, Hastings, Melbourne, Ryvere, Simeon, Trussell, Verdon, Walkington and Wilinton.

[30] Fowler, *King's Lieutenant*, p. 185, n. 115. Additional families to those already identified by Fowler: Bayouse, Beler, Blount, Burdet, Clinton, Darcy, Greasley, Hothum, Lovel, Luttrell, Mare, Mohun, Musard, Newmarch, Paynel, Ryvere, Seaton, Swinnerton, Trussell, St Pierre, Verdon, Wake, Walkefare, Walkington, Zouche.

[31] Of the men who accompanied Edmund of Lancaster on crusade in 1270, 30% either served or share their surname with men who served in the retinues of Earls Edmund and Thomas in the decade following 1294. Spencer, *Military Retinue in the Reign of Edward I*, pp. 57–8.

[32] The families of Meynell and Cuilly contributed manpower to the military retinues of the house of Lancaster from the thirteenth up to the mid-fourteenth century. For reference to the careers of men under the first two earls of Lancaster see, Madicott, *Thomas of Lancaster*, pp. 53–4; Spencer, *Nobility and Kingship in Medieval England*, p. 133, n. 109. For careers under the later earls see references in Fowler, *King's Lieutenant*.

[33] Family traditions of service with the same noble household, although over a much shorter period, are also evident among the men-at-arms who served in the retinues of Lord Percy from 1327 to the late 1330s: Ayton, *Armies and Military Communities*, p. 233–4.

Comradeship Groups

The stability of retinue-based combatants also derived from comradeship groups and individuals who had a shared campaigning experience with retinue captains other than Lancaster. In this way the stability of military personnel in one magnate's retinue might be transferred to another, and is a point nicely illustrated by the early careers of Sir Alexander Auncel and Sir Richard de Rawcliffe. From 1336 to 1340 both men had twice served together under the banners of Henry, Lord Beaumont and his son and heir John Beaumont in different theatres of war.[34] Before 1345, however, Auncel had never served with Lancaster, and Rawcliffe had taken up arms with the earl on only one previous occasion.[35] This evidence of limited or no continuity of service with the earl suggests that both knights contributed little to the retinue's stability, but their shared experience of fighting under the Beaumont banner on earlier campaigns suggests that they brought a pre-existing camaraderie and degree of stability to Lancaster's retinue in 1345.

Sir John de Lymbury also had a tradition of service with the same magnate family, having served with Henry Beaumont at Bannockburn in 1314 and on three subsequent campaigns in the same retinue up to 1319.[36] There are, indeed, not a few examples of men in Lancaster's *comitiva* who had previously served together with different retinue captains, and the benefits of their shared campaigning experience no doubt reinforced an *esprit de corps* in Lancaster's retinue in the mid 1340s.[37] Such camaraderie permeated all ranks of the retinue: the examples of large groups of esquires led by John Musard and Henry de Lalande highlight Lancaster's use of pre-formed and probably, therefore, stable units of men, while the dozen or so archers from the Lancashire village of Wolfall in Huyton are a poignant reminder that neighbourhood and locality were also potential sources of cohesion.[38] These various and sometimes opaque networks of comradeship groups which existed at different echelons of the retinue would have promoted the overall stability of the troop in 1345.

---

[34] Service with Lord Beaumont in Scotland, 1336: E 101/19/36, m. 2. Service with John Beaumont in the Low Countries, 1340: C 76/15, m. 22. Auncel also served with John Beaumont in 1338: C 76/12, m. 7.

[35] Rawcliffe (1344): C 76/19, m. 19; C 81/1724, m. 49.

[36] C 71/6, m. 3 (1314); C 71/8, m. 6 (1315); C 71/8, m. 4 (1318); C 71/10, m. 4 (1319).

[37] Hugh Trussebut and Reginald de Mohun, for example, were part of the Earl Marshal's retinue in 1327 and Robert de Causton and Norman de Swinford both accompanied the earl of Gloucester to Brittany in 1342. C 71/11, m. 5 (Trussebut and Mohun); C 76/17, m. 25 (Causton and Swinford).

[38] For discussion on these comradeship groups, see previous chapter.

Returnees from Aquitaine

The continuity of service within Lancaster's retinue can also be measured over the course of the expedition in Aquitaine rather than from one campaign to the next. The administrative records used to make a formal account of Lancaster's service, namely the particulars of account and attached retinue roll, present a somewhat artificial picture of continuous service by the same men in his retinue but, inevitably, there was some fluctuation of military personnel. Besides the usual dangers of warfare faced by every soldier, such as fatality or capture (as was the case for Sir John de Dalton and Sir William Bernak), a further drop in manpower was caused by the departure of a number of men from Lancaster's service in the duchy.[39] No fewer than eleven men-at-arms, of whom eight were knights, returned to England at some point over the course of the expedition.[40] So what were the reasons for their departure? Can we deduce from the prosopographical evidence the motivations of these individuals for military service, or gain an insight into their *mentalité*? Moreover, what impact did their departure have on the stability of the retinue composition?

The reasons for the men's departure might be explained by the activities in which they became engaged following their arrival in England. In the case of Simon Simeon, his return to England in the spring of 1346 was to be expected considering the itinerant nature of his role as *nuncius*, and it should be noted that Simeon intended to return to the duchy soon after he had brought news of events in Aquitaine to Edward III.[41] Of the ten other men who returned from Aquitaine, at least eight took part in a major military campaign in 1346. Sir Ralph de Hastings brought news of events from the duchy to Leicester corporation before leading the second division of the English army against the Scots at Neville's Cross in October.[42] Five of the knights, as well as Roger Flitcham and Hugh Courson, embarked on Edward III's expedition to Normandy in July, which culminated in the

[39] E 403/338, m. 34; payment of 100 marks by Edward III for part of Dalton's redemption. *Crécy and Calais*, p. 145; William's father, John Bernak, had spent a large sum for his release.

[40] Returns: John Blount, Robert Burdet, Henry de Caldecotes, Hugh Courson, Richard Fitzsimon, Roger Flitcham, Ralph de Hastings, Ralph de Neville, Nicholas de Peyvre, Thomas Ramesbury, Simon Simeon.

[41] A letter close made on 17 May 1347 states that Simeon 'is now about to return to Gascony on the King's order': *CCR, 1346–49*, p. 76.

[42] *Records of the Borough of Leicester: Being a Series of Extracts from the Archives of the Corporation of Leicester, 1509–1603*, ed. Mary Bateson, 7 vols (London: C. J. Clay, 1899–1974), II (1901), p. 65. Michael Prestwich, 'The English at The Battle of Neville's Cross', in *The Battle of Neville's Cross, 1346*, ed. Michael Prestwich and David Rollason (Stamford: Shaun Tyas, 1998), (pp. 1–14), p. 11.

battle of Crécy.[43] A writ of exoneration for military service reveals that Sir
John Blount stayed *in partibus Vasconie* until the third week after Easter (7
May 1346), but there is no evidence to suggest that he took up arms again
that year. The confirmation of a grant by Sir Robert de Neville of Hornby in
the Chancery on 28 September 1346, the day before he was issued a protection for service at the siege of Calais, suggests that he too was absent from
the king's military exploits in Normandy.[44]

    Those men who left Lancaster's *comitiva* to take part in Edward III's
expedition found service in various different retinues. Sir Thomas Ramesbury and Roger Flitcham both served in the retinue of William de Kildesby,
king's clerk, while Sir Henry de Caldecotes served under the earl of Salisbury's banner.[45] Interestingly, there is no evidence to suggest that any of
the men had served with their captains on a previous campaign. Sir Robert
Burdet was among the men who were recruited into the ranks of Sir Richard
Talbot's retinue for the first time.[46] Ayton points out that in 1346 Talbot
'seems to have lacked a stable core of personnel' due to the frequent garrison
service he had undertaken earlier in his career;[47] a 'new' knight such as
Burdet, therefore, would probably have been a welcome recruit.[48] Sir Nicholas de Peyvre is another knight who joined a retinue captain with whom
he had no history of service; in 1346 Peyvre served with Geoffrey Say, a
banneret who led his own company in the earl of Northampton's retinue.
There is no known connection between the two knights, however it may have
been Say's service with Lancaster in 1338 which influenced Peyvre's choice of
captain.[49] Sir Richard Fitzsimon served with the Black Prince at Crécy, in
the opening campaign of the young prince's military career. Although there
was no history of service between the soldier and his captain, Fitzsimon's
role as the prince's standard-bearer suggests that he must have already been
affiliated with the prince's household.

    So what motivated these men to leave the duchy of Aquitaine? In the
case of Ralph de Hastings it seems reasonable to speculate that his sense of

---

[43] Ayton's suggestion that Courson may have been the only soldier to take part in the
major battles in Aquitaine and in Normandy the following year seems very unlikely:
Ayton, *English Army at Crécy*, p. 203.

[44] *CCR, 1346–49*, p. 151; C 76/23, m. 14.

[45] C 76/22, mm. 8, 15d (Ramesbury); *Crécy and Calais*, p. 158, C 76/22, m. 9 (Flitcham);
C 76/25, m. 20d (Caldecotes).

[46] C 76/22, m. 12; E 159/123, m. 123d.

[47] Ayton, *English Army at Crécy*, pp. 212–13.

[48] It is interesting that three of the men-at-arms mentioned above served in retinues
led by a royal clerk or, in Talbot's case, the steward of the royal household. This might
suggest that members of the king's household struggled to meet an unusually high
recruitment target and therefore relied more heavily on men with whom they had little
or no association.

[49] C 76/25, m. 26d; E 159/123, m. 154d (Peyvre). C 76/ 12, m. 8 (Say).

duty as head of one of the prominent Yorkshire gentry families and strong regional ties to the northern county were among the reasons for his return to England. Hastings had previously served as constable and steward of the honour of Pickering for Lancaster's father, as well as sheriff of Yorkshire from 1337 to 1340.[50] He was a man firmly embedded in the social fabric of the county but, more importantly, he was an integral part of the military community in northern England which is reflected by his command of the army's second division at the battle of Neville's Cross.[51] Such important factors are likely to have influenced his decision to return to England, which was probably made sometime during the spring of 1346.[52] Although the Scots did not cross the border until the beginning of October, the threat of an attack would have been realised by the English much sooner. Perhaps another feeling which resonated in Hastings' mind was a desire to defend his family estates and protect his property in Yorkshire against the devastation which would have ensued had the Scottish invasion succeeded. The threat of financial loss and the prospect of being unable to defend his land-holdings must also have contributed to Hastings' decision to withdraw from Aquitaine.

In the instance of Richard Fitzsimon it was possibly his loyalty to the Black Prince that inspired his return to England. However, it is difficult to establish his association with the prince's household prior to 1346 and perhaps, therefore, an ambition to become established in a retinue whose leader was heir to the throne caused Fitzsimon's return.[53] Conversely, he may have been 'parachuted' in to the young prince's retinue at the request of Edward III in order to bolster its ranks with the experience of a veteran knight who was well known to the king. Fitzsimon's career in arms had progressed since the mid 1330s when he had served in John de Norwich's retinue, and he had twice served with Lancaster before serving as the prince's standard-bearer in 1346.[54] He was retained by the Black Prince and served with him again in the following year; and although he received the grant of an annuity for 'good service' at Crécy, namely his heroic defence of the

---

[50] *CPR, 1330–34*, p. 364; *Somerville*, p. 356.

[51] He shared the command with the earl of Angus, Lord Deyncourt, Roger la Zouche and the provost of Beverley: Prestwich, *Battle of Neville's Cross*, p. 11.

[52] *Oeuvres*, IV, p. 337. According to Froissart, Hastings was one of the knights sent to recapture the castle of Villefranche prior to the siege of Aiguillon which probably began at the end of March.

[53] David Green suggests that Fitzsimon may have come to the prince's attention through his earlier service with Reginald de Cobham in 1338 (personal correspondence, 12 November 2012). Interestingly, Fitzsimon is not mentioned in the incomplete account of the prince's household foreign expenses for 1344: BL, Harleian MS 4304.

[54] Richard Barber, *Edward, Prince of Wales and Aquitaine: A Biography of the Black Prince* (Woodbridge: Boydell, 1978), p. 67; David Green, *Edward the Black Prince: Power in Medieval Europe* (Harlow: Longman, 2007), p. 38.

prince's banner, the greatest reward was bestowed on him in 1348 when he became a Knight of the Garter.[55]

For the other six men-at-arms who took part in the Normandy expedition after having served with Lancaster, perhaps it was a simple desire for warfare, or more specifically, a desire for the rewards of warfare, which inspired their departure. The psychological impact of Lancaster's twin victories against the French in 1345, first at Bergerac and then at Auberoche, should not be underestimated. The huge profits amassed from the booty and ransoms of prisoners following the military success were unprecedented in the Hundred Years' War and demonstrated the potential rewards of a successful campaign. Obviously, Lancaster's men who departed early from Aquitaine during the course of the campaign could not have known that the expedition in the north of France would culminate in the victory at Crécy. However, they would have been aware that the king intended to lead a much larger army on a military enterprise of a grander scale which could provide another opportunity to further their career in arms and, potentially, allow them to reap the rewards of war. The prospect of campaigning in a different theatre of war must have seemed even more appealing to these men, considering that the possibility of another decisive victory in Aquitaine was unlikely following the arrival of the duke of Normandy's large army. For men like Hugh Courson who had never taken up arms before, the extraordinary military success which he experienced as part of Lancaster's retinue in 1345 must surely have had a dramatic effect on his attitude to warfare and helped spark a desire to serve on Edward III's expedition.[56] It is unlikely that the profits of war and the chance of participating in the glory of victory did not motivate such men.

Some of the soldiers who left Aquitaine to serve in Normandy, however, were not only veteran soldiers, but also among Lancaster's most trusted knights. Sir Nicholas de Peyvre, for example, was 'a beloved valet' of Lancaster. The fact that he and Sir Robert Burdet both returned to Lancaster's service during the siege of Calais in 1347 demonstrates their loyalty to the earl and reinforces the notion that the theatre of war, or more specifically, perhaps, the nature of an expedition could be the determining factor

---

[55] He was granted a £20 annuity from the honour of Wallingford on 1 September 1346, and on 17 May 1347 he was requested to go to join the prince at Calais with his retinue 'in accordance with his retainder': *BPR*, I, pp. 14, 80. Barber suggests it may have been the single act of saving the prince's banner which led to him being chosen as a Knight of the Garter. Barber, *The Triumph of England*, p. 302.

[56] C 47/6/1, no. 99. Courson served on at least three military campaigns after the expedition to Aquitaine.

in an individual's choice of retinue.[57] Such loyalty, however, does not appear to have been greater than their desire to serve on another campaign in a different theatre of war, which was grander in scale and could potentially offer greater rewards than those gained in Aquitaine. And even for Ralph de Hastings who was a retainer of Lancaster and a knight 'in whom he placed much confidence', it seems that the prospect of personal loss and, perhaps, his obligations as a prominent northern knight proved more important than his attachment to his lord.[58] Alternatively, it may have been the case that the earl had agreed with Edward III to send some of his men-at-arms home if the opportunity presented itself, as the king would have been all too aware of the challenges that he would face in raising a large field army for the Normandy expedition. It is possible, therefore, that Lancaster encouraged his own men to return to England, although the evidence suggests that other important and perhaps more 'personal' factors influenced their decision to leave Aquitaine.

The examples discussed above suggest that the reasons why men departed from Lancaster's retinue in the duchy varied depending upon the status, the ambition and the attitude to warfare of each individual. Those men who engaged in major warfare within a short period of their return to England may have shared a mentality based on profit, career progression and personal gain, but it is impossible to establish how representative these men were of other soldiers. In a period of intense militarisation in England, however, when campaigning opportunities were in abundance for those inclined to take up arms, it is likely that the motivations aforementioned were typical of the medieval soldier in the mid 1340s. Moreover, the departure of those closest to Lancaster provides food for thought on the dynamics of the relationship between a knight and his lord and, indeed, on the contemporary perception of loyalty.

When it comes to assessing the impact of the departure of Lancaster's men on the stability of the retinue composition we are on more uncertain ground. The knights who returned to England constituted 8% of the earl's known *milites* which, as we have seen, included those who belonged to his core group of men. It is difficult to quantify the loss of individual personnel although, naturally, the absence of an experienced and trusted knight such

---

[57]   C 76/25, m. 25 (Burdet); C 76/24, mm. 6, 12 (Peyvre). It is tempting to view the decisions made by other soldiers in the mid 1340s, who left the service of a retinue captain whom they had served consistently for more than a decade, as also being determined by the theatre of war or the opportunities they perceived were offered by a particular expedition. Sir Robert Marney, for example, had been a loyal comrade-in-arms of the earl of Northampton for more than a decade, but missed the battle of Crécy because he had joined Lancaster's expedition to Aquitaine in the retinue of Walter Mauny. Ayton, *English Army at Crécy*, p. 209; Ayton, *Edward III and the English Aristocracy*, p. 174, n. 8.

[58]   Froissart, *Chronicles of England*, I, p. 146.

as Hastings (and presumably his own following of men) would have had a negative impact on the stability of the retinue. Nevertheless, the proportion of retinue personnel who returned home is relatively small, and it should be borne in mind that the composition of any retinue is unlikely to have remained exactly the same over the course of a campaign – moreover, the departure of individuals from the retinue would probably have been offset by the arrival of new combatants. We might presume, then, that the returnees' impact on the stability of the retinue was minimal. And considering the length of time that the retinue spent in the field and the course of events of the campaign, which included notable battles, sieges and chevauchées, there would have been numerous occasions when men experienced hard fighting alongside one another. The experiences of an eventful campaign, therefore, would have perpetuated a strong sense of camaraderie and strengthened the stability of the retinue, which in all likelihood would not have been under-mined to any great extent by the departure of a handful of men.

Horizontal Ties: Kinship

The evidence of prior service with Lancaster and the continuity of military personnel has shown that the retinue he led to Aquitaine in 1345 was rela-tively stable in its composition. A shared campaigning experience with the same captain, whether it be Lancaster or someone else, and family loyalty of service to the same noble household should have cultivated a sense of camaraderie amongst the men and almost certainly enhanced their fighting capability. The stability and subsequent strength of a retinue, however, was also rooted in the various connections and 'horizontal' ties which existed between the men themselves, rather than their direct relationship with the retinue leader or, indeed, their *indirect* relationship with that leader via his sub-captains. An exploration of these internal and natural bonds of association between the retinue combatants based on family and friend-ship, marriage, landholdings and neighbourhood, among other things, can provide a valuable insight into the different forms of cohesion exhibited by the troop.

The importance of family ties in creating a large and stable following is reflected by the examples of the seventy-nine families who provided two or, in some cases, up to five men for military service in 1345.[59] Of the 103 iden-tifiable bannerets and knights in Lancaster's retinue, no fewer than forty-

[59] The Pommiers family, for example, provided five men-at-arms for service in 1345. The sample includes family names which, particularly in the case of archers, may denote a man's occupation, or place of origin or residence rather than a tie of kinship, although two groups of men who are known by the obvious Lancashire place names, 'of Standish', 'of Langtree' and 'of Wolfall', have been discounted.

three served alongside paternal relatives, including five Gascon lords.[60] And within the rank of esquire, forty-nine men are known to have taken up arms with their kin. In most instances, however, it is difficult to determine the relationship between family members, especially when two generations of one family share the same name and when both men were militarily active during the 1340s. A Sir William Scargill, for example, served at Halidon Hill in 1333 before his appointment as steward of John de Warenne, earl of Surrey, in Wakefield (Yorkshire) and then became steward of Lancaster's honour of Pontefract in the same county in 1343.[61] This man should not be confused with his son and namesake who served in Lancaster's retinue alongside his brother, Sir Warren Scargill, in 1345.[62] Only by building up a career profile of each member of the Scargill family can we be certain that it was the siblings rather than the father and son who accompanied Lancaster to Aquitaine and, furthermore, the nominal evidence of both brothers shows that other connections existed between them besides kinship and military service. The good service of Sir William Scargill to the earl of Surrey from the 1330s onwards does not appear to have been continued by his two sons who, in 1342, were accused by the earl of poaching and having burnt his houses at night in his parks in Wakefield.[63] The brothers also appointed the same attorneys to represent them during the expedition to Aquitaine, and in 1348 the king pardoned both men for holding jousts in Wakefield contrary to a royal proclamation.[64] The Scargill brothers are an example of men whose personal connection based on kinship was strengthened through different types of martial activity and whose association is evident in contexts other than warfare. Interestingly, although both men appear to have been part of the same social network in Yorkshire and, indeed, were part of the same military community in that county, William did not share the same status

[60] Two members of the Chetewynde family would also have served with Lancaster had John, father of Robert, de Chetewynde not been infirm at the time of the expedition. C 76/24, m. 3d.

[61] In 1333 Sir William was appointed steward of Warenne's lands in Wakefield and Sowerbyshire for life for his good service in the 'present' Scottish war and was the earl's main representative from 1338 to 1340: *CPR, 1330–34*, p. 458; *The Court Rolls of the Manor of Wakefield: From October 1338 to September 1340*, ed. and calendared by K. M. Troup (Leeds: Yorkshire Archaeological Society, 1999), p. xxi. He was also Lancaster's steward in the honour of Pontefract on 10 March 1343, and held numerous other appointments of local office in Yorkshire during the 1330s and 1340s: *Somerville*, p. 363; Richard Gorski, *The Fourteenth-Century Sheriff: English Local Administration in the Late Middle Ages* (Woodbridge: Boydell, 2003) pp. 190–1.

[62] Fowler mistakenly records the service of Sir William Scargill, knight, in Lancaster's retinue in 1345: Fowler, 'Henry of Grosmont', II, p. 259.

[63] *CPR, 1340–43*, p. 540.

[64] C 76/20, m. 15; John, son of Thomas Frere and John de Barneburgh were appointed as their attorneys in 1345. *CPR, 1348–50*, p. 117 (pardon). William was also pardoned for homicide in 1349: *CPR, 1348–50*, p. 253.

as his brother.[65] It is possible that William had eschewed knighthood in the hope of avoiding the potential administrative burden which accompanied the title, as was the case for Peter de la Mare, or perhaps he was a landless younger son with no substantial property or income to support such rank and status.[66] However, the fact that Sir William Scargill had granted land in Wakefield to Warren sometime before 1347, but not to William, might suggest that the latter was the reason why William remained an ordinary man-at-arms in 1345.[67]

The Scargills were not the only family from which men-at-arms of different rank served with Lancaster in 1345. In total there are twenty-nine examples of knights who served alongside a family member (often a brother or son) who was of inferior status.[68] That a little more than a quarter (28.2%) of knights were related to esquires is perhaps indicative of an enthusiasm to wage war amongst gentry families whereby esquires aspired to the superior status of their kin, or, in some instances, it may reveal men's attitude towards knighthood.[69] Interestingly, the retinue roll of 1336 reveals a much higher proportion of knights in Lancaster's retinue a decade earlier – 9 out of 18 – who were related to an esquire.[70] An extrapolation of the evidence, therefore, shows that the proportion of knights who served alongside paternal relatives of lower rank in 1336 was halved on the expedition to Aquitaine. And, if we focus on knights who served with kinsmen of any rank, esquire or otherwise, a greater proportion is evident again in the earlier retinue.[71] Does this suggest that stronger family ties underpinned the retinue which Lancaster recruited for the Scottish expedition? It would seem safe to assume so, although the evidence of a slightly higher proportion of families in 1345 than in 1336 which provided clusters of three, four

[65] Warren is listed as a knight and William as an esquire on Lancaster's retinue roll in 1345. E 101/25/9, m. 3; E 101/35/2/10, m. 1.

[66] Saul, *Knights and Esquires*, pp. 46–7.

[67] The earl of Surrey alienated land in Wakefield to Sir William Scargill sometime before the earl's death in 1347, from which William granted nine acres to his son Warren: *CIPM*, X, p. 53.

[68] In addition to Warren Scargill, the following knights served alongside an esquire who belonged to their own family: Astley, Berton, Burdet, Causton, Clifton, Cok, Everingham, Favell, Grailly (Johan and Peys), Hastings (William and Ralph), Havering, Hotham, Loring, Lovel, Mare (Peter and Robert), Meynell (Hugh and William), Mohun, Paynel (John and Ralph), Pommiers (Guilhem-Sans, Hélias, Guilhem), Rye, Scargill.

[69] Of 103 known knights banneret and bachelor (eight Aquitanians included), 29 served alongside relatives of lower rank.

[70] E 101/15/12. Knights who served with an esquire of the same family: Cok, Grey, Hastings (Hugh and Ralph), Meynell, Mohun, Seaton, Twyford (John the brother, and the son).

[71] Nine out of 18 knights (50%) served alongside a relative in 1336, compared with 42 out of 103 known knights (41%) in 1345.

or sometimes up to five soldiers of different rank implies that elements of cohesion among the men-at-arms in 1345 remained firmly rooted in bonds of kinship.[72] It should also be borne in mind that the retinue raised in the mid 1340s comprised two and a half times the number of men-at-arms as that led by Lancaster nine years earlier, and the latter expedition was undertaken during the early stages (and was possibly the first campaign) of the earl's career.[73] We might expect these two factors to have affected the prevalence of family ties among the retinue personnel as the earl may have relied more heavily upon the recruitment of family-based units of men at a time when nascent relationships with members of different military communities were yet to develop, and his cross-channel status and reputation as a retinue leader was only beginning to grow.

The bonds of kinship which brought a familiarity of personnel and subsequent cohesion to Lancaster's men-at-arms in 1345 permeated all levels of his war retinue, including mounted archers, retinue-based pardon recipients and others who were not military combatants in the strictest sense. The proportion of archers who shared their surname with another combatant is almost identical to that of the esquires, with 1 out of 4 archers serving with a family member.[74] If we include the archers of Standish-with-Langtree and Wolfall in the sample, then the level of kinship increases whereby roughly a third of archers can be shown to have served with relatives.[75] This degree of kinship is comparable to the family ties which are known to have existed in the retinue of the absentee Sir James Lord Audley of Heighley, one of the other four principal retinue leaders of the English army in 1345. Around one third of the mounted archers and ordinary men-at-arms in Audley's *comitiva* served alongside paternal relatives, a trend which might be explained by the fact that such a large proportion of Audley's retinue (as much as half), was recruited from his tenantry, where we would expect strong family networks to exist.[76] In contrast, parts of Lancaster's retinue were recruited indirectly through his bannerets and therefore drawn from regions where he had little or no tenurial connection. The extent to which

---

[72] In 1345 five families contributed 3 men-at-arms (Clifton, Everingham, Hastings, Paynel, Zouche), three contributed 4 men (Grailly, Mare, Meynell) and one contributed 5 men (Pommiers), compared with 1336 when just two families provided 3 men-at-arms (Cresswell and Seaton) and 4 men-at-arms (Hastings and Twyford), respectively.

[73] The 1336 retinue comprised 100 men-at-arms (excluding Lancaster himself), and in 1345 the earl contracted to provide 250 men-at-arms.

[74] Out of 269 mounted archers, 71 (26.4%) and out of 201 known esquires, 48 (23.9%) shared their surnames with another combatant in Lancaster's retinue.

[75] The proportion increases to 99 out of 269 (36.8%), Standish-with-Langtree and Wolfall inclusive.

[76] Twelve out of 39 esquires (30.8%) and 13 out of 40 mounted archers (32.5%) served alongside paternal relatives in Audley's retinue: Gribit, *Accounting for Service at War*, pp. 165–6. Morgan, *War and Society*, p. 76.

kinship underpinned Lancaster's archers and esquires is all the more impressive considering that the earl's retinue was more than six times the size of Audley's troop.

When it comes to the individuals who are likely to have been attendants of Lancaster, at least 6 out of 39 served alongside relatives who were fellow attendants. Two men from each of the families of Birkoure, Mulne and Wite accompanied Lancaster to Aquitaine, which demonstrates that family relationships also existed within the earl's household.[77] And if the analysis of attendants' surnames is broadened to include combatants, we find that a quarter of men served with their kinsmen, of whom five were archers.[78] This degree of kinship evident among the non-combatants is wholly consistent with that of the archers and esquires. In the instance of the pardon recipients, similar hereditary bonds of association also can be shown to have existed. Of the seven men granted a royal pardon for service in the sub-retinues of Lancaster's bannerets, there are two pairs of men who share the same surname.[79] The enrolled letters of pardon seldom reveal the rank, occupation or status of the pardon recipients, but in the case of John son of William Halden we know that he was a clerk and also a cousin of John son of John Halden.[80] The relationship between these men, like those between the archers and attendants of Lancaster, reflects the social diversity of particular families whose kinsmen provided the earl and indeed his bannerets with different types of service.

Interestingly, the evidence of family ties also provides an insight into the extent to which the boundaries between distinct social groups of the military community, as determined by military rank and social status, were blurred and imprecise in the 1340s.[81] For example, 12 out of 69 archers in our sample share their surname with an esquire, although among these men are individuals who hold occupational surnames such as 'Falconer', or 'Parker', and place names such as Hallam or Leicester.[82] When deciding whether John de Leicester (archer) and William de Leicester (esquire) were recruited from within the same family, for example, we are faced with an intractable problem.[83] In the cases of Coleman, Vernoun, Sholl and several others, however, we can be more certain that these families contributed

---

[77] E 101/25/9, m. 3d. There are several other men who possibly served alongside relatives, but we cannot be certain whether men such as Nicholas filz Hugh, for example, was the son of Hugh Frattun or Hugh le Keu.

[78] Surnames shared by archers and probable attendants: Baker, Birkoure (two men), Butler and Preston.

[79] Two men share the surname of Halden, and two share the surname of Kelyng.

[80] *CPR, 1345–48*, p. 558.

[81] Ayton, *Dynamics of Recruitment*, pp. 216–17.

[82] For names shared by archers and esquires, see Appendix B.

[83] E 101/35/2/10, m. 1 (William), m. 3d (John).

manpower to the different troop types of archers and men-at-arms, although the precise relationship between the men is unknown. It may have been, as Ayton suggests, that younger scions of minor gentry families could not afford to equip themselves to the same standard as elder siblings, or perhaps the soldiers aforementioned were distant cousins (in lineage rather than residence) who belonged to families of different economic standing.[84] Whatever the case, the examples of the Burton and Damport families, each of which provided different types of soldiers for service in Audley's retinue, implies that such patterns of recruitment were not unusual in the 1340s and, perhaps, that the economic and social origins of the mounted archer were not too far removed from that of the ordinary man-at-arms.[85] Indeed, it is interesting to note that no instances of knights can be found in the retinues of Audley or Lancaster who share their surname with an archer, and we might presume from the plethora of such examples later in the fourteenth century that the social distinctions between members of England's military community had become even less pronounced than they were in the second quarter of the century.[86]

Horizontal Ties: Marriage Alliance

A network of family connections and ties which existed in a war retinue was not always based on men who shared a direct blood line, as kin groups often expanded through the marriage alliances made between families. It is not unusual, therefore, to find men serving in the same company or sub-retinue as their father-in-law, for example, as was the case for Roger Beler in 1345. The latter married Margaret, daughter of John de Grey of Codnor, sometime before 1344, and it was probably this new marriage alliance which prompted Beler to serve with his father-in-law in Aquitaine.[87] Furthermore, the sum of 200 marks which Grey owed to Beler in the month prior to their embarkation to the duchy shows that both men had pre-existing financial ties as well as ties of kinship.[88] It was not only the Grey family, however, to which Beler had a matrimonial connection. He had previously married

---

[84] Andrew Ayton, 'Military Service and the Development of the Robin Hood Legend in the Fourteenth Century', *Nottingham Medieval Studies*, 36 (1992), 126–47, pp. 136–7.

[85] Gribit, *Accounting for Service at War*, p. 157, n. 52 (Burton and Damport). For a discussion of the heterogeneous origins of the mounted archer, see Ayton, *Dynamics of Recruitment*, pp. 40–1; Baker, *The Socio-Economic Origins of English Archers*, pp. 173–216.

[86] For multiple examples of knights and mounted archers being recruited from within the same family in the second half of the fourteenth century, see Bell et al., *The Soldier in Later Medieval England*, p. 162.

[87] *CPR, 1343–45*, p. 364. There is no evidence of previous service by Beler in Grey's company.

[88] *CCR, 1343–46*, p. 569.

the eldest daughter of Richard de la Ryvere, who was probably the father of Lancaster's loyal esquire, Thomas de la Ryvere.[89] It was very likely, therefore, that Beler served alongside his ex-brother-in-law and father-in-law in 1345, and the bonds of matrimony (both past and present) no doubt provided an added, if somewhat complex, dimension of cohesion to the retinue personnel.

Sir Adam de Everingham was also tied to the baronial family of Codnor through the marriage of his eldest son, William, and Alice, the daughter of John de Grey.[90] We cannot be sure whether the date of their matrimony preceded the expedition to Aquitaine; but Grey's request for letters of protection for Everingham, possibly for service in Brittany in 1342, implies that the inter-marriage of the two families strengthened an association which had initially been founded on a shared history of military service.[91] Everingham also formed an alliance with Sir Richard de Rawcliffe based on the latter's marriage to Everingham's daughter, Elizabeth.[92] The union between the two households is of no surprise as both men shared a strong association with Lancaster, having accompanied him overseas on several occasions, and the equally extensive careers in arms of both knights are described in their depositions at the Court of Chivalry in 1385.[93] Whether the marriage alliance was made before the knights had first taken up arms under Lancaster's banner we cannot be certain, but had this been the case we might expect Rawcliffe to have served in his father-in-law's company in 1345. The union, therefore, was probably rooted in bonds of association between father and son-in-law which had been shaped and, indeed, strengthened by previous military service.

There is also evidence of inter-marriage between the families of ordinary knights in Lancaster's retinue. Sir Thomas Ramesbury, for example, wed the sister of Sir Edmund Everard, although in this case the natural connections between the men based on the proximity of their landholdings in the county of Dorset, as well as a shared campaigning experience in Aquitaine, had long been established before the matrimonial bond was made.[94] Moreover, there are not a few examples of marriages between the

---

[89] John Burke, *A Genealogical and Heraldic History of the Commoners of Great Britain and Ireland, Enjoying Territorial Possessions or High Official Rank; But Uninvested with Heritable Honours*, 4 vols (London: H. Colburn, 1835–38), IV (1838), pp. 230–1.

[90] *CIPM*, XVI, p. 208.

[91] C 81/1727/65; Everingham is one of four knights recorded in Grey's undated bill of request for protections. William and Alice had married before 28 January 1353: *CP*, V, p. 191.

[92] *Scrope and Grosvenor*, II, p. 351.

[93] *Scrope and Grosvenor*, I, pp. 240–1 (Everingham); *Scrope and Grosvenor*, II, p. 351 (Rawcliffe).

[94] *CIPM*, XIII, p. 20; Margaret Everard was born *c.* 1346.

relatives of men of Lancaster's retinue. The sister of Sir John de Norwich, for instance, married Sir Robert de Ufford, earl of Suffolk, who was a close relative (and possibly the elder brother) of the eponymous knight in Lancaster's retinue – and, thus, Norwich served alongside his cousin in 1345.[95] The families of other men in Lancaster's retinue that were united by matrimony include Darcy and Meynell, Neville and Percy, Zouche and Roos and Grey and Fitzpayn.[96] The grant of a marriage licence to Henry of Lancaster in 1348 for the union of one of his daughters with Sir John de Verdon reflects the close relationship of the two men and typifies how the institution of marriage could strengthen 'vertical' ties between the retinue leader and his men, as well as internal bonds of association between the men themselves.[97]

The evidence of marriage alliances within the ranks of banneret and knight suggests that inter-marriage was a means of shaping and building upon pre-existing ties between men, based on landholding and a shared history of prior service, rather than creating a 'new' association between them. Furthermore, the case of Everard and Rammesbury shows that the practice of forging marriage alliances was not just the preserve of the baronial class or social elites. Indeed, we would expect inter-marriage to have been prevalent within the lower echelons of the retinue owing to the nature of the dynamics of recruitment. Among the constituency of esquires led by John Musard, for example, were probably brothers or fathers-in-law, or cousins, no doubt, and it would be surprising not to find similar family ties between the archers of Wolfall. Conversely, the marriage of Lancaster's daughter to the son and heir of Ralph, Lord Stafford in 1344 demonstrates that the unification of two households in such a way was also evident at the command level.[98] The bond of matrimony, therefore, was a potentially strong cohesive force that augmented existing connections between individuals and groups of men in Lancaster's war retinue and the military community as a whole.

---

[95] Anthony Verduyn, 'Norwich, John, first Lord Norwich (c.1299–1362)', *ODNB*, 2004 [accessed 17 Dec 2014]. It is impossible to establish the exact relationship between the earl of Suffolk and his namesake who appears 7th in the nominal list of knights on the 1345 retinue roll.

[96] James S. Bothwell, *Edward III and the English Peerage: Royal Patronage, Social Mobility and Political Control in Fourteenth-Century England* (Woodbridge: Boydell, 2004), pp. 185–91.

[97] Marriage rights were granted on 24 April 1348: Bothwell, *English Peerage*, p. 186.

[98] *CP*, XII, p. 177.

Horizontal Ties: Landholding and Locality

One of the principal sources of cohesion for a war retinue was landholding. Whether it was lordship exercised by a retinue captain, or tenurial connections between retinue members, property and territorial possession often provided a strong thread of unity among military personnel. The localities and regions in which men were resident, or held land, shaped an important part of their identity and could often influence an individual's decision to serve in a certain *comitiva*, or with a particular captain. To understand the territorial cohesion of Lancaster's retinue in 1345 and, indeed, to identify the regions from which the earl drew his military support it is necessary to assess the landholdings of his men. A previous survey of annuities granted by Lancaster has shown that the prominent men of his retinue were not connected with his father's lands, as the largest endowments were tied to manors which the earl had inherited by way of his mother, Maud Chaworth, during the 1330s.[99] A significant number of men who formed the core of Lancaster's retinue, however, were never in receipt of an annuity and the date on which the fee or land was granted is unknown in the vast majority of cases.[100] The evidence of annuities, therefore, is limited in what it reveals of the territory related cohesion of the earl's troop. In turn, an assessment of all land held by Lancaster's men at the time of the expedition to Aquitaine can provide a more accurate insight into the regional composition of the retinue in 1345. Does the evidence of landholdings relate to the distribution of Lancaster's estates? Furthermore, is there evidence of connections between the men themselves based on tenure of land in the locality of their property? An investigation of the geographical dimension of the retinue can throw important light on several aspects of the dynamics of recruitment, but more importantly, for the purpose of this chapter, it can reveal the nuances of retinue stability and cohesion.

Table 12 shows the location and geographical spread of land held by Lancaster's men in 1345. The evidence is largely derived from documentary sources produced in connection with the military assessment of the mid 1340s and the writs of return of landholders who had not taken up knighthood prior to the expedition to Aquitaine.[101] The figures show that

---

[99] Fowler, *King's Lieutenant*, p. 186. Fowler's assertion that Lancaster's retinue was distinct from that of his father is partly based on the fact that several of the earl's most prominent annuitants were granted fees assigned to manors (in the counties of Hampshire and Wiltshire) which he had inherited from his mother, in or before 1337.

[100] There is no indication of when the annuities recorded in Lancaster's inquisition post mortem were originally granted by Lancaster: *CIPM*, X, pp. 92–116.

[101] The writs of exoneration are enrolled in the Treaty and Memoranda Rolls and the allowance of the fine is recorded in the Pipe Rolls. In addition, there are several extant privy seal writs directed to the Chancery and to the Exchequer ordering that the writs of exoneration be made. There are also the writs of return themselves which record the

landholders in the region of the North Midlands are the most represented, then those in East Anglia, followed closely by those in the South Midlands. At county level, most men held land in Norfolk, followed by the North Midlands counties of Lincolnshire and Leicestershire. The high number of landholders in the former county is of some surprise considering that Lancaster was not in possession of the Norfolk manors which had been enfeoffed to his uncle, Thomas of Lancaster, by John de Warenne, earl of Surrey, more than twenty years earlier, until after Warenne's death in 1347.[102] At the time of the expedition, therefore, Lancaster's estate in the county was limited to a single manor and the hundred of North Greenhoe.[103]

The possibility of the Norfolk landholders having a tenurial connection with their retinue leader, other than that they held land in the same county, seems remote and, in this instance, the normal association of neighbour-hood or proximity of landholdings would have been less pronounced as the earl was probably seldom resident in Norfolk. It is more likely that Lancaster was able to extend his recruiting reach into the county by utilising the connections of Sir John de Norwich, who served as the earl's banneret in 1344 and 1345.[104] Of the fourteen men who possessed property in Norfolk, at least five served in Norwich's sub-retinue in 1345, or had done so on a previous occasion. The example of Sir Richard Fitzsimon, who had served with Norwich in 1335 and then with Lancaster in 1344 having led his own company of five men-at-arms, suggests that Lancaster had gained access to Norfolk knights through the employment of Norwich who, as his name might suggest, was a prominent member of the military community in the county.[105] It was probably the lack of resident magnates in the region that enabled the greater gentry, such as Norwich, to become prolific recruiters in their localities on behalf of greater lords who had no strong local ties in the region.[106] Interestingly, Edward the Black Prince also drew a signifi-

---

valuation of lands in 1345, C 47: Chancery Miscellanea. The evidence of property owner-ship summarised in the *Calendars of Inquisition Post Mortem* relating to Lancaster's men was only partially utilised because the inquisitions only reveal landholdings at the time of an individual's death. In most cases therefore it is impossible to establish whether men in Lancaster's retinue had actually been in possession of their land in 1345.

[102] *Somerville*, p. 36.

[103] *CPR, 1334–38*, p. 538; the hundred and the manor of Whyton were granted upon his creation as earl of Derby in 1337.

[104] C 81/1724/49; E 101/25/9, m. 3.

[105] The company of Yorkshiremen which Sir Thomas Ughtred brought into the earl of Warwick's retinue in 1346 is a similar example of how a magnate captain could gain access to a regional pool of manpower through his bannerets. Ayton, *Dynamics of Recruitment*, p. 22; Ayton, *Sir Thomas Ughtred*, pp. 122–5.

[106] Caudrey, *War, Chivalry and Regional Society*, p. 122. This distinctive characteristic of East Anglia's military community should not overshadow the natural 'pulling power' of Norwich, which derived from his reputation and status as a formidable war captain.

Table 12. Counties and Regions in which Lancaster's Men Held Land
in or before 1345

Region	County	No. of men
North	Yorkshire	5
	Lancashire	2
	Cheshire	1
	Cumberland	1
	Northumberland	1
	Westmorland	1
	Sub-total	11
North Midlands	Lincolnshire	13
	Leicestershire	12
	Nottinghamshire	7
	Rutland	6
	Derbyshire	2
	Staffordshire	2
	Sub-total	42
South Midlands	Northamptonshire	6
	Warwickshire	6
	Bedfordshire	4
	Buckinghamshire	4
	Hertfordshire	3
	Sub-total	23
East Anglia	Norfolk	14
	Suffolk	8
	Essex	4
	Cambridgeshire	2
	Sub-total	28
South East	Oxfordshire	7
	Hampshire	4
	Berkshire	2
	Kent	1
	Surrey	1
	Sussex	1
	Sub-total	16
South West	Wiltshire	7
	Somerset	5
	Dorset	4
	Devon	3
	Cornwall	1
	Sub-total	20
Wales and Welsh Borders	Herefordshire	2
	Anglesey	1
	Monmouth	1
	Sub-total	4
Total	-	144

Note: 'Sub-totals' represent landholdings rather than individuals as some men held land in
more than one county.

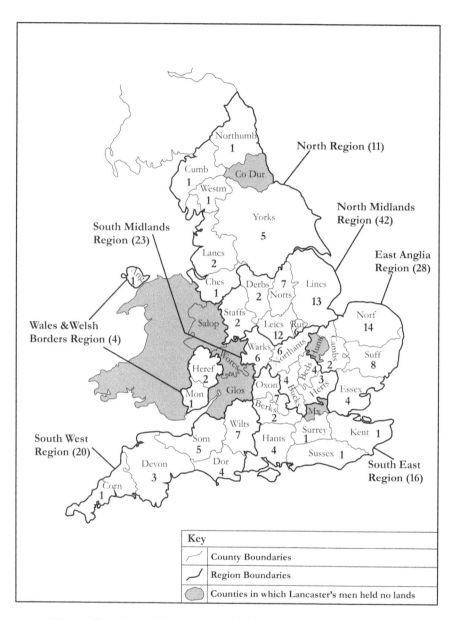

Map 7. Counties and Regions in which Lancaster's Men Held Land
in or before 1345

cant number of his affinity from East Anglia, particularly from Norfolk, despite having no landed interests in the region. David Green argues that the recruitment of the prince's Norfolk retainers is 'an example of bastard feudalism *par excellence*', and it is apparent that some of the region's land-holders had entered into Lancaster's service through similar means.[107]

The concentration of landholders in Lincolnshire and Leicestershire is interesting because the earl of Lancaster himself did not hold any property in either county, with the exception of the manor of Hallaton (Leicester-shire) before taking up his father's inheritance at the beginning of 1347 and his revival of the earldom of Lincoln in 1349.[108] The earldom of Leicester, however, had been restored to the elder Henry of Lancaster in 1324 and it is no surprise that some of his son's most prominent knights, such as Thomas Cok, Hugh Meynell and John de Seaton, were all landholders in the county. Another knight, Thomas de Verdon, had been granted a £20 annuity by the elder Henry assigned to the honour of Leicester which was subsequently confirmed by his son and, furthermore, no fewer than seven of the twelve Leicestershire landholders had served or their progenitors had served the two previous earls. In 1345 Lancaster relied upon landholders whose property was located within his father's earldom to provide military service, some of whom had not taken up the order of knighthood by 1343 despite being in possession of a substantial landholding.[109] It seems, therefore, that the lord-ship of his father, as earl of Leicester, may have been an important factor that influenced the decision of some of the gentry from the eponymous county to join his retinue in 1345, and it may have been a similar case for some of the landholders in the South-East and South-West considering that the honour of Leicester included manors in the counties of Berking, Dorset and Wiltshire.[110] And that four of the Leicestershire landholders also had property in the neighbouring county of Rutland suggests that Lancaster had access to a regional military community which expanded beyond his father's estates.[111]

In contrast, the vast estates which Thomas of Lancaster had inherited by way of his marriage to Alice Lacy, including the earldom of Lincoln, were not restored to the house of Lancaster during his son's lifetime. There-fore the association between the Lincolnshire landholders and their retinue

---

[107] David Green, 'Edward the Black Prince and East Anglia: An Unlikely Association', in *Fourteenth Century England, III*, ed. W. M. Ormrod (Woodbridge: Boydell, 2004), pp. 83–98.

[108] The Leicestershire manor of Hallaton was conveyed to Lancaster in fee by William Dexter sometime between 1337 and 1345; *Somerville*, p. 39.

[109] C 47/1/11, m. 14; John de Boyville, John Boson and Robert Burdet are listed in a returned writ of persons holding £40 of land in Leicestershire in 1343 who are not yet knights.

[110] Spencer, *Nobility and Kingship in Medieval England*, p. 15.

[111] *CIPM*, VI, pp. 442–5 (Beler); C 47/2/39, m. 8 (Boyville, John de Seaton, Richard de Seaton).

leader in 1345 was unlikely to have been based on a shared proximity with the Lancastrian estates. Two men with property in Lincolnshire belonged to families that had served Thomas (and for whom old landholding ties with the Lancastrian household may have existed), but there is evidence of direct tenurial ties between the men themselves rather than with their retinue captain. Sir Nicholas de Rye and Simon Simeon, for example, both held land of Thomas, son of Robert de Gosberkirk in their home county of Lincolnshire before the latter was hanged for felony in 1345.[112] Another neighbour of Nicholas de Rye was Sir Hugh Cressy, who held the manor of Risegate, also known as 'Gosberton Risegate', in Surfleet where Rye was also a landholder.[113] Sir Hugh aptly served at the battle of Crécy, but his relative and namesake was among Lancaster's esquires in Aquitaine who also held land in the same county.[114] Such natural ties of neighbourhood and proximity of landholding must have been a powerful cohesive force on the military personnel.

The high number of Lincolnshire landholders in Lancaster's retinue might also be explained by those men whose families had transferred into Lancaster's service from the retinue of Henry Beaumont. The latter had not only been a prominent landholder in the county before his death in 1340, but also Lancaster's father-in-law.[115] Sir John de Lymbury, for example, was a veteran of the Scottish wars of all three Edwardian kings and had served with Beaumont on numerous occasions, and it is perhaps significant that his son, Philip de Lymbury, held land in Lincolnshire of Henry Beaumont's cousin and namesake.[116] Sir Richard de Rawcliffe was also a tenant of Beaumont's cousin in the same county and he too had served with Lord Beaumont in Scotland and John Beaumont in the Low Countries before joining Lancaster's retinue in 1342.[117] There are not a few examples of other men from Lancaster's retinue who had held land directly of the Beaumont family in Lincolnshire which shows that territory related cohesion can sometimes correspond to the estates of both past and present retinue leaders.[118] The individuals who had a connection of tenure with the Beaumonts

---

[112] E 159/123, m. 163d; *CCR, 1343–46*, p. 532.

[113] *CIPM*, VII, p. 450.

[114] Hugh Cressy took out a letter of protection for service in Lancaster's retinue in 1345 and was more than likely an esquire. C 76/20, m. 15. He held land in Braytoft and Fryseby (Lincolnshire): *CIPM*, VIII, p. 194.

[115] *CP*, XII, p. 177.

[116] *CIPM*, XII, p. 294.

[117] *CIPM*, XII, p. 292. See Chapter 9 for history of military service.

[118] Hugh Cressy held a sixth of a knight's fee in Braytoft and Fryseby of Henry Beaumont in Lincolnshire, although there is no evidence of his service with Beaumont: *CIPM*, VIII, p. 194. Edmund de Swinford and a relative of Alexander Auncel held land in Lincolnshire of John Beaumont: *CIPM*, XVII, pp. 284–91. John Boson held land of Henry Beaumont, knight, in Poynton (Lincolnshire): *CIPM*, XII, p. 294.

also demonstrate how ties of association were often deep-rooted and more enduring than the life of one magnate.

In the counties where Lancaster held estates inherited by way of his mother, that is Hampshire and Wiltshire, there were four and seven men who held land in each county respectively. The number of landholders in Hampshire equalled those men with landholdings in the counties of Bedford and Dorset, amongst whom was one of Lancaster's most loyal knights, Sir Edmund Everard, who had property in all three of the southern counties.[119] The latter held land in Manshead hundred in Bedfordshire along with Nicholas de Peyvre, but their possessions must have seemed a trifle in comparison to that of William la Zouche whose land in the same hundred was valued at twelve men-at-arms, equivalent to the sum of £240.[120] When all three knights took up arms together for the first time in 1345, we can assume that they were already closely associated with one another. Other examples of tenurial connections between men include land held by Peter de la Mare of Nicholas de Peyvre in Hertfordshire, while John Boson and Richard de Walkefare were both tenants of John Roos in his Nottinghamshire manor.[121] The evidence has shown that men often held land in the same locality; indeed, in twenty-six counties at least two men from Lancaster's retinue were landholders, and four or more men had property in sixteen counties. It is likely, therefore, that many men in Lancaster's retinue would have served alongside their landlords, neighbours, tenants or men who had landed interests in the same county which, in turn, would have created familiarity with one another and contributed to the *esprit de corps*.

When it comes to the territory related cohesion of the mounted archers in Lancaster's retinue, the tabulated evidence is of little use. Some archers would have had small landholdings, but their landed possessions are not revealed by the administrative records. The dominance of Cheshire and Lancashire archers within the retinue, however, suggests that there was a strong regional focus of the North-West among the men. It is not surprising to find numerous examples of archers who originated from villages and townships that were part of, or situated nearby, the Lancastrian estates in north-western England. The township of Standish-with-Langtree and the manor of Wolfall, for example, where thirteen archers originated, belonged to the hundreds of Leyland and West Derby which constituted part of the

---

[119] C 47/2/41, no. 2 (Bedford). *CFR, 1337–47*, p. 338 (Dorset). E 372/192, m. 40 (Hampshire).

[120] C 47/2/58, m. 5.

[121] *CIPM*, IX, pp. 309–10; Mare held land in Offeleye of Peyvre and Sir Edward Kendale by service of half a knight's fee 3d. yearly for annual rent. Walkefare and Boson both held a moiety of a knight's fee in the manors of Orston, Screveton and Skerington in Nottinghamshire of William de Roos of Hamelak, in 1343: *CIPM*, VIII, p. 338.

earldom of Lancaster.[122] Similarly, the honour of Tutbury, which overlapped the counties of Derby and Stafford, brought further cohesion to the men commensurate with the estates that Lancaster had held as earl of Derby since 1337.[123]

The landholdings of men in Lancaster's retinue were spread over forty counties or lordships in England and Wales and although a significant number of men held land in the south, particularly Oxfordshire and Wiltshire, the largest concentration of landholders was in the North Midlands as well as the neighbouring counties of Norfolk and Suffolk. The geographical spread of the landholdings reflects the extent of the social networks and military communities (local, regional, and national) that underpinned the war retinue. It is surprising, perhaps, that the evidence of land tenure does not relate to the distribution of estates held by Lancaster in 1345, as earl of Derby, in the same way that landholdings of members of other magnate retinues do.[124] Indeed, it is impossible to find evidence of any men who were direct tenants of their retinue leader at the time of the expedition to Aquitaine, which reflects the breadth of his recruitment and the multitude of recruitment avenues utilised to mobilise a large retinue contingent.[125] However, considering that Lancaster's father had retired from military and public affairs during the late 1330s it is likely that some of the men in Lancaster's retinue would have been raised among the tenantry close to his father's lands and, as the evidence suggests, the estates previously held by his uncle. In spite of the lack of direct tenurial ties between the retinue leader and his men, there is considerable evidence of land based connections between the men themselves. The underlying territorial cohesion of Lancaster's war retinue derived largely from the spheres of influence and regional networks of his bannerets, such as John de Norwich, the networks of the closely affiliated Beaumont household and, of course, the estates of the current and previous earls of Lancaster.

---

[122] *Victoria History of the County of Lancaster*, III, (1907), pp. 172–4 (Wolfall), VI, (1911), pp. 192–3 (Standish-with-Langtree).

[123] *Somerville*, pp. 36–9.

[124] For examples of strong tenurial ties between magnate captains and their retinue members in the thirteenth and fourteenth centuries, see Spencer, *Military Retinue in the Reign of Edward I*, p. 53; Ayton, *English Army at Crécy*, pp. 211–14; Bell, *War and the Soldier*, pp. 117–25.

[125] In contrast, in the reign of Edward I, on average one in ten members of comital retinues were also tenants of the respective earl: Spencer, *Military Retinue in the Reign of Edward I*, p. 53.

Conclusion

The evidence of military service has shown that Lancaster's war retinue in 1345, in spite of its extraordinary size, was of a relatively stable composition and exhibited a good deal of cohesion. An unprecedented high recruitment target of retinue manpower caused a natural fall in the proportion of men who had previously served the earl, but a more nuanced approach to the evidence has revealed that the rates of re-service among Lancaster's knights in the mid 1340s were on par with those of other magnate retinues of the time, and that the continuity of service in Lancaster's retinue was much higher than has previously been thought. In spite of the influx of 'new' military personnel in 1345, who had not previously served under Lancaster's banner, it was not detrimental to the overall stability of the retinue due to the continuity of service of a core group of men. The natural bonds of association between individuals and groups of men based on a shared campaigning experience were augmented further by underlying personal and pre-existing ties of kinship, neighbourhood and a shared proximity of landholdings. In sum, the cohesion and stability of the retinue was vital to its performance in the field over the course of the campaign, a fact no more clearly demonstrated than by the successful deployment of small task forces (itinerant and sedentary) which could break away from the retinue and reform on command. The overall cohesion and stability of Lancaster's war retinue are all the more impressive considering its unprecedented size and, in many respects, were the principal sources which provided the strength to such a formidable fighting force.

9

An Era of Military Professionalism: Careers and Patterns of Service

The study of an English army raised during an important period of transformation in the organisation of war would not be complete without an investigation of the development of professional soldiering. The careers of the most renowned professional soldiers such as the Cheshire knights Robert Knolles and Hugh Calveley have been well documented in both contemporary and modern literature, and there can be little doubt of their single-minded commitment to a martial lifestyle.[1] The task of establishing traits of professionalism amongst less well-known soldiers, however, is more difficult. It is the aim in this final chapter to investigate the extent to which professional soldiering is evident in the retinue of Henry of Lancaster in 1345–46. How many of Lancaster's men should be considered as professionals in warfare, and how many different retinue captains had they previously served under before joining Lancaster's *comitiva*? The answers to these questions may give an insight into men's attitudes towards warfare and their aspirations to different types of careers in arms during the first half of the fourteenth century. It is important to remember that professional soldiers were not a homogeneous group, as the paths and progression of a military career could vary greatly from one man to the next, and a focus, therefore, on the underlying patterns of service of individuals can often help elucidate the various motivations and campaigning habits of military careerists.

If we broaden the analysis to include military service performed after 1345 then we can also capture the careers of men who were inexperienced and relatively new to the business of warfare at the time of Lancaster's first expedition to Aquitaine. By reconstructing the entire careers of the earl's men, as far as the sources permit, and focusing on those individuals who served on the largest number of campaigns, we can also assess the different types of military professionals that emerged in the fourteenth century. The loyal warrior who might be considered a 'one household soldier', for example, who served exclusively with the same retinue leader during his lifetime, was

---

[1] See references in Kenneth Fowler, 'Calveley, Sir Hugh (*d.* 1394)', *ODNB*, Oct 2007 [accessed 18 March 2015]; Michael Jones, 'Knolles, Sir Robert (*d.* 1407)', *ODNB*, May 2009 [accessed 18 March 2015].

clearly of a different cut of cloth from the roaming careerist or freelance soldier who served in the companies of multiple captains. In addition, an investigation of the martial activities or social duties undertaken by men after the Treaty of Brétigny (1360), which might be considered a watershed for service in English armies owing to the nine-year truce that ensued, can throw important light on the different mentalities of professional soldiers and contribute to the wider debate on when military professionalism first emerged in England.

In the broadest sense, all men who performed military service in return for wages can be considered as professional soldiers because they profited financially from the service which they performed. A military professional might also be defined as someone who was competent in warfare and who gained wealth or status from a successful martial lifestyle, such as the two captains mentioned at the beginning of the chapter. Other factors such as aspiration, equipment, experience, lifestyle and outlook are also important considerations for defining such a person. For our purpose, however, the term 'professional soldier' is used to refer to an individual whose main occupation was warfare and as such pursued a career at arms. Although it is important to distinguish between men, on the one hand, who loyally served with the same captain on one campaign after another, and on the other, men who frequently served under a different banner with no apparent attachment to a captain, both should be regarded as professional soldiers in terms of their commitment to, and participation in, warfare.

To measure or to detect signs of professionalism can be less straightforward, despite the variety of methods utilised by historians over the years. In his study of the Gloucestershire gentry, Nigel Saul used the number of campaigns undertaken to identify those men who 'made an active profession of arms' during the fourteenth century, while Adrian Bell adopted an alternative approach by utilising the evidence of continuity of service to suggest that a level of professionalism was evident among the men who served in the two naval expeditions led by Richard, earl of Arundel, in 1387 and 1388.[2] More recently, Andrew Ayton has made a qualitative assessment of army professionals based on the military careers of deponents who supported Thomas, Lord Morley in his armorial dispute with John, Lord Lovel in the mid 1380s.[3] For the first part of our study a similar methodology to that of Saul has been used to enable an initial selection of the personnel in Lancaster's retinue and provide a refined sample comprising men who served repeatedly on military expeditions and, therefore, might be considered professionals. Thus our analysis is based on the corpus of men who served on four campaigns and upwards over the course of their career.

---

[2]   Saul, *Knights and Esquires*, p. 52. Bell, *War and the Soldier*, p. 97; 49% of knights and peers, and 15% of esquires from 1387 served again in the following year.
[3]   Ayton, *Dynamics of Recruitment*, pp. 45–59.

Military Careers up to 1345

Table 13 shows the careers of twenty-four men who had served on four or more campaigns before joining Lancaster's retinue in 1345. The names of men are listed chronologically by the date of their earliest expedition, and the number of captains under whom each man had served is also shown. All the men, except for Payn de Mohun and Simon Simeon, are of a knightly status and if we put them in the context of the ninety-five identifiable

Table 13. Military Careers of Men in Lancaster's Retinue before 1345

Names	Campaigns	No. of Captains	Earliest Date
John de Lymbury	9	3+	1301
Peter de la Mare	6	3+	1318
John de Norwich	5	3+	1322
Reginald de Mohun	6	3	1324
John de Dalton	4	2+	1324
Ralph deHastings	5	2+	1327
John Blount	4	3	1329
John de Seaton	6	2	1332
Richard Fitzsimon	4	3+	1333
Nicholas Goushill	5	2+	1333
Adam de Everingham	6	3+	1333
John de Walkington	5	1+	1333
John de Grey of Codnor	8	2+	1333
Neil Loring	6[a]	3+	1335
Thomas Cok	5	1	1336
Philip de Lymbury	6	6	1336
Richard de Rawcliffe	5	4	1336
Simon Simeon	5	1	1336
Theobald Trussell	5	2	1336
Alexander Auncel	4	3	1336
Hugh Meynell	4	1	1336
Payn de Mohun	4	1	1336
William la Zouche of Totnes	4	2+	1337
Nicholas de Rye	4	2	1338

Note: '+' indicates the minimum number of captains.
[a] Loring's diplomatic mission to the papal court in February 1345 to obtain a dispensation for the marriage of the prince of Wales with a daughter of the duke of Brabant has not been included as the tabulated evidence is based entirely on service undertaken as part of a military retinue.

knights in Lancaster's *comitiva* then we find that around one quarter of that group had served on at least four campaigns.[4]

How many of these soldiers showed a loyalty or exclusivity of service towards Lancaster? Interestingly, only five individuals can be shown to have served exclusively with the earl prior to 1345 and it is no surprise to find the marshal of his army, his trusted *nuncius* and one of his bannerets among these men.[5] However, there are other soldiers who should be considered as having been both professional and loyal to Lancaster. Although the majority of our sample of twenty-four men (70.8%) served with either two or three different captains, eight of these soldiers had already taken part in a military expedition before Lancaster had first taken up arms himself (and in the instance of John de Lymbury, before the earl was born).[6] John de Seaton, for example, began his military career with Sir William la Zouche of Mortimer in 1332 before entering into Lancaster's service in 1336; thereafter Seaton served with the same retinue captain on four further campaigns prior to the expedition to Aquitaine.[7] Reginald de Mohun also served with Lancaster for the first time on the same Scottish expedition of the mid 1330s after having first taken up arms in the *comitiva* of Sir John de Segrave during the War of Saint-Sardos in 1324.[8] Mohun had also served with Thomas de Brotherton, earl of Norfolk, in 1327 following Segrave's death in 1325 but Mohun continued his family's tradition of support for the house of Lancaster and established himself in Henry's retinue from 1336 onwards.[9] In total Reginald had served on six military campaigns before 1345 while his brother Payn also entered into Lancaster's service at the same time and exclusively served with his retinue leader on four campaigns during that period.[10]

Another example of an individual whose career in arms saw him serve under the banners of different captains before settling into Lancaster's retinue is that of Peter de la Mare. The earliest record of his service is in 1318 with a Gloucestershire knight, John de Giffard of Brimpsfield, and he served with Richard Damory, steward of the king's household, four years

---

[4] The sample of ninety-five identifiable knights banneret and bachelor was presented in Table 9.

[5] Names: Thomas Cok, Simon Simeon, Hugh Meynell.

[6] Lancaster's first military expedition was to Scotland in 1333, although it is uncertain whether he took part in the fighting at Halidon Hill: Fowler, *King's Lieutenant*, p. 30.

[7] *CPR, 1330–34*, p. 279 (1332); E 101/15/12 (1336); C 76/12, mm. 3, 8 (1338); C 76/15, m. 24 (1340); C 76/17, mm. 27, 29 (1342); C 81/1724, m. 49; C 76/19, m. 19 (1344).

[8] E 101/17/2, m. 1; *CPR, 1324–27*, pp. 12, 178 (1324); E 101/15/12 (1336). Segrave was the father of Reginald's sister-in-law: *CP*, IX, p. 23; *CPR, 1301–07*, p. 327.

[9] C 71/11, m. 5 (1327). Reginald's father, John, first Lord Mohun was pardoned in 1313 as an adherent of Thomas of Lancaster and forbidden to attend the meeting of 'Good Peers' summoned by Lancaster in 1321: *CPR, 1313–17*, p. 21; *CP*, IX, p. 23.

[10] E 101/15/12 (1336); C 76/12, m. 7, E 36/203, fol. 125v (1338); C 76/17, mm. 25, 29 (1342); C 81/1724/49, C 76/19, m. 19 (1344).

later before taking part in the Scottish expedition of 1333.[11] Interestingly, de la Mare was granted a respite of knighthood in 1326 and he did not take up the order until 1337, after he had been granted an exemption for life from taking up the relevant local offices and duties against his will in 1333.[12] If, as Saul suggests, de la Mare regarded the administrative duties of knighthood as an obstacle to his military lifestyle, then it does not seem to have been a view shared by the majority of knights in the fourteenth century.[13] David Simpkin has, indeed, shown that 84% of knights bachelor in England performed military service under Edward I and Edward II, although the numerous instances of esquires in Lancaster's retinue who had eschewed knighthood up to 1345, despite having the appropriate wealth to maintain such rank, is a reminder that administrative appointments were regarded by some, at least, as a hindrance to their military endeavours.[14] By the time de la Mare assumed knighthood he was possibly already affiliated with Lancaster, and he went on to serve the earl on at least three separate occasions from 1338 to 1342.[15] De la Mare's commitment to warfare suggests that he was a professional soldier in every respect, and it seems that his proficiency at arms was matched by his administrative and diplomatic skills. In 1340 he played a part in securing Lancaster's release from prison in Mechelen, where he had been held as surety for Edward III's debts, and the Gloucestershire knight became steward of Lancaster's lands in the south after serving on his final campaign in 1347.[16]

The professionalism of all three knights discussed above cannot be doubted and the underlying patterns of their service reveal a commitment to serve continuously with Lancaster once they had first taken up arms with him. Although the start of their military careers preceded that of Lancaster, which meant that they learnt their trade, so to speak, under different retinue

---

[11] C 71/10, mm. 4, 12 (1318); *CPR, 1321–24*, p. 199 (1322); *CPR, 1330–34*, p. 456 (1333).

[12] *CPR, 1324–27*, p. 247 (respite of knighthood). *CPR, 1330–34*, p. 456; the exemption was granted 'in consideration of his service to the late king and the king in his wars in Gascony and Scotland'. Saul interprets the grant as evidence of service by de la Mare in Gascony before this date, but the clause may not specifically relate to all of the men whose names are grouped together in the Patent Rolls and there is no other nominal evidence of his service in the duchy in 1324: Saul, *Knights and Esquires*, p. 46.

[13] Saul, *Knights and Esquires*, p. 46.

[14] Simpkin, *English Aristocracy at War*, pp. 22–4. The multitude of men in the mid 1340s whose names are recorded in the sheriffs' writs of return for those who held £40 of land but had not taken up knighthood shows that some men were not eager to assume knighthood. The 50 marks owed to Robert Chippelegh by Sir Thomas Courtney in 1344 suggests that Chippelegh is another example of an esquire whose wealth probably exceeded that of most *strenui milites*. *CCR, 1343–46*, p. 366.

[15] C 76/12, m. 7; E 36/203, fol. 126r (1338); C 76/15, m. 18 (1340); C 76/17, m. 25; C 81/1724/40 (1342).

[16] E 159/123, mm. 145, 154; *CPR, 1340–43*, pp. 176–7 (delivery of Lancaster). *CPP*, p. 133 (steward).

captains, it was knights such as Mohun, Seaton and de la Mare who formed the stable core of the earl's retinue. It is perhaps significant that more than a quarter (29.2%) of the men in the sample group exclusively served with Lancaster from 1336 onwards and that three of them had already fought with another retinue captain on a previous occasion.[17] The launch of Lancaster's military career therefore provided an opportunity, for these men at least, to join the newly-formed retinue of a magnate. Whether these men aimed to pursue a martial lifestyle from the outset or whether their continuous service at war resulted from Lancaster's ability and commitment to the role of Edward III's leading war captain we cannot be sure but, certainly in Peter de la Mare's instance, a desire to pursue a profession at arms was evident before joining Lancaster's *comitiva*.

At the opposite end of the spectrum of military professionalism are those men who showed little or no loyalty towards a particular lord and who served under a different banner from one campaign to the next. Table 13 shows that Philip de Lymbury and Richard de Rawcliffe fought under various captains more than anyone else during the period up to the mid 1340s and, like most men in the sample, their first military action was in the Scottish war of 1336.[18] Lymbury served continuously from the opening campaign of his career up to 1340 with no fewer than four different retinue captains, including Richard Fitzalan, earl of Arundel, John de Eltham, earl of Cornwall, Henry Burghersh, bishop of Lincoln, and Sir John Molyns.[19] In 1342 he accompanied Sir Robert Ferrers to Brittany before finally joining Henry of Lancaster's expedition to Spain in 1344.[20] The Yorkshire knight Richard de Rawcliffe had entered into Lancaster's service in 1342 after having already served in Scotland, firstly with Sir Henry Beaumont in 1336, and then with Sir Henry, Lord Percy in 1338 when the earls of Arundel and Salisbury failed to take Dunbar.[21] He also campaigned overseas in 1340 under the banner of Sir John Beaumont and continued to serve with Lancaster in 1344.[22] In his deposition at the Court of Chivalry in 1385 Rawcliffe claims to have been 'armed' since he was thirteen years old, which suggests that he chose to

---

[17] Seven out of 24 men only served Lancaster after 1336. Names: Thomas Cok, Ralph de Hastings, Hugh Meynell, Payn de Mohun, Reginald de Mohun, Simon Simeon, John de Walkington.

[18] It is interesting to note that Lancaster's military career started at the same time, and on the same Scottish expedition (1336), as most of the men in the sample.

[19] E 101/19/36, m. 8 (1336, Cornwall); E 101/35/3, m. 2d (1337, Arundel); E 36/203, fol. 127r (1338, Molyns); C 76/15, m. 22 (1340, Lincoln).

[20] C 76/17, m. 25 (1342, Ferrers); C 76/19, mm. 19, 22; *CCR, 1343–46*, p. 361 (1344, Lancaster).

[21] E 101/19/36, m. 2 (1336, Beaumont); E 101/35/3, m. 2 (1338, Percy); C 76/17, m. 20 (1342, Lancaster).

[22] C 76/15, m. 22 (1340, Beaumont); C 76/19, m. 19; C 81/1724/49 (1344, Lancaster).

pursue a military career from a very young age.[23] Such youthful aspirations might well have been shared by many among the military community in the first half of the fourteenth century.

For both Lymbury and Rawcliffe, however, it is not only the number of occasions that they took up arms but also the frequency of their service that reflects their professionalism. Rawcliffe, for example, served on five campaigns with four captains in eight years and Lymbury served on no fewer than six campaigns during the same period, but he never served with the same captain more than once. The fact that both men fought in a different retinue on almost every campaign reflects their own desire to pursue a martial lifestyle, rather than make a career in the affinity of one particular magnate. The two soldiers might be regarded as what Ayton terms 'gentleman military careerists'[24] but after entering Lancaster's service in the 1340s neither of the men served with another captain thereafter and, in Lymbury's case, he consistently served in the same retinue up until Lancaster's death in 1361.[25] The examples of Lymbury and Rawcliffe, therefore, suggest that some professional soldiers who served under various captains, to whom they appear to have had no real attachment or loyalty, would settle in a magnate's retinue if the latter was able to offer them the campaigning opportunities they desired.

Military Careers beyond 1345

The evidence of military service suggests that none of Lancaster's men who can be considered as independent military professionals were completely unattached from their retinue captain. However, the evidence presented in Table 13 does not account for military service performed in the duchy of Aquitaine (1345) or on any subsequent campaigns. Therefore, any professionals who were at an early stage of their career, or who were perhaps serving for the first time in 1345, are missing from view. If we are to extrapolate the full extent of professional soldiering from the military careers of the individuals in Lancaster's retinue then we need to look beyond the mid 1340s and analyse the entire histories of service of the earl's men. By maintaining the same sample criteria, to include only men who served on four or more campaigns, the sample group expands to 71 men, comprising 6 bannerets, 8 esquires and 57 knights. It should be noted, however, that the coverage of histories of service is limited to the knights banneret and bachelor and the handful of men who were identified as 'probable' esquires

---

[23] *Scrope and Grosvenor*, II, p. 351.

[24] Ayton, *Dynamics of Recruitment*, pp. 56–9.

[25] Lymbury went on to serve in a further six campaigns with Lancaster after 1344.

before the recent rediscovery of the missing portion of Lancaster's retinue roll, which contains a complete nominal list of esquires. The latter, therefore, are underrepresented in the sample.

Table 14 shows the military service of 71 of Lancaster's men who served on four or more campaigns during their military careers. It displays the number of men and the number of campaigns on which they served, as well as the mean period of time that they were militarily active. The most striking feature of the evidence is that, when compared with the sample of known retinue personnel used in the previous chapter, it shows that two-thirds (66.3%) of the 95 identifiable knights banneret and knights bachelor in Lancaster's retinue can be considered as professional soldiers who consistently took up arms in what were often different theatres of war.[26] From the sample of 71 men, the majority served on a total of four campaigns and three groups of 10 men each served on five to seven campaigns. A substantial minority of men (13.7%) served on ten campaigns and upwards, including 2 men who served on no fewer than sixteen and nineteen occasions, respectively. The mean length of career of each group who served on the same

Table 14. Military Careers of Men who Served on Four or More Campaigns

Number of Campaigns	Number of Men	Mean Length of Career (yrs)
4	22	14.75
5	10	39.4
6	10	18.9
7	10	21.4
8	1	24
9	5	25
10	2	32.5
11	1	33
12	4	34.8
13	3	29.7
14	1	34
15	0	-
16	1	31
17	0	-
18	0	-
19	1	34

[26] Out of the sample of 95 identifiable knights banneret and bachelor, 63 served on four or more campaigns.

number of campaigns generally increases commensurate with the number of campaigns undertaken, with the exceptions of men who served respectively on five and twelve campaigns. The surprisingly high mean values of years of service for these groups, however, might be explained by the unusual longevity of individual careers. Sir Thomas Mountjoy, for example, who served on at least five campaigns, probably first took up arms with Sir Robert Mohaut in 1310 and was still enjoying a martial career in 1349 as part of a garrison force at Calais.[27] Similarly, among the men who served on twelve campaigns is Andrew Luttrell, an exemplar of the medieval knight who had been armed for fifty-one years since 1337 and represents the longest serving soldier from the sample.[28]

The evidence of service is predominantly based on men who belonged to the higher echelons of the military retinue, although the illustrative examples of esquires such as Edmund de Bulstrode, Walter de Bintree and Thomas de la Ryvere who served on six, seven and nine campaigns respectively suggest that professionalism was also prevalent among ordinary men-at-arms.[29] It is perhaps significant that all three men were annuitants of, and exclusively served with, Henry of Lancaster.[30] The careers of these soldiers elucidate the strong connection between repeated service and loyalty to a single captain that was evident within all ranks of men-at-arms. Bulstrode and the other esquires mentioned above were 'household careerists' and, as such, benefited from the patronage of their lord in return for the good and loyal service which they provided but, first and foremost, they were professional soldiers who embraced a martial lifestyle that was inherent to Lancaster's own military career. Why they were never promoted to knighthood is something of a conundrum, as we cannot be certain whether they aspired to knighthood, like most ordinary men-at-arms, or if it was through personal choice that they remained esquires. Whatever the reason for maintaining the same rank, the men's professionalism and commitment to warfare cannot be doubted.

The career progression of soldiers who had served as esquires prior to

---

[27] C 71/4, m. 12 (1310); C 76/27, m. 10 (1349).

[28] *Scrope and Grosvenor*, I, p. 243.

[29] Other esquires who are not included in the sample, but who exclusively served with Lancaster on four or more campaigns, are, among others, Richard Sholl and Robert Wickham. Thomas de la Mare, a veteran from the War of Saint-Sardos and son of Sir Peter de la Mare, is another esquire who served on four campaigns and became a trusted member of the earl's household. He is described as Lancaster's valet in 1353 when he delivered two premium warhorses (destriers) to Edward III. E 403/368, m. 11 (destriers).

[30] For their annuities, see Chapter 7. The esquires exclusively served with Lancaster throughout their careers, except for Walter de Bintree, who twice served in Walter Mauny's retinue before entering into Lancaster's service in 1344. John de Newmarch, esquire, was another annuitant of Lancaster who should be considered as a 'household careerist', and the fact that he served on only three campaigns, all of which were with the earl, might well be down to the patchiness of the military service records.

Lancaster's expedition to Aquitaine and subsequently gained wealth and status through consistent campaigning may also be indicative of professionalism among ordinary men-at-arms. There are several examples of men who began their military career as esquires during the mid 1330s but who had become knights by the time they served with Lancaster in 1345.[31] Conversely, virgin soldiers such as Thomas Florak who served as an esquire for the first time on the expedition to the duchy went on to fulfil eventful and rewarding military careers. Florak had been made a knight by the time of the Reims expedition (1359–60), and his wealth, which grew commensurate with the development of his career in arms, is reflected by his appointment of four attorneys in 1366, whilst serving in the retinue of the Black Prince.[32] Other esquires from Lancaster's retinue such as Thomas Mountjoy, William Scargill and Richard de Walkefare went on to become knights later in their careers, and all of them should be considered as professional soldiers. However, not until an attempt has been made to reconstruct the military careers of all of the esquires in Lancaster's retinue based on a systematic study of the administrative records can we be certain how representative their professionalism was among their fellow comrades of the same rank. It should be noted that these illustrative examples roughly tally with the levels of professionalism that have been shown to have existed among ordinary men-at-arms later in the fourteenth century.[33]

If it is possible to gain only a partial insight into military professionalism among the ordinary men-at-arms in Lancaster's retinue, then when it comes to the mounted archers we are faced with an even greater quandary. The careers in arms of archers, as we have already seen, are more diffi-

[31] William de Hastings, Theobald Trussell, Richard de Seaton, Avery de Sulny and John Walkington all served as esquires with Lancaster in 1336, but had become knights by 1345. Neil Loring is described as the 'king's yeoman' in 1335, and registered as an esquire in 1338 before being knighted in 1340 for his role in the battle of Sluys: *CPR, 1334–38*, p. 169 (1335); Ayton, *Knights and Warhorses*, p. 187 (1338); *Oeuvres*, III, p. 197 (1340).

[32] Florak served on at least four expeditions with Lancaster from 1345 to 1359, and on four expeditions with the Black Prince in the 1360s, all of which were in Aquitaine. In 1366 the Wiltshire knight appointed John Bridmore, John Brunning, John Frisel and William Pain as his attorneys. C 61/79, mm. 4, 8, 15. Service with Lancaster: E 101/35/2/10, m. 1 (1345); C 76/27, m. 1; E 403/355, m. 19; E 404/508/77 (1349); E 101/174/12 (1356); C 76/38, m. 16 (1359). Service with the Black Prince: C 61/76, mm. 6, 7 (1363); C 61/79, mm. 4, 8, 15 (1366); C 61/80, m. 1 (1367); C 61/82, m. 3 (1369).

[33] Ayton's study of the military experiences of the deponents who testified in support of Lord Morley at the Court of Chivalry in the mid 1380s demonstrates the prevalence of military professionalism among his sample group of 52 men, 42 of whom had not been knighted and therefore were probably esquires. Ayton, *Dynamics of Recruitment*, pp. 45–59. We can also infer from a case study of 100 ordinary men-at-arms in the retinue of the earl of Hereford in 1372 that 23% of esquires were 'professional', based on their participation in four or more campaigns from 1369 to 1399. See Table 3.3a in Bell et al., *The Soldier in Later Medieval England*, p. 121.

cult to construct than those pertaining to men of higher status due to the unevenness of the military service records which are generally less favourable to men at the lower echelons of the retinue. However, the numerous examples in Lancaster's retinue of archers and men-at-arms being recruited from within the same family suggest that there was potential in the mid 1340s for archers to move between troop types.[34] The career progression of mounted archers who fought as mercenaries in France in the late 1350s is attested by the contemporary chronicler Sir Thomas Gray, who observed that men of obscure origins throughout England had risen to prominence after 'beginning as archers, and then becoming knights, and some of them captains'.[35] It would, indeed, be of little surprise to find a similar commitment to warfare among the retinue-based archers who served in English armies, or that similar aspirations for career development, regardless of the service context, were rooted in military service undertaken in the previous decade. For those who began their career with a bow and aspired to promotion through the ranks of different retinues, there were no doubt others who served consistently with the same captain. Unfortunately, there are no surviving retinue rolls pertaining to Lancaster's *comitive* except for those of 1336 and 1345, and therefore it is impossible to identify archers who, like some men-at-arms, had traditional service ties to the earl or to the house of Lancaster.[36] However, it is tempting to think that archers who fought later in the fourteenth century such as Robert Fishlake, for example, who has been shown to fit into a 'careerist model of military service', and who served consistently with the same gentry family, might reflect the dispositions shared by men forty years earlier.[37] Certainly some men, whose main occupation was warfare with the bow, would have hoped for social betterment as a result of their deeds on the battlefield.

We should also remember that the development of military professionalism was not limited to retinue combatants alone, as some clerks and other necessary personnel such as surgeons, carpenters and engineers would have accompanied a captain on multiple campaigns. Should these men who performed their 'civilian' duties on numerous occasions in a wide geographical range of warfare also be considered as military professionals? In some respects it would seem to be appropriate to do so. The three clerks Henry de Campden, John de Welbourne and Peter de Wotton, for example, served Henry of Lancaster on at least three (and in Campden's case four)

---

[34] For discussion of twelve families who contributed both archers and esquires, see Chapter 8.

[35] Gray, *Scalacronica*, p. 157.

[36] Note that Lancaster's retinue roll for 1336 lacks the names of archers.

[37] Bell et al., *The Soldier in Later Medieval England*, pp. 164–9. For a detailed study of Fishlake's career, see his 'Soldier Profile', by David Simpkin: <www.medievalsoldier.org/February2008.php>

separate overseas campaigns, including the expedition to Aquitaine in 1345.[38] In peacetime these men would have performed a variety of administrative duties, but whilst on campaign the clerks operated in a military context and fulfilled roles that were specific to war such as receiving money and victuals, valuing warhorses, reviewing troops, distributing wages and, above all, accounting for service. To perform such duties with some degree of regularity no doubt precipitated a form of military professionalism within the pool of active clerks and administrators in England. If a magnate captain was to choose between two household clerks to accompany him on an overseas expedition: one whose only experience was as a 'quill pusher' on his estate, while the other was accustomed to the rigours of campaigning life – battle, siege, chevauchée and all – then the latter would be the favourable choice on account of his specialist knowledge and experience of warfare. The clerk Henry de Walton, for instance, who was with Lancaster in Aquitaine, served three different retinue captains in less than a decade.[39] Indeed, he is someone whom we might consider as a 'professional military administrator', in that he switched from the Exchequer into Lancaster's employment in the 1340s, became the earl's treasurer and, later on, lieutenant of the palatinate of Lancaster. This reflects a 'careerist model' among administrators whose skills were honed, at least in part, in the context of war.[40]

Beyond the military retinue, we find that the service performed by men who belonged to infantry divisions, or at least the officers who commanded such contingents, can also be characterised by professionalisation. A recent study of the military service of *centenars* during Edward I's reign has, indeed, shown that a considerable number of the infantry officers repeatedly led companies of foot soldiers on royal expeditions, and sometimes they served over the course of a decade.[41] Clearly military professionalism had already emerged among the officers of infantrymen more than half a century before Lancaster's expedition to Aquitaine.

---

[38] Campden: C 76/12, m. 7 (1338); C 76/19, mm. 11, 23 (1344); C 76/20, m. 25; C 81/1724/34 (1345); C 76/26, m. 9 (1348). Welbourne: E 404/508/47 (1345); C 76/26, m. 9 (1348); C 76/27, m. 4 (1349). Wotton: C 76/17, mm. 22, 25; C 81/1724/36 (1342); C 76/20, m. 15 (1345); C 76/33, m. 1 (1355).

[39] Walton served with John Charnels in the Low Countries (1338), the earl of Pembroke in Brittany (1342) and with Henry of Lancaster in Aquitaine (1345) and at Calais (1347). E 36/203, fol. 128; C 76/17, m. 27; C 76/20, m. 15; C 76/25, m. 25.

[40] For Walton's career, see Fowler, *King's Lieutenant*, pp. 180–1; *Somerville*, pp. 358–9; Tout, *Chapters*, IV, pp. 136–8, 140–4. An illustrative example of a 'professional military administrator' from the fifteenth century is the clerk John Fishlake. The latter served on the Agincourt campaign (1415) as a mounted archer in the retinue of Sir John Mowbray, earl marshal of England, and was later appointed as the earl's attorney who drew up his particulars of account. Curry, *Personal Links and the Nature of the English War Retinue*, pp. 157, 165.

[41] Bachrach, *Edward I's Centurions*, pp. 109–28.

So far the discussion of military professionalism has focused on the careers of 'English' soldiers in Lancaster's retinue, but among the Aquitanians, who often escape the gaze of historians, are a plenitude of soldiers whose martial lifestyle brought them advancement and reward.[42] In the case of Hélias de Pommiers a rare type of soldier comes into view. This Gascon, who hailed from that famous knightly clan of Pommiers, had originally pursued a clerical career and held the canonry of Bazas before he chose to abandon the Church in order to take up arms against the French in Aquitaine during the late 1330s.[43] Although it was not unknown for clergymen to divest their robes in order to pursue a military career, it was often a claim to family inheritance, following the death of an older sibling, which induced their departure from the Church.[44] But for Hélias there was no prospect of a substantial family inheritance, only the potential rewards of war.[45] The early stages of his military career, however, brought him near to financial ruin following the service he performed in the duchy from 1337 to 1339, for which he still awaited payment three years later.[46] On account of his martial activities Hélias was made 'incapable by the pope', which meant he was prohibited from holding ecclesiastical benefices (such as the canonry of Bazas).[47] His loss of goods, lands and benefices caused such impoverishment that by 1344 he was no longer able to continue in the king's service.[48] It was not until 1345, when he served as a knight in Lancaster's retinue, that his fortunes changed. Following the success of the earl's expedition in Aquitaine, Hélias was created seneschal of Périgord (1347) and made lord of Arbanats by 1349.[49] He was also later appointed seneschal of Limousin and Quercy, but perhaps the greatest reward of war came with the capture of the count of Eu at the battle of Poitiers (1356), whom he subsequently sold

---

[42] Pey de Grailly, founding knight of the Order of the Garter, and Guilhem-Sans III, lord of Pommiers, are prime examples of Aquitanians who accrued land, wealth and prestige on account of the success of their military careers.

[43] He held ecclesiastical benefices before 1344, but we cannot be certain exactly when he was made canon of Bazas: C 61/56, m. 12.

[44] The 'cynical ex-priest', Galhart de Durfort, for example, left the Church to take up knighthood and marriage and to promote his family's interests in the duchy following the death of his brother, Aimeric, in 1345. Sumption, *Trial by Battle*, p. 478.

[45] A fourth part of the place of Civrac ('Sivrak') came to Hélias by inheritance after the death of his father, lord of Pommiers. C 61/72, m. 9.

[46] In 1340 the constable of Bordeaux was ordered to pay Hélias his annual fee and compensation for one horse lost in 'the Gascon war' because he had been retained by the king. C 61/52, m. 21.

[47] *CPR, 1343–45*, p. 217.

[48] In 1344 the king ordered that Pommiers be granted money from the wine custom of Bordeaux, and any void benefices in England, in payment of arrears for money granted to him in 1342 on account of the losses incurred as a result of the war in Aquitaine. C 61/56, m. 12; *CPR, 1340–43*, p. 4; *CPR, 1343–45*, p. 217.

[49] Bériac, *Guillaume-Sanche, Elie de Pommiers et leurs frères*, pp. 214–15.

to the Black Prince for the enormous sum of 30,000 écus (about £5650).[50] A man once committed to the Church was now committed to war, and by the mid 1350s Hélias, like other Gascon lords, had become virtually a full-time soldier.[51] For someone who held the titles of knight, canon and lord over the course of an ecclesiastical and military career, his endeavours are a persuasive reminder of how incessant warfare provided the opportunities for professional soldiering and opened up alternative career paths to men who would otherwise not have pursued a career in arms. Indeed, the final reward for Pommiers' long-term service came in 1365 when he was granted a royal annuity of £100 for his allegiance to the king during the wars in the duchy.[52]

Such career progression is also evident among the Aquitanians who served as ordinary men-at-arms in Lancaster's retinue. Hélias' relative, Amaniu de Pommiers, for example, who is listed as an esquire on the earl's retinue roll in 1345, was subsequently promoted to knighthood and was one of the Black Prince's companions at Poitiers.[53] Three years later he served as retinue captain in his own right during the expedition to Reims. Indeed, the rise in status of Amaniu is reflected by the quality of his men's horses in 1359, and by his appointment as a royal official in Aquitaine to investigate any breaches of the truce that was made between England and France at Brétigny in 1360.[54]

Another native of the duchy who can be seen to have acquired greater status and presumably, therefore, wealth, since serving with Lancaster in 1345 was Arnaut Micol of Bazas. Although he had pursued a mercantile career for most of his life, and served as chief butler and sergeant of Edward III in the early 1330s, it was his decision to bear arms in Lancaster's retinue as an esquire that brought him to the earl's notice and probably led to his appointment as prévôt of Bazas and Bazadais sometime before 1347.[55]

---

[50] Sumption, *Trial by Fire*, p. 248; E 403/388, m. 22. Hélias actually received the slightly smaller sum of £4877 in thirteen instalments, the last payment was made on 24 February 1369: Chris Given-Wilson and Françoise Bériac, 'Edward III's Prisoners of War: The Battle of Poitiers and its Context', *EHR*, 116 (2001), 802–33 (p. 831).

[51] Sumption, *Trial by Fire*, p. 190.

[52] C 61/78, mm. 2, 3.

[53] Amaniu de Pommiers is listed 29th and 76th among the esquires: E 101/35/2/10, mm. 1, 2. Sumption, *Trial by Fire*, p. 493 (Poitiers).

[54] Pommiers' retinue has the third highest mean horse value (£20 0s 53d) out of 119 retinues that received horse restoration for service in 1359. It should be noted that the high horse value may be accounted for by the fact that Pommiers' men were only compensated for the loss of three mounts. Ayton, *Knights and Warhorses*, pp. 265–7; E 101/393/11, fol. 86. In 1361 Pommiers was appointed with Amaniu d'Albret, lord of Langoiran, to investigate any violations of the truce: C 61/74, m. 10.

[55] For his activities as Edward III's butler and sergeant, see numerous references in *CPR, 1330–34*; *CPR, 1334–38*; C 61/44, m. 7. He is described as a burgess of Bordeaux in 1344 and listed 41st among the esquires on the 1345 retinue roll. C 61/35, m. 15d; E 101/35/2/10, m. 1. On his appointment as prévôt, see C 61/64, mm. 2, 3, 4, 7.

Arnaut, therefore, like Hélias, provides another example of how men from a range of social backgrounds and occupations were induced to take up arms by the potential rewards of war, whether it was the grant of lordships or the appointment to local offices.

Prolific Military Careers

The evidence thus far has shown that three-quarters of Lancaster's bannerets in 1345 served on at least four campaigns during their lifetimes and 56 out of 87, or 64.4%, identifiable 'English' knights also served on the same minimum number of occasions throughout their military careers. We can conclude therefore that the majority of Lancaster's men who were of a knightly status or above led a military lifestyle and might be considered as professional soldiers. However, although the number of campaigns on which a soldier served is an important means of identifying military professionals, it is also a crude methodology which often provides only a general view of the soldier. The military service evidence alone, for example, particularly for a relatively large sample, fails to reveal the nuances of an individual's attitude to warfare, his attachment to a particular captain, or indeed his desire to continue fighting in different theatres of war during times of peace. To understand these attributes of soldiers, which can be used to further investigate military professionalism in Lancaster's retinue, it is paramount to consider the careers of individual soldiers.

The careers of a more focused sample of nineteen men from Lancaster's retinue, based on those with the most campaigning experience, are tabulated below. Table 15 also shows the number of captains under whom the soldiers served, as well as the period and length of their careers.

This crop of seasoned warriors, all of whom served on eight or more campaigns, forms a distinguishable subset out of the sample group of seventy-one men used earlier in the chapter. The most striking feature of the evidence is that more than three-quarters (78.9%) of the men had already served on a minimum of four campaigns before the mid 1340s.[56] That fifteen of the men listed in Table 15 might already have been considered as military professionals before serving with Lancaster in 1345 reveals two things. First, the evidence does support Ayton's view that the fifteen-year period of intensive warfare from 1332 onwards was fundamental to the development of military professionalism and 'encouraged careerism in a recognisable form'.[57] Indeed, just around 10% of the seventy-one professional soldiers had taken up arms before 1332, and John de Lymbury is the only example

---

[56] Compare names with those listed in Table 13.
[57] Ayton, *Dynamics of Recruitment*, p. 57.

Table 15. Military Careers of Men who Served on Eight or More Campaigns

Name	Campaigns	No. of Captains	Dates
Norman de Swinford	8	4+	1342–66
Thomas Cok	9	2	1336–52
Reginald de Mohun	9	3	1324–49
John de Norwich	9	2	1322–59
Thomas de la Ryvere	9	2	1338–61
John de Seaton	9	2	1332–56
John de Lymbury	10	4+	1301–45
Nicholas de Rye	10	2	1338–59
William la Zouche of Totnes	11	2+	1337–70
Alexander Auncel	12	4	1336–59
Nicholas Goushill	12	6+	1333–75
Theobald Trussell	12	2	1336–59
Andrew Luttrell	12	5+	1337–88
Adam de Everingham	13	3+	1333–59
Simon Simeon	13	2+	1329–59
Stephen de Cosington	13	4+	1334–67
John de Grey of Codnor	14	4+	1333–67
Philip de Lymbury	16	7+	1336–67
Neil Loring	19	7+	1335–72

Note: '+' indicates the minimum number of captains.

of a soldier who had already served on at least four military enterprises by the early 1330s.[58] This low percentage, however, might be explained by the nature of English warfare which had become sporadic during the reign of Edward II, particularly after the battle of Bannockburn in 1314.[59] Second, that such a high proportion of men listed in Table 15 can be considered as professional soldiers by 1345 reflects the men's long-term commitment to warfare. Indeed, the mean career length of men from the sample is thirty

[58] See Table 13 for men who served before 1332. Lymbury's service up to 1333: C 67/14, m. 4 (1301); E 101/13/7, m. 1 (1306); C 71/4, m. 4 (1311); C 71/6, m. 3 (1314); C 71/8, m. 6 (1315); C 71/8, m. 4 (1318); C 71/10, m. 4 (1319); C 71/13, m. 28 (1333). Interestingly, the percentage also implies that most of the knights were contemporaries of Lancaster.
[59] The only royal overseas campaign undertaken during this period was to Aquitaine in 1324, and other warfare after 1314 was largely limited to small-scale expeditions to Scotland. For military expeditions in the reign of Edward II, see Phillips, *Edward II*.

years, which shows that the majority of soldiers led a martial lifestyle over a protracted period of time.[60]

Another distinctive feature of the evidence is that that 10 out of the 19 men never served on campaign again after the Treaty of Brétigny was concluded in 1360 and, thus, their military careers had finished by the end of the first phase of the Hundred Years' War. So why did around half of the men not serve again after 1360, and can an extrapolation of the evidence give an insight into the nature of their military professionalism? In the instances of Thomas Cok, John de Lymbury, Reginald de Mohun and John de Seaton, it was not a personal choice but death which brought an end to their military careers.[61] However, the withdrawal from the military stage by the six other soldiers seems to have resulted from different reasons. Alexander Auncel disappears from view amongst the administrative records after a letter of protection was issued to him in 1359, but the remaining five men were still alive and fully engaged in gentry life after the expedition to Reims.[62] The Northamptonshire knight, Theobald Trussell, for example, served on several commissions of oyer and terminer in his home county during the mid 1360s and was possibly still living in the early 1370s.[63] John de Norwich and Nicholas de Rye were also appointed as local commissioners in their home counties from 1360 to 1361, while the former knight was also summoned to parliament and thus became a peer of the realm two years prior to his death in 1362.[64] Similarly, Adam de Everingham was summoned to parliament (1370) and appointed to various commissions in Nottinghamshire from the 1360s to the 1380s, including a commission of the peace to suppress any rebellious factions against Richard II in 1382.[65] He was on an oyer and terminer commission in 1386, the same year that he testified at the Court of Chivalry on behalf of Richard Scrope, the year before his death in 1387.[66] Simon Simeon, or 'little Simon' (*Simkyn*), as he was commonly known, continued to serve the house of Lancaster after Henry's death in 1361, although we cannot be certain whether he served on

[60] A total of 567 campaigning years by 19 men gives a mean career length of 29.8 years.

[61] The expedition to Aquitaine in 1345 was Lymbury's final campaign, Mohun disappears from the records after Lancaster's second expedition to the duchy in 1349, as does Seaton in 1356. Cok died around 1352.

[62] C 76/38, m. 16 (Auncel).

[63] *CIPM*, XIII, pp. 236–7.

[64] Rye was appointed as a commissioner 'de wallensis et fossatis' on the sea coast in Lincolnshire in 1360 and as a commissioner of the peace in the same county in the following year: *CPR, 1358–61*, p. 417; *CPR, 1361–64*, pp. 65–6. In 1360 Norwich was appointed as commissioner of array with Robert de Causton and others in Norfolk: *CPR, 1358–61*, p. 415. Norwich's summons to parliament: *CP*, IX, p. 765.

[65] See *CPR* for various commissions from 1360s to 1380s. *CP*, V, p. 189 (summons to parliament).

[66] *CPR, 1385–89*, p. 262; *Scrope and Grosvenor*, I, pp. 240–1; *CIPM*, XVI, pp. 207–9.

any overseas campaigns with John of Gaunt, duke of Lancaster, as he had done on so many occasions under the duke's predecessor.[67] Simeon died the same year as Everingham.[68]

We cannot be certain why the six individuals discussed above withdrew from active service following the Treaty of Brétigny, although retirement through old age, at least in the case of John de Norwich, seems to have been a likely cause.[69] The customary ailments and injuries incurred over the course of a campaigning life may have taken their toll on some of the men. However, that at least three individuals continued to live for more than a decade, and in two instances, for more than twenty years after their last overseas campaign suggests that it was not through physical impairment that they had retired from active warfare. Indeed, all of the men, except for Auncel, were of sound enough health to take active roles as local commissioners in the years and decades that followed 1360. For these men who first took up the sword in the 1320s or 1330s the peace concluded with France must have provided a natural caesura in their military careers, particularly as most of their previous campaigning experience had been part of the Anglo-French conflict. It should be borne in mind, however, that other theatres of war and contexts of warfare such as Ireland, the Iberian peninsula or crusading expeditions to Alexandria or the Baltic, for example, provided further opportunities for military service if soldiers so desired.[70]

Another reason why some soldiers no longer served after 1360 may have been due to Lancaster's death. It is perhaps significant that of the six men, four had exclusively served with Lancaster once they entered into his service.[71] And in Theobald Trussell's case, he too consistently served under Lancaster's banner except for two occasions in 1337 and 1341 when he accompanied his father, Sir William Trussell of Flores, on important diplomatic missions to the Low Countries.[72] Five of the six soldiers, therefore, were attached to Lancaster through a continuance of service during the first phase of the Hundred Years' War and for half of the men their loyalty was rooted

---

[67] Simeon appears as 'Simkyn' in Lancaster's two extant retinue rolls for 1336 and 1345. He was Gaunt's steward in Lincolnshire and Bolingbroke and disappears from view around 1385: Fowler, *King's Lieutenant*, p. 176. Simeon also served on commissions in Lincolnshire in the late 1360s: Walker, *Lancastrian Affinity*, p. 242, n. 36.

[68] *CIPM*, XVII, p. 52.

[69] Norwich was fifty years old at the time of the Reims expedition in 1359.

[70] Note that crusading expeditions to Alexandria and the Baltic would have required a considerable financial outlay, either by the individual participating in the crusade or a sponsor, and therefore were not opportunities available to all soldiers.

[71] Names: Auncel, Everingham, Rye, Simeon.

[72] *CPR, 1334–38*, p. 421 (1337). C 76/16, m. 26; C 81/1740/91 (1341).

in their families' tradition of service with the same noble household.[73] The importance of this tradition and loyalty is typified by Simeon's decision to continue to serve with John of Gaunt after having begun his career with the elder Henry, third earl of Lancaster. It was perhaps, therefore, the men's attachment to their lord and their family loyalty to the same noble lineage that influenced as much a soldier's decision of when to serve, as when not to serve on a certain campaign or with a particular captain. The local commissions and offices which five of the men had taken up from 1360 onwards are also revealing of the type of professionals these men were. Shire administration seems to have been a natural occupation and 'next step' for men of gentry stock who had retired from the battlefield; all the men, besides Simeon, might be considered as being 'gentlemen warriors', and as such were an important part of the social fabric and traditional structures of regional and national society in England.[74] The reasons for not continuing to serve beyond the Treaty of Brétigny varied among our group of veteran soldiers; death and old age played an inevitable part, and the lure of provincial life following a lengthy military career would have been enticing for some men, but for others the death of their lord and retinue captain may have been an important factor in retiring from their profession at arms.

The evidence has shown that at least six of the nineteen men from our sample can be regarded as belonging to the traditional warrior class, men of genteel birth who were firmly embedded in medieval society with ties of loyalty to a regional magnate; but what of those who continued to serve beyond the first phase of the war with France?[75] Did these men share the same cultural origins and loyalties as those who never served on campaign again after 1360? Should they be considered as being more specialist or professional in warfare, or did they have a stronger careerist mentality? Of the nineteen men listed in Table 15, nine can be shown to have continued to serve overseas after the Treaty of Brétigny. Interestingly, the expeditions in which roughly half of these men took part during the interim period of peace (1360–69) in the French war were part of a pilgrimage or crusade rather than a secular military enterprise. Andrew Luttrell, for example, appointed general attorneys in the summer of 1360 because he was 'going on pilgrimage to the Holy Land' and William la Zouche of Totnes went on the same pilgrimage two years later.[76] Luttrell set out overseas again in 1362 but, unfortunately, the evidence does not reveal the purpose or destination

---

[73] Simeon and the fathers of Everingham and Trussell had served the elder Henry of Lancaster, while William Trussell had also served with Thomas of Lancaster.

[74] Phrase used in Ayton, *Dynamics of Recruitment*, p. 57.

[75] Simeon is included among the six men on account of his prolific military career and attachment to the house of Lancaster, but strictly speaking he would probably not have been considered as someone of 'genteel birth'.

[76] *CPR, 1358–61*, p. 446 (Luttrell); *CPR, 1361–64*, pp. 249–50 (Zouche).

of his intended expedition. Other soldiers, such as John de Grey of Codnor, joined the ill-fated crusade of Pierre de Lusignan, king of Cyprus, against Alexandria in 1365, and on this occasion the banneret acted as the standard-bearer of the papal legate throughout the expedition.[77] Philip de Lymbury, the veteran soldier who had served on no fewer than seventeen expeditions before his death in 1367, may also have served on the same crusade as Grey.[78] The stalwart knight had appointed four attorneys in 1365 because he was going 'beyond the seas', and his death at Constantinople two years later suggests that he may well have been on pilgrimage to the Holy Land at that time.[79] None of these men continued to take part in secular warfare when England was at peace with France, but instead appear to have sought religious atonement through pilgrimage or crusade. Indeed, such faith-based expeditions were common in truce periods, or times of peace, as crusading was often prohibited in wartime on account of the negative effect it had on the pool of military manpower available to the king.[80]

Some soldiers may have regarded fighting during times of peace as being unjust or unworthy, and for men of such thinking the campaigning opportunities which arose elsewhere, such as the Castilian dispute between Pedro the Cruel and Enrique of Trastámara, for example, or fighting in Ireland, would probably have had little appeal. As Fowler points out, according to the laws of war of the fourteenth century, only when men 'were fighting for a lord "with just title" were their activities considered to be legal'.[81] Whether the four men discussed above shared this view, or whether it was coincidental that they had not participated in secular fighting during the 1360s we do not know, but the fact that Andrew Luttrell immediately took up arms again at the beginning of the resumption of the Hundred Years' War suggests that he was of this moral mindset. The latter's service with John of

[77] Although Grey went on crusade in 1365, his protection states simply that he was 'going beyond the seas on pilgrimage': *CPR, 1364–67*, p. 127. Anthony Luttrell's assertion that Grey carried the standard of the Church for the legate is based on a fifteenth-century manuscript of a Carmelite legendary: Anthony Luttrell, 'English Levantine Crusaders, 1363–67', *Renaissance Studies*, 2 (1988), 143–53, (p. 149, n. 44). Note that caution should be taken if evidence of military service is based solely on a chronicle, and cannot be corroborated by other types of 'firmer' evidence such as royal administrative records. The danger of historians' assumptions of military service performed by men during the Alexandria crusade is highlighted by Bell: Adrian R. Bell, 'The Soldier, "hadde he ridden, no man ferre"', in *The Soldier Experience*, ed. Bell et al., pp. 209–18 (pp. 211–12).

[78] *CIPM*, XII, p. 129; he died at 'Constantyn Noble' on 6 July 1367.

[79] *CPR, 1364–67*, p. 180; one of Lymbury's four attorneys, John Repynghale, had also represented Andrew Luttrell in 1360 and 1362.

[80] In the fourteenth century the English Crown allowed crusading to flourish most during truce periods in the king's wars. Ayton, *Dynamics of Recruitment*, p. 35; Christopher Tyerman, *England and the Crusades, 1095–1588* (Chicago: University of Chicago Press, 1988), p. 266.

[81] Kenneth Fowler, *Medieval Mercenaries* (Oxford: Blackwell, 2001), p. 1.

Gaunt in Aquitaine (1369) at the age of forty-nine demonstrates his innate enthusiasm to return to the military arena, and reflects a commitment to warfare that he maintained well into mid-life.[82] Moreover, his subsequent place on Arundel's expedition in 1388 is a testimony to the military professionalism that epitomised the career of an exceptional soldier.[83]

The five remaining men from the sample of nineteen professional soldiers all embarked overseas on some campaign or other during the 1360s. Thomas de la Ryvere, a former esquire of Henry of Lancaster with whom he had served on at least eight campaigns, set out for Aquitaine in 1361, although we cannot be sure of the nature of his mission.[84] In the months that immediately followed the conclusion of peace in 1360 Stephen de Cosington and Neil Loring were both involved in overseeing the transfer of lands and castles in France in accordance with the terms of the Treaty of Brétigny.[85] Their efforts to redress any violations of the treaty often involved negotiations with various garrison captains who were reluctant to surrender their strongholds, which could last several weeks.[86] Cosington and Loring were longstanding members of the Black Prince's retinue; it is of no surprise, therefore, that both knights served in the latter's army against the Trastámaran forces at the battle of Nájera in 1367.[87] As one of the prince's marshals, Cosington led a contingent in the vanguard of the army and Chandos Herald recounts that he was one of the 'worthy knights, who did their duty well', while Loring reportedly served in the main battle with the prince.[88]

In the preceding year Cosington and a Lincolnshire knight, Norman de Swinford, both served under the command of Hugh Calveley during the invasion of Castile which was led by Bertrand du Guesclin.[89] That both men became annuitants and retainers of Charles II, king of Navarre, in 1366

[82] C 76/52, m. 15 (1369).

[83] *Scrope and Grosvenor*, I, p. 243; Bell, *War and the Soldier*, p. 141 (1388).

[84] *CPR, 1358–61*, p. 574; E 101/28/11, m. 3.

[85] *Foedera*, III, p. 504 (Cosington), p. 507 (Loring).

[86] Fowler, *Medieval Mercenaries*, pp. 25–6, 40, n. 64. In 1361 Cosington and Loring were commissioned to receive the lands and castles in Aquitaine which had been ceded to the English by the French.

[87] David Green, 'The Military Personnel of the Black Prince', *Medieval Prosopography*, 21 (2000), 133–52 (pp. 149, 151). Both men were 'in attendance on the prince's person' at the battle of Poitiers in 1356 and became prominent members of his council and household. Cosington was an annuitant for life and bachelor of the prince while Loring was retained for life and served as his chamberlain. C. L. Kingsford, 'Loring, Sir Neil (*c*. 1315–86)', rev. by Richard Barber, *ODNB*, Oct 2005 [accessed 18 March 2015]; *BPR*, IV, pp. 179, 206 (bodyguard at Poitiers).

[88] *The Life and Campaigns of the Black Prince*, ed. and trans. Richard Barber (Woodbridge: Boydell, 1986), p. 126; *Oeuvres*, VII, p. 214. Green notes that Loring served in the rearguard of the prince's army: Green, *Military Personnel*, p. 149.

[89] Fowler, *Medieval Mercenaries*, p. 149.

and had decided to take up arms in the Castilian civil war highlights the rewards of, and their motivation for, military service in mercenary armies.[90] Although Fowler suggests that Cosington's part in du Guesclin's expedition was intended to maintain liaison with the Black Prince, nevertheless Cosington's participation in warfare in the Iberian peninsula reflects the mentality of some professional soldiers who, despite having a tradition of service in English royal armies, were fully prepared to take advantage of the campaigning opportunities provided by private wars on the continent.[91] The latter had also served with the prince in Aquitaine a few years earlier and Norman de Swinford's participation in the battle of Auray in 1364, which proved a decisive victory for Jean de Montfort in the Breton dispute, suggests that he too had no intention of relaxing his campaigning habits during the period of peace with France.[92] The commitment to warfare by Stephen de Cosington and Neil Loring is evident by their service with the Black Prince in 1369. Loring also served with the earl of Pembroke in Poitou the following year and, had Norman de Swinford not died in 1368, we might imagine that he too would have endeavoured to take up arms at the resumption of the Hundred Years' War.[93]

The evidence of military service of Cosington, Loring and Swinford is indicative of their professionalism and highlights the different avenues available to men who wished to continue to pursue a martial lifestyle in the 1360s. In that decade new campaigning opportunities emerged through the activities of mercenary companies and the intervention of the Black Prince in the Castilian dispute. For Nicholas Goushill, however, the English governance of Ireland provided an alternative theatre of war to Aquitaine

---

[90] Fowler, *Medieval Mercenaries*, p. 176, n. 65, n. 66. Cosington and Loring both did homage to the king of Navarre; the former knight was retained with an annuity of 1000 florins and the latter was granted an annual fief-rent of 200 *livres tournois*. From 1350 to 1380 the florin was worth about 3s 0d sterling: Peter Spufford, *Handbook of Medieval Exchange* (London: Offices of the Royal Historical Society, University College London, 1986), pp. 220–1.

[91] Fowler, *Medieval Mercenaries*, p. 149.

[92] Cosington: *Foedera*, III, p. 738; C 61/77, m. 2. Swinford: Fowler, *Medieval Mercenaries*, p. 149.

[93] Cosington: C 61/82, m. 3 (1369). Loring: C 61/82, m. 4 (1369); Kingsford, 'Loring, Sir Neil', *ODNB*. A Neil Loring, knight, also took out letters of protection and attorney for service overseas with the Black Prince in 1372: C 76/55, mm. 17, 23; www.medievalsoldier.org [accessed 7 December 2012]. Swinford's death: *CIPM*, XII, pp. 232–3. Simon Walker's claim that Swinford's military career stretched into the 1380s is incorrect; Walker, *Lancastrian Affinity*, p. 29. Kingsford claims that Loring served with Robert Knolles during his expedition into Agenais and at the siege of Dommes in 1369, but Loring took out letters of protection and attorney for service in the prince's retinue in the same year: Kingsford, 'Loring, Sir Neil', *ODNB*; C 61/82, m. 4.

and Iberia.[94] In 1362 he set out to Ireland in the retinue of William de Windsor after having already served with Robert Herle in Brittany two years earlier.[95] At the Court of Chivalry in 1386 during the heraldic dispute between the lords Lovel and Morley, Goushill claimed to have taken part in John of Gaunt's chevauchée in 1369.[96] The deponent's long and eventful military career which had started in the 1330s stretched up to the mid-1370s, when he returned to Ireland to serve once again under Windsor's command.[97]

It has been shown that Goushill, like the other men discussed above, was an experienced soldier who continued his martial activities during the peace with France. There can be little doubt that the war veteran who had first taken up arms at Halidon Hill in 1333 had become as much a specialist in warfare as had Stephen de Cosington or Norman de Swinford, for example, but it is important to make the distinction between the types of professionals that these men represented. Cosington and Swinford maintained strong attachments to prominent noble households and retinues in which they regularly provided military service. Cosington's career was firmly rooted in his loyalty to the two most powerful English magnates of his time, Henry of Lancaster and Edward the Black Prince. He served with Lancaster on possibly four different expeditions and with the Black Prince on at least five separate occasions throughout his military career.[98] Norman de Swinford was a retainer of Lancaster whom he had served continuously until the expedition to Reims in 1359, when he switched into the service of the Black Prince, and it has already been shown that after the death of his lord Swinford continued to participate in warfare under different captains in two different theatres of war. Although Table 15 shows that Cosington and Swinford both served with at least four different retinue captains during their careers, on the majority of campaigns they served either with Lancaster

---

[94] The English colonisation of Ireland was part of Edward III's wider aim to establish imperial power in the 1360s: David Green, 'Lordship and Principality: Colonial Policy in Ireland and Aquitaine in the 1360s', *Journal of British Studies*, 47 (2008), 3–29.

[95] *CPR, 1361–64*, pp. 219, 428; E 101/28/11, m. 2 (1362). C 76/40, m. 10; *CPR, 1358–61*, p. 542; *CCR, 1360–64*, pp. 106, 111 (1360).

[96] C 47/6/1, no. 29.

[97] Goushill served as part of a standing force in Ireland from 1374 to 1376: E 101/33/35, m. 1; E 101/33/38, m. 11; www.medievalsoldier.org [accessed 7 December 2012]. A namesake, probably his son, who was also a knight took out letters of protection for service in the retinues of John de Hastings, earl of Pembroke, in 1369, and Edmund of Langley, earl of Cambridge, in 1374: C 61/82, m. 11 (1369); C 76/57, m. 12 (1374); www.medievalsoldier.org [accessed 7 December 2012].

[98] Lancaster: C 76/19, m. 23 (1344); C 76/20, m. 15, E 101/25/9, m. 3 (1345); C 76/25, m. 25 (1347?); C 76/27, m. 4; E 404/508/52 (1349). Black Prince: *BPR*, I, p. 80 (1347?); *BPR*, IV, pp. 178–9 (1355); C 76/40, m. 12 (1359); C 61/77, m. 2 (1364); see above (1367); C 61/82, m. 3 (1369).

or the prince. Thus, the military careers of both men were largely under-pinned by a loyalty to two magnates who were among Edward III's most prominent captains, and their place in the respective affinities enabled the men to pursue sustainable and rewarding careers in arms.

The service history of Nicholas Goushill, however, suggests that he was a 'gentleman military careerist' who never attached himself to a particular magnate nor established himself within a prominent affinity. He served under six different captains during the course of his career and only ever returned to the same retinue on three occasions.[99] Although Goushill was a well-established member of the military community and shared the same social origins as most of the men discussed above, who belonged to gentry families, there is no evidence that he ever held a local office and on only two occasions did he serve as a commissioner in his home county.[100] Should we regard him, therefore, as the 'socially disengaged military professional' who, as it has been suggested, was part of the reason for the demilitarisation of the gentry after the mid-1380s?[101] If Goushill had inherited his family's lands in Derbyshire before 1374, when he was already sixty years of age and his military career was drawing to an end, he may indeed have embraced the traditional values of gentlemen and become embedded in the social structures of his locality.[102] However, that is not to say that he would not have pursued a martial lifestyle with the same tenacity had he become a landholder at an earlier point in his life. It seems accurate, therefore, to regard him as a soldier who was socially disengaged (unlike his father), and whose motivations for an extensive military career may have been rooted in the lack of prosperity at home or his long awaited inheritance.[103] Of more importance to the historian, perhaps, are the reasons why Goushill never

---

[99] He served twice with William Montague, earl of Salisbury, Henry of Lancaster and William de Windsor. Montague: E 36/203, fol. 125v (1338); C 47/6/1 (1340). Lancaster: C 76/17, m. 27; C 81/1724/59 (1342); E 101/25/9, m. 3 (1345). Windsor: *CPR, 1361–64*, pp. 219, 428; E 101/28/11, m. 2 (1362); E 101/33/35, m. 1; E 101/33/38, m. 11 (1375); www.medievalsoldier.org [accessed 20 December 2012].

[100] In 1362 Goushill served as a commissioner of array to recruit archers in Derbyshire for the expedition to Ireland. It is interesting to note that he was commissioned (with William la Zouche of Lubbesthorpe and Robert Twyford) to arrest John de Araby who had intended to serve with Goushill in Ireland but deserted before the army's embarkation after having already received an advance payment of wages. *CCR, 1360–64*, p. 340; *CPR, 1364–67*, p. 151; C 81/1727/56 (Goushill's request for protection on behalf of Araby). Goushill also served as a collector of the parochial subsidy in Derbyshire in 1371: *CFR, 1369–77*, pp. 111, 127.

[101] Ayton, *Dynamics of Recruitment*, pp. 56–9.

[102] *CIPM*, XIV, p. 29. Ayton, *Knights and Warhorses*, p. 236, n. 191; Goushill entered into part of his inheritance in 1370.

[103] Nicholas's father, Sir Thomas Goushill, was appointed to various commissions in Derbyshire and Nottinghamshire from 1334 to 1347. C 47/2/25, m. 5 (commissioner of array, 1334); *CCR, 1339–41*, p. 647 (justice of the peace, 1340); *CCR, 1341–43*, p. 275

established himself in the retinues of powerful magnates such as Lancaster or the Black Prince, under whose banners he had served during the 1350s. On this point, however, the evidence reveals little.[104] We cannot be certain whether it was Goushill's personal choice or careerist mentality which caused him to switch between numerous retine captains or if it was the latter who did not value his worth. Indeed, the offences which Goushill caused against men whom he had served alongside on previous campaigns may be telling of his disruptive and criminal character, but whether captains considered him to be detrimental to the cohesion and stability of their military retinue we do not know.[105] Although, in truth, it is difficult to imagine that the experience which a veteran soldier such as Goushill brought to a military retinue could be outweighed by his incorrigible behaviour.

There are only two other men from our sample who served with more retinue captains than Goushill over the course of their careers. Table 15 shows that Neil Loring and Philip de Lymbury had both served with a different captain on at least seven occasions. On this evidence alone the two knights appear to be independent careerists like our socially disengaged soldier above but, despite their service with numerous captains, they represent the traditional warrior class whose careers had progressed through their attachment to Lancaster, Edward III or the Black Prince. In Loring's case he was an annuitant of all three royal figures, a life-retainer of the prince and a Knight of the Garter, while the loyalty shown by Lymbury after he had settled in Lancaster's service has been discussed earlier. The stark contrast between the career progression of both Loring and Lymbury and that of Goushill may have resulted from the luck or exceptional talent of an individual, but it is tempting to attribute Goushill's lack of prosperity to his seemingly detached and independent status.

(justice of oyer and terminer, 1341); *CFR, 1337–47*, p. 482; *CFR, 1347–56*, p. 44 (collector of lay subsidies, 1346 to 1347).

[104] Goushill served with the Black Prince at Poitiers in 1356: C 47/6/1, no. 29. For service with Lancaster, see above.

[105] Goushill was pardoned in 1361 for entering the close of Sir John Boson at Screveton (Nottinghamshire) and stealing his goods and kidnapping two of his servants; as well as other crimes of theft, castle rustling and rape: *CPR, 1358–61*, p. 542. Any bonds of comradeship which may have existed between the two knights during their service together in Lancaster's retinue in 1345, do not seem evident in the following decades. Goushill was also part of gang which terrorised tenants of John of Gaunt in Nottinghamshire in 1379 and at seventy-six years of age, he (and his son, Robert Goushill) found mainprise not to harm William Birkes in 1386: *CPR, 1377–81*, p. 360; *CCR, 1385–89*, p. 144. Goushill was accused of committing various other offences which date back to 1336.

Conclusion

The military careers of Henry of Lancaster's men provide a valuable insight into professional soldiering during the fourteenth century. Almost a quarter of the knights from Lancaster's retinue in 1345 had already served on at least four campaigns by the time of the expedition to Aquitaine, which suggests that warfare had become a main and, indeed, desirable occupation for a significant proportion of men who belonged to the knightly class by the mid 1340s. More importantly, these men had taken up arms with some regularity prior to the extraordinary success of the series of English campaigns from 1345 to 1347. The evidence suggests, therefore, that despite the 'militarisation' of the gentry in England which began during Edward I's reign, it was the decade and a half of intense warfare from 1332 which gave greater impetus to the emergence of military professionalism. Moreover, the extent to which professionalism had developed during the middle third of the fourteenth century is emphatically borne out by the fact that two-thirds of the 'English' knights in Lancaster's retinue served on four or more campaigns over the course of their careers. That these men had become 'experts at arms' there can be little doubt. The real specialists in warfare, however, were the veteran soldiers who fought on multiple campaigns over a protracted period, or in some instances men became specialists in certain theatres of war. All nine expeditions which John de Lymbury served on before 1345, for example, were undertaken in Scotland, while more than half of Stephen de Cosington's campaigns were either in the duchy of Aquitaine or the neighbouring regions.[106] In some instances men's long careers reflect their commitment to warfare, but for others, such as Thomas Cok, it is the frequency of their service that is indicative of their professionalism.[107]

The careers of some men illustrate both the nuances and shared mentality of soldiers who continued their martial lifestyle in different contexts and theatres of war during the peace with France in the 1360s. A wide variance in the attributes that characterised 'professionalism' is evident among Lancaster's men, although nearly the entire sample of nineteen men who served on the most campaigns has been shown to be largely representative of the traditional warrior class. Only Nicholas Goushill can be characterised as an independent military professional who had little attachment to a magnate captain, and his career seems to have been untypical of his comrades. The extent to which professionalism had emerged among the sub-knightly ranks of Lancaster's retinue is a subject that requires further investigation. However, the illustrative examples of esquires who repeatedly served on campaigns, aspired to knighthood and accrued wealth through

---

[106] For references of military service, see above.
[107] Cok served on nine campaigns in sixteen years, during which time he was elevated to the status of banneret and became seneschal of Aquitaine in 1349.

a career in arms suggests that professionalism had emerged at the lower echelons of the military retinue. The endeavours of Hugh Courson in the mid 1340s, for example, epitomise a careerist mentality and it is tempting to believe that his pursuit of a profession at arms was commonly embraced by others of the same rank.[108]

In conclusion, the emergence of professionalism was naturally linked to the intensive periods of warfare in the fourteenth century. The careers of Lancaster's men show that military professionalism existed on a small scale before the early 1330s but had developed further by the mid 1340s, which no doubt resulted from the successive wars in Scotland and on the Continent. The professionalism that prevailed among the knightly class later in the fourteenth century was rooted in the campaigning experience of soldiers earlier in the century, and the patterns of service of men from our sample implies that an era of professionalism had fully emerged by the time of the Treaty of Brétigny.

---

[108] In his deposition at the Court of Chivalry in 1386 Courson claimed to have taken part in the famous victories in Aquitaine (1345), the battle of Crécy (1346), the subsequent siege of Calais, the naval battle of Winchelsea in 1350 and other campaigns, but unfortunately no further details are given. C 47/6/1, no. 99.

Conclusion

The detailed study of Henry of Lancaster's expedition in 1345–46 has attempted to add to our understanding of the army, the expedition, and the careers and lives of the individuals who took up arms in Lancaster's retinue. A close scrutiny of the royal administrative records has provided fresh insights into the military preparations prior to the army's embarkation, and has thrown new light on the shipping of the earl's expeditionary force. Overall the assembling of Lancaster's army was impressive and the time in which it was mobilised is a testament to the efficacy of England's military organisation. A new analysis of the arrival and departure of different retinues and military contingents in the duchy has highlighted the changes in the army's composition and, indeed, the changes in the nature of warfare over the course of the expedition. The decision to send infantry-based reinforcements to Aquitaine in 1346 was clearly a response to Lancaster's anticipation of siege warfare on account of the arrival of the duke of Normandy's huge army in the duchy. The earl's need for soldiers who possessed the 'shooting power' to defend a castle's walls is borne out by the arrival of the contingent of 300 Welshmen which was entirely made up of archers.

It has been shown that 1345 was a crucial year for military developments in England, not least in the Crown's use of the indenture system to recruit magnates for military service. That three retinue captains in Lancaster's army accounted for their service directly at the Exchequer is indicative of the development of the indenture system which, by the time of the Agincourt campaign (1415), was used to recruit all royal armies.[1] The Crown's use of contract management fulfilled an important role in the financing of multiple expeditionary forces in the mid 1340s and demonstrates the professionalism of the royal administration. A systematic study of the extant pay records has shown that the finances of Lancaster's army were administered efficiently, despite the fact that the multi-front warfare launched by Edward III inevitably put an enormous strain on the royal system of finance. The reconstruction of a schedule of royal payments for each of Lancaster's retinue captains also highlights the importance and flexibility of the Wardrobe in financing an army which was recruited and predominantly financed by the Exchequer;

---

[1]   Curry, *Armies in the Fifteenth Century*, pp. 41–2.

neither of the administrative departments functioned independently of one another, which underlines the complexity and overall professionalism of the medieval royal administrative system.

The army of Lancaster also serves as an important benchmark for the changes in the structure and character of royal armies which fought in the wars of Edward III. The earl's expeditionary force represents a hybrid structure, half of which comprised retinue-based contingents and the other half infantry divisions. Its composition demonstrates that the Crown was as much dependent on foot soldiers during the mid 1340s as it was on the military retinues recruited by magnates. However, the most distinctive structural feature of Lancaster's army is the extraordinary size of the commander's own retinue (250 men-at-arms and 250 mounted archers), which constituted one quarter of the army's total manpower. A retinue of this size was unprecedented and it signified the beginning of the consolidation of manpower in royal armies around fewer retinue contingents of superior strength. However, it was not until near the end of the first phase of the Hundred Years' War and after the resumption of the war in 1369, in particular, that the dependence upon such 'super' retinues becomes clearly evident.

The analysis of the formation and structure of Lancaster's retinue has illustrated the various means by which the earl was able to assemble such a large retinue for war in 1345. The extensive recruiting reach of Lancaster largely derived from his ability to exploit an expanse of social networks which he had built up in various 'military communities' at a regional, national and international level. It was on account of the geographical range of the earl's spheres of influence that his retinue had an international identity, composed as it was of soldiers from Aquitaine, Brabant, Wales and the Iberian peninsula as well as from England. It was no doubt his attendance at tournaments and royal councils, his visits to the Continent and the constant tours of his family's estates and neighbouring counties during his early years of manhood that provided Lancaster with the opportunity to establish and build up such a wide range of networks that could be utilised for military recruitment in later years.[2] He also had the ability to reignite old loyalties and ties of service to the Lancastrian dynasty that had long since been established by his uncle and grandfather.

It was above all else his esteemed reputation as a retinue captain and military leader which provided him with the 'pulling power' not only to maintain a core group of military followers, but to attract new men into his service. When Lancaster was faced with the task of raising a retinue of an extraordinary size he relied on his friends and followers – which included bannerets who acted as recruiting middle-men – and, of course, the king.

---

[2] On the itinerant movements of Lancaster at home and abroad up to the early 1330s, see Fowler, *King's Lieutenant*, pp. 27–8.

Henry's intimate relationship with Edward III had built up over the previous decade through continuous military and diplomatic service, as well as in a personal capacity as his kinsman and confidant. The earl's imprisonment in the Low Countries (1340) as a surety against the king's debts is a prime example of the affection and admiration which he held for his cousin, and the benefits of his close connection with Edward are clearly demonstrated by the recruitment of 'the king's knights' into his retinue and the propitious terms of service offered to him in 1345. First and foremost, then, it was Henry of Lancaster's unrivalled reputation, status and talent as a military captain and his intimate relationship with the king that enabled him to assemble such a large war retinue, and it would be prudent to question which (if, indeed, any) other military commanders of Edward III would have been able to accomplish the same feat.

A prosopographical study of the men who served under Lancaster's banner in 1345–46 has shown that much higher levels of cohesion and retinue stability existed in the earl's troop than has previously been thought. That nearly three-quarters of Lancaster's men-at-arms in 1344 returned to his service for the expedition in 1345, and that more than a third of his bannerets and knights in the duchy served with him again on the following expedition (Calais, 1347) reflects a high level of continuity which is all the more remarkable considering the prodigious size of his retinue in Aquitaine. In addition, this evidence has demonstrated that the cohesion of the troop was underpinned by 'horizontal ties' based on landholdings, kinship and marriage. The cohesion and stability which permeated all levels of the retinue enhanced camaraderie, discipline and communication, and by extension improved the retinue's overall effectiveness in the field. An additional strength of the war retinue was its flexibility which derived from the nature of its formation and structure – comradeship groups and sub-retinues could break away into smaller task forces and later rejoin the main retinue without having a negative effect on the cohesion of the different military contingents. It was these attributes of the retinue, therefore, combined with the collective experience of veteran soldiers and captains such as Sir John de Norwich, that made Lancaster's war retinue a cogent and formidable fighting force.

The military careers of Lancaster's men have shown that they were both recruited and fought in an era of professionalism. That most of the 'English' knights who can be considered as professional first took up arms in the 1330s, either in Scotland or the Low Countries, suggests that the wars fought in the first two decades of Edward III's reign provided the opportunity and experience for men to pursue a long-term martial lifestyle. The scarcity of evidence for 'professional soldiers' who were completely unattached from a particular lord or magnate's affinity suggests that, on the whole, their motivations for service were based as much on loyalty to a lord as on the profits and rewards of war. The possibilities of career progression through successful soldiering is exemplified by the career of Sir Neil Loring whose rapid rise from humble origins resulted from his military endeavours which brought him into the service of the king and important noblemen of the realm.

The importance of the expedition in Aquitaine and the implications of its success in the outcome of other military events during the mid 1340s have been considered from a more nuanced view point. The events in the duchy in 1345 were a precursor to the battle of Crécy the following summer; it was the remarkable victories at Bergerac and Auberoche which drew the duke of Normandy's huge army into the south west of France at the beginning of 1346 and effectively divided Philippe VI's forces as had been Edward III's overall strategic aim in the previous year. It was the absence of the duke's forces in his eponymous duchy that facilitated Edward's landing there, and the significance of Lancaster's earlier victories in the chain of military events has accordingly been attested by chroniclers and historians. It was, indeed, during Edward's sea-crossing to France that Sir Godfrey Harcourt is reported to have advised the king to land in Normandy on account of its vast riches and because 'the whole cream of the Norman knights are at the siege of Aiguillon with the duke [of Normandy]'.[3]

It was Edward III's subsequent and emphatic victory at Crécy, however, which largely overshadowed the true significance of Lancaster's expedition in Aquitaine. Apart from the strategic advantage of dividing the French forces, Lancaster's remarkable success in the duchy handed the English an important psychological advantage in the war. An English force had not defeated the French in a decisive battle on French soil since the reign of Richard I, and yet Lancaster had achieved this feat twice within two months. Furthermore, his capture of Bergerac and La Réole effectively ensured English control of the duchy until the resumption of the war in 1369.

The only historian to consider the psychological impact of Lancaster's success was Alfred Burne, who briefly notes that Lancaster had 'established the moral superiority of the English army', but the effects of such dramatic victories on the medieval soldier should not be underestimated.[4] All the more so, considering that the victories were unprecedented and had indeed been accomplished by an outnumbered force. It was not only the first time that men realised the potential profits which could be gained from warfare, but it was also their first experience of the glory of triumph against the French in an overseas campaign. The victories at Auberoche and Bergerac may not have reverberated around the whole of Christendom, as did that at Crécy, but news of Lancaster's early success in the duchy would have reached England by the end of November in 1345 at the latest. We can imagine that the news, accounts and stories of the campaign would have been shared amongst the military community throughout the entire country

---

[3]   Jean Froissart, *Chronicles*, ed. and trans. by Geoffrey Brereton (London: Penguin, 1978), p. 69.
[4]   Burne, *Crécy War*, p. 117.

and left an indelible mark on the imaginations of thousands of people. The combined prospect of military glory and private profit was no doubt a potent cause to motivate and inspire men back home to serve on an overseas campaign. Lancaster's overwhelming success in Aquitaine, therefore, provided an impetus for military recruitment and a commitment to overseas warfare prior to Edward III's expedition to Normandy in 1346. The brilliance of the victories went a long way in legitimising Edward III's pursuit of war with France and, most notably, it started a winning momentum for English armies that continued over the next two years and into the following decade.

The king's lieutenant was central to the recruitment of the English army in 1345 and, ultimately, he was responsible for the extraordinary success of the expedition in the duchy which marked the beginning of a fifteen-year period of English dominance in the Hundred Years' War. Although Fowler concluded that Lancaster's real achievement in Aquitaine 'was above all as an administrator who could draw upon the resources of his enormous wealth', this certainly was not the case in 1345 as Henry had yet to come into his family's inheritance or, indeed, accrue the huge profits of war which awaited him.[5] As an administrator and diplomat Lancaster was clearly an exceptional talent, but this study has attempted to show that his most important attributes were as a retinue captain and military commander. On landing in the duchy his immediate rebuff of the conventional tactics of gradual siege warfare, castle by castle and town by town, adopted by the English seneschal, Ralph Stafford, set the tone for military operations for the rest of the expedition. The speed with which Lancaster's army attacked, avoided and outmanoeuvred the enemy allowed the earl to capitalise on the weak positions of the French forces, capture a plenitude of towns and cities and lead an outnumbered force to two decisive victories. It was his innovative use of tactics involving archers and men-at-arms which, according to the *Saint-Omer* chronicler, led to the defeat of the count of Eu's forces prior to the capture of Bergerac. The deployment of small task forces and his use of coordinated chevauchées enabled Lancaster to bring large swathes of the duchy under English control either by the sword or by economic and political inducements. The earl had the military acumen to know when to attack the enemy or lay siege to a town, and when to avoid a military engagement – a quality not exhibited by the duke of Normandy when he arrived outside the walls of Aiguillon in the spring of 1346. Indeed, the ineptitude demonstrated by the duke did not bode well for his future military career, and presaged his capture (as king of France) at the battle of Poitiers ten years later.

---

[5] Fowler, *King's Lieutenant*, p. 220.

At the heart of the English army was Lancaster's war retinue, formidable in size and in fighting capability. Few other captains had the means or the ability to recruit and command such a sizeable force which included a substantial body of men who were indigenous to the duchy. He provided inspirational leadership not just to his own retinue, but to the entire Anglo-Gascon coalition forces. Indeed, contrary to the view of Michael Prestwich, that Lancaster 'for all his merits, was no innovative commander', a reassessment of the earl and his army has shown that it was exactly for his innovation as a military commander that the expedition in Aquitaine was such a remarkable success.[6] The importance of Lancaster to Edward III's regime and the significance of his achievements at this juncture in the Hundred Years' War are evident by the substantial royal grants made to him in 1347 and his position as third founder knight of the Order of the Garter in 1348. The greatest honour was bestowed on him three years later when he was elevated to the rank of duke and palatine powers were granted to him in his county of Lancaster, modelled on those that his cousin, the Black Prince, exercised in Cheshire and Flintshire. In conclusion, Henry of Lancaster was an administrator, diplomat and nobleman renowned throughout the whole of Europe, but above all he was an exceptional military commander and arguably the most talented of Edward III's captains. His death in 1361 was a significant loss for the king and there can be little doubt that it greatly undermined the English war effort when the war with France resumed in 1369.

[6] Prestwich, *Armies and Warfare*, p. 300.

Appendix A

Transcription of an Indenture of War made between Henry of Lancaster, Earl of Derby, and Edward III on 13 March 1345. E 159/123, m. 254d

Ceste endenture faite entre nostre seigneur le roi d'une parte et monsieur Henri de Lancastre, conte de Derby, d'autre parte, tesmoigne que le dit conte, par comaundement nostre seigneur le roi, ad empris d'aler en Gascoygne a y demorer come lieutenant le roi pur un demy an, si guerre soit, et a faire le bien q'il poet ove cink centz hommes d'armes, milles archers, dont cink centz serront a chival et cink centz a pie, et outre cink centz Galeys a pie. Et du nombre susdit deux centz et cinquante homes d'armes et deux centz et cinquante archers a chival serront a la retenance propre du dit conte, c'est assavoir soi, oytisme a banere, quatre vintz et douze chivalers et cent et cinquante esquiers. Et nostre seigneur le roi lui perfournira des gentz d'armes, archers et gentz Galeys tanque au nombre susdit. Et le dit conte ove sa retenance susnomee serra au port de Southamptoun le veille de Pentecost proschein avenir pour passer versus les dites parties de Gascoigne. Et Southamptoun la veille de Pentecost soit le primer jour de demy an avantdit pour acompter des gages et pour touz autres convenances comprises en ceste endenture, s'il ne soit garni par maundement du roi par convenable temps de prendre autre jour par defaute de navire que ne soit mye pleynement venue. Et est l'entencion toutes voies que le jour q'il vendra a la meer sur son passage il commencera d'aconter. Et le dit conte prendra pour lui meismes sys soldz et oyt deniers le jour, pour chescun baneret quatre soldz, pour chescun chivaler deux soldz, pour chescun esquier douze deniers, et pour chescun archer a chival sys deniers; les qeux gages pour sa retenue proper pour le demy an avantdit amontent a quatre mille quatre centz quatre vintz douze livres sept soldz et quatre deniers, et ovesque ce il prendra pour regard pour meisme le temps troys mille treys centz trente et trois livres sys soldz et oyt deniers; les queles summes amontent en tout a sept mille oyt centz vint et cynk livres quatorz soldz, dont il serra paie dedeinz un moys apres la Pasque proschein avenir de cynk mille livres.

Item, il avera assignement sur la disme de Seint Eglise de terme de Seint Barnabe proschein suant de mille oyt centz vint et cynk livres quatorze soldz.

Item, sur la quinzisme de la commune du terme des Touz Seintz proschein suant, mille livres.

Item, le dit contre avera eskippeson pour lui, ses gentz, chivaux et vitailles en alant et venant as custages nostre seigneur le roi.

Item, les chivaux du dit conte et de sa retenance serront prisez a convenable pris devant lour eskippeson en manere acustumee; et en cas q'aucuns des ses gentz d'armes ne se voillent monter des chivaux decea la meer, mes faire le pourveance par delea, que adonques meismes ceux chivaux soient prisez illoeques par le conestable de Burdeux en la manere suisdite et a quell heure que nul home d'armes perde chival avant prise que de temps en temps lour chivalx q'ils pourvoierent soient prisez par le dit conestable en convenable manere come dessus est dit.

Item, est ordene que un clerc suffisant soit assigne pour paier gages a les communes qi serront en la compaignie du dit conte, aussibien decea la mer come delea; et serra meisme clerc convenablement estuffe d'argent pour faire meisme les payementz, et si ne ferra nul payement saunz l'avis et comaundement du dit conte.

Item, le roi voet que en cas que prisons soient pris et dites parties par le dit conte ou les soens, q'il puisse faire d'eux sa volente et q'il puisse avoir toutes autres avantages de guerre, forspris villes, chastelx, terres, rentes et homages, a quiconque q'ils soient; pour queux choses le dit counte avera pleyn poair par commission de les doner ou lesser selonc ce q'il verra que mieux soit pour le profit nostre seigneur le roi.

Item, il avera pleyn poair par commission de seisir en la mein le roi toutes terres, tenementz, villes, chastelx, franchises, custumes, profitz des monoies et toutes autres choses en quecunque manere a la duche de Guyenne, en nul temps regardantz en qi meins q'il soient devenuz, par la ou il verra q'il le puisse faire par bone et juste cause, et de les tenir ensi en pees en la mein nostre seigneur le roi tanque il lui ent eutrement certifie, issint que par son avis il eut puisse ordener ce que mieux soit.

Item, il avera poair par commission de prendre treives et soeffrances en les parties susdites quant il verra que busoigne soit pour l'onour du roi et la sauvete de lui et de ses gentz et du pays.

Item, il avera poair par commission a surveer les faitz de touz les ministres le roi es dites parties, et de les nient convenables remuer et autres mettre en lour leux a toutes les foitz q'il verra q'il soit affaire, reservant nepraignant au roi les offices du seneschal et du conestable.

Item, il avera poair par commission de granter vie et membre et de faire mise de rebealx et disobeissantz aussibien par meer comme par terre es dites parties durant le demy an avantdit, et aussint q'il puisse receivre a la pees nostre seigneur le roi les rebealx et desobeissantz en celles parties et a eux pardoun faire de lour trespass; et la convenances q'il ferra ovesque eux tenuz et perfourniz par nostre seigneur le roi et par touz autres qi y serront après le dit conte.

Item, le roi voet que si nul poair soit grante a aucun autre accordant a nul des pointz compris en ceste endenture, que meisme cel poair soit repelle et anienty.

Item, en cas que apres le demy au susdit il plese a nostre seigneur le roi que le dit conte demoerge en les dites parties de Gascoigne come son lieutenant ove tut sa retenance et les gentz d'armes et archers susditz a faire le bien q'il poet pour le demy an ensuant, que adonques soient gentz suffisantes assignez par commission d'aconter ovesque lui aussibien de ses gages come de restor de ses chivalx perduz, et de lui paier quant que lui serra duz par meisme l'aconte et aussint ses gages et regard devant la mein pour le temps q'il demora illoeques, et q'il eit touz autres convenances sicome est dit plus pleynenement pour le primer demy an.

Item, voet le roi que en cas que nul des convenances susdites ne soit tenuz au dit conte, que adonques au chief de primer demy an il soit de tut descharge et ove toutes ses gentz puisse venir en Engleterre ou aler par aillours queu parte que lui perra saunz empeschement de nostre dit seigneur le roi ou de nul autre en son noun. Il est accorde que le trewes nadgaires prises en Bretaigne soient suspendues par convenable temps, issint que le dit conte ent puisse estre certifie en Gascoigne devant q'il chivauche de guerre.

Item, le roi ad grante que en cas que aucunes terres ou tenementz puissant avenir droiturelement au dit conte, par descent d'eritage ou en autre quecunque manere resonable durant le temps q'il demorra issint en service nostre seigneur le roi, que par defaute de homage ou foialte ou aucun autre service tieux terres et tenementz ne soient retenuz en la mein le roi par eschetour ne par autre ministre, einz soient delivere par duz proces as attornez le dit conte, franchement, pour faire ent son profit saunz contredit ou empeschement de nullui; et soient les homages et foialtees respitees tanque a sa venue en Engleterre.

Item, le roi ad grante que s'il aviegne que le dit conte soit assiege ou presse par si grant force des gentz q'il ne se pourra eider saunz ester rescous par le poair du roi, que le roi soit tenuz de lui rescoure par une voie ou par autre, issint q'il soit rescous convenablement.

Item, en cas que ceste viage du dit conte soit par aucune cause chaunge ou destourbe, le roi ad promis q'il avera regard a les custages queux le dit conte covient faire par ceste cause, come en retenance des gentz, pourveances faire et en autre manere, et ferra ensi devers lui q'il s'agreera par reson. En tesmoignance de queu chose a ceste partie de l'endenture demorrante devers nostre seigneur le roi le dit conte ad mys son seal.

Donne a Westminstre, le xiii jour de marz, l'an du regne nostre seigneur le roi d'Engleterre disnoefisme et de France seisme.

An Indenture of War made between Henry of Lancaster, Earl of Derby, and Edward III on 13 March 1345. E 159/123, m. 254d

This indenture made between our lord the king, on one part, and lord Henry of Lancaster, earl of Derby, on the other part, witnesses that the said lord, by command of our lord the king, undertakes to go to Gascony and remain there as the king's lieutenant for half a year, if there is to be war, and to do as well as he can with 500 men-at-arms, 1000 archers (of which 500 are to be mounted and 500 on foot) and another 500 Welsh on foot. And of the aforesaid number, 250 men-at-arms and 250 archers on horse are to be in the retinue of the said earl, that is to say, 8 bannerets, 92 knights and 150 esquires. And our lord the king will himself provide the remaining men-at-arms, archers and Welshmen up to the number aforesaid. And the said earl with his aforementioned retinue should be at the port of Southampton on the vigil of Pentecost next [14 May 1345] for passing to the said parts of Gascony. And the same vigil of Pentecost is to be the first day of the half year aforesaid to account for the wages and all other agreements included in this indenture, unless he is warned by mandate of the king by a suitable time to take another day because for the lack of shipping that cannot come in full strength. And it is always the intention that on the day which he goes to the sea on his passage he will begin to account. And the said earl takes for himself 6s 8d per day, for each banneret 4s, for each knight 2s, for each esquire 12d, and for each mounted archer 6d; the cost of wages for his own retinue for the half year aforesaid amounts to £4492 7s 4d, and with this he takes for *regard* for the same time £3333 6s 8d; the cost of sums in total amounts to £7825 14s, of which he will be paid in part one month before Easter next an advance of £5000.

Likewise, he will have an assignment on the tenth of the Holy Church of the term of St Barnabas following of £1825 14s.

Likewise, on the fifteenth of the Commons of the term of All Saints next following, £1000.

Likewise, the said earl will have freightage for himself, his men, horses and victuals in coming and going as customary from our lord the king.

Likewise, the horses of the said earl and of his retinue are to be appraised at an appropriate value before their freightage in the customary manner; and in case any of his men-at-arms do not wish to mount their horses on this side of the sea, but make the purveyance on the other side of the sea, then those same horses are to be appraised by the constable of Bordeaux in the aforesaid manner and when any man-at-arms loses a horse that has been appraised, then the horses that they have purveyed should be appraised by the constable from time to time, in a suitable way as it is said above.

Likewise, it is ordered that a sufficient clerk shall be assigned to pay wages to those in general who shall be in the company of the said earl, on this side of the sea as well as the other; and the same clerk shall take enough money to make the same payments, and he should not make any payment without the advice and command of the said earl.

Likewise, the king wishes that when prisoners are taken in the said parts, by the said earl or his own men, then he may do with them as he wishes, and that he is to have all other advantages of war, besides towns, castles, lands, rents and homages, whoever they may belong to; for those things the said earl is to have complete power by commission to grant or lease them according to whichever person is better for the profit of our lord the king.

Likewise, he will have complete power by commission to seize into the king's hand all lands, tenements, towns, castles, franchises, customs, profits of mint(s), and all other things of whatever type in the duchy of Guyenne, regardless of whose hands they have ended up in, and he is to see how to proceed justly and reasonably, and to keep them peaceably in our lord the king's hand until it is to him otherwise certified, so that he may be able to ordain by the advice of our council what may be best.

Likewise, he will have the power by commission to make truces and armistices in the parts aforesaid when he should see the need, for the honour of the king and the safety of himself, his men and the country.

Likewise, he will have power by commission to assess the work of all the ministers in the said parts, and to remove anyone unsuitable, and to put others in their place immediately, then he should see what is to be assessed, nevertheless assigning by the king the offices of seneschal and constable.

Likewise, he will have power by commission to grant life and limb and to accept pleas from rebels and contrariants, by sea as well as by land in the said parts during the half year aforesaid, and also he is to receive into the peace of our lord king the rebels and contrariants in these parts, and by them to make a pardon of their trespasses; and the agreements which he is to make with them are to be held and performed by our lord the king and by all others who will come after the said earl.

Likewise, the king wishes that if any power is granted to any other person in connection with any of the points included in this indenture, then that same power is to be repealed and annulled.

Likewise, in the event that after the half year aforesaid it satisfies our lord the king that the said earl remain in the said parts of Gascony as his lieutenant with all his retinue and the men-at-arms and archers aforesaid, and to do as well as he can for the half year ensuing, that then there should be men sufficiently assigned by commission to account with him both for their wages and for restoration of their lost horses, and to pay him whatever he will be owed by the same account and also his wages and *regard* in advance for the same time that he remains in those parts, and he is to have all other agreements just as is said more fully for the first half year.

Likewise, the king wishes that in the event that none of the agreements aforesaid are carried out by the said earl, then at the end of the first half of the year he is to be discharged of everything, and with all his men he may come to England or go elsewhere to whatever part pleases him, without hindrance of our lord the king or of any other in his name. It is agreed that the truces lately made in Brittany are to be suspended by a suitable time, in order that the said earl shall have been able to certify in Gascony before he rides to war.

Likewise, the king is to grant that when any lands or tenements may come reasonably to the said earl by descent of heritage or any other reasonable manner during the time that he remains in the service of our lord the king, that by reason of default or homage, or fealty, or any other such service for land and tenements they are not to be returned to the king's hand by the escheator or by another minister, but are to be delivered by due process by the attorneys of the said earl, freely so that he may have his profit without contradiction or hindrance from anyone; and the homage and fealties will be respited until his coming to England.

Likewise, the king is to grant that if he discovers that the said earl is besieged or oppressed by such a great force of men that he cannot aid himself without being rescued by the king's power, the king will be obliged to rescue him by one way or another, so that he should be rescued appropriately.

Likewise, if this voyage of the said earl is by whatever cause changed or disrupted, the king promises that he will have regard to the costs that the said earl needs to make for this reason, as in retaining his men, making purveyances and in other things, and will behave reasonably towards him. In testimony of which matters in the presence of our lord the king the said earl has put his seal to this part of the indenture.

Given at Westminster on the thirteenth day of March in the nineteenth year of the reign our lord the king of England and the sixth of France [13 March 1345].

Appendix B

Prosopographical Catalogue of Men
in Lancaster's War Retinue, 1345–46

This catalogue provides key information on individuals who served, or who intended to serve, in Lancaster's retinue on the Aquitaine expedition of 1345–46. The entries are not complete biographies, but provide a summary of qualitative evidence of each person. Entries are arranged in alphabetical order by surname and are given in the following format:

Line one: name; year of birth/death; rank/troop type/status; county of origin.

Line two: source reference of service in Lancaster's retinue (where applicable, position of name in retinue roll is indicated by number in parentheses).

Line three: notes on the individual generally based on his military career, landholdings, kinship, office-holdings or commissions at home or abroad and his connections with other individuals in Lancaster's retinue.

Note that evidence of county of origin is tentative when based solely on a locative surname which has several toponyms. For example, it is feasible that the archer Thomas de Ashley may have originated from either Cheshire or Northamptonshire, as there are places named Ashley located in both counties. Forenames are given in their modern indigenous form, except where ambiguity remains. Locative surnames are given in their modern form if the place-name can be identified with certainty (e.g. Blakschaue is rendered as Blackshaw, Yorkshire), as are descriptive (e.g. Broun as Brown) or occupational names (e.g. Cok as Cook), except where a more common form of the surname exists in the sources. Sir Thomas Cok, for example, is rendered as Cok rather than Cook.

For the purpose of brevity entries have been kept short and generally do not include information which can be found in the main text of this work, or in well-known secondary literature. Evidence of military service is not referenced in detail, nor are the administrative commissions undertaken by men at county level which has been largely sourced from the online *Calendar of Patent Rolls*. Similarly, the evidence of landholdings is often duplicated with the evidence of service in Lancaster's retinue (line two), and therefore is usually only referenced once.

Catalogue

Alan, John (archer)
E 101/35/2/10, m. 2d (92)

Aldeby, Walter de (esquire) Norfolk
E 101/35/2/10, m. 2 (87)

Altas, John (esquire)
E 101/35/2/10, m. 2 (110)

Altofts, Adam de (archer) Yorkshire
E 101/35/2/10, m. 2d (89)

Altrincham, Hugh de (archer) Cheshire
E 101/35/2/10, m. 1d (264)

Andwaryn, Andelyn (archer)
E 101/35/2/10, m. 1d (240)

Anteley, Henry de (archer)
E 101/35/2/10, m. 3d (54)

Antingham, Bartholomew de (esquire) Norfolk
E 101/35/2/10, m. 2 (126)

Archenfield, Robert de (archer) Herefordshire
E 101/35/2/10, m. 3d (66)

Ardemschal, Richard de (archer)
E 101/35/2/10, m. 2d (159)

Ardsley, William de (archer) Yorkshire
E 101/35/2/10, m. 2d (90)

Arley, Roger de (archer) Cheshire
E 101/35/2/10, m. 2d (132)

Arnold, John (esquire)
E 101/35/2/10, m. 2 (115)

Arnold, Thomas (archer)
E 101/35/2/10, m. 1d (218)

Arnold, Richard (esquire)
E 101/35/2/10, m. 3 (153)

Artonstall, John de (archer) Cheshire
E 101/35/2/10, m. 1d (195)
John and Thomas Artonstall may have belonged to the Artonstall family of
Timperley (Cheshire).

Artonstall, Thomas de (archer) Cheshire
E 101/35/2/10, m. 1d (197)

Arwafeld, Richard de (archer)
E 101/35/2/10, m. 2d (149)

Ash, William de (archer) Derbyshire
E 101/35/2/10, m. 2d (124)

Ashbourne, Thomas (esquire) Derbyshire
E 101/35/2/10, m. 2 (103)

Ashley, Robert de (archer) Cheshire
E 101/35/2/10, m. 2d (176)

Ashley, Thomas de (archer) Cheshire
E 101/35/2/10, m. 2d (139)

Ashow, John de (archer) Warwickshire
E 101/35/2/10, m. 3d (21)

Astley, Ralph de (knight) Norfolk
E 101/25/9, m. 3 (37)
Ralph, possibly the son of Sir Ralph de Astley (*d*. 1341) and Margaret, belonged to a
family that had a tradition of service with the earls of Lancaster.[1] He was knighted
by 1342 when he served in Henry of Lancaster's retinue in Brittany, and he may
have been the Sir Ralph 'Dastele' who was detained in Brabant for forty-three days
in 1340 as surety for Edward III's debts.[2]
1 Francis Blomefield, 'Holt Hundred: Melton Constable', in *An Essay Towards A Topographical History of the County of Norfolk*, 11 vols (London: W. Miller, 1805–10), IX
(1808), pp. 415–26 (p. 418).
2 Astley received 5s per day during his time as hostage: E 101/389/8, m. 4.

Astley, Thomas de (esquire) Norfolk
E 101/35/2/10, m. 2 (133)

Audley, Peter de (knight) Staffordshire
E 101/25/9, m. 3 (53)
Peter was probably related to the Audley family, lords of Heighley, from the north
Staffordshire township from which they took their name. Soon after the expedition
to Aquitaine (1345–46), he seems to have become associated with Edward, the Black
Prince, who gave Audley a silver cup (made in Paris) and 10 marks as a gift some-
time in 1348.[1] The following year he took a retinue of nine men-at-arms and twenty

mounted archers to garrison Saint-Jean-d'Angély.[2] He may have been the same person who, together with Eustache d'Aubricourt and a German mercenary named Albrecht (probably Albert Sertz), operated as captains of a mercenary company in southern Champagne in 1359.[3]

1 *BPR*, IV, pp. 73, 90.
2 E 403/341, mm. 13, 14.
3 Sumption, *Trial by Fire*, pp. 406, 410.

Auncel, Alexander (knight) Lincolnshire

E 101/25/9, m. 3 (18); E 159/123, m. 126

Auncel is known to have first taken up arms in 1336 with Henry, Lord Beaumont (serving with a horse valued at £10),[1] and continued to serve under different captains before he was recruited by Henry of Lancaster in 1345, with whom thereafter he served consistently and exclusively up to 1360. In 1349 he was paid £13 6s 8d for horse restoration.[2] He had small landholdings in Lincolnshire and Oxfordshire, and served as a justice of oyer and terminer in the latter county in 1343.[3] Auncel and Sir Richard de Hebden appointed the same attorney, Thomas Sleford, as their legal representative in 1355, but a closer association seems to have existed between Auncel and Sir Philip de Lymbury.[4] Both men held property in Lincolnshire (and were exonerated from providing military service in 1346 by the same royal writ), shared administrative duties in Brittany (1356–58) during Lancaster's lieutenancy in the duchy and, in the following year, testified to the good service of Thomas de Ruston, who was pardoned for the murder of John Forester and John Lister.[5] Auncel probably died in or around the time of the Reims expedition (1359).

1 E 101/19/36, m. 2.
2 E 404/508/79.
3 C 47/2/36, no. 10; E 159/123, m. 126. *CPR, 1343–45*, p. 79 (oyer and terminer).
4 C 76/33, m. 9 (Sleford).
5 *CPR, 1358–61*, p. 225 (pardon).

Auncel, Thomas (esquire) Lincolnshire

E 101/35/2/10, m. 2 (121)

Bacoun, Thomas (esquire) Norfolk

Crécy and Calais, p. 152; E 372/192, m. 16d

Thomas Bacoun may well have been the man who served as 'sergeant' on numerous Scottish expeditions from 1297 to 1316. He and Sir Hugh Trussebut were exonerated from an assessment of their lands in Norfolk and Suffolk by the same writ because they had served continuously with Henry of Lancaster in Aquitaine (1345–46) and at Calais (1347). He inquired in 1333 into a charge made against the bailiff of Lothingland and the constable of Lowestoft (Suffolk) of having allowed Scots and others to take silver out of the realm. Two years later he inquired into the discovery of treasure buried under a pear tree in a garden formerly owned by Thomas, earl of Lancaster, in the parish of St Clement Danes (London).[1] Thomas's estate included lands in Cambridgeshire and Essex.[2] He was possibly the brother of Sir Edmund de Bacoun, a household knight of Edward II. He predeceased his wife, Denise, who died in 1349.

1 *Foedera*, II, pp. 869, 914.
2 *CIPM*, X, p. 257; *CIPM*, XI, p. 12.

Bag, Andrew (archer)
E 101/35/2/10, m. 1d (258)

Baguley, Ronald de (archer) Cheshire
E 101/35/2/10, m. 2d (130)

Baker, Matthew le (archer)
E 101/35/2/10, m. 3d (60)

Baker, William (attendant)
E 101/25/9, m. 3d (22)

Balle, William (attendant)
E 101/25/9, m. 3d (10)

Banham, Bartholomew de (esquire) Norfolk
E 101/35/2/10, m. 2 (70)

Barthomley, Thomas de (archer) Cheshire
E 101/35/2/10, m. 1d (182)

Baskerville, Richard (knight) Herefordshire
E 101/25/9, m. 3 (12)
Richard or, more likely, his father (and namesake) regularly served as a commissioner of array and justice of oyer and terminer in Herefordshire in the reign of Edward II.[1] He was a retainer of the Black Prince, whom he served at Calais in 1347 after having first returned to England with Henry of Lancaster on New Year's Day.[2] Richard held land of the honour of Webbele in Herefordshire worth £17 10d yearly.[3] He was probably the father of Richard Baskerville the younger, who boldly defended himself against the French outside the walls of Paris in 1360 and was dubbed knight by the Black Prince.[4] This younger Richard married Joan, and died in 1374.[5]
1 C 61/36, mm. 19, 27d; C 71/10, m. 13; *CPR, 1307–13*, p. 66; *CPR, 1324–27*, pp. 8, 85, 352.
2 *BPR*, I, pp. 67, 80.
3 *CCR, 1343–46*, pp. 276, 343.
4 Gray, *Scalacronica*, p. 183.
5 *CPR 1374–77*, p. 199 (Joan); *CIPM*, XIV, p. 14.

Bastret, William Hounhull (archer)
E 101/35/2/10, m. 2d (119)

Bate, John (archer)
E 101/35/2/10, m. 2d (88)

Bayouse, Walter de (esquire)
E 101/35/2/10, m. 1 (28)

Beaufou, William (esquire) Lincolnshire
C 81/1760/13
William was exonerated, together with Roger de Trykingham, from an assessment of his small landholding in Lincolnshire because he served with Henry of Lancaster in 1345–46. He is probably not the person who held the keepership of Taunton castle (1345), nor the son of John Beaufou of Seaton who held land in Salisbury. A William Beaufou served as a local commissioner in Rutland in the 1360s and as sheriff of that county (1361–62). He may have been the officer tasked with arresting members of the Dalton gang who had attacked the manor of Beams (Berkshire) in 1347.[1]
1 *CCR, 1346–49*, pp. 444, 451.

Bedford, Walter de (attendant) Bedfordshire
E 101/25/9, m. 3d (36)

Bedwardine, Hugh de (archer) Worcestershire
E 101/35/2/10, m. 1d (201)

Beler, Roger (*d.* 1380) **(knight)** Leicestershire
C 76/20, mm. 16, 19; C 76/23, m. 20; C 81/1730/14; E 101/25/9, m. 3 (48)
Roger Beler, the son of Alice and Roger, was the grandson and namesake of the chief baron of the Exchequer who was infamously murdered by the Folville gang in Leicestershire in 1326. After having served exclusively in the retinue of Henry of Lancaster from 1340, he served on commissions in Nottinghamshire in the 1360s and was granted an exemption from holding local offices in the following decade. In 1369 Beler and Sir Gervase de Clifton were involved in a transaction of feoffment with Sir Robert de Tibetot concerning lands in London and Suffolk.[1] Beler died in 1380, holding lands in Derbyshire, Leicestershire (majority), Lincolnshire, Nottinghamshire, and Rutland.[2] His daughters Margaret, wife of Sir Robert de Swilington, and Thomasina, were his heiresses.
1 *CIPM*, XIII, pp. 190–4.
2 *CIPM*, XV, pp. 130–4.

Belgrave, John de (esquire) Leicestershire
E 101/35/2/10, m. 2 (85)

Belk, Thomas (archer)
E 101/35/2/10, m. 1d (239)

Bell, John (archer)
E 101/35/2/10, m. 3d (73)

Bénesse, Menaut de (esquire) Dax (Landes)
E 101/35/2/10, m. 3 (183)

Bennet, Thomas (archer)
E 101/35/2/10, m. 3d (61)

Beorefeld, John de (esquire)
E 101/35/2/10, m. 1 (64)

Bernak, William (knight) Lincolnshire
E 101/25/9, m. 3 (73)
William, born around 1322, was the son of John Bernak of Sudbrook (Lincolnshire).
His brother John died (*c.* 1348) a minor in the king's wardship.[1] He served on the
expedition to Aquitaine (1345) in place of his father, who held lands in Leicestershire, Lincolnshire and Northamptonshire.[2] He is possibly the William Bernak of
Barkeston who took out royal protection for service in the king's retinue in 1359,
and who served on local commissions with Roger Beler in the Midlands, including
the collection of subsidies in Leicestershire (1373).[3] In 1357 Bernak rendered an
annual fine at the Exchequer for lands held in Lincolnshire.[4] He married Mary (*b.
c.* 1343), sister and heir of Sir Thomas de Engayne.[5]
1 *CIPM*, XII, p. 431–3.
2 *Crécy and Calais*, p. 145; E 372/191, m. 36d.
3 C 76/38, m. 15 (Barkeston); *CPR, 1370–74*, p. 102, *CPR, 1374–77*, p. 228 (commissions); *CPR, 1370–74*, p. 227 (subsidies).
4 BL, Additional MS 26588.
5 *CIPM*, XII, p. 113.

Berteville, Richard (esquire)
C 76/20, m. 15; C 81/1724/49; E 101/35/2/10, m. 1 (5)
Richard first took up arms as an esquire in Henry of Lancaster's retinue in 1344,
serving together with Robert Berteville on the earl's diplomatic mission to Avignon.[1]
He may be related to Nicholas Berteville who served as a *centenar* of 100 infantrymen from Yorkshire in 1339.[2]
1 C 81/1724/49.
2 E 101/15/25.

Berton, William de (esquire)
E 101/35/2/10, m. 1 (30)

Bickerton, John de (esquire) Cheshire
E 101/35/2/10, m. 3 (167)

Bintree, Walter de (*d.* 1381) **(esquire)** Norfolk
C 76/20, m. 15; E 101/35/2/10, m. 1 (4)
Bintree, a native of the Norfolk village of that name, was one of the most trusted
members of Henry of Lancaster's household. He twice served with Walter Mauny
(1337, 1342) before taking up arms exclusively in Lancaster's retinue (1344–55). On
several occasions he acted as the earl's envoy; he delivered Lancaster's instructions
and letters to Charles, king of Navarre, at Évreux following the murder of Charles
of La Cerda (1354), and he was responsible for the delivery of crucial documents
on the governance of Brittany to Edward III in 1356.[1] Bintree and Edmund, the
son of Richard de Peres, intended to accompany the earl to Avignon in January
1345, but the mission was abandoned.[2] He was compensated with 40 marks for

a warhorse lost during the Breton expedition (1342), and served as a justice of oyer and terminer in Suffolk (1354).[3] Bintree was granted a marsh near Yarmouth (Norfolk) by Lancaster, which he held until his death in 1381.

1 Fowler, *King's Lieutenant*, pp. 123–5, 164.
2 C 66/212, m. 3; *CPR, 1343–45*, p. 380.
3 Ayton, *Knights and Warhorses*, p. 240; *CPR, 1354–58*, p. 59.

Birchoure, Nicholas de (attendant)
E 101/25/9, m. 3d (25)

Birchover, Thomas de (archer) Derbyshire
E 101/35/2/10, m. 1d (187)

Birkoure, John de (attendant)
E 101/25/9, m. 3d (28)

Biron, Adam (archer)
E 101/35/2/10, m. 1d (230)

Blackburn, John de (archer) Lancashire
E 101/35/2/10, m. 1d (237)

Blackburn, William de (archer) Lancashire
E 101/35/2/10, m. 1d (266)

Blackshaw, Robert de (archer) Yorkshire
E 101/35/2/10, m. 2d (129)

Blakeknave, John de (archer)
E 101/35/2/10, m. 3d (42)

Blaunc, Peryn (esquire)
E 101/35/2/10, m. 1 (45)

Blount, John (knight) Worcestershire
C 76/23, m. 11d; E 101/25/9, m. 3 (24); E 372/197 (Worcester)
The Blounts were loyal servants of the house of Lancaster; John was a valet of the third earl, Henry, witnessing an indenture of retainer made between the earl and Philip d'Arcy in 1327, and serving with him overseas in 1329. He became part of the earl's court and was an executor of his will.[1] John's attachment to the Lancastrian dynasty continued under the younger Henry, who made him an annuitant. In 1330 John hunted with the earl's hounds at Duffield and Needwood together with Simon Simeon.[2] He was possibly one of the justices who inquired into the serious attack on Derbyshire foot archers during their journey to Southampton in 1345.[3] He acted as constable of Kenilworth in 1348 and undertook numerous commissions in the south Midlands in the 1340s. His lands were in Gloucestershire, Herefordshire, Leicestershire, Oxfordshire, Rutland, Salisbury, Staffordshire and Worcestershire.[4]

John and Sir Hugh Meynell were justices of oyer and terminer in Derbyshire in 1349 and went on pilgrimage together to Compostella the following year; this pious journey marked the end of long and illustrious careers in arms for both men.[5]
1 *Somerville*, p. 356.
2 Fowler, *King's Lieutenant*, p. 27.
3 *CCR, 1346–49*, p. 63.
4 Lands: *CCR, 1346–49*, p. 423; *CIPM*, X, pp. 340–1; *CPR, 1330–34*, p. 258; *CPR, 1354–58*, p. 442; C 76/23, m. 11d.
5 *CPR, 1348–50*, pp. 312, 572.

Bolewyk, John de (pardon recipient) Northamptonshire
CPR, 1345–48, p. 557
John, as well as John and Matthew Kelyng, were pardoned for the death of Richard Boye.

Bonevent, John (esquire) Cheshire
E 101/35/2/10, m. 2 (75)

Booston, John de (archer)
E 101/35/2/10, m. 2d (145)

Bordeaux, a companion of Reynold de Bixley, mayor of (knight)
E 101/25/9, m. 3 (85)
Bixley was mayor of Bordeaux, 3 March 1344–49; his companion is unknown.

Bordeaux, Oliver de (esquire)
E 159/123, m. 161; E 372/198 (Norfolk)
He was a loyal and well-rewarded valet of the royal household during the first half of the fourteenth century. Oliver first served on the Scottish expedition in 1310, and is described thereafter as the 'king's yeoman' (1310–49). He went on pilgrimage to Compostella in 1316.[1] He held the prévôté of Bayonne from the late 1330s until 1344, and was keeper of the castle of Bayonne in 1345. He was assigned by Edward III, together with the lord of Albret and eleven other royal commissaries, to treat with the king of Castile concerning a truce and war reparations in 1347.[2] Oliver had substantial land interests in Aquitaine and England.[3] He was the brother of Guilhem-Bergunh and Lop-Bergunh.
1 *CPR, 1313–17*, p. 390.
2 C 61/59, m. 2.
3 For his career see Chapter 7.

Boseville, Robert (esquire) Yorkshire
E 159/123, m. 102; E 372/192 (Norfolk, Suffolk)
Boseville led a retinue of fifteen mounted archers to Scotland in 1335, and may have served on a Scottish expedition the previous year.[1] He acted on various commissions in Yorkshire from 1327 to 1344, and was exempted from holding local offices in 1345, the year that he served on the Aquitaine expedition. He was granted the keeping of the castle and gate of Pontefract for life by Queen Isabella in 1328, and was pardoned in 1336 for the escape of a Scottish prisoner of war, Henry Douglas,

and other prisoners, from the castle during his constableship.[2] In 1340 Boseville was permitted to repair a bridge at Ferrybridge (Yorkshire), a village at an important crossing of the river Aire.[3] He was an annuitant of Edward III (1354), and is described as 'the king's yeoman' from 1327. He held lands in Norfolk, Suffolk and Yorkshire.

1 BL, Cotton MS Nero C VIII, fol. 253r.
2 *CPR 1327–30*, p. 248; *CPR, 1334–38*, p. 334.
3 *CPR 1338–40*, p. 432.

Boson, John (knight) Nottinghamshire
C 76/25, m. 15d; E 101/25/9, m. 3 (72)
There are problems of homonymity concerning Boson and the esquire Bozoun. Sir John held lands in the Lincolnshire, Leicestershire and Nottinghamshire.[1] One of his properties in the latter county (Screveton) was attacked by Nicholas Goushill sometime in the 1350s; Goushill stole jewellery, expensive cloth and other valuable items during a night-time raid in which two of Boson's servants were kidnapped and robbed.[2]

1 *CIPM*, VII, pp. 432, 437; *CIPM*, VIII, p. 338; C 47/1/11, m. 14.
2 *CPR, 1358–61*, p. 542.

Bowdon, John de (archer) Cheshire
E 101/35/2/10, m. 3 (2)

Boyville, John de (*d.* 1375) **(knight)**
E 101/25/9, m. 3 (64)
John, like his father of the same name (*b. c.* 1296),[1] was regularly appointed to commissions in the counties of Leicester and Rutland; he served as justice of the peace and commissioner of array with Sir John de Seaton in the 1340s.[2] He held property in those counties, as well as Norfolk, where he performed administrative duties.[3] Henry of Lancaster granted him the manor of Marchington (Staffordshire) at some point before 1361.[4] Two of his horses were stolen at 'Cranehowe' by Geoffrey and William Cut in 1369.[5] In 1374 he and Sir William la Zouche of Harringworth inquired into assaults on the king's tenants in Oakham (Rutland).[6]

1 *CIPM*, VII, p. 481.
2 *CPR, 1340–43*, p. 107; C76/22, m. 25; C 76/24, m. 33.
3 *CIPM*, XIV, p. 240; *CFR*, V, p. 515; C 47/2/39, m. 8.
4 *CPR, 1361–4*, p. 50.
5 *CPR, 1374–77*, p. 95.
6 *CPR, 1374–77*, p. 56.

Bozoun, John (of Claxton) (esquire) Norfolk
C 76/20, mm. 16, 21
John probably originated from the Norfolk village of the same name. He served as an esquire in Lancaster's retinue in 1344.

Bradshaw, Richard de (archer) Lancashire
E 101/35/2/10, m. 1d (200)

Bradshaw, Roger de (archer) Lancashire
E 101/35/2/10, m. 1d (198)

Bras, Henry (archer)
E 101/35/2/10, m. 2d (101)

Bredecork, Richard de (archer)
E 101/35/2/10, m. 3 (18)

Bredon, John de (esquire)
C 76/20, m. 15
Bredon spent his entire military career (1338–59) in the service of Henry of Lancaster. A John de Bredon was pardoned for the death of Thomas de Seytone in 1347.[1] He is not to be confused with his namesake, a merchant of the staple of Lincoln, who was indicted for the murder of three men at Nottingham in 1362.[2]
1 *Crécy and Calais*, p. 273
2 *CPR, 1361–64*, p. 286.

Bridd, Geoffrey (attendant)
E 101/25/9, m. 3d (29)

Brigham, John de (esquire) Norfolk
C 76/22, m. 16d
Brigham had experience of warfare in Aquitaine, having served in the duchy as an esquire in John de Norwich's retinue in 1337. He held lands in Norfolk and Cambridgeshire.[1] Brigham was convicted of smuggling wool from the port of London in 1343, but was released from Newgate prison at the end of the year because Sir William Trussell and others acted as his mainpernors.[2] He is probably not the John de Brigham who was associated with Edward III, and who led his own retinue on the Reims expedition (1359).
1 C 76/22, m. 16d.
2 *CCR, 1343–46*, pp. 243, 256.

Brown, Richard (archer)
E 101/35/2/10, m. 3d (85)

Brown, Robert (esquire)
E 101/35/2/10, m. 3 (170)

Brown, William (archer)
E 101/35/2/10, m. 2d (113)

Brown, William (archer)
E 101/35/2/10, m. 2d (120)

Bruggewod, Robert atte (archer)
E 101/35/2/10, m. 1d (228)

Buckland, John de (esquire)
E 101/35/2/10, m. 3 (176)

Bulstrode, Edmund de (esquire) Bedfordshire/Buckinghamshire
C 76/20, m. 15; E 101/35/2/10, m. 1 (9)
Edmund served exclusively with Henry of Lancaster on military campaigns for more
than a decade (1336–47). He was paid 20 marks for horse restoration relating to his
service in the Low Countries (1340).[1] He was granted an oven in Leicestershire for
life by Lancaster, and was exempted from holding local offices in 1350.[2] Edmund,
together with his two relatives, John and Thomas de Bulstrode, and others, allegedly assaulted John Chenduit at Banbury (Oxfordshire) in 1338.[3] He was granted a
licence to alienate in mortmain some of his lands in Bedfordshire to a chaplain to
celebrate divine service daily at St Mary's church, Flitwick, and to pray for his and
his family's souls.[4] It was probably his son and namesake who served in Aquitaine
with Master John de Streetly in 1362.[5]
1 *Norwell*, p. 312.
2 *CPR, 1350–54*, p. 54; *CPR, 1361–64*, p. 50.
3 *CPR, 1338–40*, p. 73.
4 *CPR, 1350–54*, p. 496.
5 C 61/75, m. 1.

Burdet, Robert (of Huncote) (knight) Leicestershire
C 76/20, mm. 15, 16; E 101/25/9, m. 3 (65)
His father and namesake was a local commissioner in Leicestershire from the 1310s
to 1330s, who inquired into Roger Beler's murder (1326) and the possible reprisal
attacks against the Foleville family.[1] Robert held lands in his home county and
Warwickshire.[2]
1 *CPR, 1327–30*, pp. 73, 209, 213.
2 E 159/123, m. 123d; E 372/192 (Warwick).

Burdett, Robert (esquire)
E 101/35/2/10, m. 2 (84)

Burgoyne, Hurtaud de (knight)
E 101/25/9, m. 3 (92)

Burleys, John de (archer)
E 101/35/2/10, m. 3d (24)

Burton, Thomas de (esquire)
E 101/35/2/10, m. 1 (21)

Burton, William de (knight)
E 101/25/9, m. 3 (74)
Several men of this name were militarily active in the first phase of the Hundred
Years' War. Burton served with Sir John Beaumont in the Low Countries (horse
valued at £20, 1338)[1] and Scotland (1341), and on an oyer and terminer commission
in Rutland in 1354.[2] He probably held land in Leicestershire and Yorkshire, but is

unlikely to have been the knight of the same name closely associated with Edward III.[3]

1 E 36/203, fol. 128v.
2 *CPR, 1354–58*, p. 124.
3 *CIPM*, VIII, p. 346; *CIPM*, XI, p. 81.

Butler, John de la (attendant)
E 101/25/9, m. 3d (4)

Butler, William de la (archer)
E 101/35/2/10, m. 2d (115)

Calboc, Alan (archer)
E 101/35/2/10, m. 2d (121)

Caldecotes, Henry de (knight) Norfolk
C 76/20, m. 20; E 101/25/9, m. 3 (35)
His family probably originated in the Norfolk township from which they took their name. Henry was associated with the families of Norwich and Ufford, embarking on his first overseas military campaign with John de Ufford 'the son' in 1338. He had minor landholdings in Suffolk.[1]

1 C 76/25, m. 20d.

Caltoft, John (esquire)
E 101/35/2/10, m. 2 (152)

Camoys, Ralph de (knight)
C 76/20, m. 15; C 76/23, m. 24; E 101/25/9, m. 3 (33)
Ralph is a little-known member of the Camoys family, which was of East Midlands origin. His uncle, Sir Hugh de Camoys, was a prominent donee of Henry of Lancaster, who granted him the manor of Longstock (Hampshire) in 1350.[1] He is not to be confused with his grandfather (*d.* 1335) and namesake who enjoyed an exceptionally long military career beginning in the reign of Edward I.[2] Ralph served in Lancaster's retinue on the expeditions to Aquitaine (1345, 1349) and Calais (1347). He married Elizabeth and held land in Norfolk and Hampshire.[3] He died before 1372.

1 *CPR, 1348–50*, p. 573.
2 Nigel Saul, 'Chivalry and Art: The Camoys Family and the Wall Paintings in Trotton Church', in *Soldiers, Nobles and Gentlemen*, ed. Coss and Tyerman, pp. 97–111 (p. 102).
3 *CPR, 1367–70*, p. 368; E 372/192, m. 40.

Campden, Henry de (clerk) Suffolk
C 76/20, m. 25; C 81/1724/34
Campden served with Lancaster on four overseas campaigns (1338–48). He was parson of a church in Sudbury (Suffolk) – probably St Peter's – and canon of St Paul's cathedral (London).[1]

1 C 81/1724/34. His name appears on a small plaque mounted on the wall near the main entrance of St Peter's church which lists the names of 'rectors'.

Carles, John (archer) Norfolk
E 101/35/2/10, m. 2d (157)

Carles, John (of Sholl) (archer) Norfolk
E 101/35/2/10, m. 3d. (62)
John, like the esquire Richard Sholl, may have originated from the village of Scole, near Diss (Norfolk).

Carpenter, Thomas le (attendant)
E 101/25/9, m. 3d (38)

Catour, Henry (archer)
E 101/35/2/10, m. 1d (268)

Catterall, Henry de (archer) Lancashire
E 101/35/2/10, m. 3d (44)

Catterall, John de (archer) Lancashire
E 101/35/2/10, m. 3d (34)

Catterall, Robert de (archer) Lancashire
E 101/35/2/10, m. 3d (35)

Causton, Ranulf de (esquire) Norfolk
E 101/35/2/10, m. 2 (73)

Causton, Robert de (knight) Norfolk
C 76/20, m. 15; E 101/25/9, m. 3 (10)
Causton's family probably originated in the Norfolk parish of the same name, which is near Aylsham. It is unclear whether Robert was the person who held the dual shrievalty of Norfolk and Suffolk and keepership of Norwich castle (1337–41), or was this man's son and namesake.[1] It was probably the latter who served with Lancaster in Aquitaine (1345–46), although a 'Robert son of Robert de Causton' intended to serve with Hugh Audley, earl of Gloucester, in 1345.[2] He and Peter de la Mare were among the witnesses to Lancaster's indenture concerning the grant of a hospital in Thetford in 1348.[3] Robert held various commissions in Norfolk, including the maintenance of part of the county's coastal defences (*wallis et fossatis*), and was appointed joint admiral of the fleet north of the Thames which set out to sea in response to an attack on Winchelsea in 1360.[4] On two commissions he acted alongside Richard de Walkefare, an esquire who, like himself, served in John de Norwich's sub-retinue on the expedition in Aquitaine.[5] Causton possessed land in his home county.[6]

1 *CFR*, V, pp. 23, 213; *CPR, 1334–38*, p. 76.
2 C 76/17, m. 14.
3 *CPR, 1348–50*, p. 19.
4 *CPR, 1358–61*, p. 415; *CPR, 1361–64*, p. 206.
5 *CPR, 1361–64*, pp. 206, 285.
6 *Crécy and Calais*, p. 169; E 372/195 (Norfolk).

Cavel, Walter (esquire)
E 101/35/2/10, m. 2 (146)

Caynell, John (pardon recipient) Northamptonshire
CPR, 1345–48, p. 557
Pardoned for the death of William Donnel of Gretton (Northamptonshire).

Chaddesden, Thomas (esquire) Derbyshire
E 101/35/2/10, m. 2 (101)

Chadesley, Adam de (archer) Worcestershire
E 101/35/2/10, m. 2d (152)

Chamber, Robin de la (esquire) Norfolk
E 101/35/2/10, m. 1 (47)

Chamber, William de la (attendant)
E 101/25/9, m. 3d (1)

Chamberlain, Robert (esquire)
C 76/20, m. 15; E 101/35/2/10, m. 2 (105)
Robert first served as an esquire with Henry of Lancaster in 1344, and the earl requested a royal pardon for him, in or before 1345.[1] He was imprisoned, with Sir Ralph de Hastings, Sir William de Hastings, Sir Richard de Rawcliffe and others, at York castle in 1332 for the death of Edmund Darel.[2] He may have been the individual who committed a number of other offences, including besieging the priory of Gisburn (Yorkshire) in 1336.[3] A Robert Chamberlain whose arrest was sought in 1354 for raiding a ship at Sully (South Wales) is described as a soldier of Brittany.[4] Men of the same name were landholders in Buckinghamshire, Wiltshire and Lincolnshire.[5]
1 C 81/1724/46.
2 *CPR, 1330–34*, p. 289.
3 *CPR, 1334–38*, p. 355.
4 *CPR, 1354–58*, p. 56.
5 *CIPM*, VII, pp. 150–1, 272, 357; *CIPM*, VIII, p. 432; *CIPM*, IX, p. 119.

Cheadle, Adam de (archer) Cheshire
E 101/35/2/10, m. 2d (167)

Chester, Richard de (attendant) Cheshire
E 101/25/9, m. 3d (35)

Chetewynde, Roger de (knight)
E 101/25/9, m. 3 (31)
A probable relative of Sir John de Chetewynde, who was too ill to serve on the expedition to Aquitaine in 1345.[1] He may also have been related to Philip de Chetewynde, esquire, who contracted to serve in 1319 for one year with Ralph, Lord Basset of Drayton.[2]

1 C 76/24, m. 3d.
2 Jones and Walker, *Private Indentures*, p. 63.

Chetewynde, three esquires of Sir John de (esquires)
C 76/24, m. 3d
Three unknown esquires served as proxy for Sir John de Chetewynde, who was deemed 'weak and incapable' of service in 1345.

Chippelegh, Robert Somerset
E 372/196 (Somerset)
He first took up arms with Henry, bishop of Lincoln in 1338, and served in the company of Sir Thomas Courtney in Aquitaine (1345–46) and Calais (1347). Robert and Thomas were both landholders in Somerset; the latter was a debtor (50 marks) of Robert in 1344.[1] Robert had still not taken up knighthood by 1356, despite holding land worth £40 in Somerset.[2] He was commissioned to levy a tax (*moiety*) in his home county, and store it in Glastonbury abbey (1360).[3] He witnessed the Black Prince's indenture with Sir Thomas Fichet in 1353, and he may have been the same Robert Chippelegh who hunted in Dartmoor forest without licence in 1371.[4]
1 *CCR, 1343–46*, p. 366.
2 C 47/1/15, m. 12.
3 *CPR, 1358–61*, p. 345.
4 *BPR*, IV, p. 105; *CPR, 1370–74*, p. 172.

Chortrey, Adam (archer)
E 101/35/2/10, m. 1d (255)

Clayton, Hugh de (esquire) Lancashire
E 101/35/2/10, m. 3 (186)

Clerk, Henry le (archer)
E 101/35/2/10, m. 1d (191)

Clerk, John le (archer)
E 101/35/2/10, m. 1d (178)

Clifton, Gervase de (*b.* 1313) (knight) Nottinghamshire
C 76/20, m. 16; E 101/25/9, m. 3 (46)
Gervase, son of Robert de Clifton (of Clifton in Nottinghamshire) testified at the Court of Chivalry in 1386 that he had been armed for fifty-two years.[1] He claimed to have served with Edward III at Antwerp (1340) and may have been the same Sir Gervase de Clifton who had been ordered to raise men from Nottinghamshire for service in Scotland in 1334.[2] He inherited his father's lands in Nottinghamshire in 1327, and was a commissioner of array there in 1339 and 1344.[3] Clifton held the dual shrievalty of Derbyshire and Nottinghamshire in 1345, and was made escheator in the counties the same year.[4] He seems to have oppressed the people of the two counties during his tenure as sheriff; complaint was made by 'the whole commonalty' in 1346 against the various extortions, oppression and evils committed by him.[5] Clifton continued to serve on local commissions in his home county until the

1370s. He was involved with Sir Roger Beler and other men in an enfeofment of land to Sir Richard Tibetot in 1370;[6] two years later Clifton and Sir John de Grey of Codnor (in whose sub-retinue Clifton had served in 1345–46) acted as justices of oyer and terminer concerning the kidnap and rape of Tibetot's wife.[7] In 1371 Clifton was commissioned (together with Roger Beler) to collect taxes in Nottinghamshire, and was granted an exemption from office–holdings six years later.[8] He married firstly Margaret, daughter of Sir Robert Pierpoint, and secondly, before 1348, Isabel, daughter of Vincent Herbert. It is not known when he died. He had a son (and heir) by Margaret, named Robert de Clifton.

1 *Scrope and Grosvenor*, II, p. 357.
2 C 47/2/25, m. 5.
3 *CIPM*, VII, p. 11.
4 *CPR, 1345–48*, p. 149; *CFR*, V, p. 461.
5 *CPR, 1345–48*, p. 241.
6 *CIPM*, XIII, pp. 190, 194.
7 *CPR, 1370–74*, p. 239.
8 *CPR, 1370–74*, p. 120; *CPR, 1374–77*, p. 484.

Clifton, Robert de (esquire) Nottinghamshire
C 76/20, m. 16; C 81/1727/60; E 101/35/2/10, m. 3 (160)

Clinton, Thomas de (esquire)
E 101/35/2/10, m. 2 (79)
Thomas first served with Henry of Lancaster in Brittany (1342).[1]
1 C 76/17, m. 22.

Clynt, John (archer)
E 101/35/2/10, m. 3d (78)

Cockfield, Robert de (esquire) Suffolk
E 101/35/2/10, m. 2 (138)

Cockfield, Thomas de (esquire) Suffolk
E 101/35/2/10, m. 3 (158)

Coddington, Thomas de (archer) Cheshire
E 101/35/2/10, m. 1d (231)

Combrehale, Henry de (archer)
E 101/35/2/10, m. 2d (117)

Cok, Adam le (archer)
E 101/35/2/10, m. 1d (188)

Cok, Piers (esquire)
E 101/35/2/10, m. 2 (100)

Cok, Thomas (*d. c.* 1352) **(knight)** Oxfordshire
C 76/20, m. 16; C 76/22, m. 16d; E 101/25/9, m. 3 (1)
Sir Thomas Cok was one of Henry of Lancaster's most trusted and capable knights; he served consistently and exclusively in Lancaster's retinue from 1336, was among the earl's charter witnesses (1344) and performed the role of a diplomat and negotiator in 1341 and in 1350–51. As marshal of the army in Aquitaine (1345–46) he was responsible for mustering the troops at Southampton and overseeing the process of horse appraisal – a role he fulfilled again in 1349. He had one horse valued at 40 marks and three sold for £86 13s 4d in 1338 and 1349, respectively.[1] In 1347 he was elevated to the rank of banneret and made seneschal of Aquitaine (1347–49).[2] Cok was retained for life by Edward III on 24 August 1349 with an annuity of 100 marks, and the king granted him 200 marks in the same year for the marriage of his ward, the heir of George Mountboucher.[3] In addition to his property in Oxford and Leicestershire, Cok held lands in Aquitaine, including Latresne, the castle of Lalinde and the commune of Clerans.[4] His pilgrimage to Rome in 1350 did not mark the end of his long and illustrious military career because two years later he 'set out speedily with men-at-arms and archers upon the sea' to protect merchant vessels from pirates.[5] He performed homage and fealty to the Black Prince for the manor of Aston Rohand (Oxfordshire) in February 1351, and employed four stone masons and three carpenters to build a chapel there the following year.[6] In 1338 the king had granted him the marriage of Miliscent, the widow of Hugh le Plecy, but she refused to consent to the union, and Cok went on to marry Eleanor.[7] He died before mid-February 1353.[8]
1 E 36/203, fol. 126; E 404/508/67.
2 C 61/59, m. 13.
3 *CPR, 1348–50*, pp. 271, 362.
4 C 61/63, mm. 9, 10.
5 *CPR, 1348–50*, p. 581; *CPR, 1350–54*, p. 244.
6 *BPR*, IV, pp. 2, 25; *CPR, 1350–54*, p. 244.
7 *CPR, 1338–40*, p. 47; *CPR, 1350–54*, p. 56.
8 C 61/65, m. 8.

Cokton, John de (esquire)
E 101/35/2/10, m. 3 (154)

Coleman, John (archer)
E 101/35/2/10, m. 2d (96)

Coleman, Thomas de (esquire)
E 101/35/2/10, m. 1 (18)

Colthorp, John de (esquire) Yorkshire
E 101/35/2/10, m. 2 (117)
A John de Colthorp was pardoned in 1321 for actions against the Despenser family.[1]
1 *CPR, 1321–24*, pp. 15–16.

Coly, William de (archer) Devonshire
E 101/35/2/10, m. 3d (59)

Cosington, Stephen de (knight) Kent
Crécy and Calais, p. 180; C 76/20, m. 15; E 101/25/9, m. 3 (2)
Cosington first took up arms with Sir Reginald de Cobham (1334) and went on to have a distinguished military career in the retinues of the Black Prince and Henry of Lancaster.[1] He was a retainer of the Black Prince (from 1347) and Charles, king of Navarre (1366); he distinguished himself at the battle of Poitiers (1355) and was rewarded with an annuity of £100 by the prince.[2] In 1348 he led a bodyguard of 130 men-at-arms to escort the entourage of Edward III's daughter, Joan, on her ill-fated mission to Castile.[3] Cosington was strongly associated with Sir Neil Loring, who was probably his brother-in-arms; in 1340 their ship, which was laden with armour, was raided off the Yorkshire coast.[4] He acted as messenger between his two most important patrons, Lancaster and the Black Prince, when the latter ordered his cousin to raise the siege of Rennes in 1357. He performed numerous high profile diplomatic roles in the 1350s, and his exemption from the appointment to local offices in 1358 enabled him to pursue his martial lifestyle in Aquitaine and the Iberian kingdoms in the following decade. His moderate wealth is reflected by the sale of a destrier in 1349 for £66, and the lands he held in his home county of Kent, as well Berkshire and Hampshire.[5] Lancaster had granted him property in all three counties before 1361.[6] Cosington was probably a relative of John de Cosington of Northfleet (Kent); both men owed a sum of £120 to the cardinal Sir Gaucelinus Johannis, bishop of Albano, and to Master Raymond Pelegrini in 1345, and John acted as Stephen's attorney in 1348.[7]

1 BL, Cotton MS Nero C VIII, fol. 234v.
2 *BPR*, IV, pp. 178, 301, 373.
3 Peter E. Russell, *Portugal, Spain, and the African Atlantic, 1343–1490: Chivalry and Crusade from John of Gaunt to Henry the Navigator* (Aldershot: Variorum, 1995), VII, pp. 327–30.
4 *CPR, 1338–40*, p. 556.
5 E 404/508/52 (destrier).
6 *CIPM*, V, pp. 95, 108; *CPR, 1361–64*, p. 50.
7 *CCR, 1343–46*, p. 484; C 76/26, m. 9 (attorney).

Coudray, Fouk de (*b.* 1314) **(knight)** Berkshire
C 81/321/18583; E 101/35/2/10, m. 1 (97); E 159/123, m. 154
Fouk was the son of Sir Thomas de Coudray, who made a name for himself in the military campaigns of Edward I and Edward II. He served in Lancaster's retinue in Aquitaine (1345–46) and Calais (1347), and with Sir Gerard de Isle in 1359. He held property in Berkshire and Hampshire, including his family's principal manor of Padworth in the former county.[1] He married Joan and died sometime before 1378.[2]
1 *CIPM*, XI, pp. 67, 117; *CPR, 1324–27*, p. 198; *CPR, 1364–67*, p. 263; *CPR, 1367–70*, p. 157; *The Victoria History of Berkshire*, ed. William Page et al., 4 vols (London: Constable, 1906–1924), III (1923), pp. 413–14.
2 *CPR, 1377–81*, p. 165.

Courson, Hugh (of Carleton) (*b.* 1326) Norfolk
C 76/22, m. 7d; C 47/6/1, no. 99; E 101/35/2/10, m. 2 (136)
Hugh, son of William Courson, testified on behalf of Thomas, Lord Morley, at the Court of Chivalry in 1386. Hugh deposed, at sixty years of age, that he had

first fought under Sir John de Norwich's banner (1345–46), before serving with the Black Prince at Crécy (1346), and that he had taken part in the siege of Calais (1347) and the battle of Winchelsea (1350).[1] He had minor landholdings in Norfolk; he delivered twenty-five fresh herrings to the steward of the royal household in 1347 as service for his manor of Carleton.[2] Hugh committed numerous crimes in his home county, including felonies made against the Black Prince. In 1356 he was accused of being one of the 'evildoers', who harboured an outlaw (Walter ate Felde) indicted for murder, and is the only one of the gang named specifically in the assault on the Black Prince's clerk, John de Carleton, and the theft of his goods.[3] Two years later Hugh was accused of breaking into the prince's property at East Carleton, where he assaulted the prince's servants and stole his cattle.[4]

1 C 47/6/1, no. 99.
2 CPR, 1345–48, p. 402.
3 CPR, 1354–58, p. 401.
4 CPR, 1358–61, p. 159.

Courtney, Thomas (*d. c.* 1352) **(knight)** Devonshire
Crécy and Calais, p. 172; E 372/196 (Somerset)
Thomas was probably a relative of Hugh Courtney, earl of Devon. The only evidence of his military service is that with Lancaster in Aquitaine (1345–46) and Calais (1347), although it seems that he had originally intended to serve in the earl of Pembroke's retinue on the former expedition.[1] His estates were scattered across the southern counties of Devon, Hampshire, Oxford and Somerset.[2] Thomas was appointed as warden of Devon in 1346 and served as a justice of oyer and terminer in that county from 1338 to 1351.[3] He married Muriel, daughter and heir of John de Moels, before 1337.[4]

1 C 76/20, m. 16 (Pembroke).
2 CCR, 1343–46, p. 420; CIPM, X, p. 78; CIPM, XI, pp. 242–4; CPR, 1343–45, p. 254.
3 C 76/22, m. 27; CPR, 1343–45, p. 181.
4 CPR, 1334–38, p. 507.

Crane, Richard de (esquire)
E 101/35/2/10, m. 2 (151)

Crawbarwe, William de (archer)
E 101/35/2/10, m. 2d (142)

Cray, John (knight)
E 101/25/9, m. 3 (45)
He may be the John de Cray who was part of an armed gang which in 1350 alleg-edly broke into Roger Jolyf's property in Abingdon (Berkshire), and subsequently assaulted and robbed the said Roger.[1]
1 CPR, 1350–54, pp. 25–6.

Cresswell, Richard de (archer) Derbyshire
E 101/35/2/10, m. 1d (181)

Cressy, Hugh (esquire)
CPR, 1345–48, p. 183: C 76/20, m. 15
Hugh Cressy served as an esquire with Henry of Lancaster in Scotland (1336) and Brittany (1342) and with Sir John de Norwich in Aquitaine (1337), and he may have been part of the English garrison at Berwick in 1335. He received £8 for horse restoration in 1336.[1] He is not to be confused with his namesakes of Risegate, or of Selston (Nottinghamshire). Cressy and others broke into the property of Sir Hugh Meynell near Waltham (Leicestershire) and stole his goods; Cressy was required to pay a fine of only 10s on account of his service in Aquitaine.[2] He had small land-holdings in Lincolnshire.
1 E 101/15/12.
2 *CPR, 1345–48*, p. 183.

Crewe, Richard de (archer) Cheshire
E 101/35/2/10, m. 1d (186)

Crier, Richard le (archer)
E 101/35/2/10, m. 2d (126)

Croket, Hendekyn (archer)
E 101/35/2/10, m. 1d (219)

Croket, Ralph (archer)
E 101/35/2/10, m. 1d (213)

Crossley, Roger de (archer)
E 101/35/2/10, m. 1d (225)

Croule, Thomas (archer)
E 101/35/2/10, m. 2d (97)

Crouther, Richard le (archer)
E 101/35/2/10, m. 1d (212)

Crupeland, Gord[1] de (esquire)
E 101/35/2/10, m. 3 (177)
1 A very unusual forename of the fourteenth century.

Cuilly, Walter de (esquire) Norfolk
E 101/35/2/10, m. 2 (142)

Cundall, William de (archer) Yorkshire
E 101/35/2/10, m. 3d (80)

Dacre, John (archer) Yorkshire
E 101/35/2/10, m. 3d (76)

Dafydd, Hywel ap (archer)
E 101/35/2/10, m. 3d (69)
Dafydd was a Welshman and may have been brought into Lancaster's retinue by the Welsh esquire Gruffudd Dwn.

Dalton, John de (*d.* 1369) **(knight)** Lancashire
C 76/22, m. 26; C 76/23, m. 8; E 101/25/9, m. 3 (30)
John de Dalton of Bispham, son of Sir Robert de Dalton, is not to be confused with Sir John de Dalton of Kirkby Misperton, who probably founded the Yorkshire branch of the Dalton family and who served as bailiff of Pickering for Thomas of Lancaster. John regularly served on military campaigns during the first phase of the French war and was granted an annuity of 20 marks by Edward III at Antwerp in 1338, which was increased to £50 in 1350.[1] He was captured during Lancaster's expedition in Aquitaine (1345–46), and his subsequent ransom was partly paid by the king.[2] In what seems to have been his last military campaign (1359) John captured James de Penquadyk.[3] He appointed Geoffrey de Wrightington, an esquire whom he had served alongside in Aquitaine, as his attorney in 1356 whilst on service in Brittany.[4] In 1347 he led an armed gang in an attack on the manor of Beams (Berkshire), during which Michael de Poynings the elder and one of his servants were murdered, and Margaret de la Beche was abducted and goods worth in excess of £1000 stolen. Among John's confederates were the knights Matthew de Haydock, Edmund de Manchester and William Trussell who had also fought in Lancaster's retinue the year before. His main landholdings in Lancashire were supplemented by property in Northamptonshire.[5] In 1369 he was murdered by Richard Garstene.[6] He married Ellen, and later Margery de la Beche. He had two sons named John and Robert.
1 *CPR, 1338–40*, p. 396; *CPR, 1348–50*, pp. 540, 552.
2 E 403/338, m. 34; E 403/339, m. 34.
3 *Feodera*, III, p. 439.
4 C 76/34, m. 14.
5 *CIPM*, XII, pp. 330–1.
6 *CPR, 1367–70*, p. 405.

Darcy, Roger (knight)
E 101/25/9, m. 3 (56)
Roger was the son of Sir John Darcy, and most likely a relative of another John Darcy who held the positions of steward of the royal household, constable of the Tower of London and justice of Ireland in the 1330s and 1340s. It is possible, although unlikely, that he is the same Roger Darcy, 'king's yeoman', who was made constable of Dublin castle for life (1339), and was granted the manor of Esker in Ireland by Edward III in 1342.[1] He held land in Kindale, Yorkshire.[2]
1 *CPR, 1338–40*, p. 397; *CPR, 1340–43*, p. 502.
2 *CIPM*, IX, p. 317.

Darrington, William de (esquire) Yorkshire
E 101/35/2/10, m. 1 (16)

David, Peter (archer)
E 101/35/2/10, m. 2d (99)

Dean, John (archer)
E 101/35/2/10, m. 3d (77)

Delves, Richard de (archer)
E 101/35/2/10, m. 1d (206)

Delves, Richard del (esquire)
E 101/35/2/10, m. 3 (187)

Derewelsch, John de (archer)
E 101/35/2/10, m. 2d (175)

Derewelsch, William de (archer)
E 101/35/2/10, m. 2d (165)

Despaigne, Vascomede (knight)
E 101/25/9, m. 3 (93)
Several men of this surname appear in the administrative records of the fourteenth century. A Ralph Despaigne, for example, was bailiff of the High Peak in the honour of Tutbury in 1332.[1]
1 *Somerville*, p. 357.

Destor, Henry (knight)
E 101/25/9, m. 3 (43)

Dodleston, Richard de (archer) Cheshire
E 101/35/2/10, m. 2d (162)

Dodleston, William de (archer) Cheshire
E 101/35/2/10, m. 2d (161)

Dorgyn, Lewis (esquire)
E 101/35/2/10, m. 3 (182)

Dragon, Thomas (archer)
E 101/35/2/10, m. 2d (93)

Drinkale, Adam (archer)
E 101/35/2/10, m. 3d (72)

Dudley, Hugh de (archer) Worcestershire
E 101/35/2/10, m. 3d (70)

Dudrinton, Thomas de (archer)
E 101/35/2/10, m. 1d (236)

Durfort, a companion of Arnaut de (knight)
E 101/25/9, m. 3 (88)
An unknown companion of Arnaut de Durfort III.

Durfort, Arnaut de (knight) Frespech (Lot-et-Garonne)
E 101/25/9, m. 3 (78)
Arnaut III de Durfort, lord of Castelnoubel and Frespech, was the son of Arnaut II (*d.* 1340). Both father and son had loyally served both Edward I and Edward II, and had taken out loans from Edward I's Wardrobe.[1] In 1328 the constable of Bordeaux was ordered to pay Arnaut the younger £100 out of the duchy's revenues for his expenses of war – the other half had already been paid at the Exchequer.[2] He held two of the strongest castles in Agenais, Castelnoubel and Bajamont. Other prominent branches of the Durfort family included Galhart de Durfort, lord of Duras, Bertran de Durfort, lord of Clermont, and Ramon-Bernat de Durfort (known as Dosina), lord of Fenholac and Gaynhac.
1 C 61/36, m. 24; C 61/50, m. 16.
2 C 61/40, m. 4.

Dutton, Robert de (archer) Cheshire
E 101/35/2/10, m. 3 (15)

Dwn, Gruffudd (of Kidwelly) (esquire) Carmarthenshire
E 101/35/2/10, m. 1 (57)
Gruffudd originated from Lancaster's lordship of Kidwelly (Carmarthenshire). He served as commissioner of array in South Wales and the March of Wales in 1338, and was appointed to lead Welshmen from the South to Southampton in 1345. He was a relative of the notorious rebel, Henry Dwn, and of Sir Gruffudd Dwn, who fought at Agincourt (1415) and became a prominent Welsh captain during the period of the English occupation of Normandy.

Dyket, Roger (archer)
E 101/35/2/10, m. 1d (259)

Elmsall, John de (esquire) Yorkshire
E 101/35/2/10, m. 1 (46)
John first served with Henry of Lancaster in the Low Countries (1338), and was granted an annuity of 10 marks from the manor of West Derby (Lancashire) by the earl on 1 May 1345.[1]
1 C 76/12, m. 8; *JGR*, I, p. 623.

Ely, John (attendant) Cambridgeshire
E 101/25/9, m. 3d. (11)

Emue, Hanck (esquire)
E 101/35/2/10, m. 1 (40)

Enderbourne, William de (esquire) Berkshire
E 101/35/2/10, m. 2 (96)

Englefield, John de (esquire) Flintshire
E 101/35/2/10, m. 2 (99)

Erdeleye, Peter de (archer)
E 101/35/2/10, m. 1d (214)

Ermyn, John (archer)
E 101/35/2/10, m. 1d (263)

Escoussans, Johan d' (esquire) Escoussans (Gironde)
E 101/35/2/10, m. 3 (180)
A likely relative of Bernat d'Escoussans, lord of Langoiran.

Esterley, Richard de (esquire)
E 101/35/2/10, m. 3 (155)

Estissac, Fergant d' (knight) Estissac (Dordogne)
E 101/25/9, m. 3 (84)
Fergant originated from the honour of Estissac, which included the communes of Saint-Jean-d'Estissac (where the castle of its lords lay), Saint-Hilaire-d'Estissac and Saint-Séverin-d'Estissac. In 1323, Fergant and other members of the Estissac family – Archambaud and Gui – were among a group of Gascon nobles requested to raise men-at-arms for service on Edward II's proposed Scottish expedition.[1] He was pardoned in 1325 along with another relative, Hélias, for his adherence to the French.[2]
1 C 61/35, m. 11d.
2 C 61/37 m, 10d.

Ethere, Henry de (attendant)
E 101/25/9, m. 3d. (12)

Everard, Edmund (*d.* 1370) **(knight)** Dorset
Crécy and Calais, p. 156; C 76/24, m. 2; E 101/25/9, m. 3 (13)
Edmund, son of William Everard, started his military career at the beginning of the Hundred Years' War, serving exclusively with Henry of Lancaster up until the Reims expedition (1359). He was compensated £20 for the loss of a warhorse during the Breton expedition of 1342.[1] In 1343 he was granted respite of homage because he was with Lancaster in Grenada and the following year he served as an assessor of land in his home county of Dorset.[2] Everard was affiliated with Sir Nicholas de Peyvre; both men held land in the hundred of Manshead (Bedfordshire) and were issued royal protections on the same day (6 June 1345) prior to the Aquitaine expedition.[3] In 1347 his 'palyfreyman', David, was accused, along with Everard's brother–in–law, Sir Robert de Loundres and others, of assaulting the bishop of Salisbury's servants.[4] Everard served as a justice of the peace in 1362, and was endowed with an annuity of

40 marks from Edward III in 1369.[5] His landholdings were spread across Bedford-shire, Berkshire, Dorset, Hampshire, Somerset and Wiltshire.[6] He married Felicia and died on 16 August 1370.

1 E 36/204, fol. 83r.
2 *CFR, 1337–47*, p. 338; *CPR, 1343–45*, p. 415.
3 C 47/2/58, m. 5.
4 *CPR, 1345–48*, p. 306.
5 *CPR, 1361–64*, p. 293; *CPR, 1367–70*, p. 302.
6 *CIPM*, XIII, pp. 20–1; C 47/2/41, no. 2; E 372/192, m. 40.

Everingham, Adam de (of Laxton) (*c.* 1307–87) **(banneret)** Nottinghamshire
C 61/58, m. 2; C 76/20, m. 15; E 101/25/9, m. 3 (5)
Adam, the last baron of Everingham (Yorkshire), held lands in Lincolnshire, Nottinghamshire and Yorkshire upon his death on 8 February 1387.[1] At the Court of Chivalry in 1386 he testified to being 'armed for sixty years', having first taken up arms at the age nineteen.[2] He was compensated with 25 marks and £20 for the loss of two warhorses in 1337 and 1342 respectively.[3] Everingham and Sir Hugh Meynell were both captured during the siege of Tournai in 1340 and subsequently ransomed.[4] He was frequently engaged in local administration having regularly served as a justice of the peace in Nottinghamshire from the 1340s to the 1360s.[5] In 1351 he was imprisoned in Nottingham castle, having been indicted of various trespasses.[6] He witnessed the foundation charter for the college of Newark issued by Lancaster in 1355.[7] His son and heir apparent, Sir William de Everingham, married Alice, daughter of John de Grey of Codnor, before 1354, by whom William had a son, Robert (and two daughters, Joan and Katherine). Robert, like his father, prede-ceased Sir Adam de Everingham who died on 8 February 1387 at Laxton, whereupon the hereditary barony went into abeyance.

1 *CIPM*, XV, pp. 207–9.
2 *Scrope and Grosvenor*, I, pp. 240–1.
3 E 101/35/3, m. 1 (Scotland, 1337); E 36/204, fol. 83r (Brittany, 1342).
4 E 403/341, m. 22.
5 See *CPR* for relevant years.
6 On his imprisonment and career in general, see *CP*, V, pp. 189–93.
7 Thompson, *History of the Hospital and New College of the Annunciation of St Mary in the Newarke*, p. 29.

Everingham, John de (esquire) Nottinghamshire
E 101/35/2/10, m. 2 (109)

Everingham, Robert de (esquire) Nottinghamshire
E 101/35/2/10, m. 2 (108)

Eye, Thomas de (archer) Herefordshire
E 101/35/2/10, m. 2d (106)

Eye, Walter de (archer) Herefordshire
E 101/35/2/10, m. 2d (107)

Facoun, Hugh (attendant)
E 101/25/9, m. 3d (24)

Falconer, Bertam le (esquire)
E 101/35/2/10, m. 1 (20)

Fauconer, John le (archer) Derbyshire
E 101/35/2/10, m. 2d (118)
John belonged to the Fauconer family, who were granted small annuities by Henry of Lancaster from the manor of Melbourne (Derbyshire). He was probably the son of Amy and Ingram Fauconer; the latter was one of Lancaster's lesser officers and constable of Melbourne castle (1361). John was probably the younger brother of Damel Fauconer, who served as an esquire in Lancaster's retinue (1336, 1338), and possibly a sibling of William Fauconer. The earl granted annuities to John (5 marks), Ingram (£10), Amy (5 marks) and William (£1 10s) in Melbourne manor.[1]
1 *CIPM*, XI, pp. 93, 96.

Favell, Richard (esquire) Northamptonshire
E 101/35/2/10, m. 2 (114)

Favell, William (knight) Northamptonshire
E 101/35/2/10, m. 1 (96)
Favell's name is grouped together with those of Simon Secre, George de Hotham and Fouk de Coudray at the end of the list of knights' names on Lancaster's retinue roll (1345–46). Interestingly, the men's names are also written, but subsequently struck through, in the 'esquires' section of the roll which might indicate that they were knighted at some point in the course of the expedition in Aquitaine.

Ferrers, Ralph de (knight) Leicestershire
C 76/20, m. 15; C 76/23, m. 4; E 101/25/9, m. 3 (80)
Ralph belonged to the Ferrers family, lords of Groby in Leicestershire. He is not to be confused with his relative and homonym who testified during the Scrope v. Grosvenor armorial dispute, or with other namesakes who were militarily active during the fourteenth century. Ralph was a veteran of the Scottish wars, having served there with the elder Henry of Lancaster in 1327. He was paid £10 for horse restoration relating to his service in Scotland in 1336.[1] Like several men from Lancaster's retinue, Ferrers became an associate of the Black Prince; he received a gift of a silver gilt cup (1353), as well as furs and gold cloth (1357) from the prince.[2] Ralph was appointed commissioner of array in his home county of Leicester (1344), where he also held land.[3] He had other small landholdings in Staffordshire, Yorkshire and Salisbury. Ralph married Joan and died some time before 1369.[4]
1 E 101/19/36, m. 5d.
2 *BPR*, III, pp. 99, 229.
3 C 76/19, mm. 9, 11.
4 *CIPM*, XIII, p. 60.

Field, John de la (archer)
E 101/35/2/10, m. 3d (67)

Fitz Henry, Ingram (esquire)
E 101/35/2/10, m. 1 (6)

Fitz John de Hole, Robert (archer)
E 101/35/2/10, m. 3d (37)

Fitzpayn, Robert (knight)
E 101/25/9, m. 3 (47)
Robert was probably a son or close relative of Sir Robert, second Lord Fitzpayn (*c.* 1285–1354), who was an adherent of Thomas of Lancaster and a substantial land-holder in Dorset and Somerset.[1] It is possible that Lord Fitzpayn is the person who served with Lancaster in 1345–46, but the position of Robert Fitzpayn towards the middle of the nominal list of knights on the retinue roll suggests not.
1 *CP*, V, pp. 451–3.

Fitzsimon, Richard (KG 1349) **(knight)** Norfolk
C 76/20, m. 15; E 101/25/9, m. 3 (6)
Richard first took up arms in the retinue of Sir John de Norwich (1335), but he may have served on an expedition to Scotland two years earlier.[1] He was at the Dunstable tournament of 1334. He fought under the banner of Sir Reginald de Cobham in the Low Countries (1338) and was with Henry of Lancaster at the siege of Algeciras in 1344. On 11 June 1345 he was at Chelworth (Wiltshire), where he witnessed an enrolment of a release of land between Sir Walter Pavely, Sir Adam de St Philbert and Richard le Forester, before setting out to Aquitaine in Lancaster's retinue a few weeks later.[2] He returned from the duchy in 1346 to serve on the Normandy expedition in the retinue of Sir Robert de Ufford but evidently fought alongside (and carried the standard of) the Black Prince at the battle of Crécy. Thereafter he was retained by the prince and, like Sir Richard Baskerville and Sir Stephen de Cosington, was ordered to join the prince at Calais (1347).[3] He was made a Knight of the Garter in 1349, probably as a reward for his services to the prince at Crécy.[4] Richard held lands in Essex, Hertfordshire, Norfolk, Suffolk and Sussex.[5] He died sometime before 1359, probably without an heir.
1 C 71/13, m. 6 (1333).
2 *CCR, 1343–46*, p. 589.
3 *BPR*, I, p. 80.
4 Barber, *The Triumph of England*, p. 513.
5 *Crécy and Calais*, pp. 160, 185; *CCR, 1346–49*, p. 258; E 372/193, (Sussex); E 372/200 (Norfolk); E 372/203 (Essex).

Flegg, John (esquire) Norfolk
E 101/35/2/10, m. 1 (26)

Flesschere, Henry le (archer)
E 101/35/2/10, m. 1d (242)

Flitcham, Roger (esquire) Norfolk
C 61/57, m. 5
Roger son of Roger Baron of Flitcham first served in the retinue of Robert de

Ufford, earl of Suffolk, in 1344. He returned from Aquitaine to fight under William de Kildesby's banner on the Normandy expedition (1346), and at the siege of Calais (1347), although he switched to the earl of Suffolk's retinue during the siege following Kildesby's death. He held land in Norfolk.[1]

1 E 372/191 (Norfolk).

Florak, Thomas (esquire) Wiltshire
E 101/35/2/10, m. 1 (43)

Thomas, son of Pounz and Joan Florak, belonged to a Wiltshire family who were longstanding supporters of the Lancastrian dynasty. He served exclusively with Henry of Lancaster from 1345 to 1359, by which time he was knighted and led his own small company. Thereafter he established himself in the retinue of the Black Prince, serving with the prince in Aquitaine in 1363, 1366–67 and 1369. He sold a horse in the duchy for £10 in 1350.[1] The patronage given to the Florak family by Thomas, earl of Lancaster, continued under Henry (fourth earl) who granted Thomas (esquire) an annuity of 10 marks from the manor of Collingbourne (Wiltshire) for life in 1350.[2] Thomas was an officer and valet of Lancaster, who witnessed the earl's foundation charter of Newarke college (Leicester). His rise in status and wealth from the beginning of his military career is reflected by his appointment of four attorneys in 1366.[3] He was probably related to Thomas Florak of London, who acted as mainpernor for a pardoned outlaw, Thomas Chisenhale, in 1344.[4]

1 E 404/508/52.
2 *CPR, 1350–54*, p. 8.
3 C 61/79, mm. 8, 15.
4 *CPR, 1343–45*, p. 194.

Fog, Hugh (archer)
E 101/35/2/10, m. 2d (133)

Folifeld, Thomas (archer)
E 101/35/2/10, m. 1d (246)

Ford, John de la (archer)
E 101/35/2/10, m. 2d (171)

Forseer, Franscekyn (esquire)
E 101/35/2/10, m. 1 (32)

Gamel, Thomas (archer)
E 101/35/2/10, m. 1d (269)

Thomas may be a relative of John Gamel of Norton (Leicestershire), who was pardoned for the murder of Sir Edmund de Manchester's servant in 1356.[1]

1 *CPR, 1354–58*, p. 377.

Gayton, John de (esquire) Cheshire
E 101/35/2/10, m. 2 (89)

Gerbergh, John (esquire) Norfolk
E 101/35/2/10, m. 2 (131)
John was granted a general pardon in 1344 at the request of William de Bohun, earl of Northampton, on condition that he serve in the king's wars.[1] He twice served in the retinue of Henry of Lancaster (1345–46, 1359).
1 *CPR, 1343–45*, pp. 304–5.

Gerbergh, Thomas (esquire) Norfolk
E 101/35/2/10, m. 2 (132)

Gernoun, William (archer)
E 101/35/2/10, m. 1d (177)

Gerst, William othe (attendant)
E 101/25/9, m. 3d (23)

Gilling, Thomas (knight) Yorkshire
C 76/20, m. 15; C 81/1724/38; E 101/25/9, m. 3 (77)
Gilling probably originated from Gilling East in north Yorkshire from where his family took their name. He served in John Charnel's retinue in the Low Countries (1338), and his royal protection for service with Lancaster in Aquitaine (1345–46) was enrolled together with protections for William and Warren Scargill and Theobald Trussell on 4 June 1345. He was granted a general pardon in 1347 on account of the 'good service' he had performed in Aquitaine.[1] Gilling was a landholder in Leicestershire.[2] His wife Agnes, daughter of John Giles of York, was abducted by Hugh Bonhumme of Bugthorp in York (1362) and forced to marry a Simon Porter. Gilling's goods were stolen in the same attack.[3]
1 *CPR, 1348–50*, p. 24.
2 *CCR, 1343–46*, p. 79.
3 *CPR, 1361–64*, p. 515.

Goushill, Nicholas (1310–93) **(knight)** Derbyshire
E 101/25/9, m. 3 (70)
Goushill had a colourful career in arms spanning more than thirty-five years, during which he served in a wide range of theatres of war. At the armorial dispute between Lord Lovel and Lord Morley (1386), despite admitting to having a defective memory, he claimed to have first taken up arms at Halidon Hill in 1333; he continued to serve on overseas campaigns until the mid 1370s.[1] Goushill was paid £10 and £8 for horse restoration relating to military campaigns in 1338 and 1362 respectively.[2] He appears to have been an incorrigible individual and his indictment along with his father, Sir Thomas Goushill, for breaking into the property and stealing livestock of John de Leicester in 1336 was one of numerous felonies committed by him during his lifetime.[3] He acted as commissioner of array in his home county of Derby (1362) and was appointed in 1365 together with Robert de Twyford and William la Zouche of Lubbesthorpe to arrest John de Araby of Scalford (Leicestershire), who deserted from an English army with 'a great sum of the king's money' before it had embarked for Ireland.[4] Araby had intended to serve on the said Irish expedition in Goushill's company.[5] The latter collected parochial subsidies in 1371.[6] He inherited

his father's estate in Derbyshire at sixty years of age and had two sons named Robert and Nicholas.[7]

1 C 47/6/1, no. 29.
2 E 36/203, fol. 125v; E 101/28/11, m. 2.
3 *CCR, 1333–37*, p. 727; *CCR, 1337–39*, p. 397. For examples of Goushill's felonies see *CPR*.
4 *CCR, 1360–64*, p. 340; *CPR, 1364–67*, p. 151.
5 C 81/1727/56.
6 *CFR, 1369–77*, pp. 111, 127.
7 *CIPM*, XIV, p. 29.

Glayve, Hugh (archer) Cheshire
E 101/35/2/10, m. 2d (128)

Glayve, Thomas (of Booths) (archer) Cheshire
E 101/35/2/10, m. 2d (131)

Glayve, Thomas (of Mobberley) (archer) Cheshire
E 101/35/2/10, m. 2d (125)

Goldeborgh, John de (archer) Yorkshire
E 101/35/2/10, m. 1d (241)

Grafton, Robert de (archer) Dorset
E 101/35/2/10, m. 2d (146)

Grailly, a companion of Johan de (esquire)
E 101/35/2/10, m. 1 (50)
An unknown companion of the esquire Johan de Grailly, or possibly of the knight Johan III de Grailly.

Grailly, a companion of Pey de (esquire)
E 101/35/2/10, m. 1 (52)
An anonymous companion of the esquire, Pey de Grailly, or possibly of the knight of the same name.

Grailly, Johan de (esquire)
E 101/35/2/10, m. 1 (49)
A relative of his namesake, Johan III de Grailly, known as Captal de Buch.

Grailly, Johan III de, Captal de Buch (*d.* 1377) (KG 1349) **(knight)** Buch (Gironde)
E 101/25/9, m. 3 (81)
The Grailly family were perhaps the most influential and loyal supporters of the English kings among the Gascon nobility.[1] Johan III de Grailly, more commonly known as Captal de Buch, was the fifth-generation descendant of Johan I (*d.* 1303), who served as Edward I's lieutenant and seneschal in Aquitaine in 1266–68 and 1278–87. The expedition to Aquitaine (1345–46) signalled the beginning of the Captal de Buch's distinguished career in arms which continued up to the naval

defeat of the English off La Rochelle in 1372. He played crucial roles at the battles of Poitiers (1356), where he captured the duke of Bourbon, and Nájera (1367), and participated in the supposed 'massacre' of Limoges in 1370. He was twice captured by the French (1364, 1372), but refused to switch from his English allegiance despite generous offers of inducement to join the French cause. He was made Knight of the Garter in 1349. His coat-of-arms appears in the decorative frame of the opening page of *Le Livre de Seyntz Medicines* (The Book of Holy Medicines), which demonstrates his close ties with its author, Henry of Lancaster.[2] Grailly held the lordships of Buch, Castillon, Bénauges, and other strongholds in Aquitaine, and was granted the comté of Bigorre by the Black Prince in 1370. He married Rose, daughter of Bernat-Etz II, lord of Albret. Grailly died in captivity in 1377, and was succeeded by his son and heir Archambaud de Grailly.

1 See Vale, 'Grailly, Jean (III) de', *ODNB*.
2 Émile Jules François Arnould, *Le Manuel des péchés: étude de littérature religieuse anglo-normande (XIIIme siècle)* (Paris: E. Droz, 1940), lxvii–viii.

Grailly, Pey de (knight)
E 101/25/9, m. 3 (82)
He is possibly Pey II de Grailly, vicomte of Bénauges and Castillon (*d.* 1357) and grandfather of the Captal de Buch, although his position below that of the latter on Lancaster's retinue roll (1345–46) suggests that he is another relative of lesser standing.

Grailly, Pey de (esquire)
E 101/35/2/10, m. 1 (51)
A Pey de Grailly was reportedly knighted by Henry of Lancaster on the day that Bergerac surrendered (24 August 1345).[1]
1 AL, *Livre velu de Libourne*, fol. 133v.

Greasley, Robert de (knight) Nottinghamshire/Staffordshire
E 101/25/9, m. 3 (41)
Sir Robert de Greasley may have originated from the manor of the same name in Nottinghamshire, or perhaps belonged to the notorious Greasley family of Staffordshire which became embroiled in a number of criminal activities throughout the fourteenth century. He was possibly one of the younger sons of Joan of Greasley, who was raped and forced to re-marry but exacted revenge by murdering her new husband in 1323.[1]
1 Prestwich, *The Three Edwards*, p. 204.

Grete, John de (archer)
E 101/35/2/10, m. 2d (122)
A John de Grete was pardoned for outlawry in 1367, and was an executor of William de Overton's will.[1]
1 *CPR, 1364–67*, p. 409.

Grey, John de (of Codnor) (*c.* 1305–92) (banneret) Derbyshire
C 76/20, m. 15; C 76/22, mm. 10d, 16; E 101/25/9, m. 3 (2)
The eldest son of Richard, second Lord Grey of Codnor. His scattered estates were

concentrated in the East Midlands, but included manors in Essex, Hampshire and Kent.[1] A problem of homonymity exists between this John de Grey and his relatives and namesakes, who often served on the same military campaigns in the 1330s and 1340s.[2] He first served on Edward III's Scottish expedition in 1334, was knighted by 1341 and, despite a grave illness in 1350, continued to pursue an active military career up to the Alexandria crusade in 1365.[3] As a reward for his services Grey was granted the keepership of Rochester castle, together with the farm of the town, for life in 1359.[4] In 1338 he was compensated 40 marks for the loss of a warhorse.[5] Whilst on service in Aquitaine (1345–46) his men were attacked in Kent and his goods were stolen. In 1347 Richard de Wylougby, who had served as one of Grey's four attorneys during the recent expedition, was appointed to act on an oyer and terminer commission relating to the incident.[6] Grey was regularly appointed as justice of the peace in his home county from the 1340s onwards; he served alongside Sir Hugh Meynell on administrative commissions in Derbyshire and was appointed with Sir Roger Beler, Sir Adam de Everingham and Sir Gervase de Clifton as commissioners of array in Nottinghamshire in 1367.[7] He married Eleanor (before 1325), and secondly, Alice (1330), daughter of Sir Warren de Lisle. He was succeeded by his son, Sir Henry de Grey.

1 *CIPM*, XVII, p. 131.

2 In 1335, for example, two men named John de Grey served separately in the retinues of the Nicholas de Cantilupe and Hugh Audley, earl of Gloucester, and in 1340 the two namesakes served as knights in the retinues of William Montague and Henry of Lancaster, respectively. 1335: C 71/15, mm. 33, 42. 1340: E 36/203, fols 125v–26. Note that he had a brother and son named John.

3 For his career, see Walker, 'Grey of Codnor, *ODNB*; *CP*, VI, pp. 125–7.

4 *CFR, 1356–68*, p. 97.

5 E 36/203, fol. 126.

6 *CPR, 1345–48*, p. 315.

7 *CPR, 1348–50*, p. 383 (service with Meynell); *CPR, 1364–67*, p. 431 (service with Beler and others).

Greystoke, William Lord (1321–59) **(banneret)** Cumberland
CCR, 1346–49, p. 320; E 101/25/9, m. 3 (7); E 159/123, m. 170; E 372/191 (Bedfordshire)
Born and baptised at the family residence at Grimthorpe in Yorkshire, he held lands in that county as well as Bedfordshire, Cumberland, Hertfordshire, Northumberland and Westmorland.[1] After achieving his majority in 1342 he participated in the Breton expedition (with a warhorse valued at £50) in the same year, which signalled the beginning of his military career.[2] He took out royal protection for service on Lancaster's crusade to Prussia in 1351–52, and took part in the unsuccessful Anglo-Scottish negotiations concerning the release of David II, king of Scots, the following year.[3] In 1354 Greystoke was appointed captain of Berwick-upon-Tweed, and later pardoned for the town's surrender during his absence on Edward III's expedition to Reims (1359). He was accused of seizing land in Yorkshire from Hamo de Hessay 'by force of arms' in the mid 1340s and was appointed to serve as a justice of oyer and terminer in the same county the following decade (1353–54).[4] Sir John Boson, who served in Greystoke's sub-retinue in 1345–46, was appointed as one of his attorneys in 1349 and in 1351, as was Sir Ralph de Neville in the latter year.[5] Neville became

godfather of Greystoke's son, Ralph, in the same year.[6] Greystoke married, first, Lucy, daughter of Sir Anthony de Lucy, and secondly, Joan, daughter of Sir Henry Fitzhenry of Ravensworth. He died at the age of thirty-eight and was buried in Greystoke church (Cumberland).

1 *CIPM*, X, pp. 420–7.

2 E 36/204, fol. 83r (warhorse). On his career, see *CP*, VI, pp. 192–4; Keith Dockray, 'Greystoke family (per. 1321–1487)', *ODNB*, 2004.

3 *CPR, 1350–54*, p. 172; C 66/235, m. 16 (Prussia).

4 *CCR, 1346–49*, p. 585 (Hessay); *CPR, 1350–54*, p. 541; *CPR, 1354–58*, p. 68.

5 C 76/27, mm. 4, 5; *CPR, 1350–54*, p. 172.

6 Louis Hass, 'Social Connections between Parents and Godparents in Late Medieval Yorkshire' in *Studies on the Personal Name in Later Medieval England and Wales*, ed. Dave Postles and Joel T. Rosenthal (Kalamazoo, MI: Medieval Institute Publications, Western Michigan University, 2006), pp. 159–75 (p. 167).

Gumby, Stephen de (knight) Lincolnshire

E 101/25/9, m. 3 (17); E 159/123, m. 79; E 372/195 (Lincoln)

Stephen de Gumby, often recorded as Tumby in the administrative records, took out royal protection for service in John Montgomery's retinue in the Low Countries (1338).[1] He had small landholdings in Lincolnshire, and in 1348 was granted a royal licence to fell trees in the manors of Dene and Ingham after he had bought the custody of the lands following the death of Sir Oliver de Ingham.[2] Stephen married Mary, daughter and heir of Sir John de Courzoun (and relative of Ingham). He died before 1351.[3]

1 *CPR, 1334–38*, p. 539.

2 *CPR, 1348–50*, p. 95.

3 *CPR, 1350–54*, p. 113.

H(a)[..]heth, Edward de (archer)

E 101/35/2/10, m. 1d (207)

Halden, John le clerk son of William (pardon recipient) Nottinghamshire

CPR, 1345–48, p. 558

A native of Stanton on the Wolds; pardoned for the death of Simon son of William de Sibthorp.

Halden, John son of John (pardon recipient) Nottinghamshire

CPR, 1345–48, p. 558

John also originated from Stanton on the Wolds; pardoned for the death of Simon de Sibthorp.

Hale, John del (attendant) Lancashire

E 101/25/9, m. 3d (6)

Halen, Frank van (KG 1359) **(banneret)** Halen (Brabant)

E 101/25/9, m. 3 (6)

A first-generation Brabantine (not Flemish, as commonly thought), he was probably born in the 1320s. He was the brother of Sir Simon van Halen, lord of Perwez

(Brabant), and son of a Lombard money lender named John de Mirabello.[1] Frank first served with Edward III in the Low Countries (1340) and was retained by the king for life in 1347. As a reward for his services, most notably during Henry of Lancaster's expedition in Aquitaine (1345–46), he was granted the manors of Weston Patrick and Winchfield-by-Odiham and an annuity of £20 out of the manor of King's Somborne (Hampshire) for life by Lancaster, prior to 1361. Frank was appointed seneschal of Aquitaine in 1349; he was responsible for enlisting troops in preparation for Lancaster's arrival in the duchy and participated in the ensuing expedition (1349–50).[2] He and Sir Stephen de Cosington were sent by Lancaster to treat with Louis, count of Flanders, in 1351 concerning an extension of the Peace of Dunkirk. He had been made keeper of the castle of Rochefort in 1346 and seems to have resided there over the following decades; he was granted royal protection for two ships carrying corn from Sluys to Rochefort in 1353.[3] In 1355 the Black Prince paid him £66 13s 4d as a repayment of a loan.[4] He was made Knight of the Garter in 1359. Frank's connection with the house of Lancaster continued in the 1370s at which time he was also attendant at the court of the count of Flanders. He probably died soon after 1375.

1 On van Halen's career, see discussion and corresponding references in Chapter 7; Barber, *The Triumph of England*, pp. 515–16.
2 C 61/61, m. 5.
3 C 61/65, m. 6.
4 *BPR*, IV, p. 166.

Hall, John atte (esquire)
E 101/35/2/10, m. 1 (22)

Hall, John de la (archer)
E 101/35/2/10, m. 1d (184)

Hallam, William de (esquire) Yorkshire
E 101/35/2/10, m. 1 (34)

Hallum, Hugh de (archer) Lancashire
E 101/35/2/10, m. 2d (166)

Hallum, William de (of Warrington) (archer) Lancashire
E 101/35/2/10, m. 2d (173)
In 1360 William and his wife, Margaret, together with two others, allegedly disseised land from Elizabeth, daughter of Robert de Medburn, in Warrington. The following year William complained that John son of Gilbert de Haydock had stolen cattle from him.[1]
1 *Victoria History of the County of Lancaster*, III, p. 321, n. 4.

Halugh, John de (archer)
E 101/35/2/10, m. 3d (86)

Hardes, Thomas de (esquire)
E 101/35/2/10, m. 3 (175)

Harold, William (archer)
E 101/35/2/10, m. 2d (144)

Harper, Hamond le (archer)
E 101/35/2/10, m. 2d (168)

Harper, Hugh le (archer)
E 101/35/2/10, m. 2d (135)

Harper, John le (archer)
E 101/35/2/10, m. 1d (208)

Haslingden, Thomas de (archer) Lancashire
E 101/35/2/10, m. 3d (79)

Hastings, a companion of Ralph de (knight)
E 101/25/9, m. 3 (87)
An unknown companion and knight of Ralph de Hastings.

Hastings, Ralph de (*d.* 1346) **(knight)** Yorkshire
C 76/20, m. 15; E 101/25/9, m. 3 (4)
Ralph de Hastings was a veteran of the Scottish wars, having first served on a campaign with Sir William de Latimer in 1327.[1] He was a retainer of both Henry, third earl of Lancaster, and his successor, in whose retinue he regularly served from 1336.[2] He acted as constable and steward of the earl's honour of Pickering and held the shrievalty of Yorkshire and keepership of York castle (1337–40), where he had himself been imprisoned in 1332 along with two relatives (Edmund and William de Hastings), Robert le Chamberlain, Richard de Rawcliffe and others for their involvement in the murder of Edmund Darel.[3] Ralph served on numerous commissions in his home county, and was attacked at Beverley during his investigation of a concealed wool store in 1342.[4] He enlarged his family's estates, which included lands in Leicestershire, Norfolk, Northamptonshire and Yorkshire. He died in November 1346, within a month of leading the rearguard division against the Scots at Neville's Cross, and was buried at Sulby abbey (Northamptonshire). His son and heir of the same name continued the family's close association with the house of Lancaster through military service, first with Henry and then John of Gaunt.
1 C 71/11, m. 5.
2 See Simon Walker, 'Hastings family (*per. c.*1300–*c.*1450)', *ODNB*, Jan 2008; *Somerville*, p. 356.
3 *CPR, 1330–34*, p. 289.
4 *CPR, 1338–40*, p. 146.

Hastings, William de (knight)
C 76/20, m. 15; E 101/25/9, m. 3 (90)
He first appears as an esquire in Henry of Lancaster's retinue on the expedition to Scotland in 1336.[1] Two men of this name, one of whom is known as 'nephew' (*nepot*), were paid horse restoration of £30 and £20 respectively relating to service with Lancaster in 1338.[2] He was probably the relative and donee of Laurence de

Hastings, earl of Pembroke, and held lands in Berkshire, Cambridgeshire, Kent, Oxford and Wales.[3] In 1348 Sir William de Hastings and Robert de Elford, the former lieutenant of the late earl of Pembroke, owed 400 marks to William Clinton, earl of Huntingdon; the money was to be levied from their lands in Oxford.[4] He died sometime before 1352.[5]

1 E 101/15/12.
2 E 36/203, fol. 126.
3 CCR, 1346–49, p. 582; CPR, 1340–43, p. 515; CPR, 1348–50, pp. 274, 535; CPR, 1354–58, p. 58.
4 CCR, 1346–49, p. 587.
5 CPR, 1350–54, p. 280.

Hastings, William de (esquire)
E 101/35/2/10, m. 1 (54)
This William is probably the man described as 'nephew' who served in Lancaster's retinue in Scotland (1336) and the Low Countries (1338); he was paid £20 horse restoration for the latter campaign.[1] A William de Hastings, esquire, gave testimony at the armorial dispute between Lords Lovell and Morley in 1386.[2]

1 E 36/203, fol. 126.
2 C 47/6/1, no. 171.

Hatton, Henry de (archer) Cheshire
E 101/35/2/10, m. 2d (150)

Havering, Richard de (knight) Essex
C 76/20, m. 15; C 81/321/18522; E 101/25/9, m. 3 (14); E 159/123, m. 173d
Richard, son of William de Havering, probably originated from Havering-atte-Bower (Essex).[1] He first took up arms with Henry of Lancaster in the Low Countries (1338), and continued to serve exclusively with the earl up to the Reims expedition (1359). The patronage of his retinue captain was demonstrated in 1341 when Havering was pardoned at Lancaster's request for the issues of £7 3s 4d, which had been deemed forfeit by justices of oyer and terminer in Hertfordshire.[2] In 1364 he allegedly committed waste on the lands of John de Sayer in Essex, and his own servants were robbed in Oxford in the same year.[3] He had small landholdings in the counties of Bedford, Essex, Lincoln and Wiltshire, and was appointed as a local commissioner in the latter county in 1366 and 1375.[4]

1 E 372/191, m. 6.
2 CPR, 1341–43, p. 281.
3 BPR, IV, pp. 521–2; CPR, 1361–64, p. 542.
4 CPR, 1364–67, p. 359; CPR, 1374–77, p. 153.

Havering, Thomas de (esquire) Essex
E 101/35/2/10, m. 2 (102)

Hawe, John de la (archer)
E 101/35/2/10, m. 3d (71)

Haydock, Matthew de (knight) Lancashire
E 101/25/9, m. 3 (75)
Matthew de Haydock served with Ralph, Lord Stafford on the Breton expedition in 1342 and had intended to fight under the same banner in Aquitaine (1345–46) but changed to Lancaster's retinue.[1] Matthew and two of his relatives (Gilbert and William), along with comrades from the recent expedition in Aquitaine, formed part of the infamous 'Dalton gang' which attacked the manor of Beams (Berkshire) in 1347. He may be the same person who served as a justice of oyer and terminer in Lancashire in 1318.[2]
1 C 61/57, m. 5; C 76/17, m. 32.
2 CPR, 1317–21, p. 184.

Hebden, Richard de (knight) Lincolnshire
C 61/58, m. 1; C 76/20, m. 15; E 101/25/9, m. 3 (20); E 159/123, m. 139
Hebden first took up arms on the Aquitaine expedition (1345–46), and thereafter served on three campaigns in Lancaster's retinue. He was a trusted knight of the earl and member of his council of war; Hebden was among the men who recaptured the town of Villefranche in 1346. He appointed the same attorney (Thomas Sleford) as did Sir Alexander Auncel to represent him during Lancaster's intended Breton expedition in 1355.[1] Hebden's property in Lincolnshire was supplemented by land in Coniston (Yorkshire) which he held of Isabel, widow of Robert de Clifford, by homage and fealty and by doing suit to the court of Skipton every three weeks.[2]
1 C 76/33, m. 9.
2 CIPM, XI, p. 248.

Helden, Thomas de (archer)
E 101/35/2/10, m. 3d. (30)

Helpiston, Robert de (clerk) Norfolk
CCR, 1346–49, p. 67; C 76/20, m. 20
For his administrative role in 1345–46, see Chapter 4. He may have served in Aquitaine with Edmund, earl of Kent, in 1325.[1]
1 C 61/34, m. 5.

Henan, Sansset de (esquire)
E 101/35/2/10, m. 1 (24)

Hending, Walter (archer)
E 101/35/2/10, m. 3d (68)

Henhull, Henry de (esquire) Cheshire
E 101/35/2/10, m. 2 (129)

Henley, Henry de (esquire) Shropshire
E 101/35/2/10, m. 3 (169)

Henry, Yevan ap (archer)
E 101/35/2/10, m. 3d (55)

Yevan was a Welshman, probably of mixed birth given that 'Henry' is not a Welsh patronym.

Herscy, John de (knight) Yorkshire
E 101/25/9, m. 3 (71)
John was most likely a relative of Sir Hugh Herscy, who served on several campaigns during Edward I's Scottish wars. The Aquitaine expedition (1345–46) may have been the only occasion that John performed military service. He was the receiver of Sir Thomas de Furnivall and Robert Torald of Gayneburgh. In 1361 Herscy was pardoned for non-appearance before the King's Bench concerning pleas to render account during his time as receiver for Furnivall and Torald because he had submitted himself to Fleet prison.[1]
1 *CPR, 1361–64*, p. 12.

Hethersett, Esmund de (esquire) Norfolk
E 101/35/2/10, m. 2 (69)

Hey, Robert le (esquire)
E 101/35/2/10, m. 3 (184)

Higham, John de (clerk) Northamptonshire
C 76/20, m. 15
John only served twice overseas with Lancaster (1345–46, 1359). He was parson of Denford church (Northamptonshire). In 1345 John son of John Higham held a small piece of land in the Bedfordshire hundred of Flitt.[1]
1 C 47/2/41, no. 3.

Hok, Roger (attendant)
E 101/25/9, m. 3d (21)

Holdington, John de (archer)
E 101/35/2/10, m. 1d (235)

Holland, Thomas de (archer) Lincolnshire
E 101/35/2/10, m. 3d (31)

Hornby, Edmund de (archer) Lancashire
E 101/35/2/10, m. 3d (53)

Horshale, William de (archer) Cheshire
E 101/35/2/10, m. 2d (154)

Hotham, George de (knight)
E 101/35/2/10, m. 1 (95)
Hotham, like Favell, Coudray and Secre, may have been knighted at some point during the expedition in 1345–46. He is possibly a native of Yorkshire, where Hotham manor is situated.

Hotham, Robert de (esquire)
E 101/35/2/10, m. 2 (120)

Howath, Edmund de (archer)
E 101/35/2/10, m. 3d (50)

Howergh, John (archer)
E 101/35/2/10, m. 2d (94)

Howes, John de (pardon recipient) Northamptonshire
CPR, 1345–48, p. 557
Pardoned for the death of Edmund le Bruer of Mithelar.

Hugh, Nicholas fitz (attendant)
E 101/25/9, m. 3d (27)

Hull, Walter (attendant) Yorkshire
E 101/25/9, m. 3d (14)

Hunt, John (of Altofts) (archer) Yorkshire
E 101/35/2/10, m. 2d (112)

Hunt, William le (archer)
E 101/35/2/10, m. 2d (123)

Hunte of Burghton, John (archer) Norfolk
E 101/35/2/10, m. 2d (114)

Hunter, Nicholas le (archer)
E 101/35/2/10, m. 1d (216)

Hurell, William (attendant)
E 101/25/9, m. 3d (5)

Hurleton, John de (archer)
E 101/35/2/10, m. 3d (27)

Hurleton, William de (archer)
E 101/35/2/10, m. 3d (26)

Huwet, John (attendant)
E 101/25/9, m. 3d (13)

Hykeden, Robert de (archer)
E 101/35/2/10, m. 3d (19)

Ilketshall, Robert de (esquire) Suffolk
E 101/35/2/10, m. 2 (143)

Illey, Richard de (esquire) Norfolk
E 101/35/2/10, m. 2 (134)
He may have been the man who was a knight bachelor of the Black Prince by 1359.[1]
1 *BPR*, IV, p. 320.

Joete, Walter (archer)
E 101/35/2/10, m. 2d (98)

John, Richard son of (attendant)
E 101/25/9, m. 3d (9)

Kelyng, John (pardon recipient) Somerset
CPR, 1345–48, p. 557
John and Matthew Kelyng, and John de Bolewyk were pardoned for the death of
Richard Boye.

Kelyng, Matthew (pardon recipient) Somerset
CPR, 1345–48, p. 557
Matthew and John Kelyng were pardoned, together with John de Bolewyk, for the
death of Richard Boye.

Kenilworth, Henry de (archer) Warwickshire
E 101/35/2/10, m. 2d (104)

Keu, Hugh le (attendant)
E 101/25/9, m. 3d (2)

Killinghall, Thomas de (archer) Yorkshire
E 101/35/2/10, m. 3d (75)

Kippye, Nichol (esquire)
E 101/35/2/10, m. 1 (60)

Kirkby, Roger de (archer) Lancashire
E 101/35/2/10, m. 3d (23)

Knap, William (archer)
E 101/35/2/10, m. 2d (109)

Knutsford, John de (archer) Cheshire
E 101/35/2/10, m. 2d (137)

Knutsford, Stephen de (archer) Cheshire
E 101/35/2/10, m. 2d (138)

Knypersley, Richard de (archer)
E 101/35/2/10, m. 2d (148)

Lalande, eight esquires with Henry de (esquire)
E 101/35/2/10, m. 1 (53)
Henry was probably indigenous to Aquitaine, although his anglicised forename is highly unusual, probably resulting from a clerical whim. He was accompanied by eight esquires.

Lalande, Ponset de (esquire)
E 101/35/2/10, m. 1 (66)
Ponset, a native of Aquitaine, was a likely relative of Henry de Lalande.

Langton, William de (esquire) Leicestershire
E 101/35/2/10, m. 2 (111)

Lamothe, Johan de (esquire) Langon (Gironde)
E 101/35/2/10, m. 1 (11)
Johan belonged to the family of the lords of Roquetaillade and the co-lords of Langon.

Lancaster, Thomas de (esquire) Lancashire
Froissart, *Chronicles of England*, p. 140
Thomas' service in Aquitaine (1345–46) is not corroborated by the royal administrative sources but, nevertheless, his service in Lancaster's retinue and his command of Montpouillan (1345) should not be dismissed.

Landefey, Roger (archer)
E 101/35/2/10, m. 2d (111)

Landon, Richard de (archer)
E 101/35/2/10, m. 1d (261)

Langshaw, Adam de (archer)
E 101/35/2/10, m. 2d (140)

Langtree, William de (archer) Lancashire
E 101/35/2/10, m. 3 (17)
William originated from Langtree, which formed part of the township of Standish-with-Langtree.

Lawton, Richard de (archer) Northumberland
E 101/35/2/10, m. 1d (224)

Lawton, William de (archer) Northumberland
E 101/35/2/10, m. 1d (223)

Lee, Richard de la (esquire)
E 101/35/2/10, m. 3 (172)

Leicester, John de (archer) Leicestershire
E 101/35/2/10, m. 1d (211)

Leicester, William de (esquire) Leicestershire
E 101/35/2/10, m. 1 (59)

Lese, Esmund de (esquire)
E 101/35/2/10, m. 2 (140)

Leuthenour, Petray (d'Aguillon) (esquire) Aiguillon (Lot-et-Garonne)
E 101/35/2/10, m. 1 (67)

Leynthale, William de (archer)
E 101/35/2/10, m. 3d (58)

Lilley, John (archer) Hertfordshire
E 101/35/2/10, m. 3d (28)

Lillibrook, Ranulf de (esquire) Berkshire
E 101/35/2/10, m. 1 (10)

Lindsey, Robert de (esquire) Suffolk
E 101/35/2/10, m. 3 (164)

Lolles, Galfrey (attendant)
E 101/25/9, m. 3d (17)

Londsdale, John de (archer) Lancashire
E 101/35/2/10, m. 1d (247)

Loring, Neil (*c.* 1315–86) (KG 1349) **(knight)** Bedfordshire
C 76/20, m. 15; C 76/22, m. 6; E 101/25/9, m. 3 (11)
The Loring family had been established in Bedfordshire since the twelfth century. Neil, son of Roger de Loring of Chalgrave, was perhaps the most celebrated and accomplished knight in Lancaster's retinue. He first appears as an esquire on the Scottish expedition of 1335, and went on to distinguish himself on several occasions over the course of a long and colourful career in arms; most notably at Sluys (1340), after which he was knighted and granted a royal annuity of £20, and at Romorantin during the Black Prince's chevauchée (1356) which culminated in the battle of Poitiers.[1] It was during this battle that Loring was 'appointed to be in attendance on the prince's person'. He was compensated £8 for a horse and £21 for two horses (and one of his esquires' mounts) lost during his service in 1338 and 1340.[2] Loring performed several diplomatic roles in the 1350s and 1360s. He was closely associated with the Black Prince, Lancaster and Edward III, all of whom endowed

him with pensions and lands, although it was the former who became his greatest patron, and he served as chamberlain and a member of the prince's council from 1351. He benefited greatly from the largesse of the prince who bestowed a multitude of gifts on him, including furs, horses and armour.[3] Loring, like Grailly, van Halen and Fitzsimon, was a founding knight of the Order of the Garter but did not serve at the battle of Crécy; his close ties with the Black Prince are reflected by his occupation of the tenth stall of the Order on the prince's side. Loring held land in Bedfordshire, Cornwall, Devonshire and Norfolk. He was associated with the Peyvre family, who also originated from Bedfordshire; he served alongside Sir Nicholas de Peyvre in Aquitaine (1345–46), and his youngest daughter, Margaret, married Thomas de Peyvre. Thomas Loring, clerk, and probably a relative, acted as his attorney in 1348, 1349 and 1351, and also for Sir John de Loring, who also served in the Black Prince's retinue (1348).[4] Loring was a pious man who invested in several churches and religious foundations. He died on 18 March 1386 and was buried at Dunstable priory church. He married Margaret, daughter and heir of Ralph Beauple of Cnubestone (Devon), by whom he had two daughters, Isabel and Margaret.

1 *CPR, 1334–8*, p. 169 (1335); Kingsford, 'Loring, Sir Neil', *ODNB*.
2 E 101/35/3, m. 1d; E 101/389/8, m. 4.
3 See *BPR*.
4 *CPR, 1350–54*, p. 179 (Neil); C 76/26, m. 4; C 76/26, mm. 4, 5 (John).

Loring, Piers (esquire)
E 101/35/2/10, m. 3 (174)

Lostock, Thomas de (archer) Lancashire
E 101/35/2/10, m. 1d (267)

Loudam, Thomas de (esquire) Suffolk
E 101/35/2/10, m. 2 (145)

Lovedale, John de (knight)
E 101/25/9, m. 3 (59)
John is mentioned by Froissart as one of the knights who served in the garrison at Auberoche under van Halen's captaincy in 1345. He is not to be confused with a Brabantine of a similar name who was part of Edward III's household and served with the king at Crécy. He may have married Joan (*b.* 1331), daughter of Thomas de Northwood.[1]
1 *CIPM*, XI, pp. 16–47.

Lovel, Philip (knight) Wiltshire
E 101/25/9, m. 3 (66)
A probable relative of John, Lord Lovel (*c.* 1314–49) who served in Henry of Lancaster's retinue in 1344. Philip was also a likely relative of the Lovel family of Titchmarsh. He fought with Lancaster on the Reims expedition (1359).[1] The daughter and heir of a Philip Lovel married Nicholas de Seymore; this Philip Lovel held land in Wiltshire and died before 1362.[2]
1 C 76/37, m. 2; C 76/38, m. 17.

2 *CIPM*, X, p. 514.

Lovel, Philip (esquire) Wiltshire
E 101/35/2/10, m. 2 (80)

Ludlowe, Adam de (archer) Shropshire
E 101/35/2/10, m. 2d (153)

Lutelere, Ralph de (archer)
E 101/35/2/10, m. 1d (238)

Luttrell, Andrew (*c.* 1313–90) **(knight)** Lincolnshire
CCR, 1343–46, p. 540; C 76/25, mm. 12d, 14d; E 159/123, m. 124; E 372/190, m. 14d.
Andrew was the son of Sir Geoffrey Luttrell of Irnham (Lincolnshire), who is famously depicted in the Luttrell psalter. A deponent at the Scrope v. Grosvenor dispute, his career spanned more than half a century and, like Cosington and Loring, he established himself in the Black Prince's retinue having served regularly in Aquitaine after his first expedition there with Henry of Lancaster.[1] He was paid 12 marks and 20 marks for horse restoration in 1337, and compensated with £10 13s 4d for loss of a horse relating to his service in 1359.[2] He received a gift of £20 from the Black Prince (1358) as a reward for his 'good service in Gascony', and numerous other gifts including a tun of wine for his passage to Aquitaine in 1363.[3] He is described as the king's sergeant-at-arms (1354), and was awarded £10 by Edward III for bringing news of the Reims expedition to England in 1359.[4] In the following year he went on pilgrimage to the Holy Land, and he later granted land to the Austin friars of Stamford and founded a chantry at Croxton abbey (Leicester).[5] He was a justice of the peace in his home county of Lincoln in the 1350s and 1360s. Luttrell held lands in the counties of Leicester, Lincoln, Nottingham and York.[6] He married, Beatrice, daughter of Geoffrey Scrope, by whom he had a son and heir of the same name (*d.* 1397), and secondly Hawise, daughter of Philip le Despenser. He died on 6 September 1390 and was buried at St Andrew's church, Irnham.[7]
1 *Scrope and Grosvenor*, I, p. 243.
2 E 101/20/17, m. 10d; E 101/388/5, m. 19 (1337); E 101/393/11, fol. 71r (1359).
3 *BPR*, IV, pp. 251, 500–1.
4 *CPR, 1354–58*, p. 162; E 101/393/11, fol. 73r.
5 Robert W. Dunning, 'Luttrell family (*per. c.*1200–1428)', *ODNB*, 2004 [accessed 29 May 2015].
6 *CCR 1343–46*, pp. 597–8, 602; *CIPM*, VIII, pp. 422–3.
7 *CIPM*, XVI, pp. 406–7; *CP*, X, pp. 287–8.

Luttrell, a companion of Andrew (knight)
E 101/25/9, m. 3 (86)
An unknown companion of Sir Andrew Luttrell.

Lymbury, John de (knight) Cambridgeshire/Lincolnshire
E 101/25/9, m. 3 (22)
Sir John de Lymbury was perhaps the oldest serving knight in Lancaster's retinue; a veteran of the Scottish wars in the reigns of Edward I and Edward II, he first

took up arms as a 'sergeant' with Philip Darcy in 1301, was knighted by 1329, and continued to fight regularly on Scottish campaigns up to the mid 1330s. The Aquitaine expedition (1345–46) was the only occasion when John served overseas. He was closely associated with the families of Beaumont and Darcy, both of whom were supporters of Thomas, earl of Lancaster. He served on commissions of array and of oyer and terminer in Cambridgeshire in the 1320s and, despite being granted an exemption from holding local offices in 1333, he was appointed to raise troops in Lincolnshire and lead them to Newcastle for service in Scotland in 1335.[1] He was accused of breaking into Sir Robert Darcy's manor of Scott Willoughby (Lincolnshire) and stealing timber from there in 1329, along with his relative (Edmund de Lymbury), Alexander Auncel, Roger de Trykingham and others.[2] He held land in Cambridgeshire but probably originated from the Lincolnshire manor of Great Limber. He married Juliana Darcy.

1 Cambridgeshire: *CPR 1321–24*, pp. 268, 274, 424; *CPR, 1324–27*, p. 350. Lincolnshire: C 71/15, m. 46d; *CPR, 1330–34*, p. 457 (exemption).
2 *CPR, 1327–30*, pp. 476, 564. Edmund had served with Sir John in Henry Beaumont's retinue in Scotland (1315): C 71/8, m. 6.

Lymbury, Philip de (*d.* 1367) (knight) Lincolnshire

C 76/20, m. 15; E 101/25/9, m. 3 (21); E 159/123, m. 126

Philip was probably the son of Sir John de Lymbury. His military career spanned 1336 to 1359, during which he lost horses valued at 5 marks (1337), £8 (1338) and £30 (1342).[1] He went on pilgrimage twice, including at least once to the Holy Land.[2] Philip was a witness to several of Henry of Lancaster's charters. He received gifts of a silver cup and a piece of silver called a 'biker' (enamelled on the bottom, with lids with boats, and gilt on one side), from the Black Prince in 1348.[3] In the following year Roger de Trykingham, who had served as an esquire in Lancaster's retinue (1345–46), was appointed as Philip's attorney.[4] Sir Alexander Auncel, who like Trykingham, was affiliated with Sir John de Lymbury, performed administrative duties in Brittany with Philip (1356–57).[5] The latter was appointed as a justice of the peace in Lincolnshire (1361–65), where the majority of his landholdings lay.[6] He also held property in Bedfordshire, Cambridgeshire and Wiltshire.[7] He married Joan, by whom he had a son also named Philip. He died at Constantinople on 6 July 1367.[8]

1 E 101/19/36, m. 8; E 101/35/3, m. 2d; E 36/203, fol. 127.
2 *CPR 1345–48*, p. 422 (1347); *CIPM*, XII, p. 129 (1367).
3 *BPR*, IV, pp. 68, 73.
4 C 76/27, m. 3.
5 Fowler, *King's Lieutenant*, p. 183.
6 *CPR, 1361–64*, pp. 65, 67.
7 *CIPM*, XII, pp. 128–9; E 372/191, m. 17d.
8 *CIPM*, XII, pp. 128–9.

Magot, John (archer)

E 101/35/2/10, m. 1d (217)

Mallerbe, William (archer)

E 101/35/2/10, m. 2d (116)

Mallory, William (esquire)
E 101/35/2/10, m. 2 (83)

Manchester, Edmund de (knight) Lancashire
E 101/25/9, m. 3 (61)
Edmund was pardoned (1347) for his part in the attack on the manor of Beams led by Sir John de Dalton in 1347.[1] He became an indentured retainer of the Black Prince in 1351 and contracted to serve the prince with one esquire at peace and war.[2] He was granted an annuity of 20 marks in 1351 as a retaining fee, increased to £40 two years later.[3] Edmund's servant, Nicholas Hurley, was murdered by John Gamel of Norton (Leicestershire) who was pardoned for the crime in 1356.[4]
1 *CPR, 1348–50*, p. 339.
2 *BPR*, IV, p. 12.
3 *BPR*, IV, pp. 91, 103.
4 *CPR, 1354–58*, p. 377.

Mandeville, Richard de (esquire)
E 101/35/2/10, m. 2 (137)

Manion, Ferdinand (of London) (esquire) London
C 76/23, m. 15
Ferdinand took out royal protection on 27 September 1346 for service in Aquitaine with Henry of Lancaster, which suggests that he did not arrive in the duchy until the later stages of the expedition.[1] A Ferdinand Manion had served together with Pedro de Loupes Manion of Spain in the retinue of Master John Galiciano, king's clerk, in 1325.[2] Ferdinand, or a namesake, was married to Margaret in 1338.[3]
1 C 76/23, m. 15.
2 *CPR, 1324–27*, p. 181.
3 *CPR, 1338–40*, pp. 10–11.

Marbury, Richard de (archer) Cheshire
E 101/35/2/10, m. 2d (156)

Marbury, Simon de (archer) Cheshire
E 101/35/2/10, m. 2d (155)

Marchemond, Robert (esquire)
E 101/35/2/10, m. 1 (35)

Marchys, Roger (esquire)
E 101/35/2/10, m. 2 (150)

Mare, Peter de la (*c.* 1292–1349) **(knight)** Gloucestershire
C 76/20, m. 15; E 101/25/9, m. 3 (8); E 159/123, m. 140; E 372/192 (Oxford)
Peter de la Mare began his military career in 1318 in the retinue of the marcher lord, John de Giffard of Brimpsfield, and was among the most experienced of Lancaster's knights. His considerable wealth is reflected by the destrier with which he served in 1338, valued at £100.[1] Peter was appointed as keeper of the peace in Wiltshire 1332,

but was granted an exemption from holding local offices the following year, and thus did not take up a local commission again until the 1340s.[2] He was a renowned and trusted office of Lancaster, serving as an attorney when the earl was detained as surety against the king's debts in 1340.[3] He retired from active warfare after the Aquitaine expedition (1345–46), but continued to perform important administrative duties for the Lancastrian household, serving as the earl's attorney in 1347 and as steward of his lands in 1348–49.[4] He was a prominent donee of Lancaster and was naturally associated with other members of the earl's entourage, serving with Simon Simeon on an oyer and termier commission in 1347.[5] Peter's estates were scattered across Gloucestershire, Hertfordshire, Oxfordshire and Wiltshire.[6] In the last county he held land directly of the king in return for the keeping of a tower at Devizes castle, with a partner in wartime, and a 20s fee, for the tower's upkeep, in time of peace. He also held land of Sir Nicholas de Peyvre in Hertfordshire. He married Joan and had two sons, Robert and Thomas, who served as a knight and esquire, respectively, alongside their father in Aquitaine.

1 E 36/203, fol. 126.
2 *CPR, 1330–34*, pp. 294–6.
3 Fowler, *King's Lieutenant*, p. 37.
4 *Somerville*, p. 362.
5 *CPR, 1345–48*, p. 318.
6 *CIPM*, IX, p. 309.

Mare, Piers de la (esquire) Gloucestershire
E 101/35/2/10, m. 2 (88)

Mare, Robert de la (*c.* 1314–82) **(knight)** Gloucestershire
C 76/20, m. 15; E 101/25/9, m. 3 (28)
Robert, son of Peter de la Mare, fought under Henry of Lancaster's banner in 1338 and continued to serve exclusively in the earl's retinue up to the Treaty of Brétigny (1360). He received 40 marks for horse restoration whilst on campaign in the Low Countries (1338), and acted as one of three horse appraisers in Aquitaine in 1350.[1] Robert continued his family's tradition of service with the Lancastrian household; he was among the earl's charter witnesses and executors and, like his father, was appointed steward of the earl's lands.[2] He was granted a portable altar by Pope Clement VI in 1355, who also prayed for Robert's wife, Matilda, during her absence from church on account of her pregnancy in the same year.[3] His majority landholdings in Wiltshire were augmented by property in Gloucestershire, Hertfordshire and Oxfordshire.[4] Despite a grant of exemption from holding local offices against his will (1358), Robert served on local commissions in the 1360s and 1370s, including a charge of coastal defences in his home county.[5] He had a son by Matilda named Robert.

1 E 36/203, fol. 126.
2 *Somerville*, pp. 47, 360.
3 *CPP*, p. 271.
4 *CIPM*, XV, pp. 215–16; C 47/2/41, no. 5.
5 See *CPR, 1374–77*, pp. 152–3 and numerous other references in *CPR*.

Mare, Thomas de la (esquire) Gloucestershire
E 101/35/2/10, m. 1 (19)
Thomas may have been the esquire of that name who served with Reynold de la
Mare during the War of Saint-Sardos (1324). He was part of Henry of Lancaster's
retinue in Aquitaine (1345–46), at Calais (1347) and on the Reims expedition (1359).

Marshal, Alan le (esquire)
E 101/35/2/10, m. 2 (77)

Marshal, Thomas le (archer)
E 101/35/2/10, m. 1d (202)

Martin, Hughy (esquire)
E 101/35/2/10, m. 1 (44)

Martinscroft, Robert de (archer) Lancashire
E 101/35/2/10, m. 2d (164)

Marton, Adam de (archer) Cheshire
E 101/35/2/10, m. 3d (49)

Marton, William de (archer) Cheshire
E 101/35/2/10, m. 3d (48)

Melbourne, Thomas de (esquire) Derbyshire
E 101/35/2/10, m. 3 (165)

Melton, John de (esquire) Leicestershire
E 101/35/2/10, m. 2 (122)
John served as an esquire in Lancaster's retinue in 1336.[1]
1 E 101/15/12.

Meoblese, Gilbert de (archer)
E 101/35/2/10, m. 3d (38)

Merlin, John (esquire)
E 101/35/2/10, m. 2 (97)

Mess, Hugh de (archer)
E 101/35/2/10, m. 1d (193)

Meynell, Hugh (c. 1302–1363) **(banneret)** Derbyshire
E 101/25/9, m. 3 (4); C 47/2/58, m. 2d; C 76/22, mm. 6, 11; C 76/25, m. 24d; *CPR,
1345–48*, p. 183; E 159/123, m. 127d; E 372/195 (Stafford); C 76/20, m. 15
Meynell's family were longstanding supporters of the earls of Lancaster. Hugh probably first took up arms on the Scottish expedition in 1336; he was compensated
20 marks for a lost warhorse in 1338 and was captured along with Sir Adam de

Everingham during the siege of Tournai (1340) – Edward III helped secure both men's ransoms.[1] A week before Lancaster's army was due to muster at Southampton in 1345, Meynell was in London, where he witnessed an indenture made between the earls of Huntingdon and Pembroke.[2] He does not appear to have served on a military campaign after the expedition to Aquitaine (1345–46), but was regularly appointed to serve on various commissions in the East Midlands in the 1340s and 1350s. His appointments included assessor and collector of wool, justice of the peace (with John de Grey of Codnor) and commissions of array and of oyer and terminer in Derbyshire (with John Blount), Staffordshire and Nottinghamshire.[3] On several occasions Meynell was commissioned to inquire into crimes committed against Henry of Lancaster, such as hunting and felling trees on the earl's lands.[4] Meynell's landholdings were spread across nine counties: Berkshire, Derbyshire, Lancashire, Leicestershire, Nottinghamshire, Oxfordshire, Staffordshire, Warwickshire and Worcestershire.[5] In 1345 he became entangled in a legal dispute with Joan, widow of Sir Ralph Basset of Drayton, concerning land in Nottinghamshire which he had inherited through his wife, Alesia.[6] Joan led reprisal attacks on his property in Leicestershire in 1346. He was succeeded in 1363 by his son and heir, Sir Richard Meynell.

1 E 36/203, fol. 126 (1338).
2 *CCR 1343–46*, p. 567.
3 *CCR, 1341–43*, p. 229; *CFR*, V, p. 285 (collector of wool); *CCR, 1349–54*, p. 436 (tax collector); *CCR, 1349–54*, p. 181 (Grey); *CPR, 1348–50*, p. 312 (Blount).
4 *CPR, 1348–50*, p. 173; *CPR, 1358–61*, p. 410.
5 *CIPM*, XI, pp. 394–96; E 159/123, m. 127d; E 372/195 (Stafford).
6 *CCR, 1343–46*, p. 568; *CPR, 1345–48*, p. 183.

Meynell, John (esquire) Derbyshire
E 101/35/2/10, m. 1 (58)

Meynell, Richard (esquire) Derbyshire
E 101/35/2/10, m. 2 (106)

Meynell, William (knight) Derbyshire
E 101/25/9, m. 3 (69)
William, son of Sir Hugh Meynell, first appears in Henry of Lancaster's retinue in Brittany (1342), and remained in the earl's service up to the Normandy-Brittany expedition in the following decade. We cannot be certain whether this William, or a namesake, served as a steward of Laurence de Hastings, earl of Pembroke, in 1346.[1] He is not to be confused with William, son of Sir Richard Meynell (*d.* 1376).[2] A William Meynell 'and many others of his confederacy' attempted to burn the abbey of Burton-on-Trent (Staffordshire), and attacked the abbot's servants at his property in Burnedston.[3]

1 *CPR, 1348–50*, p. 199.
2 *CIPM*, XIV, p. 272–3.
3 *CPR, 1354–58*, pp. 164–5.

Michel, Adam (archer)
E 101/35/2/10, m. 3d (56)

Michel, Thomas (archer)
E 101/35/2/10, m. 1d (229)

Micol, Arnaut (esquire) Bazas (Gironde)
E 101/35/2/10, m. 1 (41)
Arnaut Micol of Bazas was exiled from his home town in 1325. He was a merchant who became a sergeant and butler of Edward III in the 1330s.[1] He was twice robbed of his goods in England (1328).[2] Arnaut is described as a burgess of Bordeaux in 1344 and was made prévôt of Bazas and Bazadais by Henry of Lancaster after having served in the earl's retinue (1345–46). He was pardoned as an adherent of Thomas, earl of Lancaster, in 1322 and was granted a general pardon in 1333.[3]
1 For his career, see Chapter 9.
2 *CPR, 1327–30*, pp. 281, 284.
3 C 61/35, m. 15d; *CPR, 1327–30*, p. 489.

Middleton, Ellis de (archer)
E 101/35/2/10, m. 3d (88)

Misterton, William de (esquire) Leicestershire
E 101/35/2/10, m. 3 (159)

Mohun, Payn de (esquire) Somerset
C 76/20, m. 15; E 101/35/2/10, m. 1 (1)
Payn was the fourth son of John, Lord Mohun and the older brother of Sir Reginald de Mohun. He spent his entire military career (1336–49) in the retinue of Henry of Lancaster, who granted Payn the manor of Ebboth (Monmouthshire) and a life annuity of £20 from the manor of Godmanchester (Huntingdonshire).[1] He held land in Somerset. He was compensated £16 and 1 mark for horse restoration (1338), and he sold two horses in Aquitaine (1350) for £11 13s 4d.[2] Payn was among the witnesses to Lancaster's indenture with Sir Edmund de Ufford and a grant of charter in 1348.[3] His social status and prominence in the earl's household is reflected by his position at the top of Lancaster's retinue roll for the Scottish expedition in 1336. He was indicted for various felonies and trespasses in his home county in 1344.[4] Despite his adequate wealth, Payn never took up knighthood.
1 *CPR, 1361–64*, p. 50.
2 E 36/203, fol. 126; E 404/508/52.
3 *CPR, 1348–50*, p. 201.
4 *CCR, 1343–46*, pp. 361, 376.

Mohun, Reginald de (knight) Somerset
C 61/58, m. 3; C 76/20, m. 15; C 81/1730/23; E 101/25/9, m. 3 (27)
Reginald was the youngest son of John, Lord Mohun (1330) and a veteran of the War of Saint-Sardos (1324–25). He served consistently with Henry of Lancaster from 1336 up to the earl's second expedition in Aquitaine (1349). He was paid £10 and 40 marks for horse restoration relating to service in 1324 and 1338, and was compensated with £30 for his destrier lost on the Breton expedition (1342).[1] Reginald was a donee of Lancaster and among the witnesses to the earl's indenture with Sir Edmund de Ufford (1347). He held lands in Dorset and Huntingdonshire.[2] In

1349 he appointed four attorneys before setting out on campaign overseas.[3] He was the younger brother of Payn de Mohun.

1 E 101/17/2, m. 1; E 36/203, fol. 126; E 36/204, fol. 83r.
2 *CFR*, V, p. 403; *CIPM*, VIII, p. 373.
3 C 76/27, m. 4.

Mondesleygh, John de (archer) Norfolk
E 101/35/2/10, m. 3d (36)

Montferrand, Bertran de (*d. c.* 1361) **(knight)** Montferrand (Gironde)
E 101/25/9, m. 3 (83)
Bertran de Barès, lord of Montferrand, more commonly known as Bertran I de Montferrand, was the son of Amaubin III de Barès (*d. c.* 1341). He twice served in Henry of Lancaster's retinue in Aquitaine (1345 and 1349), and was part of the earl's council at Avignon in 1353. He was reportedly among the Aquitanians dubbed knights before the battle of Bergerac on 24 August 1345. As a reward for his service to Lancaster Bertran was made captain and governor of the castle and town of La Rochelle, an office he held up until his death in 1361.[1] He was also captain and governor of the castle, town and jurisdiction of the land of Aunis. He was the elder brother of Johan de Montferrand and the father of Bertran II de Montferrand.
1 See references in C 61/74.

Moore, Henry de la (archer) Cheshire
E 101/35/2/10, m. 3d (22)

Moore, John de la (archer) Cheshire
E 101/35/2/10, m. 3d (47)

Moore, Robert de la (archer) Cheshire
E 101/35/2/10, m. 3 (14)

Moore, Robert de la (archer) Cheshire
E 101/35/2/10, m. 1d (215)

Mortimer, Constantine (knight) Norfolk
C 81/322/18663
Constantine belonged to the Norfolk branch of the Mortimer family. He was associated with the household of Aymer de Valence, earl of Pembroke, and was one of the hostages held by Jean de Loumilly in the county of Bar as surety against Pembroke's ransom (£10,400) following the earl's release in 1317.[1] He is not to be confused with his father of the same name who was steward of Edward III's sister, Eleanor, and who served on numerous commissions in Norfolk in the 1320s and 1340s. It was his father's yeoman, William le Peyntour, who was sent to procure the younger Constantine's release from prison in October 1324.[2] He was knighted by 1335, and served with Henry of Lancaster at Calais in 1347 after having returned from Aquitaine with Henry at the beginning of that year. Constantine had a small landholding in his home county.

1 On Pembroke's capture and ransom: J. R. Seymour, 'Valence, Aymer de, eleventh earl of Pembroke (*d.* 1324)', *ODNB*, Jan 2008 [accessed 29 May 2015].
2 *CPR, 1324–27*, p. 39.

Morton, Robert de (archer) Derbyshire
E 101/35/2/10, m. 1d (222)

Morton, Roger de (archer) Derbyshire
E 101/35/2/10, m. 1d (220)

Morton, William de (archer) Derbyshire
E 101/35/2/10, m. 1d (221)

Mounteney, Teobaud de (esquire) Essex
E 101/35/2/10, m. 1 (55)

Mountjoy, Thomas (esquire)
C 61/58, m. 3; C 81/1730/26; E 101/35/2/10, m. 2 (71)
Thomas may have served on expeditions to Scotland (1310, 1311) in the retinue of Robert Mohaut. A protection granted to Thomas in February 1346 is the only evidence of his service with Henry of Lancaster in Aquitaine, which suggests that he may have joined the earl's retinue half way through the expedition. He served as a knight with Sir John de Beauchamp at Calais (1349).

Mubie, Adam atte (attendant)
E 101/25/9, m. 3d (18)

Mulle, William atte (attendant)
E 101/25/9, m. 3d (7)

Mulne, Galfrey atte (attendant)
E 101/25/9, m. 3d (20)

Murydene, Thomas de (esquire)
C 76/20, m. 15; E 101/35/2/10, m. 1 (12)
The royal protection granted to Thomas and his position in Lancaster's retinue roll implies that he was an esquire of moderate wealth and status.

Musard, eleven companions of John (esquires)
E 101/35/2/10, m. 1 (63)
Eleven unknown esquires who served in the company of John Musard.

Musard, John (esquire) Gloucestershire
E 101/35/2/10, m. 1 (62)
John was a relative, possibly the younger brother, of the notorious gentry criminal Malcolm Musard.[1]
1 See Chapter 7 and Hunt, 'Musard family', *ODNB*.

Neville, John de (knight) Lancashire

E 101/25/9, m. 3 (49)

John belonged to a gentry family prominent in Lancashire and Yorkshire. It is sometimes difficult to distinguish him from his relatives and namesakes based in Raby (Durham) and Essex. He served in Lancaster's retinue on two expeditions to Aquitaine (1345–46, 1349), and is probably the same person who entered into John of Gaunt's service and fought at Nájera (1367). He is also probably the grandson of Sir John de Neville (*d.* 1336) who held the castle and town of Hornby (Lancashire) of Henry of Lancaster, and various other lands in Yorkshire.

Neville, Robert de (knight) Lancashire

E 101/25/9, m. 3 (60)

Robert, son of Sir Robert de Neville, was probably the cousin and heir of Sir John de Neville of Hornby (*d.* 1336), and uncle of Sir John de Neville who served in Lancaster's retinue (1345). He is not to be confused with Sir Robert son of Philip de Neville of Stotton, who served with Lancaster in 1344.[1] He acted as a justice of the peace in Lancashire (1344, 1346) and Yorkshire (1350). A Robert de Boseville, possibly an esquire who had served in Lancaster's retinue (1345), was among the witnesses of an enrolment of a grant made by Neville to Sir William de Scot in 1346.[2] Neville was imprisoned in Newgate (released in 1362) and then committed to Fleet prison on account of his debts which led to the forfeiture of his lands in Kent.[3] He granted his right and claim of the manor and castle of Hornby, as well as the manor of Melling and the free chase of Roubendale, to Henry of Lancaster in 1351.[4] He married firstly Joan, daughter and heir of Henry Atherton of Lancashire, and secondly, Elizabeth, widow of Sir Roger Kirkby of Horton Kirkby (Kent). His son by Joan, Sir Robert de Neville (*d.* 1413), became an annuitant of the Black Prince and later established himself in the retinue of John of Gaunt.

1 C 76/19, m. 19.

2 *CCR, 1346–49*, p. 151.

3 Peter McNiven, 'Neville family (*per c.* 1267–1426)', *ODNB*, 2004 [accessed 29 May 2015].

4 *CCR, 1349–54*, pp. 372, 374.

Newmarch, John de (esquire)

E 101/35/2/10, m. 1 (8)

John was one of Henry of Lancaster's household esquires; he served with the earl in Aquitaine (1345–46), Brittany (1356–58) and on the Reims expedition (1359). He was granted an annuity of £14 from the issues of Cridling (Yorkshire) by Lancaster in 1354 and was granted the entire manor for life in 1361.[1] John was appointed as one of the earl's executors, and he was later retained by John of Gaunt.[2]

1 ; *CPR, 1354–58*, p. 114; *CPR, 1358–61*, p. 543.

2 Fowler, *King's Lieutenant*, p. 217.

Nichol, William (esquire)

E 101/35/2/10, m. 1 (13)

William served with Lancaster in Aquitaine (1345–46) and Brittany (1356–58); he is described as 'the king's yeoman' in 1348, and was sent to Aquitaine with men-at-arms, archers and grain supplies for the munitioning of the town of Saint-Jean-d'Angély (Charente-Maritime) that year.[1] William had been granted the property of Master Andriu Moirusson in that town for life by Lancaster – unless Moirusson should come back into Edward III's service – following its capture in October 1346.[2] He is described as a *damoiseau* (1346).

1 *CPR, 1348–50*, p. 147.
2 C 61/60, mm. 7, 19.

Norris, Hugh le (archer) Lancashire
E 101/35/2/10, m. 2d (170)

Norton, Adam de (archer) Cheshire
E 101/35/2/10, m. 2d (134)

Norwich, John de (*c.* 1299–1362) **(banneret)** Norfolk
C 47/2/58, m. 1d; C 76/20, m. 15; E 101/25/9, m. 3 (1)
John, brother of Sir Roger and Sir Thomas de Norwich, was the most experienced of Lancaster's bannerets, and led a colourful career in arms which began in Scotland (1322) and continued in various theatres of war up to the Reims expedition in 1359. He was knighted in 1320 with the assistance of a gift of £100 from the king's Wardrobe, and as a reward for recent service in Aquitaine and elsewhere he received an annuity of 50 marks in 1339, which increased to £40 the following year.[1] He inherited his father's estates in 1329 in Norfolk and Suffolk, including Great Massingham (Norfolk), where he secured the grant of a weekly market and annual fair in 1334. Despite a grant of exemption in 1343 from holding local offices against his will,[2] Norwich continued to serve on numerous commissions over the next two decades; he served as commissioner of array (with Robert de Causton),[3] of oyer and terminer and of the peace (with Causton and Constantine Mortimer) in Norfolk.[4] In 1345 he made an assessment of landed property in his home county as part of the Crown's land-based recruitment for the Normandy expedition (1346).[5] An important family alliance was established with the Uffords following the marriage of his sister, Margaret, and Robert de Ufford, earl of Suffolk. John was a pious man who founded a college at Raveningham church and built part of the church of Norton Subcourse. He served the king's council before his summons to parliament in 1360. He died two years later and was succeeded by his grandson and namesake, whose death in 1373 marked the end of the direct family line.

1 On career, see Verduyn, 'Norwich, John, first Lord Norwich', *ODNB*; *CP*, IX, pp. 763–5.
2 *CPR, 1343–45*, p. 4.
3 C 76/33, m. 1; C 76/34, m. 12.
4 *CPR, 1354–58*, p. 388 (Causton); *CPR, 1348–50*, p. 457 (Mortimer).
5 *CPR, 1343–45*, pp. 414–16.

Ockendon, Simon de (archer) Essex
E 101/35/2/10, m. 1d (260)

Oldfield, Richard de (archer) Yorkshire
E 101/35/2/10, m. 1d (199)

Oldfield, William de la (archer) Yorkshire
E 101/35/2/10, m. 1d (194)

Oxton, Randle de (archer) Cheshire
E 101/35/2/10, m. 2d (136)

Parker, Thomas (esquire)
E 101/35/2/10, m. 2 (148)

Parker, William le (archer)
E 101/35/2/10, m. 1d (257)

Payn, John (archer) Norfolk
E 101/35/2/10, m. 2d (103)

Paynel, Gilbert (esquire) Lincolnshire
E 101/35/2/10, m. 2 (112)

Paynel, John (knight) Lincolnshire
C 76/20, m. 17; E 101/25/9, m. 3 (42)
Sir John Paynel is probably the person from Gobion (Lincolnshire) who served in
Sir Adam de Everingham's retinue in 1345–46. Two namesakes, one of whom is from
Boothby, Lincolnshire, served at Crécy (1346) in the retinues of Robert de Ufford,
earl of Suffolk, and Sir Michael de Poynings. He may have first taken up arms as
an esquire in the retinue of William Frank in the Low Countries (1338), receiving
£13 6s 8d for horse restoration, and after the Aquitaine expedition (1345–46) Paynel
returned to Lancaster's service in 1356–58 and 1359.[1] We cannot be certain of his
relationship to Sir Ralph and Gilbert Paynel who also served in the same retinue
in Aquitaine.
1 E 36/203, fol. 128.

Paynel, Ralph (knight) Lincolnshire
E 101/25/9, m. 3 (68)
Ralph served at least three times in Lancaster's retinue together with John Paynel,
in Aquitaine, Normandy and Brittany. He may be the same Ralph who served
with John of Gaunt in 1369. He held land in Lincolnshire, and was appointed on
local commissions there and in Yorkshire in the 1360 and 1370s.[1] He was accused of
breaking into the castle and manor of Greasley in 1366 and assaulting the servants,
stealing goods and raping the wife of Sir Nicholas de Cantilupe.
1 *CIPM*, IX, p. 121; *CIPM*, XII, p. 88; *CPR, 1364–67*, p. 73; *CPR, 1370–1374*, p. 478.

Pecok, Robert (archer)
E 101/35/2/10, m. 1d (205)

Pemberton, Robert de (archer) Lancashire
E 101/35/2/10, m. 3 (1)

Pemberton, Thomas de (archer) Lancashire
E 101/35/2/10, m. 3d (39)

Pemberton, William de (archer) Lancashire
E 101/35/2/10, m. 3d (40)

Pepercorn, Thomas (archer)
E 101/35/2/10, m. 2d (147)

Perbourne, John de (esquire)
E 101/35/2/10, m. 1 (36)

Percy, Nicholas (esquire)
E 101/35/2/10, m. 3 (161)

Peyvre, Nicholas de (*c.* 1318–61) **(knight)** Bedfordshire/Buckinghamshire
C 76/20, m. 15; C 81/1724/58; E 101/25/9, m. 3 (67)
Peyvre was born at Quarrendon (Buckinghamshire). His relatively short military career began with service in Sir Neil Loring's retinue (1342) and ended with Henry of Lancaster at Calais (1347). He was one of Lancaster's valets and a tenant of the Black Prince, holding lands in Bedfordshire, Buckinghamshire and Hertfordshire.[1] In 1353 the prince's yeoman and keeper of the fees of the honour of Wallingford and St Wallery (Oxfordshire) was ordered to cease making demands of Peyvre for payment of relief.[2] Sir Robert de la Mare held land in Hertfordshire of Peyvre for an annual rent (*shrievshot*) of 3d.[3] A Thomas Fitzneil and William Sime were among the witnesses who gave testimony to Peyvre's proof of age in 1339. The wardship of Peyvre's son and heir, Thomas (*b.* 1344), was granted to the Black Prince.[4] Thomas continued the family's martial tradition, serving in the retinues of John of Gaunt (1369) and Robert Knowles (1370).
1 *CIPM*, XI, pp. 162–3; C 47/2/41, no. 2; C 76/25, m. 26d; E 159/123, m. 154d; E 372/192 (Bedford).
2 *BPR*, IV, pp. 94–5.
3 *CIPM*, IX, pp. 309–10.
4 *BPR*, IV, pp. 551–2.

Pierpoint, John le (archer)
E 101/35/2/10, m. 3d (41)

Pierpoint, Jordan (archer)
E 101/35/2/10, m. 3d (33)

Piper, Lorekyn le (esquire)
E 101/35/2/10, m. 1 (37)

Plays, Thomas (esquire) Norfolk
E 101/35/2/10, m. 2 (90)
Thomas first served with Lancaster in 1336.[1]
1 E 101/15/12.

Polone, John de (archer)
E 101/35/2/10, m. 1d (265)

Pommiers, Amaniu de (esquire) Saint-Sulpice-de-Pommiers (Gironde)
E 101/35/2/10, m. 1 (29)
Amaniu served as a knight in Brittany (1352), was with the Black Prince at Poitiers (1356), and led his own company on the Reims expedition in 1359.[1] For his career, see Chapter 9.
1 E 403/362, m. 27.

Pommiers, Amaniu de (esquire) Saint-Sulpice-de-Pommiers (Gironde)
E 101/35/2/10, m. 2 (76)
This Amaniu may be the same as the person listed above or another of the same name in Lancaster's retinue (1345–46).

Pommiers, Guilhem de (knight)
E 101/25/9, m. 3 (51)
Guilhem, recorded in the 1345 retinue roll as 'William', belonged to the Pommiers family although we cannot be certain of his exact relationship with his kinsmen in Lancaster's retinue (1345–46). He was probably a cousin or nephew of Hélias and Guilhem-Sans III.

Pommiers, Guilhem-Sans III de, Lord (banneret) Saint-Sulpice-de-Pommiers (Gironde)
E 101/25/9, m. 3 (8)
Guilhem-Sans III, whose father was mayor of Bordeaux in 1332, continued his family's long-standing allegiance to the kings of England.[1] He consistently provided military service to the king-dukes in Aquitaine. He recruited 100 men to carry out raids into Saintonge in 1342, and was appointed by Henry of Lancaster to treat with Alfonso XI, king of Castile, in 1344.[2] On the day of the capture of Bergerac (24 August 1345) by Anglo-Gascon forces he was reportedly dubbed knight with his brother, Hélias de Pommiers, by Lancaster himself, and was made captain of La Réole after the castle was surrendered later that year.[3] He was one of four members of Edward III's 'Gascon council' to treat with the French before the pope at Avignon in 1353. In addition to his home commune of Saint-Sulpice-de-Pommiers, Guilhem-Sans held a castle at Saint-Félix-de-Foncaude (Gironde), situated on the river Vignagne, near La Réole. He married Jeanne de Fronsac, and was succeeded by his son (d. c. 1377) who shared the name of his father, and grandfather (d. c. 1335). Guilhem-Sans III died around 1368.
1 On his career, see Eric Ruault, 'La famille de Pommiers au Moyen-Age' (unpublished master's thesis, Université de Bordeaux III, 1987); references in www.gasconrolls.org.
2 Sumption, *Trial by Battle*, p. 428.
3 AL, Livre velu de Libourne, fol. 133v (dubbed knight); C 61/60, m. 14; SC 8/243/12134.

Pommiers, Hélias de (knight) Saint-Sulpice-de-Pommiers (Gironde)
E 101/25/9, m. 3 (50)
Hélias, younger brother of Guilhem-Sans III, belonged to the Pommiers family which had consistently served the English king-dukes in Aquitaine for more than a

century. He was a canon of Bazas (before 1344), but abandoned the Church in order to purse a martial lifestyle. He first fought the French in Aquitaine in the late 1330s. He captured the count of Eu at the battle of Poitiers (1356), whom he later sold to the Black Prince for 30,000 écus. Hélias was made seneschal of Périgord (1347), lord of Arbanats (1349) and granted a royal annuity of £100 (1365) as a reward for his service to Edward III. He married Regina de Got, by whom he had a daughter named Regina de Pommiers. For Hélias' career, see Chapter 9.

Pommiers, three esquires of Lord (esquires)
E 101/35/2/10, m. 3 (185)

Pommiers, three knights of Lord (knights)
E 101/25/9, m. 3 (89)
Three unknown knights of the lord of Pommiers.

Pool, Walter (esquire)
E 101/35/2/10, m. 1 (48)

Popham, Philip de (esquire)
E 101/35/2/10, m. 1 (25)
Philip was a valet and an annuitant of Lancaster, who granted him a pension of £10 for life in King's Somborne (Hampshire) in 1353, together with its bedelry, and 100s of rent from Kingston Lacy manor (Dorset).[1] He was probably the son of John Popham, who served with Lancaster in 1340 and had been an annuitant of the earl's father.[2] Philip accompanied Lancaster on the Reims expedition (1359), and served as his personal envoy to Avignon.[3] He is probably not the knight and namesake who served in Ireland during the 1360s.
1 *CPR, 1348–50*, p. 546; *CPR, 1350–54*, p. 464.
2 C 76/15, m. 24.
3 SC 1/40/109.

Poyanne, ? de (knight) Dax (Landes)
E 101/25/9, m. 3 (79)
This unidentified knight probably belonged to the original family of the lords of Poyanne (not the one of Tartas-Albret). He may have been one of two sons of Pey de Poyanne and Guirauda de Saubist, Arman and Miqueu. Pey had been mayor of Bayonne and admiral of the king's fleet of Bayonne in the 1330s but died in exile sometime before 1345. Following Pey's death, his family claimed to have been stripped of their goods and driven from Bayonne by opponents in the city.[1] In 1338 Pey had requested a grant of rents in the port of Biarritz and Bedorède in favour of his sons.[2]
1 Nicholas A. Gribit and Simon J. Harris, 'Introduction: 19 Edward III (1345–46)', *Gascon Rolls*; www.gasconrolls.org.
2 C 61/50, m. 4.

Poynte, William de (esquire)
CCR, 1343–46, p. 671

Preston, Adam de (attendant) Lancashire
E 101/25/9, m. 3d (39)

Preston, William de (archer) Lancashire
E 101/35/2/10, m. 1d (251)

Prestwich, John de (archer) Lancashire
E 101/35/2/10, m. 1d (262)

Quinton, William de (esquire)
E 101/35/2/10, m. 2 (78)
Quinton served with Lancaster in 1342.[1]
1 C 76/17, m. 22.

Rabas, John (esquire)
E 101/35/2/10, m. 2 (82)

Ramesbury, Thomas (knight) Dorset
C 76/20, m. 15; E 101/25/9, m. 3 (16)
Thomas returned from Aquitaine in time to serve on Edward III's Normandy expedition (1346) in the retinue of William de Kildesby.[1] He married Margaret, sister and heir of Sir Edmund Everard; Ramesbury and his brother-in-law served together in Lancaster's retinue (1345–46) and both held land in Dorset. He died sometime before 1370.[2]
1 C 76/22, mm. 8, 15d.
2 *CIPM*, XIII, p. 20.

Ranulf, William son of (attendant)
E 101/25/9, m. 3d (8)

Rawcliffe, Richard de (*b. c.* 1321) **(knight)** Yorkshire
E 101/25/9, m. 3 (19)
Richard deposed at the Court of Chivalry that he had first taken up arms at the age of thirteen. He served in Scotland as an esquire in the retinues of Henry, Lord Beaumont and Henry, Lord Percy before establishing himself in the retinue of Henry of Lancaster (1342).[1] He took horses valued at 10 marks and 8 marks with him on campaigns in 1336 and 1338 respectively, and was one of the witnesses to Edmund de Ufford's indenture with Lancaster (1347).[2] Rawcliffe held lands of Henry Beaumont in Lincolnshire.[3] He served on numerous commissions in his home county of York, including as a justice of oyer and terminer relating to an attack on Lancaster's lands in Scalby by men from Scarborough in 1356. Richard was appointed as John of Gaunt's steward (1382–83) and master forester of Pickering (1374, 1382).[4] He was succeeded by his son, David, as constable, steward and master forester.
1 *Scrope and Grosvenor*, II, p. 351.
2 E 101/19/36, m. 2; E 101/35/3, m. 2.
3 *CIPM*, XII, p. 294.
4 *Somerville*, p. 378.

Reppes, John (esquire) Norfolk
E 101/35/2/10, m. 2 (147)
He is probably the son of Sir John Reppes who held the manor of Kettleston (Norfolk); he served on numerous local commissions in his home county in the 1350s. John may also have been a relative of his Carmelite namesake who acted as Henry of Lancaster's private confessor and personal envoy in 1344.[1]
1 *Calendar of Entries in the Papal Letters*, III, pp. 10–11, 13–14.

Riding, John (archer) Northumberland
E 101/35/2/10, m. 2d (102)

Ripon, William de (archer) Yorkshire
E 101/35/2/10, m. 2d (172)

Rochford, Thomas de (esquire) Essex
E 101/35/2/10, m. 2 (107)
Thomas twice served, together with John de Rochford, in Lancaster's retinue (1336, 1338).[1]
1 C 76/12, m. 8; E 101/15/12.

Rode, Thomas de (archer) Cheshire
E 101/35/2/10, m. 1d (227)

Rode, Richard de (archer) Cheshire
E 101/35/2/10, m. 1d (226)

Roebuck, Gerard (esquire)
E 101/35/2/10, m. 3 (178)

Roger, Henry (archer)
E 101/35/2/10, m. 1d (244)

Romel, Stephen (esquire)
E 101/35/2/10, m. 1 (7)
Romel received from Lancaster the grant for life of the prévôté of L'Ombrière at Bordeaux with the sea-canal and the pertaining issues, profits and emoluments, confirmed by Edward III in 1346.[1] In the same year Romel was referred to as 'king's yeoman' in letters patent, and granted custody of Nottingham castle for life in 1347.[2]
1 *CPR, 1345–48*, p. 475.
2 *CPR, 1345–48*, p. 333.

Roos, William de (archer) Yorkshire
E 101/35/2/10, m. 1d (256)

Rose, Henry (esquire) Norfolk
E 101/35/2/10, m. 2 (74)
Henry was granted the property of Jean Serchemont, a rebel, at Saint-Jean-d'Angély

(Charente-Maritime) by Henry of Lancaster, following the capture of the town in October 1346.[1] The grant was conditional on Rose serving as captain in the town's garrison. He remained there when Lancaster returned to England and is known to have served there, together with four men-at-arms and eighteen archers, between November 1349 and May 1351.[2] The earl granted him an annuity of £10 from Tunstead manor (Norfolk).[3] He is possibly the person named Henry Roos who was part of Lancaster's retinue in Brittany (1356–58).

1 C 61/60, mm. 19, 20.
2 E 101/168/3, fol. 4r; E 101/170/12, fol. 55r.
3 DL 29/288/4719.

Rosingreve, Hugh de (archer) Flintshire
E 101/35/2/10, m. 2d (143)

Rothing, Thomas (esquire)
E 101/35/2/10, m. 2 (113)

Rushall, Henry de (archer) Norfolk
E 101/35/2/10, m. 1d (248)

Rushworth, William de (archer)
E 101/35/2/10, m. 1d (254)

Rydyker, Richard de (archer)
E 101/35/2/10, m. 3d (83)

Rye, Nicholas de (knight) Lincolnshire
C 76/20, m. 15; C 76/23, m. 11d, 24; E 101/25/9, m. 3 (15); E 159/123, m. 110d; E 372/195 (Lincoln)
Nicholas, son of Edmund de Rye of Gosberton (Lincolnshire), was one of Henry of Lancaster's most loyal knights. He served with John Wiloughby in the Low Countries (1338), but thereafter served in Lancaster's retinue on every overseas expedition undertaken by the earl. He was accompanied by his valet, Richard de Stainton, on campaigns in 1344 and 1345–46. He served on various commissions in Lincolnshire (1343–61). He was closely associated with two of his neighbours, Simon Simeon and William Surfleet; the latter was appointed as Nicholas' attorney in 1338, 1342 and 1355 and both men inquired into the death of John Edeson, who was killed at Surfleet (Lincolnshire) in 1348.[1] Nicholas lost a law suit in 1345 concerning the alleged unjust disseisin of 140 acres of his freehold land in Gosberton by Henry, abbot of Peterborough, and others, and in the same year complained that his mother, or possibly his mother-in-law, Elizabeth, and John Roos (a debtor of Nicholas) had raided his property in Gosberton.[2] Elizabeth was granted a general pardon in 1350 at the request of Henry of Lancaster.[3] In 1359 Nicholas testified that William Jay of Swineshead (Lincolnshire) had killed Walter de la Hete, also of Swineshead, in self-defence; Jay was subsequently pardoned on account of the testimony and because of his 'good service' in Brittany with Henry of Lancaster.[4] Nicholas held lands in his home county, and married Juliana before 1345.[5]

1 *CPR, 1348–50*, p. 167.

2 *CPR, 1343–45*, pp. 493, 570. In 1344 Roos owed £40 to Rye: *CCR, 1343–46*, p. 336.
3 *CPR, 1348–50*, p. 577.
4 *CPR, 1358–61*, p. 273.
5 E 159/123, m. 163d; E 372/191 (Lincoln); *CCR, 1343–46*, pp. 336, 532.

Rye, Thomas de (esquire) Lincolnshire
E 101/35/2/10, m. 2 (118)

Ryecroft, Thomas de (archer)
E 101/35/2/10, m. 1d (196)

Ryel, John de (archer)
E 101/35/2/10, m. 1d (190)

Ryel, William de (archer)
E 101/35/2/10, m. 1d (189)

Rymes, John de (esquire) Dorset
E 101/35/2/10, m. 2 (125)

Ryvere, Laurence de la (esquire) Wiltshire
E 101/35/2/10, m. 3 (168)

Ryvere, Thomas de la (esquire) Wiltshire
C 76/20, m. 15; E 101/35/2/10, m. 1 (3)
Thomas was one of the most notable of Lancaster's valets, serving exclusively in the earl's retinue from 1336 to 1359. He was granted an annuity of £10 from the manor of King's Somborne (Hampshire) and two water mills at Hungerford (Berkshire) by Lancaster.[1] He was closely associated with Simon Simeon. Both men acted as mainpernors for Simon de Cransley, chaplain, and were involved in an assize of novel disseisin in 1345 concerning the land held of them in Wootton (Wiltshire) by Sir Robert Bicklemore – the latter held land of Thomas in Estwick and in the village of Wootton Rivers upon his death in 1361.[2] Simeon and John de Lusteshull (appointed as Thomas' attorney in 1342) served as justices of oyer and terminer, commissioned by Lancaster, on complaint by Thomas that he had been assaulted and robbed at Marlborough (Wiltshire) in 1347.[3] He served on numerous commissions in Wiltshire in the 1350s, and may have been the person appointed as escheator and sheriff (1351–54) of that county.[4]
1 *CIPM*, XI, p. 95; *CPR, 1361–64*, p. 50.
2 *CCR, 1346–49*, p. 76; *CIPM*, XI, p. 14.
3 *CPR, 1345–48*, p. 318.
4 *CPR, 1354–58*, p. 9.

Saint John, John (esquire)
E 101/35/2/10, m. 1 (39)

Sandal, Hugh de (archer) Yorkshire
E 101/35/2/10, m. 2d (91)

Sandwich, John de (esquire) Kent
C 76/20, m. 16; C 81/1727/60; E 101/35/2/10, m. 3 (163)
John twice served in Lancaster's retinue in Aquitaine (1345–46) and at Calais (1347).
He witnessed an enrolment of release of 'la Grove' manor, near Sandwich, by
William son of Nicholas la Archer of Dover to Peter de Gildesbergh, clerk, canon
of Lincoln cathedral, in 1345.[1] A John, brother of Master Nicholas de Sandwich, was
granted the remainder of some manors in Essex and Kent by William de Clinton,
earl of Huntingdon, in 1349.[2]
1 *CCR, 1343–46*, p. 545.
2 *CPR, 1348–50*, p. 430.

Sarnesfield, John de (esquire) Herefordshire
E 101/35/2/10, m. 2 (92)

Savage, Thomas (esquire)
E 101/35/2/10, m. 2 (128)

Scargill, Warren (*d.* 1349) **(knight)** Yorkshire
C 76/20, m. 15; E 101/25/9, m. 3 (57)
Warren, son of William Scargill, was knighted at the Feast of Swans in 1306 and
served in the retinue of William Rither in Scotland in the same year.[1] He raised
troops in Yorkshire for service in Scotland (1311, 1318), and served on oyer and
terminers (1327–28). In 1349 he organised an illegal joust, along with William and
Henry Scargill, and others, at Wakefield – one of several Yorkshire manors in which
Warren held land.[2] He married Margery de Holland, by whom he had a son named
William (*b.* 1340). The latter was an incorrigible individual who served in John of
Gaunt's retinue (1369); he was pardoned for numerous felonies, including rape,
trespass and marrying without licence whilst still in the king's wardship.[3] Warren
died of the pestilence on 13 September 1349.[4]
1 C 67/16, m. 4. I am grateful to Dr David Simpkin for this reference.
2 *CPR, 1348–50*, p. 117.
3 *CPR, 1361–64*, p. 251.
4 *CIPM*, XI, p. 336.

Scargill, William (esquire) Yorkshire
C 76/20, m. 15; E 101/35/2/10, m. 1 (17)
William, son of Sir William Scargill, was the younger brother of Sir Warren Scargill. In 1345 he was named among men who were not knights but who held land
worth £40 in Yorkshire.[1] He was pardoned for holding a joust at Wakefield without
the king's licence (1348).[2] It is impossible to establish whether this William, or his
nephew and namesake, served in Lancaster's retinue in 1356–58 and 1359, and with
John of Gaunt in the 1370s.
1 C 47/1/12, m. 18.
2 *CPR, 1348–50*, p. 117.

Scot, William (archer)
E 101/35/2/10, m. 1d (250)

Seabrook, Walter (knight)
E 101/25/9, m. 3 (44)

Seaton, John de (knight) Rutland
C 76/20, m. 15; C 76/25, m. 16d; E 101/25/9, m. 3 (23); E 372/203 (Rutland)
John probably originated from the village of Seaton (Rutland). He went overseas with William la Zouche of Mortimer in 1332, and may have served on earlier
campaigns in Scotland.[1] He was a knight in Henry of Lancaster's retinue in 1336
and served consistently with the earl up to the siege of Calais (1347). He was paid
50 marks for horse restoration in 1338.[2] John arrayed troops in his home county
for service on Scottish expeditions in the 1330s, and was appointed with John de
Boyville on commissions in Leicestershire and Rutland (1340, 1346), where he also
held land.[3] He was granted an annuity of £20 from Higham Ferrers (Northamptonshire) by Lancaster in 1352 or sometime before, and held lands in Oxfordshire of
the Black Prince (1352).[4] He was the son of Sir John and the brother of Sir Richard
de Seaton; all of whom attacked the bailiff of York castle and stole £40 from him
in 1332.[5]
1 *CPR, 1330–34*, p. 279.
2 E 36/203, fol. 126.
3 *CPR, 1340–43*, p. 107.
4 *BPR*, IV, p. 64; C 47/2/36, no. 5.
5 *CPR, 1330–34*, p. 285.

Seaton, Richard de (knight) Rutland
C 76/20, m. 15; E 101/25/9, m. 3 (54)
Richard was probably the younger brother of Sir John de Seaton; both men served
together in Lancaster's retinue in 1336 (Richard as an esquire), 1340 and 1345–46.
A Richard de Seaton was pardoned as an adherent of Thomas, earl of Lancaster, in
1318 and was accused of assaulting Richard Boynton at Beverley (Yorkshire) in 1334.[1]
He held lands in the neighbouring counties of Leicester, Rutland and Lincoln.[2]
1 *CPR, 1317–21*, p. 230; *CPR, 1330–34*, p. 579.
2 *CFR*, V, p. 515; *CIPM*, IX, p. 205; C 47/2/39, m. 8.

Secre, Simon (knight)
C 76/20, m. 16; C 81/1727/60; E 101/35/2/10, m. 1 (94)
Simon's one-off service in John de Grey's sub-retinue (1345–46) was probably the
only occasion that he took up arms. He is one of four English soldiers in Lancaster's retinue who might have been knighted during the expedition in the duchy. A
Simon Secre, who appointed Thomas Dru as his executor, died in or before 1370.[1]
1 *CPR, 1367–70*, pp. 447–8.

Sesoul, John (esquire)
C 76/20, m. 20; E 101/35/2/10, m. 2 (130)
John was the son of Alan Sesoul. He and John de Wadenowe granted the manor of
Sedgebrook (Lincolnshire) to Alesia, countess of Lincoln, before her death in 1348.[1]
1 *CIPM*, IX, p. 99.

Sewerby, Thomas de (knight) Yorkshire
C 76/20, m. 15; E 101/25/9, m. 3 (40)
Thomas, son and heir of Sir Robert de Sewerby, campaigned in the Low Countries (1338, 1340) and served once in Lancaster's retinue (1345–46). His lands in Yorkshire included Sewerby, where he probably originated, and Camblesforth.[1] In 1336 he was pardoned for entering lands in Camblesforth without licence, although his family had held land there for four generations since the reign of Henry III.[2] He appointed Walter Sewerby as his attorney in 1345.[3] Thomas and his brother Stephen and others were accused of assaulting Arnold de Marton at Sewerby (1351), stealing his goods and using cattle to trample and ruin his crops.[4]
1 *CIPM*, IX, p. 459.
2 *CPR, 1334–38*, pp. 339–40.
3 C 76/20, m. 15.
4 *CPR, 1350–54*, p. 166.

Sewerby, William de (esquire) Yorkshire
E 101/35/2/10, m. 2 (104)

Seymour, William (esquire)
E 101/35/2/10, m. 2 (98)

Seyntcler, Thomas (esquire) Cornwall
E 101/35/2/10, m. 2 (93)

Sharp, Robert (archer)
E 101/35/2/10, m. 1d (233)

Sharp, Thomas (archer)
E 101/35/2/10, m. 1d (232)

Shaw, John atte (attendant)
E 101/25/9, m. 3d (16)

Shelton, John (attendant) Norfolk
E 101/25/9, m. 3d (30)

Shelton, Richard de (*d. c.* 1359) **(knight)** Norfolk
C 81/322/18661; E 101/25/9, m. 3 (26)
Richard spent his entire career in arms (1336–47) serving in the retinue of Henry of Lancaster. He was granted the manor of Hinckley (Leicestershire) by Lancaster, and served as mainpernor of a chaplain, Robert Bike of Hinckley, who served with Richard on the Breton expedition in 1342.[1] He was appointed together with Hugh Meynell to arrest John and Richard Maureward, a knight and former parson, in 1336.[2] He held lands in Shelton (Norfolk) and Holderness (Yorkshire).[3]
1 C 76/17, mm. 3, 20.
2 *CPR, 1334–38*, p. 372.
3 *CIPM*, VII, p. 405; *CPR, 1358–61*, p. 302.

Shelton, Robert de (knight) Norfolk

C 76/20, m. 15; E 101/25/9, m. 3 (36)

Robert was a veteran soldier who had fought in Scotland (1316) and on two campaigns in Aquitaine (1324, 1337) before setting out to the duchy again in 1345. He was one of the Norfolk (and Suffolk) gentry who had entered into Lancaster's service through his affiliation with Sir John de Norwich. Robert had a small land-holding in his home county.[1]

1 *CIPM*, VII, p. 405.

Shirfield, Hugh de (esquire)

C 76/20, m. 16; C 81/1727/60; E 101/35/2/10, m. 3 (157)

Hugh first served in Richard de Grey's retinue (1322), before taking up arms in John de Grey of Codnor's company, together with Richard de Strolley and Peter de Wokendon, in the retinue of Henry of Lancaster on expeditions to Brittany (1342) and Aquitaine (1345–46).[1]

1 *CPR, 1321–24*, p. 198; C 81/1727/66.

Sholl, Richard (esquire)

C 76/20, m. 15; E 101/35/2/10, m. 1 (31)

Sholl served in Lancaster's retinue on three military campaigns (1345–46, 1356–58, 1359), and was commissioned to array 40 mounted archers in his home county of Hereford and lead them to Portsmouth for service in Aquitaine (1350).[1] He was made constable of the fortress at Avranches (Manche) following its capture on the earl's return from the Loire valley in 1356.[2]

1 C 76/28, m. 13.

2 Fowler, *King's Lieutenant*, p. 184.

Sibsey, Ranulf (esquire) Lincolnshire

E 101/35/2/10, m. 2 (116)

Simeon, Simon (esquire) Lincolnshire

C 76/20, mm. 6, 15; C 76/23, m. 11d; E 101/35/2/10, m. 1 (2); E 159/123, m. 110d; E 372/195 (Lincoln)

Simeon, occasionally known as 'Simkyn' (or 'little Simon'), was a trusted confidant of Henry of Lancaster and one of the longest serving members of the earl's house-hold. He had served Henry's father, the third earl of Lancaster, and entered John of Gaunt's service after 1361. He was a valet and annuitant of Lancaster, who rewarded Simeon for his service with extensive grants of lands in Derbyshire, Lincolnshire, Yorkshire and Essex. His prominence in Lancaster's retinue is reflected by his posi-tion in second place on the retinue roll, while his wealth is reflected by a payment of horse restoration (£40 in 1338), a large debt (500 marks in 1345) owed to him by Robert de Wickham, and his appointment of four attorneys in 1344; of whom two (John de Gynewell and Walter de Power) represented Lancaster, and two others (John de Bodecote and William Harald) represented Thomas de la Ryvere on the same expedition.[1] He is described as 'the king's yeoman', and was granted William de Iselbek's lands (Yorkshire) by the king in 1341, as compensation for his ransom when he was formerly detained at Riblemont castle in Flanders.[2] His estate included lands in Berkshire, Northamptonshire and Wiltshire. He made donations to several religious houses, and founded a chantry in the chapel at the site of Thomas of Lancaster's execution at Pontefract.[3] He died in 1386.

1 *CCR, 1343–46*, p. 480; C 76/19, mm. 19, 22; E 36/203, fol. 126.

2 *CPR, 1340–43*, p. 298.

3 For more details of his career, see references in Fowler, *King's Lieutenant*.

Singer, John le (archer)
E 101/35/2/10, m. 3d (64)

Singer, Stephen le (archer)
E 101/35/2/10, m. 3d (63)

Singleton, John de (archer) Lancashire
E 101/35/2/10, m. 3d (29)

Singleton, John son of Alan de (archer) Lancashire
E 101/35/2/10, m. 3d (20)

Singleton, Thomas de (archer) Lancashire
E 101/35/2/10, m. 1d (249)

Skone, William (archer)
E 101/35/2/10, m. 2d (100)

Smaleberwe, Robert de (esquire)
E 101/35/2/10, m. 2 (141)

Smith, Roger le (of Blackburn) (archer) Lancashire
E 101/35/2/10, m. 3d (52)

Soland, William (archer)
E 101/35/2/10, m. 1d (179)

Spenser, Robert le (archer)
E 101/35/2/10, m. 2d (163)

Spink, William (archer) Norfolk
E 101/35/2/10, m. 3d (32)

Spredesham, John de (archer)
E 101/35/2/10, m. 2d (158)

St Pierre, John de (*b. c.* 1308) **(knight)** Cheshire
C 61/58, m. 3; E 101/25/9, m. 3 (29)

John was a Cheshire magnate whose principal residence was at Peckforton. He continued his family's tradition of service with the Grey family; on his first military campaign (Scotland, 1327), he served in John de Grey's company as part of the retinue of Henry, third earl of Lancaster.[1] In 1345 he was ordered to raise Cheshire archers for the Aquitaine expedition and lead them to Southampton. He was granted a gift of 100 marks by the Black Prince in 1351 for the marriage of his son and heir, Urian, to the daughter of Sir Golfard Gistels.[2] He held a substantial estate in Cheshire and North Wales, including a quarter of the Malpas barony, together with the master sergeanty of the peace of the county. The following year the office of master sergeanty was seized from John by officials as a result of a violent dispute with the Maisterton family of Nantwich. In 1353 he sold his life interest in his Cheshire property and lands in Anglesey to the Black Prince for £1000 and the office of keeper of Beaumaris castle. The sale of his estate seems to have been the result of sharp practice and 'anti-patronage' of the prince.[3] He married Isabella in or before 1332.[4]

1 C 71/11, m. 6.
2 *BPR*, III, p. 33.
3 For his career, see Paul H. W. Booth, *The Financial Administration of the Lordship and County of Chester, 1272–1377* (Manchester: Manchester University Press for the Chetham Society, 1981), pp. 130–2; *Account of Master John de Burnham the Younger, Chamberlain of Chester, of the revenues of the counties of Chester and Flint, Michaelmas 1361 to Michaelmas 1362*, ed. Paul H. W. Booth and A. D. Carr (Chester: Record Society of Lancashire and Cheshire, 1991), pp. 170–1.
4 *CPR, 1330–34*, p. 379.

Stacey, John de (esquire)
E 101/35/2/10, m. 3 (162)

Stainton, Richard de (esquire)
C 76/20, m. 15; C 81/1724/48; E 101/35/2/10, m. 2 (119)
Stainton was a valet of Sir Nicholas de Rye, with whom he served in the retinues of John Wiloughby (1338) and Henry of Lancaster (1344, 1345–46).

Stamps, William de (esquire)
E 101/35/2/10, m. 1 (56)

Standish, Richard de (archer) Lancashire
E 101/35/2/10, m. 3 (16)
Richard originated from Standish-with-Langtree, near Wigan (Lancashire).

Stanniland, John de (archer) Cheshire
E 101/35/2/10, m. 3d (82)

Starky, Thomas de (archer) Cheshire
E 101/35/2/10, m. 3d (46)

Stepworth, William de (attendant)
E 101/25/9, m. 3d (32)

Stoke, Thomas de (archer) Staffordshire
E 101/35/2/10, m. 2d (105)

Stoneham, Richard de (esquire) Suffolk
E 101/35/2/10, m. 2 (139)

Stopford, Adam de (archer) Cheshire
E 101/35/2/10, m. 1d (203)

Strolley, Richard de (esquire)
C 76/20, m. 16; C 81/1727/60
Richard served alongside Hugh de Shirfield and Peter de Wokendon in the company
of Sir John de Grey of Codnor, as part of Lancaster's retinue on the Breton (1342)
and Aquitaine expeditions (1345–46).[1]
1 C 81/1727/65.

Sulny, Avery de (knight) Derbyshire
E 101/25/9, m. 3 (58)
Avery originated from Newton Solney (Derbyshire), and is not to be confused
with his father and namesake who served in the War of Saint-Sardos. Avery first
appears as an esquire in the retinue of Henry of Lancaster (1336), and he continued
to serve exclusively with the earl, albeit sporadically, up to the Breton expedition in
1356. He was an annuitant of Lancaster and was associated with the gentry families
of Greasley and Meynell in Derbyshire.[1] He held land in Leicestershire and either
Avery, or his son of the same name, was appointed keeper of the chase and parks
at Needwood (1372) and held the office of master forester there (1374), as well as
the shrievalty of Derbyshire and Nottinghamshire (1372–73).[2] Avery served in John
of Gaunt's retinue in the 1370s.[3]
1 C 47/2/25, m. 7.
2 *Somerville*, p. 381.
3 Walker, *Lancastrian Affinity*, p. 29, n. 86.

Sumpter, Richard (esquire)
E 101/35/2/10, m. 1 (38)

Sutton, Stephen de (archer)
E 101/35/2/10, m. 2d (141)

Swan, Hugh le (archer)
E 101/35/2/10, m. 2d (160)

Swayn, John (attendant)
E 101/25/9, m. 3d (31)

Swinford, Edmund de (esquire) Lincolnshire
C 47/2/37, no. 5; C 76/24, m. 8d; E 159/123, m. 127d; E 372/191 (Lincoln)
Edmund first went on campaign in the Low Countries (1338) together with Sir
Norman de Swinford and three other family members (Sir Thomas, William and
John), and he served with Norman in the retinue of Hugh Audley, earl of Gloucester
in 1342.[1] He had minor landholdings in Lincolnshire, and acquired Herlaston manor
(Lincolnshire) in fee from Norman sometime in the 1350s.[2]

1 C 76/13, m. 6d.
2 *CPR, 1367–70*, pp. 79–80.

Swinford, Norman de (*d.* 1368) **(knight)** Lincolnshire
C 47/2/37, no. 5; C 76/24, m. 8d; E 101/25/9, m. 3 (3); E 159/123, mm. 123, 127d.
Norman was a retainer of Henry of Lancaster and Charles of Navarre (1366); he
served in a wide range of theatres of war with different captains during his military
career (1338–66).[1] He held lands in his home county of Lincoln, where he also
served on commissions of array and of oyer and terminer.[2] Norman had two sons,
John and Walter, by his wife Margaret (*d.* 1354), widow of Sir John de Brewes.[3] He
died at Lee manor (Lincolnshire) in 1368, and was succeeded by his son John (*b.*
1345).
1 See Chapter 9.
2 *CIPM*, XII, pp. 232–3.
3 *CIPM*, X, 189.

Swinnerton, John (esquire)
E 101/35/2/10, m. 1 (27)

Symesak, Arnald de (esquire)
E 101/35/2/10, m. 1 (42)
The 'ak' ending of this surname suggests that he was of Gascon or Aquitanian
origin.

Tailor, Stephen le (attendant)
E 101/25/9, m. 3d (3)

Tartas, Guiraut de (knight) Dax (Landes)
E 101/25/9, m. 3 (76)
Guiraut de Tartas, also known as Guiraut d'Albret, was lord of Poyanne and la
Libarde, and the illegitimate son of Guitart d'Albret, vicomte of Tartas (*d.* 1338). He
witnessed the sealing of the treaty between Edward III and Pedro, king of Castille,
when it was read aloud at St Paul's cathedral (London) in 1361. He was temporarily
dispossessed of his land at la Libarde in 1362 and subsequently appealed to Edward
III in person. At this time he was seneschal of Bigorre.[1] Guiraut was allowed to take
a quarter of wheat or rye each week from the mill of Saint-Esprit of Bayonne for the
term of his life.[2] He received gifts of £46 3s and £33 6s 8d from the Black Prince in
1358 and 1362.[3] As a reward for his loyalty and good service, Guiraut and his heirs
were granted the fishery of Guiche (Landes) in 1372, in return for liege homage to
the Black Prince and the delivery of a falcon annually at Bordeaux castle on the
feast of All Saints.[4] This grant was confirmed (1381) after 'detainers' occupied the
fishery following Guiraut's death.[5] In 1376 Guiraut pledged together with Ramon
de Montaut, Galhart de Durfort and Bernat de Lesparre to pay Edward III the
ransom (1000 marks) of the Lord of Poys, a French prisoner of war.[6] Guiraut died
some time between 1376 and 1379.
1 C 61/25, mm. 1, 15, 24, 28.
2 C 61/95, m. 4.
3 *BPR*, IV, pp. 251, 462.

4 C 61/85, m. 6.
5 C 61/95, m. 14.
6 C 61/93, m. 8.

Tasseler, John (attendant)
E 101/25/9, m. 3d (37)

Taverham, Baudry de (esquire) Norfolk
E 101/35/2/10, m. 2 (135)

Thedden, Roger de (esquire) Hampshire
E 101/35/2/10, m. 3 (166)

Thelwall, William (archer) Cheshire
E 101/35/2/10, m. 1d (185)

Thirkenes, John de (archer)
E 101/35/2/10, m. 1d (209)

Thornhurst, John de (archer) Yorkshire
E 101/35/2/10, m. 3d (25)

Thornton, William de (archer) Yorkshire
E 101/35/2/10, m. 3d (45)

Tiringham, John de (knight) Lincolnshire
E 101/25/9, m. 3 (63)
He may be the same person who served as a justice of oyer and terminer in South-ampton (1336).[1] John was exonerated in 1346 from an assessment of his lands in Lincolnshire because Simon Simeon testified that he was serving with Henry of Lancaster in Aquitaine.[2]
1 *CPR, 1334–38*, p. 366.
2 C 76/23, m. 20d.

Tiringham, John de (esquire)
E 101/35/2/10, m. 2 (81)

Tofts, Simon de (esquire) Cheshire
E 101/35/2/10, m. 2 (94)

Truat, Reginald (esquire)
E 101/35/2/10, m. 3 (173)

Trumwyn, John (esquire)
E 101/35/2/10, m. 1 (65)
John probably belonged to the Staffordshire family of Trumwyn, and was a likely relative of the knight and namesake who served in Sir James Audley's retinue (1345). He was probably a kinsman of Sir Roger and William Trumwyn, who acted as

lieutenant justice of North Wales and commissioner of array in Derbyshire, respectively, in 1345.

Trussebut, Hugh (knight) Norfolk
Crécy and Calais, p. 152; E 372/192, m. 16d
Hugh is possibly the knight who served in the retinues of Reginald de Cobham and Thomas, earl of Norfolk, in Aquitaine (1324) and Scotland (1327). He was exonerated, together with Thomas Bacoun, from an assessment of his lands in Norfolk because he served continuously with Lancaster in Aquitaine (1345–46).

Trussell, Theobald (knight) Northamptonshire
C 76/20, m. 15; E 101/25/9, m. 3 (25)
Theobald, son of Sir William Trussell of Flores (*d. c.* 1346), began his career in arms as an esquire in Lancaster's retinue (1336). He accompanied his father on diplomatic missions (1337, 1341) and was compensated £20 and 10 marks for horses lost on campaigns in the Low Countries (1338) and Brittany (1342).[1] Theobald was pardoned in 1352, at the 'immediate request' of Wilhelm, duke of Bavaria, for murder and his non-appearance before the royal justices at Northampton.[2] He was pardoned in 1355 for his debts and all other crimes by a fine of 100 marks.[3] Theobald served on local commissions with Simon Simeon (1366) and John de Verdon (1364, 1366) in Northamptonshire, and he held land in that county as well as Leicestershire and Warwickshire.[4] He died before 1372, John was his son and heir.
1 E 36/203, fol. 126; E 36/204, fol. 83r.
2 *CPR, 1350–54*, p. 244.
3 *CPR, 1354–58*, p. 260.
4 *CCR, 1343–46*, p. 104; *CIPM*, XI, p. 181; *CIPM*, XIII, p. 187.

Trussell, William (knight) Northamptonshire
E 101/25/9, m. 3 (55)
William was probably the son of Sir William Trussell of Flores (also known as 'of Nuthurst', and 'of Peatling'), who was a senior official of Earl Thomas and Earl Henry (the elder) of Lancaster, and a trusted diplomat of Edward III. After his one-off service with Lancaster in 1345–46 he successfully established himself in the Black Prince's retinue; he served regularly with the prince in Aquitaine (1352, 1355–56, 1363, 1369), and was granted a life annuity of £40 as a reward for his service at Poitiers (1356). William is described as the prince's bachelor; his esquire was given a full suit of mail from the prince's Wardrobe (1358) and he was granted a gift of a barding of mail (*c.* 1359).[1] A William son of Sir William Trussell died *c.* 1363.[2]
1 *BPR*, IV, pp. 245, 261–2, 323.
2 *BPR*, III, p. 459.

Trykingham, Roger de (esquire)
C 81/1760/13; E 372/195 (Lincoln)
Roger had small landholdings in Lincolnshire. In 1329 he was accused of stealing timber, along with Sir John de Lymbury and others, from Sir Robert Darcy's manor at Scott Willoughby (Lincolnshire).[1] He may have been the Roger de Trykingham who was ordered to join Edward III, with horses and armour, on the Scottish expedition in 1334.[2]

1 *CPR, 1327–30*, pp. 475–6.
2 C 71/14, m. 1d.

Twig, Edward (attendant)
E 101/25/9, m. 3d (26)

Ufford, Edmund de (knight) Suffolk
C 76/20, m. 15
Edmund, kinsman of Robert de Ufford, earl of Suffolk, may have been the royal household knight who served with Edward III in the Low Countries (1338, 1340). It is difficult to distinguish this Edmund, known as 'the brother' in 1338, from his namesakes who are sometimes described as 'the cousin' or 'the elder'. An Edmund 'son of Robert de Ufford' appointed four attorneys in 1338; two of whom (Thomas Sleford and William Surfleet) also served as legal representatives of Nicholas de Rye, Alexander Auncel and Richard de Hebden in 1338, 1342 and 1355, which suggests that this Edmund (who was possibly 'the brother') served together with his father in Henry of Lancaster's retinue in 1345–46.[1] He was an annuitant of the (third and fourth) earls of Lancaster, and was retained by the latter for life in peace and war (1347) with a fee of 40 marks. The following year he was among the witnesses, including Peter de la Mare, Robert de Causton and the earl of Suffolk, of a charter concerning Lancaster's grant of a hospital to the Friar Preachers of Thetford (Norfolk). Edmund acted as Lancaster's steward in Suffolk (c. 1351–59).[2] He held lands in Norfolk, Suffolk and Northamptonshire.
1 C 76/12, m. 9.
2 *Somerville*, p. 362.

Ufford, Robert de (knight) Suffolk
E 101/25/9, m. 3 (7)
Robert was probably the father of Edmund who also served in Lancaster's retinue in Aquitaine (1345–46). A Robert de Ufford was pardoned in 1331 for the deaths of Sir Hugh de Turpliton and Richard de Monmouth, who were killed while resisting arrest from Roger Mortimer at Nottingham castle.[1]
1 *CPR, 1330–34*, p. 74.

Unfrey, Roger (archer)
E 101/35/2/10, m. 1d (252)

Upton, Nicholas de (archer) Cheshire
E 101/35/2/10, m. 3d (74)

Urberville, John (esquire)
E 101/35/2/10, m. 2 (91)

Velthem, Lewis de (esquire)
E 101/35/2/10, m. 3 (181)
Lewis may have originated from somewhere in the Low Countries.

Verdon, John de (le Filz) **(knight)** Northamptonshire
E 101/25/9, m. 3 (39)
John de Verdon served with his father, Thomas, in Aquitaine (1345–46). He is not
to be confused with his namesakes who served at the battle of Crécy. He may
have been the John de Verdon associated with the Black Prince, who granted him
a horse called 'Grey Cologne' in 1352.[1] Several men named John de Verdon served
on various commissions in Norfolk, Northamptonshire, Leicestershire, Staffordshire
and Rutland. John had small landholdings in Lincolnshire, and temporarily held
the lands and chattels of John son and heir of Thomas de Burgo in Essex, together
with his father (Thomas) and Robert de Maule.[2]
1 *BPR*, IV, p. 66.
2 C 47/2/58; *CIPM*, IX, p. 247.

Verdon, Thomas de (*d.* 1349) **(knight)** Northamptonshire
C 61/58, m. 2; C 76/20, mm. 5, 15; C 81/322/18661; E 101/25/9, m. 3 (9)
Thomas was probably a kinsman of the Verdon family which originated from Brix-
worth (Northamptonshire). He served as a valet of John de Felton during the War
of Saint-Sardos (1324), and was paid £10 horse restoration.[1] He was an annuitant
of two successive earls of Lancaster, including the younger Henry to whom he was
closely attached. Thomas served on numerous commissions in Northamptonshire
and the neighbouring counties in the 1330s and 1340s, and was granted an exemption from holding local offices in 1348. In the same year Henry of Lancaster peti-
tioned the pope 'on behalf of his knight [i.e. Thomas]', for a plenary indulgence at
the hour of death. He held lands in Essex and Northamptonshire.[2] This Thomas
may have married Alice.[3]
1 E 101/17/2, m. 1.
2 E 372/191 (Essex).
3 *CPR, 1338–40*, p. 114.

Vernon, John (archer) Cheshire
E 101/35/2/10, m. 1d (180)

Vernoun, Geoffrey (esquire) Norfolk
E 159/123, m. 172; E 372/191 (Norfolk)
Geoffrey had a small landholding in Norfolk and was recruited by Sir John de
Norwich for service in Lancaster's retinue in Aquitaine (1345–46) and Calais (1347).
He was granted a rent of £10 from the manor of Caister for life by Sir John, Lord
Bardolf of Wormegay in 1350.[1] Geoffrey is not to be confused with his namesake
of Elm (Cambridgeshire), who served on the Normandy expedition (1346) with
Robert de Ufford, earl of Suffolk.[2]
1 *CPR, 1348–50*, p. 577.
2 C 76/22, m. 15d.

Vyeleston, William de (esquire)
E 101/35/2/10, m. 2 (86)

Wake, Thomas (knight)
C 76/26, mm. 2d, 6d; C 81/1761/54; E 101/25/9, m. 3 (52)

Wake appointed John Higham as his attorney for campaigns in 1340 and 1342; he first served with Lancaster in Aquitaine (1345–46) and returned to the earl's retinue for the siege of Calais (1347). He held property in Whissendine (Rutland), and if he was the son of Hugh Wake, then he would have inherited his mother's lands in Wiltshire upon her death in 1330.[1] He was probably a relative of Thomas, Lord Wake of Liddell, and of his namesake 'of Blisworth' (Northamptonshire) who was a household knight of Edward III.

1 *CIPM*, VII, p. 241.

Walcote, Walter de (esquire) Leicestershire
E 101/35/2/10, m. 2 (124)

Waldegrave, John de (esquire) Lincolnshire
E 101/35/2/10, m. 1 (23)

Walkefare, Richard de (esquire) Norfolk
C 76/20, m. 15; C 81/1724/42; E 101/35/2/10, m. 3 (171)

Richard first served as an esquire in Aquitaine (1337) with Sir John de Norwich, and later became established in Lancaster's retinue. After the earl's death he entered into the service of the Black Prince. He was knighted by 1349, and sold two horses in Aquitaine that year for £36 13s 4d.[1] He held land in Essex and Norfolk and in 1343 he held lands, together with John Boson and other parties, of William de Roos in Nottinghamshire.[2] Richard and Sir Robert de Causton served together as commissioners in Norfolk and Suffolk in the 1350s and 1360s, and were both appointed as attorneys of Robert Howard in 1362.[3] Richard was witness to letters of the Black Prince's business manager, Sir John de Wingfield, concerning trespasses committed by the prince's steward at Castle Rising (1359).[4] He is described as the prince's bachelor in 1362, and was made head gamekeeper at Rising, where he made a park and enclosed a chase to prevent game from disturbing the local tenants.[5] Richard acted as the prince's attorney in 1364, and he appointed four of his own attorneys whilst on campaign with the prince in Aquitaine in 1365 and 1369.[6] He had two daughters, Eleanor and Joan; the latter married the famous Sir Thomas Felton (KG).

1 E 404/508/69.
2 *CIPM*, VIII, p. 338.
3 *CPR, 1361–64*, p. 252.
4 *BPR*, IV, p. 293.
5 *BPR*, IV, p. 471.
6 C 61/77, m. 3; C 61/78, m. 4; C 61/82, m. 2; C 61/83, m. 10.

Walkington, John de (knight)
C 76/20, m. 15; E 101/25/9, m. 3 (32)

John first served as an esquire with Henry of Lancaster in 1336, but may well have fought at the battle of Halidon Hill (1333).[1] He was connected to the elder Henry, second earl of Lancaster, and established himself in the retinue of the third earl, whom he served consistently and exclusively up to the siege of Calais (1347).[2] John was still an esquire in 1344, but was knighted in the following year (probably during the Aquitaine expedition). He was witness to one of Lancaster's charters in 1350 and was granted the manors of North Standen (Wiltshire) and Rolleston (Staffordshire) by the earl as a reward for his service.[3] His kinsman, William de Walkington, was granted some Derbyshire manors.

1 C 71/13, m. 5.
2 *Somerville*, p. 84.
3 *CPR, 1348–50*, pp. 282, 366, 469.

Waltham, William de (archer) Lincolnshire

E 101/35/2/10, m. 1d (253)

Walton, Henry de (clerk)

C 76/20, m. 15

Henry was a talented administrator whose services were employed by the royal Exchequer, Edward III and Henry of Lancaster. He acted as Henry of Lancaster's attorney (1348, 1350), treasurer (1348–50) and lieutenant (1354, 1359), and was well rewarded for his services. The earl helped him secure numerous grants of canonries and prebends in Herefordshire, Leicestershire, Lincolnshire, Yorkshire, Salisbury and Exeter. Henry was a probable relative of the clerks Richard and Robert de Walton, who served in Lancaster's retinue in 1349 and 1359 respectively. For Henry's career see Chapter 9.

Warburton, Robert de (archer) Cheshire

E 101/35/2/10, m. 2d (151)

Warrington, Thomas de (attendant) Cheshire

E 101/25/9, m. 3d (34)

Warton, William de (archer) Lancashire

E 101/35/2/10, m. 2d (127)

Wastenay, John (esquire) Cheshire

E 101/35/2/10, m. 2 (95)

His relatives, Thomas and Sir Hugh Wastenay, served in Lancaster's retinue in 1342 and 1356–58, respectively.

Waure, Philip de (knight)

E 101/25/9, m. 3 (5)

Philip's high position in Lancaster's retinue roll (1345–46) suggests that he was a knight of considerable status.

Welbourne, John de (clerk)

E 404/508/47

Welbourne was one of Lancaster's clerks by 1343 and went on to become the earl's chancellor and secretary. His kinsman, Thomas de Welbourne, and Henry de Walton were among four attorneys appointed by him in 1349. He, like other clerks of Lancaster, benefited from the success of the earl's petitions to the pope; Welbourne secured canonries and prebends in Lincolnshire, Yorkshire and Salisbury.[1]

1 Fowler, *King's Lieutenant*, p. 179.

Wellington, Henry de (esquire) Somerset
E 101/35/2/10, m. 2 (127)

Wernesleye, Thomas de (archer) Yorkshire
E 101/35/2/10, m. 3d (84)

Weston, Geoffrey de (esquire)
E 101/35/2/10, m. 2 (123)
Weston returned to Lancaster's retinue in 1347.[1]
1 C 76/24, m. 1.

Whittingham, William son of William de (archer) Lancashire
E 101/35/2/10, m. 3d (43)

Whitton, William de (esquire) Cheshire
E 101/35/2/10, m. 1 (33)
William served in Lancaster's retinue in Scotland (1336) and, as *centenar*, led the
Lancashire foot archers to Southampton in 1345.

Wickham, Robert de (esquire) Berkshire
E 101/35/2/10, m. 1 (61)
Robert served as an esquire in Lancaster's retinue on campaign to the Low Coun-
tries (1338), Brittany (1342), Aquitaine (1345–46) and Calais (1347).

Wigan, Walter (archer) Lancashire
E 101/35/2/10, m. 3d (81)

Wilinton, Amory de (knight)
E 101/25/9, m. 3 (34)
Amory's service in Aquitaine was the only occasion that he took up arms on a military campaign. Three members of the Wilinton family (John, Thomas and Ralph)
served with the elder Henry of Lancaster in Scotland in 1327.[1]
1 C 71/11, m. 6.

Willaston, Thomas de (archer) Cheshire
E 101/35/2/10, m. 1d (245)

Willenhall, William de (archer) Warwickshire
E 101/35/2/10, m. 3d (65)

Willey, Robert de (esquire)
E 101/35/2/10, m. 2 (72)

Willon, John (archer)
E 101/35/2/10, m. 1d (192)

Wilmslow, Richard de (archer) Cheshire
E 101/35/2/10, m. 1d (243)

Winstanley, Roger de (archer) Lancashire
E 101/35/2/10, m. 3d (51)

Wirkhale, William de (archer)
E 101/35/2/10, m. 2d (108)

Wirswall, Hugh de (archer) Cheshire
E 101/35/2/10, m. 1d (210)

Wite, Richard (attendant)
E 101/25/9, m. 3d (19)

Wite, William (attendant)
E 101/25/9, m. 3d (15)

Witney, Roger de (archer) Oxfordshire
E 101/35/2/10, m. 2d (110)

W'lford, John de (attendant)
E 101/25/9, m. 3d (33)

Wodergrete, Walter de (esquire)
E 101/35/2/10, m. 3 (179)

Wokendon, Peter de (esquire) Essex
C 76/20, m. 16; C 81/1727/60; E 101/35/2/10, m. 3 (156)
Peter served on four campaigns overseas and in Scotland from 1338 to 1347; on at
least three occasions (1338, 1340, 1345–46) he belonged to the company of Sir John
de Grey of Codnor.

Wolfall, Adam de (archer) Lancashire
E 101/35/2/10, m. 3 (4)

Wolfall, Gilbert de (archer) Lancashire
E 101/35/2/10, m. 3 (7)

Wolfall, Henry de (archer) Lancashire
E 101/35/2/10, m. 3 (11)

Wolfall, Henry de (archer) Lancashire
E 101/35/2/10, m. 3 (12)

Wolfall, Hugh de (archer) Lancashire
E 101/35/2/10, m. 3 (10)

Wolfall, John de (archer) Lancashire
E 101/35/2/10, m. 3 (6)

Wolfall, John de (archer) Lancashire
E 101/35/2/10, m. 3 (13)

Wolfall, Richard de (archer) Lancashire
E 101/35/2/10, m. 3 (3)

Wolfall, Robert de (archer) Lancashire
E 101/35/2/10, m. 3 (8)

Wolfall, Roger de (archer) Lancashire
E 101/35/2/10, m. 3 (9)

Wolfall, Thomas de (archer) Lancashire
E 101/35/2/10, m. 3 (5)

Wormbridge, Richard de (archer) Herefordshire
E 101/35/2/10, m. 3d (57)

Wotton, Peter de (clerk) Leicestershire
C 76/20, m. 15
Peter first served with Lancaster on the Breton expedition (1342), and soon after became his chaplain, wardrober and receiver-general. Peter began his clerical career as parson of Edmondthorpe (Leicestershire), but was later able to secure canonries in Salisbury and Herefordshire upon petitions made by Lancaster.[1] He went on pilgrimage in 1350.[2]
1 Fowler, *King's Lieutenant*, p. 179.
2 *CCR, 1349–54*, pp. 271–2.

Wrenbury, John de (archer) Cheshire
E 101/35/2/10, m. 1d (234)

Wrightham, John de (esquire)
E 101/35/2/10, m. 2 (68)

Wrightington, John de (esquire) Cheshire
E 101/35/2/10, m. 1 (15)

Wych, Richard de le (archer) Cheshire
E 101/35/2/10, m. 1d (204)

Wyger, Thomas (archer)
E 101/35/2/10, m. 1d (183)

Wythil, Robert de (archer)
E 101/35/2/10, m. 2d (174)

Yndebergh, John (archer)
E 101/35/2/10, m. 2d (95)

Ynglehose, John de (esquire)
E 101/35/2/10, m. 2 (144)

Yrwiham, Adam de (archer)
E 101/35/2/10, m. 2d (169)

Zouche, Richard la (*c.* 1392) **(knight)** Northamptonshire
CCR, 1343–46, p. 671; E 101/25/9, m. 3 (62)
Richard was a relative of William la Zouche of Harringworth, in whose company he served in 1345–46 and 1359. An assize of novel disseisin against Richard concerning his tenements in Olney (Northamptonshire) was postponed because he had letters of protection in 1345 as he was overseas with Henry of Lancaster.[1] Richard acted as mainpernor for John de Launton in 1342, and he was pardoned for the death of Thomas Jankynson Maggeson in 1349.[2] In the following decade he became a retainer of Edward III, who granted him an annuity of 40 marks from the issues of Northamptonshire (1359).[3] He was granted part of the remainder of the manor of Weston Young (Bedfordshire) by William la Zouche (1359), and he held Docking manor, known as 'Zouche manor' in Norfolk.[4] Richard died in or before 1392.[5]
1 *CCR, 1343–46*, p. 671.
2 C 76/17, m. 3; *CPR, 1348–50*, p. 370.
3 *CPR, 1358–61*, p. 94.
4 *CPR, 1358–61*, p. 301; *CIPM*, XVII, p. 349.
5 *CPR, 1391–96*, p. 157.

Zouche, William la (of Totnes) (*c.* 1317–1382) **(banneret)** Devonshire
C 76/20, m. 15; *CPR 1345–48*, p. 467; E 101/25/9, m. 3 (3); E 159/123, m. 145; E 372/191 (Devon);
Zouche 'of Totnes', also known as Zouche of Harringworth, or Zouche of Harringworth 'the younger' (*juniore*), is often confused with his grandfather, as both men shared the same name and both their fathers were called Eudes. The younger Zouche took part in Henry de Burghersh's diplomatic envoy to Germany in 1337 and was probably among the English army in the Low Countries the following year, which marked the start of a military career that continued up to the 1370s.[1] He inherited a substantial estate upon his grandfather's death in 1352, and thus became the wealthiest person in Lancaster's retinue (1345–46) with lands in the counties of Bedford, Buckingham, Derby, Hampshire, Hertford, Kent, Leicester, Lincoln, London, Norfolk, Northampton, Nottingham, Oxford, Rutland, Salisbury, Warwick, Wiltshire and Worcester.[2] Zouche and Sir John de Verdon were ordered to raise troops in Northamptonshire for Edward III's intended expedition in 1345, and both men were appointed justices of oyer and terminer in the 1350s.[3] Zouche continued to serve on various commissions in his home county up to the 1380s; his last official appointment was in 1381 to inquire into the royal household.

He requested burial at Biddlesden abbey (Buckinghamshire), and was succeeded by his son and namesake who became third Lord Zouche upon his death in 1382.

1 On his career, see *CP*, XII, pp. 941–2; Eric Acheson, 'Zouche family (*per. c.*1254–1415)', *ODNB*, 2004 [accessed 29 May 2015].

2 *CIPM*, XV, pp. 259–63.

3 C 76/20, m. 4 (1345); *CPR, 1348–50*, p. 530 (1350); *CPR, 1358–61*, p. 276 (1359).

Zouche, William la (of Lubbesthorpe) (knight) Leicestershire

E 101/25/9, m. 3 (38)

William was probably a cousin of the banneret in Lancaster's retinue (1345–46), a nephew of the archbishop of York (1342–52) and a king's clerk, all of whom shared the same name. He belonged to the Leicestershire branch of the Zouche family who were involved in the infamous murder of Sir Roger Beler (1326); his father, Roger, and two brothers, Ralph and Roger, were arrested for their part in the murder.[1] He was appointed as commissioner of array in Leicestershire and Warwickshire in 1351.[2] William was pardoned for outlawry in Leicestershire (1359) and Middlesex (1365), and was accused of breaking into the archbishop of York's property at Lubbesthorpe in 1354, and assaulting his servants and ruining his crops.[3] He was appointed in 1365, together with Nicholas Goushill and others, to arrest John de Araby for desertion from William de Windsor's army before it had set out to Ireland.[4]

1 *CPR, 1324–27*, pp. 245, 250, 284.

2 C 76/28, m. 13.

3 *CPR, 1354–58*, p. 127; C 76/28, m. 13.

4 *CPR, 1364–67*, p. 151.

Bibliography

Manuscript Sources

Kew, The National Archives
Chancery
C 47 Miscellanea
C 61 Gascon Rolls
C 66 Patent Rolls
C 71 Scottish Rolls
C 76 Treaty Rolls
C 81 Warrants for the Great Seal

Duchy of Lancaster
DL 27 Deeds
DL 29 Accounts of Ministers, Receivers, Feodaries and Ministers
DL 41 Miscellanea

Exchequer
E 36 Treasury of Receipt, Miscellaneous Books
E 43 Treasury of Receipt, Ancient Deeds
E 101 King's Remembrancer, Accounts Various
E 159 King's Remembrancer, Memoranda Rolls
E 368 Lord Treasurer's Remembrancer, Memoranda Rolls
E 372 Lord Treasurer's Remembrancer, Pipe Rolls
E 403 Exchequer of Receipt, Issue Rolls
E 404 Exchequer of Receipt, Warrants for Issues

Palatinate of Chester
CHES 1 Warrants, General Liveries and Miscellanea
CHES 29 Plea Rolls

Special Collections
SC 1 Ancient Correspondence
SC 8 Ancient Petitions

Leicester, Leicestershire Record Office
26D53

Libourne, Archives municipales de Libourne
Livre velu de Libourne

London, The British Library
Additional Manuscripts
7967
25688

Cotton Manuscripts
Faustina B IV
Nero C III
Nero C VIII

Harleian Manuscripts
4304

London, Duchy of Cornwall Office
Journal (*Jornale*) of John de Henxteworth

Paris, Archives nationales
Série JJ: Trésor des Chartes, Registres
65A–79B: Principal Series [1328–50]

Paris, Bibliothèque nationale de France
Collection Doat
189: House of Albret

Manuscrits français
32510: War Accounts Various

Printed Primary Sources

*Account of Master John de Burnham the Younger, Chamberlain of Chester, of the Reve-
    nues of the Counties of Chester and Flint, Michaelmas 1361 to Michaelmas 1362*,
    ed. Paul H. W. Booth and A. D. Carr (Chester: Record Society of Lancashire
    and Cheshire, 1991)
The Anonimalle Chronicle, 1333–1381: From a MS. Written at St. Mary's Abbey, York,
    ed. V. H. Galbraith (Manchester: Manchester University Press, 1970)
Autobiography of Ousama, ed. and trans. George Richard Potter (London: Rout-
    ledge, 1929)
Avesbury, Robert de, *De gestis mirabilibus regis Edwardi tertii*, ed. Edward Maunde
    Thompson (London: Eyre & Spottiswoode, 1889)
Baker, Geoffrey, *Chronicon Galfridi le Baker de Swynebroke*, ed. Edward Maunde
    Thompson (Oxford: Clarendon Press, 1889)
Baker, Geoffrey, *The Chronicle of Geoffrey le Baker of Swinbrook*, trans. David Preest
    with introduction and notes by Richard Barber (Woodbridge: Boydell, 2012)
Barbour, John, *The Bruce*, ed. and trans. A. A. M. Duncan (Edinburgh: Canongate,
    1997) ·
Bel, Jean le, *Chronique de Jean le Bel*, ed. E. Déprez and J. Vivard, 2 vols (Paris: [n.
    pub.], 1904–05), II (1905)

Calendar of Ancient Correspondence Concerning Wales, ed. J. G. Edwards (Cardiff: University Press Board, 1935)

Calendar of Charter Rolls, 1341–1417 (London: HMSO, 1916)

Calendar of Close Rolls, Edward I, 5 vols (London: HMSO, 1900–8)

Calendar of Close Rolls, Edward II, 4 vols (Nendeln: Kraus, 1971)

Calendar of Close Rolls, Edward III, 10 vols (London: HMSO, 1896–1913)

Calendar of Documents Relating to Scotland, A.D. 1108–1516, ed. J. Bain et al., 4 vols (Edinburgh: HM General Register House, 1881–1888)

Calendar of Entries in the Papal Registers Relating to Great Britain and Ireland: Papal Letters, ed. W. H. Bliss and C. Johnson, 18 vols (London: HMSO, 1893–1989), III (1897),

Calendar of Entries in the Papal Registers Relating to Great Britain and Ireland: Petitions to the Pope, ed. W. H. Bliss (London: Eyre and Spottiswoode, 1896)

Calendar of Exchequer Memoranda Rolls Preserved in the Public Record Office, Michaelmas 1326–Michaelmas 1327 (London: HMSO, 1968)

Calendar of Fine Rolls, 22 vols (London: HMSO, 1911–62)

Calendar of Inquisitions Post Mortem, 23 vols (London: HMSO, 1904–2003) IV–XVII (1913–88)

Calendar of Patent Rolls, Edward I, 4 vols (London: HMSO, 1893–1901)

Calendar of Patent Rolls, Edward II, 5 vols (London: HMSO, 1894–1904)

Calendar of Patent Rolls, Edward III, 16 vols (London: HMSO, 1891–1916)

Calendar of Patent Rolls, Richard II, 6 vols (London: HMSO, 1895–1909), I–IV (1895–1902)

Carte, Thomas, *Catalogue des Rolles Gascons, Normans et François*, 2 vols (London and Paris: Jacques Barois, 1743)

Chandos, Herald, *Life of the Black Prince*, ed. E. C. Lodge and Mildred K. Pope (Oxford: Clarendon Press, 1910)

Chaucer, Geoffrey, *The Riverside Chaucer*, ed. Larry Dean Benson, 3rd edn (Oxford: Oxford University Press, 1992)

Chronicon Anonymi Cantuariensis, ed. and trans. Chris Given-Wilson and Charity Scott-Stokes (Oxford: Clarendon Press, 2008)

'Chronique de Bazas, 1299–1355', ed. M. E. Piganeau, in *Archives historiques du département de la Gironde*, 58 vols (Paris: Aubry, 1859–1932), XV (1874), pp. 15–84

Chronique de Guyenne, ed. H. Brackhausen, in *Archives municipales de Bordeaux*, 12 vols (Bordeaux: Gounouilhou, 1867–96), V (1890)

Chronique normande du XIVe siècle: publiée pour la Société de l'histoire de France, ed. A. and E. Molinier (Paris: Renouard, 1882)

Chronographia regum Francorum, ed. H. Moranvillé, 3 vols (Paris: Librairie Renouard, 1891–97), II (1893)

Clément VI (1342–1352): Lettres closes, patentes et curiales: publiées ou analysées d'après les registres du Vatican, ed. E. Dèprez, J. Glénisson and G. Mollat, 3 vols (Paris: E. de Boccard, 1925–59), II (1958).

The Court Rolls of the Manor of Wakefield: From October 1338 to September 1340, ed. and calendared K. M. Troup, The Wakefield Court Rolls Series of the Yorkshire Archaeological Society, 12 (Leeds: Yorkshire Archaeological Society, 1999)

Crécy and Calais, From the Original Records in the Public Record Office, ed. George Wrottesley (London: [n. pub.], 1898)

Early Lincoln Wills: An Abstract of All the Wills & Administrations Recorded in the Episcopal Registers of the Old Diocese of Lincoln, Comprising the Counties of Lincoln, Rutland, Northampton, Huntington, Bedford, Buckingham, Oxford, Leicester, and Hertford, 1280-1547, ed. Alfred W. Gibbons ([n.p.]: J. Williamson, 1888)

Foedera, Conventiones, Litterae etc., ed. T. Rymer, rev. edn A. Clarke, F. Holbrooke and J. Caley, 4 vols (London: George Eyre and Andrew Strahan, 1816–69)

'Fragments inédits d'une chronique de Maillezais', ed. Paul Marchegay in *Bibliothèque de l'École de Chartes*, 2 (1840–41), 148–68

Froissart, Jean, *Chronicles*, ed. and trans. Geoffrey Brereton (London: Penguin, 1978)

Froissart, Jean, *Chronicles of England, France, Spain and the Adjoining Countries: from the Latter Part of the Reign of Edward II to the Coronation of Henry IV*, ed. and trans. Thomas Johnes, 2 vols (London: Bradbury and Evans, 1839)

Froissart, Jean, 'Chroniques', in *Oeuvres de Froissart*, ed. Kervyn de Lettenhove, rev. edn, 25 vols (Osnabrück: Biblio Verlag, 1967)

Gray, Sir Thomas, *Scalacronica, 1272–1363*, ed. and trans. and with an introduction by Andy King (Woodbridge: Boydell, 2005)

Grosmont, Henry of, First Duke of Lancaster, *Le Livre de Seyntz Medicines: The Book of Holy Medicines*, trans. with notes and introduction by Catherine Batt (Tempe, Arizona: ACMRS, 2015)

Household Accounts from Medieval England, ed. C. M. Woolgar, 2 vols (Oxford: Oxford University Press, 1992–93)

Issue Roll of Thomas de Brantingham, Bishop of Exeter, Lord High Treasurer of England: Containing Payments Made Out of His Majesty's Revenue in the 44th Year of King Edward III, A.D. 1370, ed. and trans. Frederick Devon (London: J. Rodwell, 1835)

Issues of the Exchequer: Being a Collection of Payments Made Out of His Majesty's Revenue from King Henry III to King Henry VI Inclusive, ed. and trans. Frederick Devon (London: John Murray, 1837)

Istore et croniques de Flandres, d'après les textes de divers manuscrits, ed. Kervyn de Lettonhove, 2 vols (Brussels: [n.pub.], 1879–80)

John of Gaunt's Register, Part I, ed. Sydney Armitage-Smith, 2 vols, Camden Society, 3rd series, XX–XXI (London: Offices of the Society, 1911)

Knighton, Henry, *Knighton's Chronicle 1337–1396*, ed. and trans. G. H. Martin (Oxford: Clarendon Press, 1995)

Le 'Liber' de Raymond d'Aguilers, ed. John Hugh Hill and Laurita L. Hill (Paris: Geuthner, 1969)

The Life and Campaigns of the Black Prince, ed. and trans. Richard Barber (Woodbridge: Boydell, 1986)

Murimuth, Adam, *Continuatio chronicarum*, ed. Edward Maunde Thompson (London: Eyre & Spottiswoode, 1889)

Nicolas, N. Harris, ed., *The Scrope and Grosvenor Controversy*, 2 vols (London: Samuel Bentley, 1832)

Nichols, John, *A History of the Wills of the Kings and Queens of England* (London: J. Nichols, 1790)

Norwell, William de, *The Wardrobe Book of William de Norwell 12 July 1338 to 26 May 1340*, ed. M. Lyon et al. (Brussels: Académie Royale de Belgique, Commission Royale d'Histoire, 1983)

The Parliamentary Rolls of Medieval England, ed. and trans. Chris Given-Wilson et al., 16 vols (Woodbridge: Boydell, 2005)

The Parliamentary Writs and Writs of Military Summons, ed. Sir Francis Palgrave, 2 vols (London: George Eyre and Andrew Strahan, 1827–34)

The Pipe Roll for 1295, Surrey Membrane, Pipe Roll 140, ed. Mabel H. Mills (London: Dawson, 1924)

Reading, John of, *Chronica Johannis de Reading: et Anonymi Cantuariensis, 1346–1367*, ed. James Tait (Manchester: Manchester University Press, 1914)

Récits d'un bourgeois de Valenciennes (XIVe siècle), ed. Kervyn de Lettenhove (Louvain: P. et J. Lefever, 1877)

Records of the Borough of Leicester: Being a Series of Extracts from the Archives of the Corporation of Leicester, 1509–1603, ed. Mary Bateson, 7 vols (London: C. J. Clay, 1899–1974), II (1901)

'Recueil des documents concernant la commune et la ville de Poitiers', ed. E. Adouin, II, 1328–80, in *Archives historiques du Poitou*, 61 vols (Poitiers: Société des Archives Historiques du Poitou, 1872–1982) XLVI (1928)

'Recueil des documents concernant le Poitou contenus dans les registres de la chancellerie de france', ed. Paul Guérin, II, 1334–38, in *Archives historiques du Poitou*, 61 vols (Poitiers: Société des Archives Historiques du Poitou, 1872–1982), XIII (1883)

Register of Edward the Black Prince, ed. and trans. Michael Charles Burdett Dawes, 4 vols (London: HMSO, 1930–33)

'Registres de l'échevinage de Saint-Jean-d'Angély, 1332–1496', ed. Denys d'Aussy, in *Les Archives historiques de la Saintonge et de l'Aunis*, 50 vols (Paris: [n. pub.], 1874–1967), XXIV (1895)

Rogers, Clifford J., *The Wars of Edward III: Sources and Interpretations* (Woodbridge: Boydell, 1999)

Rotuli Parliamentorum, ed. John Strachey et al., 6 vols (London: [n. pub.], 1767–77)

Saint-Omer Chronicle, ed. and trans. Clifford J. Rogers (Typescript for edition in preparation), passage quoted from BM Saint-Omer, MS 707, fols 206–33.

Treaty Rolls Preserved in the Public Record Office, ed. Pierre Chaplais and John Ferguson, 2 vols (London: HMSO, 1955–72)

Villani, Giovanni, 'Cronica', in *Cronisti del trecento*, ed. Roberto Palmarocchi (Milan and Rome: Rizzoli, 1935)

Walsingham, Thomas, *Thomae Walsingham, quondam monachi S. Albani, Historia anglicana*, ed. Henry Thomas Riley, 2 vols (London: Longman, Green, Longman, Roberts, and Green, 1863–64)

Secondary Sources

Ailes, A., 'Up in Arms: The Rise of the Armigerous *Valettus, c.* 1300', *The Coat of Arms*, n.s., 12 (1997), 10–16.

Alis, Raymond-Louis, *Histoire de la ville d'Aiguillon et de ses environs depuis l'époque gallo-romane jusqu'à nos jours* (Agen: Ferran frères, 1895)

Allmand, Christopher T., *The Hundred Years War: England and France at War, c. 1300–c. 1450*, rev. edn (Cambridge: Cambridge University Press, 2001)

Arnould, Émile Jules François, *Le Manuel des péchés: étude de littérature religieuse anglo-normande (XIIIme siècle)*, (Paris: E. Droz, 1940)

Ayton, Andrew, 'War and the English Gentry under Edward III', *History Today*, 42 (1992), 34–40

—, 'Military Service and the Development of the Robin Hood Legend in the Four-teenth Century', *Nottingham Medieval Studies*, 36 (1992), 126–47

—, 'English Armies in the Fourteenth Century', in *Arms, Armies and Fortifications in the Hundred Years War*, ed. Anne Curry and Michael Hughes (Woodbridge: Boydell, 1994), pp. 21–38

—, 'The English Army and the Normandy Campaign of 1346', in *England and Normandy in the Middle Ages*, ed. David Bates and Anne Curry (Woodbridge: Boydell, 1994), pp. 253–68

—, *Knights and Warhorses: Military Service and the English Aristocracy under Edward III* (Woodbridge: Boydell, 1994)

—, '"Knights, Esquires and Military Service": The Evidence of the Armorial Cases before the Court of Chivalry', in *The Medieval Military Revolution: State, Society and Military Change in Medieval and Early Modern Europe*, ed. A. Ayton and J. L. Price (New York: Tauris, 1995), pp. 81–103

—, 'Edward III and the English Aristocracy at the Beginning of the Hundred Years War', in *Armies, Chivalry and Warfare in Medieval Britain and France: Proceedings of the 1995 Harlaxton Symposium*, ed. Matthew Strickland, Harlaxton Medieval Studies, n.s., 7 (Stamford: Paul Watkins, 1998), pp. 172–207

—, 'Sir Thomas Ughtred and the Edwardian Military Revolution', in *The Age of Edward III*, ed. James S. Bothwell (York: York Medieval Press, 2001), pp. 107–32

—, 'The Battle of Crécy: Context and Significance', in *The Battle of Crécy, 1346*, ed. Andrew Ayton and Sir Philip Preston (Woodbridge: Boydell, 2005), pp. 35–104

—, 'The English Army at Crécy', in *The Battle of Crécy, 1346*, ed. Andrew Ayton and Sir Philip Preston (Woodbridge: Boydell, 2005), pp. 159–253

—, 'Hastings, Laurence, twelfth earl of Pembroke (1320–1348)', *ODNB*, Oxford University Press, 2004; online edn, Oct 2008

—, 'Armies and Military Communities in Fourteenth-Century England', in *Soldiers, Nobles and Gentlemen: Essays in Honour of Maurice Keen*, ed. Peter Coss and Christopher Tyerman (Woodbridge: Boydell, 2009), pp. 215–39

—, 'Military Service and the Dynamics of Recruitment in Fourteenth-Century England' in *The Soldier Experience in the Fourteenth Century*, ed. Adrian R. Bell et al. (Woodbridge: Boydell, 2011), pp. 9–59

Bachrach, David, 'Edward I's Centurions: Professional Soldiers in an Era of Militia Armies', in *The Soldier Experience in the Fourteenth Century*, ed. Adrian R. Bell et al. (Woodbridge: Boydell, 2011), pp. 109–28

Baker, Gary, 'Investigating the Socio-Economic Origins of English Archers in the Second Half of the Fourteenth Century', *Journal of Medieval Military History*, 12 (2014), 173–216

Baker, Robert L., 'The English Customs Service, 1307–1343: A Study of Medieval Administration', *Transactions of the American Philosophical Society*, n.s., 51 (1961), 3–76

Barber, Richard, *Edward, Prince of Wales and Aquitaine: A Biography of the Black Prince* (Woodbridge: Boydell, 1978)

—, *Edward III and the Triumph of England* (London: Penguin, 2013)

Barker, Juliet R. V., *Agincourt: The King, the Campaign, the Battle* (London: Brown, 2005)

Baxter, William T., 'Early Accounting: The Tally and the Checker-Board', *The Accounting Historians Journal*, 16 (1989), 43–83

Bell, Adrian R., *War and the Soldier in the Fourteenth Century* (Woodbridge: Boydell, 2004)

—,et al., 'What Did You Do in the Hundred Years War, Daddy? The Soldier in Later Medieval England', *The Historian: The Magazine of the Historical Association*, 96 (2007), 6–13

—, and T. K. Moore, 'Divided Loyalties – Hugh de Browe, John de Calveley and Richard de Vernon at the Battle of Shrewsbury 1403', *The Soldier in Later Medieval England* (2008): <http://www.icmacentre.ac.uk/soldier/database/June2008.htm>

—, 'The Fourteenth-Century Soldier: More Chaucer's Knight or Medieval Career?', in *Mercenaries and Paid Men: The Mercenary Identity in the Middle Ages*, ed. John France (Leiden: Brill, 2008), pp. 301–15

—, et.al., eds, *The Soldier Experience in the Fourteenth Century* (Woodbridge: Boydell, 2011)

—, 'The Soldier, "hadde he riden, no man ferre"', in *The Soldier Experience in the Fourteenth Century*, ed. Adrian R. Bell et al. (Woodbridge: Boydell, 2011), pp. 209–18

—, Anne Curry, Adam Chapman, Andy King and David Simpkin, *The Soldier in Later Medieval England* (Oxford: Oxford University Press, 2013)

Bellamy, John, *Crime and Public Order in England in the Later Middle Ages* (London: Routledge and Kegan Paul, 1973)

Beltz, George Frederick, *Memorials of the Most Noble Order of the Garter* (London: William Pickering, 1841)

Bennett, Matthew, 'The Development of Battle Tactics in the Hundred Years War', in *Arms, Armies and Fortification in the Hundred Years War*, ed. Anne Curry and Michael Hughes (Woodbridge: Boydell, 1994), pp. 1–20

Bennett, Michael, *Community, Class and Careerism: Cheshire and Lancashire Society in the Age of Sir Gawain and the Green Knight* (Cambridge: Cambridge University Press, 1983)

Bériac, Françoise, and Eric Ruault, 'Guillaume-Sanche, Elie de Pommiers et leurs frères vers 1340-1360', *Journal of Medieval and Humanistic Studies*, 1 (1996), 207–27

Bertrandy-Lacabane, Martin, *Étude sur les chroniques de Froissart: guerre de Guienne, 1345-1346* (Bordeaux : Impr. centrale A. de Lanefranque, 1870)

Blomefield, Francis, 'Holt Hundred: Melton Constable', in *An Essay Towards A Topographical History of the County of Norfolk*, 11 vols (London: W. Miller, 1805–10), IX (1808), pp. 415–26

Bock, Friedrich, 'An Unknown Register of the Reign of Edward III', *EHR*, 45 (1930), 353–72

Boffa, Sergio, 'The Duchy of Brabant Caught between France and England: Geopolitics and Diplomacy during the First Half of the Hundred Years War', in *The Hundred Years War (Part I): A Wider Focus*, ed. L. J. Andrew Villalon and

Donald J. Kagay (Leiden: Brill, 2005), pp. 211–40

Booth, Paul H. W., *The Financial Administration of the Lordship and County of Chester, 1272–1377* (Manchester: Manchester University Press for the Chetham Society, 1981)

Bothwell James S., *Edward III and the English Peerage: Royal Patronage, Social Mobility and Political Control in Fourteenth-Century England* (Woodbridge: Boydell, 2004)

Boulton, D'Arcy J. D., *The Knights of the Crown: The Monarchical Orders of Knighthood in Later Medieval Europe, 1325–1520* (Woodbridge: Boydell, 1987)

Bridge, J. C., 'Two Cheshire Soldiers of Fortune: Sir Hugh Calvely and Sir Robert Knolles', *Journal of the Chester Archaeological Society*, 14 (1908), 112–231

Broome, Dorothy, M., 'Auditors of the Foreign Accounts of the Exchequer 1310–1327', *EHR*, 38 (1923), 63–71

Brown, A. L., 'The Authorisation of Letters under the Great Seal', *BIHR*, 37 (1964), 125–56

Buck, M. C., 'The Reform of the Exchequer, 1316–1326', *EHR*, 98 (1983), 241–60

Burke, John, *A Genealogical and Heraldic History of the Commoners of Great Britain and Ireland, Enjoying Territorial Possessions or High Official Rank; But Uninvested with Heritable Honours*, 4 vols (London: H. Colburn, 1835–38)

Burne, Alfred Higgins, *The Crécy War: A Military History of the Hundred Years War from 1337 to the Peace of Brétigny, 1360* (London: Eyre & Spottiswoode, 1955)

Burrows, Montagu, *The Family of Brocas of Beaurepaire and Roche Court: Hereditary Masters of the Royal Buckhounds, with Some Account of the English Rule in Aquitaine* (London: Longmans, Green, 1886)

Campbell, Bruce Mortimer Stanley, *Before the Black Death: Studies in the Crisis of the Early Fourteenth Century* (Manchester: Manchester University Press, 1991)

Carne, William Lindsay, 'A Sketch of the History of the High Court of Chancery from Its Origins to the Chancellorship of Wolsey', *The Virginia Law Register*, n.s., 13 (1927), 391–421

Carpenter, Christine, 'Law, Justice and Landowners in Late Medieval England', *Law and History Review*, 1 (1983) 205–37

Caudrey, Philip, 'War, Chivalry and Regional Society: East Anglia's Warrior Gentry before the Court of Chivalry', in *Fourteenth Century England, VIII*, ed. Jeffrey S. Hamilton (Woodbridge: Boydell, 2014), pp. 119–45.

Chaplais, Pierre, 'The Chancery of Guyenne 1289–1453' in *Studies Presented to Sir Hilary Jenkinson*, ed. J. Conway Davies (London: Oxford University Press, 1957), pp. 61–96

—, 'Privy Seal Drafts, Rolls and Registers (Edward I–Edward II)', *EHR*, 73 (1958), 270–3

—, 'The Court of Sovereignty of Guyenne (Edward III–Henry VI) and its Antecedents', in *Documenting the Past: Essays in Medieval History Presented to George Peddy Cuttino*, ed. Patricia J. Bradley and Jeffrey S. Hamilton (Woodbridge: Boydell, 1989), pp. 137–53

Chapman, Adam, 'Wales, Welshmen and the Hundred Years War', in *The Hundred Years War (Part III): Further Considerations*, ed. L. J. Andrew Villalon and Donald J. Kagay (Leiden: Brill, 2013), pp. 217–29

—, *Welsh Soldiers in the Later Middle Ages* (Woodbridge: Boydell, 2015)

Cokayne, George Edward, *The Complete Peerage of England, Scotland, Ireland, Great Britain and the United Kingdom: Extant, Extinct or Dormant*, 14 vols (London: St Catherine, 1910–98)

Contamine, Philippe, *Guerre, état et société à la fin du moyen âge: études sur les armées des rois de France 1337–1494* (Paris: Mouton, 1972)

Cooke, W. G. and D'Arcy J. D. Boulton, '*Sir Gawain and the Green Knight*: A Poem for Henry of Grosmont?', *Medium Ævum*, 68 (1999), 42–54

Coss, Peter, *The Origins of the English Gentry* (Cambridge: Cambridge University Press, 2003)

Cox, J. Charles, *The Sanctuaries and Sanctuary Seekers of Mediaeval England* (London: G. Allen, 1911)

Critchley, J. S., 'The Early History of the Writ of Judicial Protection', *BIHR*, 45 (1972), 196–213

Crouch, D., *The Image of Aristocracy in Britain, 1000–1300* (London: Routledge, 1992)

Curry, Anne, 'The Organisation of Field Armies in Lancastrian Normandy', in *Armies, Chivalry and Warfare in Medieval Britain and France: Proceedings of the 1995 Harlaxton Symposium*, ed. Matthew Strickland (Stamford: Paul Watkins, 1998), pp. 207–23

—, 'English Armies in the Fifteenth Century', in *Arms, Armies and Fortifications in the Hundred Years War*, ed. Anne Curry and Michael Hughes (Woodbridge: Boydell, 1999), pp. 39–68

—, *The Battle of Agincourt: Sources and Interpretations* (Woodbridge: Boydell, 2000)

—, *The Hundred Years War*, 2nd edn (Basingstoke: Palgrave Macmillan, 2003)

—, *Agincourt. A New History* (Stroud: Tempus, 2005)

—, 'Personal Links and the Nature of the English War Retinue: A Case Study of John Mowbray', in *Liens personnels, réseaux et solidarités*, ed. E. Anceau, V. Gazeau and F. J. Riggin (Paris: Publications de la Sorbonne, 2006), pp. 153–68

—, Adrian R. Bell, Andy King, and David Simpkin, 'New Regime, New Army? Henry IV's Scottish Expedition of 1400', *EHR*, 125 (2010), 1382–1412

Cushway, Graham, *Edward III and the War at Sea* (Woodbridge: Boydell, 2011)

Daumet, Georges, *Calais sous la domination anglaise* (Arras: Répressé-Crépel et fils, 1902)

Davis, Natalie Zemon, *Fiction in the Archives: Pardon Tales and Their Tellers in Sixteenth-Century France* (Stanford, CA: Stanford University Press, 1987)

Denholm-Young, Noël, *The Country Gentry in the Fourteenth Century, with Special Reference to the Heraldic Rolls of Arms* (Oxford: Clarendon Press, 1969)

Denifle Heinrich Suso, *La Guerre de cent ans et la désolation des églises, monastères & hôpitaux en France*, 2 vols (Paris: A. Picard et fils, 1899), I

DeVries, Kelly, *Infantry Warfare in the Early Fourteenth Century: Discipline, Tactics and Technology* (Woodbridge: Boydell, 1996)

—, 'The Hundred Years War: Not One But Many', in *The Hundred Years War (Part II): Different Vistas*, ed. L. J. Andrew Villalon and Donald J. Kagay (Leiden: Brill, 2008), pp. 3–34

Drouyn, Léo, *La Guienne militaire: histoire et description des villes fortifiées, forteresses et chateaux construits dans le pays qui constitue actuellement le département de la Gironde pendant la domination anglais*, 2 vols (Bordeaux: the author, 1865)

Dugdale, W., *The Baronage of England*, 2 vols (London: Tho. Newcomb, 1675–76)

Dyer, Christopher, *Making a Living in the Middle Ages: The People of Britain 850–1520* (New Haven: Yale University Press, 2002)

Evans, D. L., 'Some Notes on the History of the Principality of Wales in the Time of the Black Prince', in *Transactions of the Honourable Society of Cymmrodorion*, session 1924–25 (London: Honourable Society of Cymmrodorion, 1927), 25–110

Farrer, William, and J. Brownbill, eds, *The Victoria History of the County of Lancaster*, 8 vols (London: Constable, 1906–14)

Fowler, Kenneth, *The King's Lieutenant: Henry of Grosmont, First Duke of Lancaster, 1310–1361* (London: Elek, 1969)

—, 'Truces', in *The Hundred Years War*, ed. Kenneth Fowler (London: Macmillan, 1971), pp. 184–215.

—, *Medieval Mercenaries* (Oxford and Malden, MA: Blackwell, 2001)

—, 'Calveley, Sir Hugh (*d.* 1394)', *ODNB*, Oxford University Press, 2004; online edn, Oct 2007

Freeman, J. '"And He Abjured the Realm of England, Never to Return"', in *Freedom of Movement in the Middle Ages: Proceedings of the 2003 Harlaxton Symposium*, ed. Peregrine Horden (Donington: Shaun Tyas, 2007), pp. 287–304

Friel, Ian, 'Winds of Change? Ships and the Hundred Years War', in *Arms, Armies and Fortifications in the Hundred Years War*, ed. Anne Curry and Michael Hughes (Woodbridge: Boydell, 1999), pp. 183–93

Fryde, E. B., 'Materials for the Study of Edward III's Credit Operations, 1327–48', *BIHR*, 22 (1949), 105–38

—, 'Loans to the English Crown 1328–31', *EHR*, 70 (1955), 198–211

—, *Studies in Medieval Trade and Finance* (London: Hambledon, 1983)

—, et al., eds, *Handbook of British Chronology*, 3rd edn (London: Royal Historical Society, 1986)

Galbraith, V. H., *An Introduction to the Use of the Public Records* (London: Oxford University Press, 1952)

Gardelles, Jacques, *Les châteaux du Moyen Age dans la France du Sud-Ouest: La Gascogne anglaise de 1216 à 1327* (Genève: Droz, 1972)

Given-Wilson, Chris, *The Royal Household and the King's Affinity: Service, Politics and Finance, 1360–1413* (New Haven, CT: Yale University Press, 1986)

—, *The English Nobility in the Late Middle Ages: The Fourteenth-Century Political Community* (London: Routledge & Kegan Paul, 1987)

—, 'Royal Charter Witness Lists', *Medieval Prosopography*, 11 (1991), 35–93

—, and Françoise Bériac, 'Edward III's Prisoners of War: The Battle of Poitiers and its Context', *EHR*, 116 (2001), 802–33

—, Ann Kettle and Len Scales, eds, *War, Government and Aristocracy in the British Isles, c.1150–1500: Essays in Honour of Michael Prestwich* (Woodbridge: Boydell, 2008)

Gladitz, Charles, *Horse Breeding in the Medieval World* (Dublin: Four Courts Press, 1997)

Gooder, Eileen A., *Latin for Local History: An Introduction*, 2nd edn (London: Longman, 1978)

Goodman, Anthony, 'The Military Subcontracts of Sir Hugh Hastings, 1380', *EHR*, 95 (1980), 114–20

Gorski, Richard, *The Fourteenth-Century Sheriff: English Local Administration in the Late Middle Ages* (Woodbridge: Boydell, 2003)

Gransden, Antonia, *Historical Writing in England, Vol. II, c. 1307 to the Early Sixteenth Century* (London: Routledge & Kegan Paul, 1982)

Green, David, 'The Military Personnel of the Black Prince', *Medieval Prosopography*, 21 (2000), 133–52

—, 'The Later Retinue of Edward the Black Prince', *Nottingham Medieval Studies*, 44 (2000), 141–51

—, 'Edward the Black Prince and East Anglia: An Unlikely Association', in *Fourteenth Century England, III*, ed. W. M. Ormrod (Woodbridge: Boydell, 2004), pp. 83–98

—, *Edward the Black Prince: Power in Medieval Europe* (Harlow: Longman, 2007)

—, 'Lordship and Principality: Colonial Policy in Ireland and Aquitaine in the 1360s', *Journal of British Studies*, 47 (2008), 3–29

Gribit, Nicholas, A., 'Accounting for Service at War: The Case of Sir James Audley of Heighley', *Journal of Medieval Military History*, 7 (2009), 147–67

—, and Simon J. Harris, 'Introduction: 19 Edward III (1345–46)', *Gascon Rolls* (February–April 2013): http://www.gasconrolls.org/en/edition/calendars/C61_57/document.html

—, and Simon J. Harris, 'Introduction: 20 Edward III (1346–47)', *Gascon Rolls* (February–April 2013): http://www.gasconrolls.org/en/edition/calendars/C61_58/document.html

—, 'Horse Restoration (*Restaurum Equorum*) in the Army of Henry of Grosmont, 1345: A Benefit of Military Service in the Hundred Years' War', *Journal of Medieval Military History*, 12 (2014), pp. 139–63

Griffiths, Ralph A., and James Sherborne, eds, *Kings and Nobles in the Later Middle Ages: A Tribute to Charles Ross* (Gloucester: Sutton, 1986)

Guinodie, Raymond, *Histoire de Libourne et des autres villes et bourgs de son arrondissement ...*, 3 vols, 2nd edn (Paris: Chez l'Auteur, 1876)

Hadwin, J. F., 'The Medieval Lay Subsidies and Economic History', *Economic History Review*, n.s., 36, (1983), 200–17

Harari, Yuval Noah, 'Inter-frontal Cooperation in the Fourteenth Century and Edward III's 1346 Campaign', *War in History*, 6 (1999), 379–95

Hardy, Robert, 'The Longbow', in *Arms, Armies and Fortifications in the Hundred Years War*, ed. Anne Curry and Michael Hughes (Woodbridge: Boydell, 1999), pp. 161–81

Harriss, Gerald L., 'Medieval Government and Statecraft', *Past and Present*, 25 (1963), 8–39

—, *King, Parliament and Public Finance in Medieval England, to 1369* (Oxford: Clarendon Press, 1975)

—, 'Political Society and the Growth of Government in Late Medieval England', *Past and Present*, 138 (1993), 28–57

—, *Shaping the Nation: England, 1360–1461* (Oxford: Clarendon Press, 2005)

Hass, Louis, 'Social Connections Between Parents and Godparents in Late Medieval Yorkshire', in *Studies on the Personal Name in Later Medieval England and Wales*, ed. Dave Postles and Joel T. Rosenthal (Kalamazoo, MI: Medieval Institute Publications, Western Michigan University, 2006), pp. 159–75

Hay, Denys, 'The Division of the Spoils of War in Fourteenth-Century England', *TRHS*, 5th ser., 4 (1954), 91–109

Hewitt, Herbert J., *The Black Prince's Expedition of 1355–1357* (Manchester: Manchester University Press, 1958)

—, *The Organization of War under Edward III, 1338–62* (Manchester: Manchester University Press, 1966)

Highfield, J. R. L., 'The English Hierarchy in the Reign of Edward III', *TRHS*, 5th ser., 6 (1956), 115–38

Holmes, George A., *The Estates of the Higher Nobility in Fourteenth-Century England* (Cambridge: Cambridge University Press, 1957)

Hunt, Edwin S., 'A New Look at the Dealings of the Bardi and Peruzzi with Edward III', *Journal of Economic History*, 50 (1990), 149–62

Hurnard, Naomi D., *The King's Pardon for Homicide before A.D. 1307* (Oxford: Clarendon Press, 1969)

Hyland, Ann, *The Medieval Warhorse from Byzantium to the Crusades* (Conshohocken, PA: Combined Books, 1996)

Jamieson, Neil, 'The Recruitment of Northerners for Service in English Armies in France, 1415–50', in *Trade, Devotion and Governance: Papers in Later Medieval History*, ed. Dorothy L. Clayton, Richard G. Davies and Peter McNiven (Far Thrupp: Sutton, 1994), pp. 102–15

Jenkinson, C. Hilary, 'Exchequer Tallies', in *Archaeologia*, 2nd ser., 62 (1911), 367–80

—, 'Medieval Tallies, Public and Private', in *Archaeologia*, 2nd ser., 74 (1925) 289–351

—, and Mabel H. Mills, 'Rolls from a Sheriff's Office of the Fourteenth Century', *EHR*, 43 (1928), 21–32

Johnson, Charles, 'The System of Account in the Wardrobe of Edward I', *TRHS*, 4th ser., 6 (1923), 50–72

Johnson, J. H., 'The System of Account in the Wardrobe of Edward II', *TRHS*, 4th ser., 12 (1929), 75–104

—, 'The King's Wardrobe and Household', in *The English Government at Work, 1327–1336*, ed. James F. Willard et al., 3 vols (Cambridge, MA: Mediaeval Academy of America, 1940–50), I (1940), pp. 206–49

Jones, Michael, *Ducal Brittany 1364–1399: Relations with England and France during the Reign of Duke John IV* (London: Oxford University Press, 1970)

—, 'The Ransom of Jean de Bretagne, Count of Penthièvre: An Aspect of English Foreign Policy 1386–8', *BIHR*, 45 (1972), 7–26

—, and Simon Walker, eds, 'Private Indentures for Life Service in Peace and War 1278–1416', in *Camden Miscellany XXXII*, Camden Society, 5th ser., 3 (London: Royal Historical Society, 1994)

—, 'Knolles, Sir Robert (*d*. 1407)', *ODNB*, Oxford University Press, 2004; online edn, May 2009

Jones, W. R., 'Rex et Ministri: English Local Government and the Crisis of 1341', *Journal of British Studies*, 13 (1973), 1–20

—, 'Purveyance for War and the Community of the Realm in Late Medieval England', *Albion: A Quarterly Journal Concerned with British Studies*, 7 (1975), 300–16

Kaeuper, Richard W., *War, Justice, and Public Order: England and France in the Later Middle Ages* (Oxford: Clarendon Press, 1988)

Kaye, Joel, *Economy and Nature in the Fourteenth Century: Money, Market Exchange, and the Emergence of Scientific Thought* (Cambridge: Cambridge University Press, 1998)

Keen, Maurice, *The Outlaws of Medieval Legend*, rev. edn (London: Routledge and Kegan Paul, 1977)

—, 'English Military Experience and the Court of Chivalry: The Case of Grey v. Hastings', in *Guerre et société en France, en Angleterre et en Bourgogne, XIVe–XVe siècle*, ed. P. Contamine, C. Giry-Deloison and M. Keen (Villeneuve d'Ascq: Université Charles de Gaulle-Lille III, 1992), pp. 123–42.

—, *The Laws of War in the Late Middle Ages* (Aldershot: Gregg Revivals, 1993)

Kingsford, C. L., 'Loring, Sir Neil (*c.* 1315–1386)', rev. Richard Barber, *ODNB*, Oxford University Press, 2004; online edn, Oct 2005

Kusman, David, 'Entre noblesse, ville et clergé. Les financiers lombards dans les anciens Pays-Bas aux XIVe-XVe siècles: un état de la question', in *Rencontres d'Asti-Chambéry (24 au 27 septembre 1998): Crédit et société: les sources, les techniques et les hommes (XIVe-XVIe S.) Actes*, ed. Jean-Marie Cauchies (Neuchâtel: '[n. pub]', 1999), pp. 113–32

—, 'Jean de Mirabello, dit van Halen (*c.* 1280-1333). Haute finance et lombards en Brabant dans le premier tiers du XIVe siècle', *Revue belge de philologie et d'histoire*, 77 (1999), 843–931

Lacey, Helen, *The Royal Pardon: Access to Mercy in Fourteenth-Century England* (York: York Medieval Press, 2009)

Lambert, Craig L., 'Edward III's Siege of Calais: A Reappraisal', *Journal of Medieval History*, 37 (2011), 245–56

—, *Shipping the Medieval Military: English Maritime Logistics in the Fourteenth Century* (Woodbridge: Boydell, 2011)

Le Patourel, Jean, *The Medieval Administration of the Channel Islands, 1199–1399* (London: Oxford University Press, 1937)

—, 'The Treaty of Brétigny, 1360', in *Feudal Empires: Norman and Plantagenet*, ed. Michael Jones (London: Hambledon, 1984), pp. 19–39

Lewis, N. B., 'An Early Indenture of Military Service, 27 July 1287', *BIHR*, 13 (1935), 85–89

—, 'The Organisation of Indentured Retinues in Fourteenth-Century England', *TRHS*, 4th ser., 27 (1945), 29–39

—, 'The Last Medieval Summons of the English Feudal Levy, 13 June 1385', *EHR*, 73 (1958), 1–26

—, 'Recruitment and Organisation of a Contract Army. May to November 1337', *BIHR*, 37 (1964), 1–19

—, 'The Feudal Summons of 1385', with a reply by J. J. N. Palmer, *EHR*, 100 (1985), 729–46

Lodge, E. C., 'The Constables of Bordeaux in the Reign of Edward III', *EHR*, 50 (1935), 225–41

Lowry, Edith Clark, and A. E. Levett, 'Clerical Proctors in Parliament and Knights of the Shire, 1280–1374', *EHR*, 48 (1933), 443–55

Lucas, Henry Stephen, *The Low Countries and the Hundred Years' War, 1326–1347* (Ann Arbor, MI: University of Michigan, 1929)

Lunt, William E. 'The Collectors of Clerical Subsidies', in *The English Government at Work, 1327–1336*, ed. James F. Willard et al., 3 vols, (Cambridge, MA: Medieval Academy of America, 1940–50), II (1947), pp. 227–80

Luttrell, Anthony, 'English Levantine Crusaders, 1363–67', *Renaissance Studies*, 2 (1988), 143–53

Lyon, B., 'The Feudal Antecedent of the Indenture system', *Speculum*, 29 (1954) 503–11

Maddicott, John R., *Thomas of Lancaster, 1307–1322: A Study in the Reign of Edward II* (Oxford: Oxford University Press, 1970)

—, *Law and Lordship: Royal Justices as Retainers in Thirteenth- and Fourteenth-Century England* (Oxford: Past and Present Society, 1978)

—, 'The Origins of the Hundred Years War', *History Today*, 36:5 (1986), 31–8

Maitland, F. W., *The Forms of Action at Common Law: A Course of Lectures* (Cambridge: Cambridge University Press, 1936)

—, and F. Pollock, *The History of English Law: Before the Time of Edward I*, 2nd edn (London: Cambridge University Press, 1968)

Marquette, Jean Bernard, *Les Albrets: l'ascension d'un lignage gascon (XIe siècle – 1360)* (Bordeaux: Ausonius, 2010)

Masschaele, James, 'Transport Costs in Medieval England', *Economic History Review*, 46 (1993), 266–79

Maubourguet, Jean, *Sarlat et la Périgord méridional*, 3 vols (1926–1955), I (1926)

Maxwell–Lyte, H. C., *A History of Dunster and of the Families of Mohun and Luttrell* (London: St Catherine Press, 1909)

—, *Historical Notes on the Use of the Great Seal of England* (London: HMSO, 1926)

McFarlane, K. B., 'Bastard Feudalism', *BIHR*, 20 (1943–45), 161–80

—, *The Nobility of Later Medieval England* (Oxford: Clarendon Press, 1973)

McKisack, May, *The Fourteenth Century, 1307–1399* (Oxford: Clarendon Press, 1959)

McNiven, Peter, 'Neville Family (*per c.* 1267–1426)', *ODNB*, Oxford University Press, 2004

Mertes, Kate, *The English Noble Household 1250–1600: Good Governance and Political Rule* (Oxford: Blackwell, 1988)

Mills, Mabel H., 'The Collectors of Customs', in *The English Government at Work, 1327–1336*, ed. James F. Willard et al., 3 vols (Cambridge, MA: Mediaeval Academy of America, 1940–50), II (1947), 168–200

Mitchell, Shelagh, 'The Armour of Sir Robert Salle: An Indication of Social Status?', in *Fourteenth Century England, VIII*, ed. Jeffrey S. Hamilton (Woodbridge: Boydell, 2014), pp. 83–98

Moore, Thomas K., 'The Cost-Benefit Analysis of a Fourteenth-Century Naval Campaign: Margate/Cadzand, 1387', in *Roles of the Sea in Medieval England*, ed. R. Gorski (Woodbridge: Boydell, 2012), pp. 103–24

Morgan, Philip, *War and Society in Medieval Cheshire, 1277–1403* (Manchester: Manchester University Press, 1987)

Morgan, Pryce, 'From Death to a View: The Hunt for a Welsh Past in the Romantic Period', in *The Invention of Tradition*, ed. Eric Hobsbawm and Terence Ranger (Cambridge: Cambridge University Press, 1992), pp. 43–100

Morris, John E., *The Welsh Wars of Edward I: A Contribution to Medieval Military History Based on Original Documents* (Oxford: Clarendon Press, 1901)

—, 'Mounted Infantry in Medieval Warfare', *TRHS*, 3rd ser., 8 (1914), 77–102

Morris, William A., et al., eds, *The English Government at Work, 1327–1336*, 3 vols

(Cambridge, MA: Medieval Academy of America, 1940–50)

Murray, Alan V., 'Prosopography', in *Palgrave Advances in the Crusades*, ed. Helen Nicholson (Basingstoke: Palgrave Macmillan, 2005), pp. 109–29

Newhall, Richard Ager, *Muster and Review: A Problem of English Military Administration, 1420–1440* (Cambridge, MA: Harvard University Press, 1940)

Nichols, John, *A History of the Wills of the Kings and Queens of England* (London: J. Nichols, 1790)

Nicholson, Ranald, *Edward III and the Scots: The Formative Years of a Military Career, 1327–1335* (London: Oxford University Press, 1965)

Ormrod, W. Mark, ed., *England in the Fourteenth Century: Proceedings of the 1985 Harlaxton Symposium* (Woodbridge: Boydell, 1986)

—, 'The Protocolla Rolls and English Government Finance, 1353–1364', *EHR*, 102 (1987), 622–32

—, 'The English Crown and the Customs, 1349–63', *Economic History Review*, 40 (1987), 27–40

—, 'An Experiment in Taxation: The English Parish Subsidy of 1371', *Speculum*, 63 (1988), 58–82

—, *The Reign of Edward III: Crown and Political Society in England, 1327–1377* (New Haven, CT: Yale University Press, 1990)

—, 'The Western Monarchies in the Later Middle Ages', in *Economic Systems and State Finance*, ed. Richard Bonney (Oxford: Clarendon, 1995), pp. 123–60

—, 'England in the Middle Ages', in *The Rise of the Fiscal State in Europe, c. 1200–1815*, ed. Richard Bonney (Oxford: Oxford University Press, 1999), pp. 19–52

—, *Edward III* (New Haven, CT: Yale University Press, 2011)

Page, William, et al., eds, *The Victoria History of Berkshire*, 4 vols (London: Constable, 1906–1924)

Palmer, J. J. N., 'The Last Summons of the Feudal Army in England (1385)', *EHR*, 83 (1968), 771–5

—, *England, France and Christendom, 1377–99* (London: Routledge & Kegan Paul, 1972)

Partington, Richard, 'Edward III's Enforcers: The King's Sergeants-at-Arms in the Localities', in *The Age of Edward III*, ed. J. S. Bothwell (York: York Medieval Press, 2001), pp. 89–106

Peña, Nicole de, *Documents sur la maison de Durfort: XIᵉ-XVᵉ siècle*, 2 vols (Bordeaux: Féderation historique de Sud-Ouest, 1977)

Pépin, Guilhem, 'La collégiale Saint-Seurin de Bordeaux aux XIIIe-XIVe siècles et son elaboration d'une historiographie et d'une idéologie du duché d'Aquitaine anglo-gascon', in *Le Moyen Âge*, 117 (2011), 43–66

—, 'Introduction: 21 Edward III (1347–48', *Gascon Rolls* (March 2013): http://www.gasconrolls.org/en/edition/calendars/C61–59/document.html

Phillips, J. R. Seymour, *Aymer de Valence, Earl of Pembroke, 1307–1324: Baronial Politics in the Reign of Edward II* (Oxford: Clarendon Press, 1972)

—, 'Valence, Aymer de, Eleventh Earl of Pembroke (d. 1324)', *ODNB*, Oxford University Press, 2004; online edn, Jan 2008

—, *Edward II* (New Haven, CT: Yale University Press, 2010)

Powicke, Michael R., 'Edward II and Military Obligation', *Speculum*, 31 (1956), 92–119

—, *Military Obligation in Medieval England: A Study in Liberty and Duty* (Oxford: Clarendon Press, 1962)

Prestwich, Michael, *War, Politics and Finance under Edward I* (London: Faber, 1972)

—, 'English Armies in the Early Stages of the Hundred Years War: A Scheme in 1341', *BIHR*, 56 (1983), 102–13

—, 'Cavalry Service in Fourteenth-Century England', in *War and Government in the Middle Ages: Essays in Honour of J. O. Prestwich*, ed. J. Gillingham and J. C. Holt (Woodbridge: Boydell, 1984), pp. 147–58

—, *Edward I* (London: Methuen, 1988)

—, *Armies and Warfare in the Middle Ages: The English Experience* (New Haven, CT: Yale University Press, 1996)

—, 'Was There a Military Revolution in Medieval England?', in *Recognitions: Essays Presented to Edmund Fryde*, ed. Colin Richmond and Isobel Harvey (Aberystwyth: National Library of Wales, 1996), pp. 19–38

—, 'The English at the Battle of Neville's Cross' in *The Battle of Neville's Cross, 1346*, ed. Michael Prestwich and David Rollason (Stamford: Shaun Tyas, 1998), pp. 1–14

—, ed., *Liberties and Identities in the Medieval British Isles* (Woodbridge: Boydell, 2008)

—, 'Edward I's Armies', *Journal of Medieval History*, 37 (2011), 233–44

Prince, Albert E. 'The Strength of English Armies in the Reign of Edward III', *EHR*, 46 (1931), 353–71

—, 'The Indenture System under Edward III', in *Historical Essays in Honour of James Tait*, ed. J. G. Edwards, V. H. Galbraith and E. F. Jacob (Manchester: [n. pub.], 1933), pp. 283–97

—, 'The Army and Navy', in *The English Government at Work, 1327–1336*, ed. James F. Willard et al., 3 vols (Cambridge, MA: Mediaeval Academy of America, 1940–50), I (1940), pp. 332–93

—, 'The Payment of Army Wages in Edward III's Reign', *Speculum*, 19 (1944), 137–60

Ramsay, J. H., *A History of the Revenues of the Kings of England 1066–1399*, 2 vols (Oxford: Clarendon, 1925)

Richardson, H. G., 'The Commons and Medieval Politics', *TRHS*, 4th ser., 28 (1946), 21–45

Rogers, Clifford. J., 'Edward III and the Dialectics of Strategy, 1327–60', *TRHS*, 6th ser., 4 (1994), 83–102

—, '"As if a New Sun had Arisen": England's Fourteenth-Century RMA', in *The Dynamics of Military Revolution, 1300–2050*, ed. MacGregor Knox and Williamson Murray (Cambridge: Cambridge University Press, 2001), pp. 15–34

—, *War, Cruel and Sharp: English Strategy under Edward III, 1327–1360* (Woodbridge: Boydell, 2000)

—, 'The Bergerac Campaign (1345) and the Generalship of Henry of Lancaster', *Journal of Medieval Military History*, 2 (2004), 89–110

Rogers, Nicholas, *England in the Fourteenth Century: Proceedings of the 1991 Harlaxton Symposium* (Stamford: Paul Watkins, 1993)

Roskell, J. S., *Parliament and Politics in Late Medieval England*, 3 vols (London: Hambledon, 1981–83)

—, Linda Clark and Carole Rawcliffe, eds, *The History of Parliament. The House of Commons, 1386–1421*, 4 vols (Stroud: Sutton, 1992)

Ross, James, 'Document in the Spotlight: The Cost of Waging War – Accounts of the Keeper of the Wardrobe, 18–21 Edward III', in *Memris Update*, 9 (2006), 6–7

Runyan, Timothy J., 'Ships and Mariners in Later Medieval England', *The Journal of British Studies*, 16 (1977), 1–17

Russell, Peter E., *The English Intervention in Spain and Portugal in the Time of Edward III and Richard II* (Oxford: Clarendon Press, 1955)

—, *Portugal, Spain, and the African Atlantic, 1343–1490: Chivalry and Crusade from John of Gaunt to Henry the Navigator* (Aldershot: Variorum, 1995)

Saul, Nigel, *Knights and Esquires: The Gloucestershire Gentry in the Fourteenth Century* (Oxford: Clarendon Press, 1981)

—, *Scenes from Provincial Life: Knightly Families in Sussex, 1280–1400* (Oxford: Clarendon Press, 1986)

—, 'Chivalry and Art: The Camoys Family and the Wall Paintings in Trotton Church', in *Soldiers, Nobles and Gentlemen: Essays in Honour of Maurice Keen*, ed. Peter Coss and Christopher Tyerman (Woodbridge: Boydell, 2009), pp. 97–111

—, 'An Early Private Indenture of Retainer: The Agreement between Hugh Despenser the Younger and Sir Robert de Shirland', *EHR*, 128 (2013), 519–34

Sayles, George, 'A Dealer in Wardrobe Bills', *EHR*, 3 (1931), 268–73

Scargill-Bird, S. R., *A Guide to the Various Classes of Documents Preserved in the Public Record Office*, 3rd edn (London: HMSO, 1908)

Sharp, Margaret, 'The Administrative Chancery of the Black Prince before 1362', in *Essays in Medieval History Presented to Thomas Frederick Tout*, ed. A. G. Little and F. M. Powicke (Manchester: Manchester University Press, 1925), pp. 321–33

—, 'The Central Administrative System of Edward, The Black Prince', in *Chapters in the Administrative History of Medieval England. The Wardrobe, the Chamber and the Small Seals*, ed. T. F. Tout, 6 vols (Manchester: Manchester University Press, 1920–1933), V (1930), pp. 289–400

Sherborne, James W., 'Indentured Retinues and the English Expeditions to France, 1369–1380', *EHR*, 79 (1964), 718–46, reprinted in his *War, Politics and Culture in Fourteenth-Century England*, ed. Anthony Tuck (London: Hambledon, 1994), pp. 1–28

—, 'The English Navy: Shipping and Manpower, 1369–89', *Past and Present*, 37 (1967), 163–75, reprinted in his *War, Politics and Culture in Fourteenth-Century England*, ed. Anthony Tuck (London: Hambledon, 1994), pp. 29–39

—, 'The Cost of English Warfare with France in the Later Fourteenth Century', *BIHR*, 50 (1977), 135–50, reprinted in his *War, Politics and Culture in Fourteenth-Century England*, ed. Anthony Tuck (London: Hambledon, 1994), pp. 55–7

—, 'John of Gaunt, Edward III's Retinue and the French Campaign of 1369', in *Kings and Nobles in the Later Middle Ages*, ed. R. A. Griffiths and J. Sherborne (Gloucester: Sutton, 1986), pp. 41–61, reprinted in his *War, Politics and Culture in Fourteenth-Century England*, ed. Anthony Tuck (London: Hambledon, 1994), pp. 77–98

—, *War, Politics and Culture in Fourteenth-Century England*, ed. Anthony Tuck (London: Hambledon, 1994)

Simpkin, David, *The English Aristocracy at War: From the Welsh Wars of Edward I to the Battle of Bannockburn* (Woodbridge: Boydell, 2008)

—, 'Total War in the Middle Ages? The Contribution of English Landed Society to the Wars of Edward I and Edward II', in *The Soldier Experience in the Fourteenth Century*, ed. Adrian R. Bell et al. (Woodbridge: Boydell, 2011), pp. 61–94

—, 'The King's Sergeants-at-Arms and the War in Scotland, 1296–1322', in *England and Scotland at War, c. 1296–c. 1513*, ed. Andy King and David Simpkin (Leiden: Brill, 2012), pp. 77–117

—, 'Keeping the Seas: England's Admirals, 1369–1389', in *Roles of the Sea in Medieval England*, ed. R. Gorski (Woodbridge: Boydell, 2012), pp. 79–109

Somerville, Robert, 'The Duchy of Lancaster Council and Court of Duchy Chamber: The Alexander Prize Essay', *TRHS*, 4th ser., 23 (1941), 159–77

—, *History of the Duchy of Lancaster*, 2 vols (London: Chancellor and Council of the Duchy of Lancaster, 1953–2000)

Spencer, Andrew, 'The Comital Retinue in the Reign of Edward I', *Historical Research*, 83 (2010), 46–59

—, *Nobility and Kingship in Medieval England: The Earls and Edward I, 1272–1307* (Cambridge: Cambridge University Press, 2014)

Spufford, Peter, *Handbook of Medieval Exchange* (London: Offices of the Royal Historical Society, University College London, 1986)

St John, Graham E., 'War, the Church and English Men-at-Arms' in *Fourteenth Century England, VI*, ed. Chris Given-Wilson (Woodbridge: Boydell, 2012), pp. 73–93

Steel, Anthony B., 'The Present State of Studies on the English Exchequer in the Middle Ages', *The American Historical Review*, 34 (1929), 485–512

—, 'The Negotiation of Wardrobe Debentures in the Fourteenth Century', *EHR*, 44 (1929), 439–43

—, *The Receipt of the Exchequer, 1377–1485* (Cambridge: Cambridge University Press, 1954)

Strayer, J. R. 'The Costs and Profits of War: The Anglo-French Conflict of 1294–1303', in *The Medieval City*, ed. Harry A. Miskimin, David Herlihy and A. L. Udovitch (New Haven, CT: Yale University Press, 1977), pp. 269–91

Strickland, Matthew, ed., *Armies, Chivalry and Warfare in Medieval Britain and France: Proceedings of the 1995 Harlaxton Symposium* (Stamford: Paul Watkins, 1998)

—, *The Great Warbow: From Hastings to the Mary Rose* (Stroud: Sutton, 2005)

Sumption, Jonathan, *The Hundred Years War I: Trial by Battle* (London: Faber and Faber, 1999)

—, *The Hundred Years War II: Trial by Fire* (London: Faber and Faber, 1999)

—, 'Mauny, Sir Walter (*c* .1310–1372)', *ODNB*, Oxford University Press, 2004; online edn, Jan 2008

—, *The Hundred Years War III: Divided Houses* (Philadelphia: University of Pennsylvania, 2009)

Sutherland, Donald W., *The Assize of Novel Disseisin* (Oxford: Clarendon Press, 1973)

Tavormina, M. Teresa, 'Henry of Lancaster: The Book of Holy Medicines (Le Livre de Seyntz Medicines)', in *Cultures of Piety: Medieval English Devotional Litera-*

ture in Translation, ed. Anne Clark Bartlett and Thomas H. Bestul (Ithaca, NY: Cornell University Press, 1999), pp. 19–40

Taylor, John, *English Historical Literature in the Fourteenth Century* (Oxford: Clarendon Press, 1987)

Thompson, Alexander Hamilton, *The History of the Hospital and New College of the Annunciation of St Mary in the Newarke, Leicester* (Leicester: E. Backus, 1937)

Thoroton, Robert, *History of Nottinghamshire*, ed. John Throsby, 3 vols (London: B. and J. White; J. Walker, 1796)

Tout, Thomas F., 'The Chief Officers of the King's Wardrobe down to 1399', *EHR*, 24 (1909), 496–505

—, *Chapters in the Administrative History of Medieval England: The Wardrobe, the Chamber and the Small Seals*, 6 vols (Manchester: Manchester University Press, 1920–33)

Tucker, P., 'The Early History of the Court of Chancery: A Comparative Study', *EHR*, 115 (2000), 791–811

Turner, Ralph V., 'The Origins of Common Pleas and King's Bench', *American Journal of Legal History*, 21 (1977), 238–54

Tyerman, Christopher, *England and the Crusades, 1095–1588* (Chicago: University of Chicago Press, 1988)

Vale, Malcolm G. A., *The Origins of the Hundred Years War: The Angevin Legacy, 1250–1340* (Oxford: Clarendon Press, 1996)

—, 'Grailly, Jean (III) de (*d.* 1377)', *ODNB*, Oxford University Press, 2004; online edn, Jan 2008

Villalon, L. J. Andrew, '"Taking the King's Shilling" to Avoid "the Wages of Sin": English Royal Pardons for Military Malefactors during the Hundred Years War', in *The Hundred Years War (Part III): Further Considerations*, ed. L. J. Andrew Villalon and Donald J. Kagay (Leiden: Brill, 2013), pp. 357–435

Wagner, Anthony Richard, Sir, *A Catalogue of English Mediaeval Rolls of Arms* (Oxford: Printed by Charles Batey for the Society of Antiquaries, 1950)

Walker, Simon, 'Profit and Loss in the Hundred Years War: The Subcontracts of Sir John Strother, 1374', *BIHR*, 58 (1985), 100–6

—, *The Lancastrian Affinity 1361–1399* (Oxford: Clarendon Press, 1990)

—, 'Grey, John, Third Baron Grey of Codnor (1305x12?–1392)', *ODNB*, Oxford University Press, 2004

Waugh, Scott L., 'Henry of Lancaster, Third Earl of Lancaster and Third Earl of Leicester (*c.* 1280–1345)', *ODNB*, Oxford University Press, 2004; online edn, Oct 2008

—, 'Talbot, Richard, Second Lord Talbot (c.1306–1356)', *ODNB*, Oxford University Press, 2004; online edn, Jan 2008

Willard, J. F., 'The Memoranda Rolls and the Remembrancers, 1282–1350' in *Essays in Medieval History Presented to T. F. Tout*, ed. A. G. Little and F. M. Powicke (Manchester: Manchester University Press, 1925), pp. 215–29

Wilson, Richard, *Medieval Norwich* (London: Hambledon and London, 2004)

Young, Charles R., *The Making of the Neville Family in England, 1166–1400* (Woodbridge: Boydell, 1996)

Unpublished Theses

Barnabé, Patrice, 'Entre roi-duc et roi de France: fidélité et ralliement du pays gascon (1259-1360)', 2 vols (unpublished doctoral thesis, Université de Bordeaux III, 2003)

Chapman, Adam, 'The Welsh Soldier, 1282–1422' (unpublished doctoral thesis, University of Reading, 2009)

Fowler, Kenneth, 'Henry of Grosmont, First Duke of Lancaster, 1310–1361', 2 vols (unpublished doctoral thesis, University of Leeds, 1961)

Gribit, Nicholas A., 'Sources for the Organisation of War: The Gascon Expedition, 1345 and the Reims Campaign, 1359' (unpublished master's thesis, University of Liverpool, 2006)

—, 'Henry de Lancaster's Army in Aquitaine, 1345: Recruitment, Service and Reward during the Hundred Years' War' (unpublished doctoral thesis, University of Leeds, 2013)

Honeywell, Mark L., 'Chivalry as Community and Culture: The Military Elite of Late Thirteenth- and Fourteenth-Century England' (unpublished doctoral thesis, University of York, 2006)

Lambert, Craig L., 'Taking the War to Scotland and France: The Supply and Transportation of English Armies by Sea, 1320–60' (unpublished doctoral thesis, University of Hull, 2009)

Legrand, M. Franck, 'Gens d'armes et art de la guerre en le sud ouest de la France (1337-1380): oppositions et specificités', 2 vols (unpublished doctoral thesis, Université de Bordeaux III, 2008)

McLoughlin, Matthew, 'The Channel Islands during the Hundred Years War' (unpublished master's thesis, University of Liverpool, 2009)

Ross, James, 'The de Vere earls of Oxford, 1400–1513' (unpublished doctoral thesis, Oxford University, 2004)

Ruault, Eric, 'La Famille de Pommiers au Moyen-Age' (unpublished master's thesis, Université de Bordeaux III, 1987)

Shenton, Caroline, 'The English Court and the Restoration of Royal Prestige, 1327–1345' (unpublished doctoral thesis, University of Oxford, 1995)

Index

Warfare in History

DH

944.
025
GRI